Max Weber

MAX WEBER

An introduction to his life and work

DIRK KÄSLER
Translated by Philippa Hurd

The University of Chicago Press

Max Weber: An Introduction to His Life and Work is a translation of *Einführung in das Studium Max Webers*. © C. H. Beck'sche Verlagsbuchandlung (Oscar Beck), Munich 1979.

The University of Chicago Press, Chicago 60637
Polity Press, Cambridge
© 1988 by Polity Press
All rights reserved. Published 1988
University of Chicago Press edition 1988
Printed in Great Britain
97 96 95 94 93 92 91 90 89 88   54321

Library of Congress Cataloging-in-Publication Data

Käsler, Dirk, 1944–
   [Einführung in das Studium Max Webers. English]
   Max Weber: an introduction to his life and work/Dirk Käsler:
translated by Philippa Hurd. —University of Chicago Press ed.
   p.   cm.
   Translation of: Einführung in das Studium Max Webers.
   Bibliography: p.
   Includes index.
   1. Weber, Max, 1864–1920.   2. Sociology—Germany—History.
I. Title.
HM22.OSW448813 1988
301′.092′4—dc19
[B]   88–19618
   ISBN 0–226–42559–2.   ISBN 0–228–42560–8 (pbk.)   CIP

Contents

'The possibility of questioning the meaning of the world presupposes the capacity to be *astonished* about the course of events.'

Max Weber, *Ancient Judaism*, p. 207

Introduction

Max Weber (1864–1920) is universally acknowledged as one of the most significant figures in the development of modern social science. The ideas he pioneered, and the avenues of research he opened up, influenced scholars in many disciplines, ranging from history to jurisprudence. Among sociologists, Weber is recognized as one of the principal 'founding fathers' of the discipline. Weber's own writings covered an enormous intellectual realm. He not only had an encyclopaedic knowledge of Western history but also carried out extensive investigations into a range of other civilizations.

Weber was a voluminous writer, and both his interests and his intellectual outlook altered to some degree over the course of his career. Describing and analysing Weber's work, therefore, presents formidable difficulties. Weber was not an author in the mould of, say, Emile Durkheim, who set out a systematic position early in his writings and thereafter persistently maintained and elaborated it. In this book, I have attempted to convey a clear picture of the unfolding of Weber's writings over the course of his career, trying to avoid the mistake – characteristic of so many introductions to Weber's work – of seeking to compress Weber's thought within a clearly structured and systematic scheme. Of course, any secondary descriptions of the works of a major author is bound to introduce simplifications. Thus in this volume I separate out Weber's substantive works (discussed in chapters 2 to 5) from his so-called 'methodological' writings – a separation which does not fully conform to Weber's own position.

In the first chapter of the book, a fairly detailed account of Weber's life and intellectual career is presented. More than in the case of most academic authors, we can only readily understand the evolution of Weber's work if we are aware of the events which shaped his life. In chapters 2 to 5, an overview of Weber's entire academic work is presented. These chapters should be read with the biographical details of Weber's career in mind. At some points it is necessary to depart from the chronological order of individual works, in order to highlight certain crucial questions with which Weber attempts to deal.

Chapter 6 offers a discussion of the methodological observations which Weber produced at various points in his works. After Weber's death, many of Weber's methodological writings were gathered by his widow, Marianne Weber, and published as a distinct volume.[1] However, it is of the first importance to understand that Weber's methodological commentaries were never intended to make up an overall 'theoretical framework'. Most of Weber's methodological commentaries were produced as offshoots of more substantive historical and sociological concerns, and were casual projects or commissioned works which to a large extent remained fragmentary.

The partial and fragmentary character of the source material is the major reason for the controversy that has long divided interpreters of Weber's thought and which continues to smoulder today. Some authors, following Marianne Weber, have argued that there is a distinct unity and coherence in Weber's methodological standpoint. Others, by contrast, stress its diverse and incomplete nature. In this book, we shall seek to show that it is not necessary to reduce Weber's work to a uniform, integrated position in order to discuss his arguments cogently. Weber's writings on methodology are very closely connected to the biographical and intellectual backdrop in terms of which they were formulated.

One important section of Weber's writings is not directly discussed in this book. This concerns Weber's interventions into political debates of his time. These aspects of Weber's activities have been extensively discussed elsewhere and the reader specifically interested in them is advised to consult other publications.[2]

[1] *Gesammelte Aufsätze zur Wissenschaftslehre (Collected Essays on Scientific Methodology)*.

[2] Wolfgang J. Mommsen, *Max Weber and German Politics 1890–1920* (Chicago, University of Chicago Press); David Beetham, *Max Weber and the Theory of Modern Politics* (Cambridge, Polity Press).

Acknowledgements

The author, translator and publishers are grateful to the following for permission to quote from previously published material: Oxford University Press, New York, for extracts from *From Max Weber*, trans. H. H. Geron and C. Wright Mills; Unwin Hyman Ltd for extracts from *The Protestant Ethic and the Spirit of Capitalism*; Verso for extracts from *Agrarian Sociology of Ancient Civilizations*, trans. Richard Frank, originally published by Verlag J. C. B. Mohr; The Free Press, a division of Macmillan, Inc., for extracts from *The Religion of China*, trans. Hans H. Geron, copyright © 1951, 1979 The Free Press, and from *The Religion of India*, trans. Hans H. Geron and Don Martindale, copyright © 1958, 1986 The Free Press, *Ancient Judaism*, trans. Hans H. Geron and Don Martindale, copyright © 1967 by The Free Press, *The Methodology of the Social Sciences*, trans. and ed. Edward A. Shils and Henry A. Finch, copyright © 1949 The Free Press, renewed 1977 Edward A. Shils.

Note on abbreviations

The numbers in brackets throughout the text, after the titles of works or after quotations, refer to sections 1 and 3 of the bibliography. References which consist of simply a number, or number and lower case letter (e.g. 215 or 215f), refer to works listed in section 3, 'Weber's works in German'. Numbers followed by upper case E (e.g. 10E) refer to works listed in section 1, 'Works by Weber available in English'. Thus, in chapter 2, page 25, to find the reference (2, p. 17) the reader should turn to the section of the bibliography which starts on p. 242.

1

Life

Karl Emil Maximilian Weber was born in Erfurt, Thuringia on 21 April 1864.[1] He was the first of eight children (Anna, born and died 1866; Alfred, born 1868; Karl, born 1870; Helene born 1873; Clara, born 1875; Alwin Hans Arthur, born 1877; and Lili, born 1880) of Max Weber Snr, Doctor of Law, and his wife, Helene Fallenstein-Weber, whom he married in 1863. His father (born 31 May 1836) was a lawyer from a family of industrialists and tradespeople in the textiles business, who lived in Westphalia. His grandfather, Karl August Weber, was a member of the Bielefeld Chamber of Commerce and for years he remained the prime example to his grandson Max of an early capitalist entrepreneur. His uncle, David Carl Weber, later took over the factory in Oerlinghausen near Bielefeld and introduced modern business management; he was Weber's model of the modern capitalist entrepreneur. At the time of Weber's birth, his father was a magistrate in Erfurt, after previously holding a post in the Berlin City Authority.

The Fallenstein family, originally part of the Huguenot line, had for some generations dedicated itself to the vocation of teaching. Helene herself (born 15 April 1844) received her basic intellectual orientation from her father, Georg Friedrich Fallenstein (born 1790, in Kleve). He was a government advisor and later Privy Finance Advisor to the Ministry of Finance in Berlin; in 1813 he had joined Lützow's volunteer corps[2] in the Prussian war of Liberation against Napoleon, Helene's mother, Emilie Souchay (born 1805) also came from a Huguenot line (Souchay de la Duboissière), which had been resident in the Frankfurt region. The historian Gervinus had been one of Helene's teachers. She was a highly educated woman who occupied herself with religious and social problems, and from 1904 she was active in poor-law administration in the Charlottenburg City Authority.

In 1866 the young Weber fell ill with meningitis. Although he soon recovered, his illness probably had long-term effects on his health. In 1869 Weber's father became a salaried City Advisor in Berlin and settled with his family in Charlottenberg. Weber Snr began a parliamentary career (1868–82; 1884–97) as a deputy of the National Liberal Party in the Prussian Chamber of Deputies and from 1872–84 in the German Reichstag where he succeeded in acquiring an influential position. In his political stance he was no 'democrat'. He belonged at the beginning of the 1860s to the 'constitutionalists', a section of the National Liberals led by Rudolf von Benningsen, the co-founder of the German National Union of 1859 and later *Oberpräsident* (Lord Lieutenant of a province) of Hanover. The constitutionalists advocated a strong monarchy which nevertheless respected the rights of the people. Weber Snr developed into a typical bourgeois politician of that time in Germany: he was pragmatic, oriented towards contemporary politics and indulged in the 'well-fed, self-satisfied liberalism of dignitaries' (Wolfgang Mommsen). He had made his peace with Bismarck a long time previously, like almost all liberals of the time. Rather hedonistic in inclination, he often clashed with his wife, whose religious and humanitarian convictions he did not share although he was a Protestant too; religion for him always remained synonymous with hypocrisy. Early on, his mother tried to impart her piety and consciousness of social responsibility to the young Weber, although without much success. As a housewife she was completely exhausted by her husband, seven children, and a large house and a wide circle of friends.

In 1870 Max Weber entered the private Döbbelin school. Two years later he moved to the Königliche Kaiserin-Augusta-Gymnasium. During his schooldays Weber read a lot, mainly historical works, the ancient classics, philosophers (Spinoza, Schopenhauer, Kant). During Christmas 1877 he composed two essays: 'On the course of German history with particular reference to the position of Kaiser and Pope' and 'On the era of the Roman Emperors from Constantine to the *Völkerwanderung*' (migration of nations). With his older cousin Fritz Baumgarten who was studying in Berlin, the fourteen-year-old Weber cultivated an intensive exchange of letters on Homer, Herodotus, Vergil and Cicero. The teachers at the school were not pleased with Weber as a pupil: his achievements could have been greater and his attitude was felt to be lacking in respect. Weber found school boring, with the result that little by little he managed to read the complete forty-volume Cotta edition of Goethe's works under the school-bench.

The large circle of famous personalities who frequented his parents' house – among them the politicians Benningsen, Miquel, Kapp, Hobrecht and the academics Dilthey, Goldschmidt, Theodor Mommsen, Sybel and Treitschke – with whom his father took part in political and intellectual discussion, created an intellectually stimulating milieu for the young Weber. Thus the main influences during his youth can be seen as family background and the then excellent German secondary education, which provided the basis for the wide spectrum of Weber's areas of interest. In spite of his father's authoritarian and patriarchal traits, Weber identified with him more strongly during this period. He provided Weber with important incentives for his later student life.

After the death in 1876 of their four-year-old daughter, Weber's parents became more and more estranged from one another; Weber Snr at first shared his wife's grief, but soon recovered his customary composure and overcame this hiatus to carry on enjoying his life. For the first time the tensions between Weber's parents, which had been latent from the beginning, broke out openly. There was a basic incompatibility between the pleasure-loving Berlin politician and the mother who was introspective both socially and in her religious outlook. How Max coped with this division at that time remains unclear; in his time as a *Rechtsreferendar* and *Assessor* (two posts in the civil service) in Berlin, a period he spent in his parents' house (1886–93), he was fully aware of this conflict.

During Christmas 1879, he wrote another essay 'Observations on national character, development and history of the Indo-Germanic nations'. In his confirmation class, he learnt enough Hebrew to be able to read the Old Testament in the original. In spring 1882 he took his *Abitur* (school-leaving exam). The same year Weber began his studies in Heidelberg, his mother's home during her youth, where he took courses majoring in jurisprudence; also studying national economy, history, philosophy and some theology. His special subjects were the history of late Antiquity, modern commercial law and contemporary theory of constitutional law. As he himself wrote later in the preface to his dissertation, he went to lectures by Immanuel Bekker, Karlowa, Heinze and H. Schulze on jurisprudence, by Kuno Fischer on philosophy, by Karl Knies on political economy and by Erdmannsdörfer on history. Essentially at his father's suggestion, Weber joined the student fraternity 'Allemannia' and took an active part in drinking-bouts and duels. He became friendly with his cousin Otto Baumgarten, who was finishing his theology studies in Heidelberg.

Weber left Berlin a thin, shy student. During his three terms in Heidelberg he fundamentally transformed himself both physically and in his personality. His working day, which he used to spend with Baumgarten, is revealed by a quotation from a letter he wrote:

The logic course at seven in the morning forces me to rise early. Then I rush around in the fencing hall for an hour each morning and conscientiously sit through my lectures. At half past twelve I eat next door for one mark, sometimes drinking a quarter liter of wine or beer with my lunch. Then I often play a solid game of skat with Otto and Herr Ickrath, the innkeeper, until two o'clock, (Otto cannot live without skat), whereupon we withdraw to our respective lodgings. I look through my notes and read Strauss's *Der alte und der neue Glaube*. In the afternoon we sometimes go hiking in the mountains. In the evening we are together again at Ickrath's, where we get a pretty good supper for eighty pfennigs, and afterwards we regularly read Lotze's *Mikrokosmos*, about which we have the most heated arguments.[3]

In Strasbourg he visited his uncle, Hermann Baumgarten, to whom he later developed a close attachment. The worldly atmosphere of the academic life in which he participated quickly distanced Weber further from his introverted mother. In 1883 he moved to Strasbourg to perform one year of National Service. The duties were hard and Weber was unused to them, so he was relieved when he at last reached the rank of corporal. In later life he was proud of his rank of captain in the Kaiser's army. He managed to escape futile barrack-duty partly through his studies at Strasbourg University which were held at the same time. Apart from going to lectures by Sohm and Bremer, he made a point of attending the lectures of his uncle, who occupied a chair in history.

Two sisters of Weber's mother, Helene, had married Strasbourg professors: his aunt Emilie had married the geologist and palaeontologist, Ernst Wilhelm Benecke and, in time, Weber formed a bond of deep friendship with the family of his aunt, Ida, the wife of Hermann Baumgarten. His uncle was his political and intellectual mentor and confidant. He was, by contrast with Weber Snr, against making compromises with or concessions to Bismarck. Baumgarten belonged to that small minority of German liberals who had preserved the spirit of 1848 (the year which saw an unsuccessful democratic revolution) and held out no illusions about the restorative character of the Chancellor's politics. At the same time, however, he took up a very critical position towards the politically organized liberalism of his age.[4] Together with Weber's uncle Carl David Weber, whose creative entrepreneurial energies greatly impressed his nephew, Baumgarten formed a strong model of opposition to Weber's father. Like her sister, Ida Baumgarten was deeply imbued with religious and social inclinations.

Under this influence, Weber increasingly saw his father as an amoral creature of pleasure, and at the same time he began to understand better his mother's religious values. In the Baumgartens' house he met the girl who was later to become his first great love, their daughter, Emmy.

In 1884, Weber resumed his studies in Berlin, doubtless at the request of his parents who wanted to extricate him from the control and influence of the Baumgartens. In Berlin, Weber did not continue the uncontrolled, stormy student life of his Heidelberg days, which had been his only 'youth' – probably for the sake of his mother. With a few interruptions – the conclusion of his studies in Göttingen and various military exercises – he spent the next eight years at home, thus also financially dependent upon his far-from-beloved father. At Berlin University he went to lectures by Beseler on civil law, by Aegidy on international law, heard Gneist on German state law and Prussian administrative law, and Brunner and Gierke on German legal history. He also attended historical lectures by Mommsen and Treitschke, whose exaggerated patriotism Weber found unattractive. He found confirmation of his attitude in Hermann Baumgarten, in opposition to his father who at that time totally supported the glorification of the Hohenzollern regime. The demagogue Treitschke became Weber's example of the professional agitator, whom he considered to be the alternative to the historically informed scholar, who was 'free from value-judgement'.

In April 1885, Weber finished his first military exercises in Strasbourg and registered for the summer term – his fifth – in Berlin again in order to prepare for the legal *Referendar* (first year) exam in the winter term of 1885–6 in Göttingen. In Göttingen he went to lectures by Dove, von Bar, Frensdorff, Regelsberger and Schröder. Little remained of his leisurely Heidelberg student life; Weber developed the intensive manner of working that would determine the rest of his academic career. After the exam in May, he returned to his parents' house in Charlottenburg which he was to leave finally only in 1893 on his marriage. He continued his studies in Berlin, aiming for promotion, which was then very difficult to achieve there in his subject. He studied *Staatswissenschaft* (theory of the state) mainly with Levin Goldschmidt and August Meitzen and also went to lectures by Dernburg, Pernice and Wagner. From 1886 he worked in the state law and agrarian history faculty at Berlin University. The following year Weber went on his second set of exercises as an officer, once again in Strasbourg. What had been a continuing close relationship with Emmy Baumgarten was interrupted, as she became mentally ill and had to spend a long period in a mental hospital.

Weber became a doctoral student under Goldschmidt. During what was for him a very boring time as a first-year law student, he completed his third military exercise in 1888 in Posen. The district magistrate there, Nollau, afforded Weber a glimpse into the Prussian colonization policy as it had been conducted since the Treaty of Ostmark. (This was a law of colonization for the provinces of Posen and West Prussia which was passed by the German Reichstag in 1886.) In Weber's eyes, the German–Slav boundary formed a cultural and national border where a danger of the foreign infiltration of eastern Germany was threatening to appear. Weber joined the *Verein für Sozialpolitik (Association for Social Policy)*. His main academic interest at this time concerned the borderline area between economic and legal history.

In 1889 Weber graduated 'magna cum laude' under Goldschmidt and Gneist with his work on the 'Development of the principle of joint liability and the separate fund in the public trading company from the household and trade communities in the Italian cities' (1889), which he based on hundreds of Italian and Spanish sources. The dissertation, which he formally submitted to the faculty, formed the third chapter of the larger work 'On the history of trading companies in the Middle Ages, according to South-European sources' (1889). He passed the viva with flying colours on three of his submitted theses, after a much debated argument with the ageing Theodor Mommsen, who had never been his teacher and who was there more as a friend of the family than as a professor. In concluding his dispute with Weber, Mommsen said: 'But when I have to go to my grave someday, there is no one to whom I would rather say, "Son here is my spear; it is getting too heavy for my arm" than the highly esteemed Max Weber.'[5]

After his graduation, Weber began preparing for his *Habilitation* (a higher doctorate which must be accepted by a University faculty for a person to be able to lecture at German universities). At the end of his time as *Referendar* at the Royal District Court of Charlottenburg in Berlin, he finished his juridical education with further exams and was called to the bar in Berlin. In the Reichstag elections of 1890, Weber voted conservative. He visited the first *Evangelisch–soziale Kongreß* (Evangelical–Social Congress), which had been established by the Court Chaplain, Stöcker. Within the framework of this organization, Weber made friendly contacts particularly with Paul Göhre and Friedrich Naumann, and worked on the *Christliche Welt*, which was edited by Martin Rade. In the same period he received a commission from the *Verein für Sozialpolitik* (which he had already joined in 1888) to work on the planned 'Agricultural-worker Enquiry' in the East

Elbian regions. He pursued this project through collaboration on the pamphlet edited by his cousin Otto Baumgarten, entitled 'Contemporary Evangelical–Social Questions'. Weber's efforts to obtain a job as legal advisor in the city of Bremen, a position which Werner Sombart held before him, was for Weber possibly a last alternative to an academic career. He was unsuccessful. In 1891 he gained his *Habilitation* under Meitzen on 'Roman agrarian history and its importance for state and civil law'. Alongside his activity as a lawyer at the Berlin Supreme Court, Weber had, since the summer term of 1892, stood in for Goldschmidt who was ill, giving lectures and classes on commercial law and Roman legal history at Berlin University.

In spring of the same year, Weber Snr's great niece, Marianne Schnitger came to Berlin. The twenty-one-year-old daughter of a doctor and sanitation advisor in Oerlinghausen and the Lippe area wanted to conclude her vocational training there. As on previous visits, she showed her attraction to the young Weber, which he returned. After a few misunderstandings, the couple became engaged. Weber's relationship with Emmy Baumgarten, who in the meantime had recovered, developed in time into a comradely friendship.

During this period Weber concluded the enquiry into 'The conditions of the agricultural workers in East Elbian regions of Germany'. Almost 900 pages long, the work was an analysis of a broad-based empirical survey of the situation of agricultural workers in the Prussian provinces of East and West Prussia, Pommern, Posen, Silesia, Brandenburg, the grand dukedoms of Mecklenburg and the dukedom of Lauenburg. From the material collected, Weber developed conclusions of considerable political significance. He proposed that improvement of the situation of the East Elbian agricultural workers, and the defence of German nationality against foreign influence from the neighbouring Slavic countries – engendered particularly by Polish seasonal workers – could only be achieved by the dissolution of the East Elbian large-estate economy. The investigations brought him general academic recognition. Such was the opinion of G. F. Knapp, one of the leading German agrarian historians, who said on the occasion of his address to the *Verein* on the agricultural worker enquiry, 'the time of our expertise is over and we must start the learning process all over again'.[6] Weber's investigations and in particular the challenges derived from them, however, sparked off violent political controversies.

In spring 1892, at the conclusion of his *Habilitation*, Weber became university lecturer in Roman and commercial law. The following year an Extraordinary Professorship in commercial and German law at Berlin

University was conferred upon him by the Ministerial Director of the Prussian Ministry of Culture, Althoff. On 6 July 1893, in Freiburg, Weber was put forward for the professorship in political economy, and at Berlin University he was considered for a professorship in commercial law, Weber's appointment in Freiburg came about essentially on the basis of his economic-historical and political works. The first change of direction in Weber's academic work was imminent – a change from jurisprudence to political economy. At the end of his lectures on the agricultural worker enquiry to the *Verein*, together with Paul Göhre, Weber was commissioned by the *Kongreß* to compile a second enquiry on the situation of German agricultural workers, this time, however, by means of interviewing around 15,000 evangelical priests across the whole country. This corresponded to Weber's own intentions: he had been unhappy with the first survey, which was based on the interviewing of land-owners, and he wanted to elaborate on it by means of new surveys.

Weber struck up a close friendship with Friedrich Naumann, one of the leaders of the Christian–Social movement in Germany at that time, who had initiated strong movements towards social reform in German Protestantism. A certain sobering and simultaneous 'radicalization' in Naumann's attitudes can undoubtedly be traced to Weber's influence. Weber joined the Pan-German Union essentially because of its national objectives, through which he hoped to find a solution to the problem of the Polish seasonal workers. He gave lectures on this theme to the Union. However, the fixed attitude of the large land-owners who represented the Union and who did not want to do without the recruitment of cheap Polish workers, soon caused him to leave on 22 April 1899.

In family matters, 1893 brought a turning point in Weber's life; on the one hand, the death of Hermann Baumgarten and on the other, Weber's marriage to Marianne Schnitger. The union was supported by an intellectual and moral comradeship. Sexual fulfilment was denied Weber within the marriage and he was to find it only just before the First World War – in extra-marital relationships. The marriage remained childless. In the years that followed, Weber once again took part in a military exercise in Posen. In the autumn of 1894 he moved to Freiburg where he took up his professorship in political economy and lectured on national economics. Among other famous academics, like Hugo Münsterberg, Weber came across the south-west German school of neo-Kantianism in the person of Heinrich Rickert. Weber had supported Rickert's interest in a dichotomy of human science (*Geisteswissenschaft*)[7] versus natural science. This separation was meant as a defence against the dominant claims made by the 'exact' natural sciences. Weber, however, was annoyed by both 'naturalism' and 'historicism' and regarded both as a 'narrow-minded patriotism of the field'.

At the Frankfurt meeting of the *Kongreß*, Weber gave a lecture on the agricultural-worker enquiry. The conclusions of the investigation, which were directed against large-scale land-ownership, led to a rift between the left-oriented Social–Christian members (Schulze-Gaevernitz, Naumann, Göhre, Weber) and the conservatives under Stöcker.

In May 1895, his second term in Freiburg, Weber gave his inaugural academic lecture on 'The National State and Economic Policy'. The speech caused a sensation right across the academic community. Weber professed his academic and political credo in a radical and disturbing manner. In addressing the analysis of the East Elbian agrarian relationships, Weber used the occasion to direct attacks against the different schools of political economy of the time. He turned on the naively optimistic academic socialists (*Kathedersozialisten*), as much as against the ethnically and culturally oriented political economy of the Schmoller school. He charged them all with the unconsidered mixing of value-judgements with statements of fact. Against this, he demanded a clear orientation towards German national state values: 'The national economy of a German state just as much as the measure of value we give to the theoretician in German national economy can thus only be German.' In his lecture he used a nationalistic language, full of 'social–Darwinist concepts' (W. Mommsen). Weber professed himself emphatically in favour of *Realpolitik* (practical politics) and German imperialism, seeing in Great Britain the political model for Germany. Here, for the first time, political processes of development were described by means of sociological categories, as when Weber confirmed the specific failure of both the workers and the bourgeoisie in the face of national tasks. Weber's development into practical and political effectiveness, as was already apparent in this speech, found expression too in his critique of the suggestions of the Stock Exchange Enquiry Commission, which he accused of acting according to moral instead of political viewpoints and under pressure from the representatives of agrarian interests. His comprehensive academic work programme – twelve hours of lectures and two seminars per week – was followed by a journey through England and Scotland which lasted from August to October 1895.

In 1896, Weber was called to Heidelberg as a successor to Knies, one of the leading figures of the historical school of political economy, to take over his chair in political economy. His withdrawal from contemporary politics, a tactic he tried repeatedly in order to keep open his path into academia, succeeded only in part because of his activities as correspondent to the Federal Council on the provisional Stock Exchange Committee and through his vote on the corn-trade commission. He criticized the new Stock Exchange law very severely. Weber took part in the Erfurt convention of National Socialists and became a member of the National Socialist group which was founded there. As well as 'giving several lectures on agrarian problems, Weber took part in the seventh *Kongreß*. In Heidelberg he renewed his contacts with his previous teachers, Bekker, Erdmannsdörfer and Kuno Fischer. He renewed links with Jellinek, the constitutional lawyer, Troeltsch, the theologian, and the philosopher, Windelband. The Webers' house became the meeting place for Heidelberg intellectuals. Among diverse contemporary political activities in the Christian–Social movement, 1897 brought two decisive points in Weber's political development: he was not adopted on the final Stock Exchange Committee and he declined the offer of a parliamentary (*Reichstag*)[8] candidature in Saarbrücken.

For his personal development, too, the year was of central importance. In July he had a serious argument with his father, who with Weber's mother, was spending some time in Heidelberg. The dispute was over his father's authoritarian, patriarchal behaviour towards his mother, which Weber criticized sharply, as Weber regarded her personal freedom as jeopardized. Weber Snr refused his wife free access to a small part of her inheritance from her mother, who had died in 1881; he also threw out a young theology student who was to help in their son Karl's education and in whom she had found an interesting conversation partner. Without being reconciled with his wife and son, Weber Snr died on 10 August in Riga. Later Weber felt guilty because of his antagonistic outburst, and saw no possibility of righting the wrong. In the autumn, Weber began to display the first signs of a nervous attack of mental and physical exhaustion. The symptoms of the illness were physical weakness, sleeplessness, inner tension, pangs of conscience, exhaustion, bouts of anxiety, continual restlessness. 'Everything was too much for him; he could not read, write, talk, walk, or sleep without torment.'[9] After a slight improvement, 1898 began with contemporary political activities. Weber certainly found his teaching activities difficult and in the spring at the end of term he suffered a severe nervous breakdown. A convalescent trip to Lake Geneva brought some improvement which lasted until the beginning of the summer term. In the summer, Weber spent some time at a sanatorium on Lake Constance. Teaching during the following winter term became a torment for him; at Christmas he had another breakdown and it was only with great difficulty that he managed to end the term.

Several possible causes of Weber's nervous suffering could be offered, although we cannot be sure which were most important. His early meningitis could be put forward as a physiological factor, just as much as his complete exhaustion from overwork. Moreover, some possibly psychological symptoms seem to be important: Weber's deep spiritual depression and the denied and repressed feeling of guilt which, partly as a result of the argument with his father – which can be regarded without doubt as an Oedipal situation – weighed heavily on him. Weber suffered as a result of the conflicting values of his mother and aunt on the one hand, and those of his father and uncle, on the other. This conflict probably brought him considerable problems of identification – an ideal breeding ground for mental illness.

The two central models for identification were formed at the latest during Weber's time as a student; emotionally drawn to his mother, he tried to sympathize with her introspection, piety and morality and this was very noticeable in their mutual consultation over the education of her third son. As far as his father was concerned, Weber presented himself as his father's ideal – a gross, beer-drinking, duelling, cigar-smoking student. Thus he presented an image which, when faced with her bloated son who was covered in duelling scars, provoked his mother at the end of term in 1882 into giving him a resounding slap across the face.

The circumstances of his marriage to Marianne, the granddaughter of his father's eldest brother, and at the same time his separation from the other cousin, Emmy Baumgarten, stayed with Weber for a long time. The asexual relationship with Marianne Weber certainly did not contribute to Weber's mental stability.

His rigid work-discipline, too, which was rooted in an ascetic way of life, should be taken into account. Alongside the desire for career success – during the 1880s, which were very interesting years in this context, when Weber was aiming for a university career and at the same time a career as a lawyer – he himself gave as the reason for his manic working a vague fear of a 'comfortable' existence. This self-satisfied way of life was put on show to him everyday – Weber lived at home until he was twenty-nine – by his father. Nothing seems more plausible than that, as long as his father lived, Weber was driven through the pressure of confrontation from his father's example into the other extreme of a great mania for work and asceticism. With the death of his father the opposition disappeared, the whole work-machine collapsed, and Weber finally became incapable of doing anything. Some of Weber's letters prove that he too thought his energy for work displayed a pathological disposition.

In general, Weber's illness can certainly not be classified as an actual 'mental illness'. Complex causes and a variety of circumstances led to the outbreak of the nervous attack. A self-analysis written at this time, but which is no longer in existence, might have provided an interesting insight into these circumstances. Nowhere is the illness's direct influence on Weber's thinking confirmed and thus it is frequently overlooked that from 1889 to 1920 (except 1901) [10] Weber published something every year. [11]

For the summer term 1899, Weber was exempted from lecturing for reasons of health. When he resumed teaching activities in the autumn, he had another breakdown, the worst so far. Weber believed he would have to give up his teaching activities for a long time and at Christmas he submitted a request to be discharged from his post. Instead of a discharge, Weber was granted a long holiday. In July 1900 Weber visited a clinic for nervous diseases; he had reached his nadir. He was incapable of work, reading, writing letters or speaking – he was suffering from nervous exhaustion. In autumn the Webers travelled to Corsica accompanied by a young psychopathic relative (who later committed suicide). A small improvement was apparent in Weber's condition.

The following year in March, Weber travelled to Rome and southern Italy, spending the summer in Switzerland where he suffered a relapse; in autumn he returned to Rome to spend the winter there. His condition had improved to the extent that he announced a lecture at Heidelberg University for the summer term, 1902. His recovery found its expression in the resumption of reading, particularly in the library of the *Historische Institut* where he met Schellhaß and Haller. He occupied himself with works of art-history (Dehio-von Betzold), philosophy (Rousseau, Voltaire, Taine, Montesquieu) and sociology (Simmel's *Philosophy of Money* of 1900). By intensive reading of the history, constitution and economy of monasteries, Weber came across the theme of 'rationality', particularly in economic life, for the first time. At Easter 1902, he travelled to Rome and Florence, arriving in Heidelberg in April. Worried about his continued mental instability, Weber submitted another request for discharge from his job.

In Heidelberg, he began his methodological works. Weber believed that, by using the epistemological and theoretical beginnings of neo-Kantianism, he had found a way of legitimizing a non-naturalistic oriented, methodologically based social science: at first in his essay on 'Roscher and Knies and the logical problems of historical political economy' and on ' "Objectivity" in social science and social policy'. Of course his working strength was nowhere near restored yet, and in this work he had to contend with mental difficulties and occasional relapses.

The fear of working as a teacher, of working to deadlines and the great pressures of his own career as a professor became a compulsive idea to Weber. In October 1903 at the age of thirty-nine he finally resigned his teaching post; he became honorary professor with invitation to lecture, but without the right to promotion and without vote in the Faculty. In September 1903 he took part in the *Verein*'s conference in Hamburg as an observer. He initiated the series of his sociological works (in the narrow sense) by beginning his piece *The Protestant Ethic and the Spirit of Capitalism*. In this work on the sociology of religion, he was stimulated by the question of the origin of modern capitalism, the revolutionizing power of which he had already recognized in the agricultural worker studies.

In the following year, Weber travelled to the USA at the invitation of Hugo Münsterberg, his colleague from the Freiburg days now teaching at Harvard, to attend a scientific world congress on the occasion of the World Exhibition in St Louis. With his wife and his friend Ernst Troeltsch he travelled through the USA from August to December. In St Louis, Weber lectured on 'German Agricultural Problems, Past and Present', his first speech to an academic audience for six and a half years. Among the lasting experiences Weber gained on his journeys through the United States for his later works, there were in particular the Protestant sects, the organizations of the political 'machinery', bureaucratization in the USA, the office of President and the American political structure in general. America became for him the model of a new, or at least different society, against the backdrop of which many features of the contemporary society of the old world appeared to Weber to be thrown in relief. In the library of Columbia University in New York he researched further material for his work on the historical effects of the 'Protestant ethic'.

With Edgar Jaffé and Werner Sombart, Weber took over editorial control of the *Archiv für Sozialwissenschaften und Sozialpolitik* (*Archive of Social Science and Social Policy*), (which was previously the *Archiv für soziale Gesetzgebung und Statistik* edited by H. Braun in eighteen volumes), building it into the leading German journal in the social sciences. Here, in the same year, 1904, Weber's article ' "Objectivity" in social science and social policy' appeared in which he introduced his approach to scientific thought. This was a rational, critical scientific variant written in a sceptical style against what he considered to be naive positivistic or metaphysical formulations. Here for the first time his concepts of 'value freedom' of 'value relationship' and of the 'ideal-type' were introduced explicitly. For Weber, the *Archiv* was to be his new extra-university entrance into science.

The Russian revolution of 1905, which Weber welcomed, increased his hopes for a process of liberalization. He compared the Czarist regime with the Kaiser's 'personal regiment' in Berlin. He learnt Russian in three months in order to be better able to follow events. Certainly he was rather pessimistic in his prognoses: the change in circumstances in Russia would not necessarily lead to democratization, but rather to bureaucratization. In the following years too, he was intensely concerned with the events in Russia. At this time he concluded the publication of *The Protestant Ethic* with the last contributions in the *Archiv*. Weber became the leader of the left-wing of the *Verein* in the confrontation with its conservative, authoritarian leadership.

At this time Weber frequently commented on questions of university policy. He tried to smooth the way into the University for Georg Simmel, whose appointment to an ordinary professorship at Heidelberg had been rejected by Dilthey, Rickert and Windelband, essentially for anti-semitic reasons; and he tried the same for Robert Michels who was not acceptable to the University because he belonged to the Social Democrats. In 1906 Weber took part in the SPD (German Social Democratic Party) party conference, criticizing the petty-bourgeois character of the SPD and its lack of political coherence.

The pluralism of his political standpoint was perhaps seen by many of his contemporaries as the expression of a controversial, difficult character which even made them suspect him of opportunistic relativism. Even the posthumous discussion of his concept of the 'plebiscite (Führer) democracy' and its ancestral relevance for the eventual domination of fascistic authoritarianism is relevant. Such ambivalence in Weber's opinions are more superficial than real on the level of his political ethic, but their origin is totally convincing.

He published articles on the developments in Russia, and on the North American sects. At the *Verein*'s conference Weber once again criticized both the Kaiser and the Social Democrats. In spring 1907 Weber's energies for work once again hit a bad patch; in March he travelled to Lake Como. An inheritance – his grandfather Karl Weber had died – brought the solution to financial problems. His brother Alfred, a professor in Prague and a sociologist like Max, won an appointment in Heidelberg. In spring 1908 Weber stayed for some time in Provence and Florence without his wife. In the same year he travelled once again to Holland. This was the time when his interest in industrial vocational work was beginning, to which end he conducted investigations in his grandfather's textile factory; he was much concerned with statistical calculations and as a result he published two works. He pursued this with a major historical-sociological work entitled *The Agrarian Sociology of Ancient Civilizations* for the *Handwörterbuch der Sozial-wissenschaften*. Weber was given the task by the publisher Paul Siebeck of continuing the four-volume *Schönberg'sches Handbuch der Politischen Ökonomie* and of taking over the editorial direction of the *Grundriss der Sozialökonomik*, which was planned in five books and nine sections. For section 3, under the general heading 'Economy and Society', two main parts were planned: I 'The Economy and the Social Orders and Powers' by Weber; and II 'Development of the Economic and Social Political Systems and Ideals' by Eugen von Philippovich. In 1922 Marianne Weber took over the section heading for the posthumous publication of the main body of the manuscript for the planned volume, and arranged the remaining drafts according to her own judgements.

The International Philosophy Congress, which in 1908 was held in Heidelberg, saw an important event. The newly constituted *Heidelberger Akademie der Wissenschaften* offered an extraordinary membership to Weber which he refused as a criticism of their methods of selection (younger and less well-known academics were excluded). Because of his unease over the scientific–political alignment of the *Verein*, Weber took steps to set up a research organization which would work in a strictly scientific, empirical manner. Even the disappointments and experiences of the agricultural-worker enquiry must be seen in the context of the origin of such an organization. Weber recognized the necessity for independent social science research institutes which would develop methods of empirical social research. The natural science oriented Kaiser Wilhelm Institute, the institutional precursor of today's Max Planck Institute, served as a model in Weber's eyes. On January 3 1909 he co-founded the *Deutsche Gesellschaft für Soziologie* (German Society for Sociology) in Berlin, the first directorate of which was comprised by Ferdinand Tönnies as director, Georg Simmel and Heinrich Herkner (soon replaced by Werner Sombart) as committee members and Weber as treasurer. It was during this period that Weber designated himself as a 'sociologist' for the first time.

In the Heidelberg circle at this time, the ideas of Otto Groß, a Freudian scholar who had launched a major attack on Victorian concepts of marital relations and fidelity, were discussed. But Weber could not agree with him that a healthy psychical condition was the central criterion of all forms of marital behaviour. Weber's ultimate values in this context were asceticism and 'heroic ethics' even in the face of marital relations which were felt to be unsatisfying.

The episode reveals Weber's disposition and the physical problems of his relationship with his wife. He suppressed his own sexual impulses and polemicized publicly, at least until about 1910, against an ethic of sensual pleasure. There was for him only one alternative – a Puritan–Christian ethic of ascetic heroism or self-righteous hedonism. He even supported the women's movement but only against authoritarian, male dominance in marriage; it never occurred to him to question this in himself or even his own sexual monogamy. Moreover, he was inclined to acknowledge the importance of Freud's theory, but only when limited to phenomena below the level of meaningful social behaviour. However, this ethical rigour which could be interpreted as 'ascetic' underwent a certain slackening in the course of the years. After about 1893, while Weber was still in Freiburg, an intimate relationship gradually developed between Weber and Else von Richthofen, later Jaffé, Marianne's closest friend, who became one of Weber's students and graduated under him in 1901. From about 1918, the character of this relationship changed, and from this time it could be regarded as an intimate friendship which lasted until Weber's death. Furthermore Weber's relationship with Mina Tobler, which from about 1911–12 became important to him, played a significant role: she aroused his keen interest in the arts, particularly in music and contributed to the relaxation of his moral rigour. This relationship too lasted until Weber's death. [12]

Weber took part in the Vienna conference of the *Verein*. When he spoke in debates it was against Schmoller's propaganda for an attitude of bureaucratic social patronage towards the workforce. From spring till summer 1909, Weber went through another, longer nervous attack. At the first Sociology Conference in Frankfurt in 1910, the organization for which Weber was largely responsible, he delivered the business report which was to determine the future work of the *Deutsche Gesellschaft für Soziologie*. Weber had to fight out numerous personal conflicts with university colleagues and the press. At the conference he spoke out particularly against racist ideology.

At the Fourth Conference of German University Lectures in 1911, Weber attacked the educational and personal policy of the late Ministerial Director in the Prussian Ministry of Culture, Friedrich Althoff. This attack and the simultaneous sharp criticism of the whole organization in business schools aroused extensive discussion in the press. Weber countered the public replies of the Rectors of the Cologne and Berlin business schools with a written reply. In October, Weber supported an article in the *Frankfurter Zeitung* (a liberal newspaper) which criticized a Freiburg student

drinking festival with military inclinations. The Vice-Rector had polemicized against pacifist 'simpletons' and the 'cloud-cuckoo-land of peace',
and a general who was present delivered further heated words. The
Freiburg professorship reacted with a collective declaration against Weber,
which Weber again answered with a letter to his colleagues.

A further example of Weber's love of argument turned into a matter of
honour (and the threat of a duel) because of some journalistic attacks on his
wife (who was involved in women's rights campaigns) and on himself.
Weber entered into a protracted dispute, at first with the paper concerned,
which led to an accusation of slander against the editor involved (the case
cited two instances) and finally in a case of slander against a Heidelberg
professor, Adolf Koch. Weber won the case, in the process stirring up the
entire Heidelberg public and ruining his colleague's career – but not
without generously forgiving Koch after his success. This attitude and not
least his self-image as 'captain of the reserves' often brought Weber into
legal difficulties and *affaires d'honneur*, which gave him quite Quixotic
characteristics.

In 1911 he worked intensively on the sociology of religion regarding
China, Japan, India, Judaism and Islam. At the conference of the *Verein* in
Nuremberg he gave a speech on the theme of 'Problems in the Psychology
of Workers'. During this time (1911–13) the original manuscript of the
later second part of *Economy and Society* for the *Grundriss der Sozialökonomik*
was written. 1912 brought numerous political society activities for Weber:
at the Berlin Sociology Assembly he delivered a critical statement of
account; on this occasion he took issue with the concept of 'nation'.
Towards the end of the year, Weber withdrew from the directorate of the
Deutsche Gesellschaft für Soziologie because of differences of opinion on the
question of freedom from value-judgement. He justified his step in writing:

Will these gentlemen, not *one* of whom can stifle the impulse (for that's just it!) to
bother me with his subjective 'valuations', all infinitely uninteresting to me, kindly
stay in their own circle. I am sick and tired of appearing time and again as a Don
Quixote of an allegedly unfeasible principle and of producing embarrassing
'scenes'.[13]

1913 brought the pinnacle of Weber's achievement; on his desk lay the
main part of the manuscript of his contribution to the *Grundriss der
Sozialökonomik*, in particular the sections on commercial and legal sociology.
His sketch for a sociology of music was provisionally concluded. In the
course of his academic endeavours, his comparative, historical approach
which he had been working on since his student days, moved more and

more in the direction of a systematic sociological procedure. This can be seen in an exemplary way in the story of the origin of *Economy and Society*, to the second, empirically oriented section of which he added, in his last working year, a systematically oriented 'Conceptual Exposition', almost symmetrical to its first section. In this year too he published an analysis of the basic sociological concepts under the title *On some Categories of Interpretive Sociology*.

From 1909–14 Weber took a considerable part in the long debates of the *Verein*, which had become well-known as the 'value-judgement dispute'. Weber's basic opinion and central position was that it was impossible to justify (or to dismiss) a political standpoint with 'scientific' arguments. This passionate controversy took place largely behind closed doors.

His travels to Italy in the spring and autumn of 1913 brought Weber into the circle of a 'commune' of 'anarchists, nature children, vegetarians and other modern sects', who had made their home in Ascona ('Monte Verità') and were leading an independent life influenced mainly by the ideas of Otto Groß and Erich Mühsam. This did not fail to leave an impression upon Weber, which completely contradicted his previous conceptions.

After the outbreak of the First World War, Weber served in Heidelberg as a reserve officer on the Reserve Military Hospitals Commission, where he took over the function of a disciplinary officer. As such he set up altogether nine military hospitals and took over their running until the end of 1915. During this activity, which absorbed him completely, he gained valuable experience, on the one hand gaining an 'insight' into bureaucracy (one of his central objects of study), and on the other hand he proved to be a useful, practical man. His attitude to the war was subject to a few changes. If, at the start of the war, he was filled with the greatest misgivings, regarding the whole situation as unworthy of the German Empire, he was soon swept along on a wave of general national enthusiasm. He expressed his heroic affirmation of events with the words: 'Despite its final outcome, this war is great and wonderful.' His application to become a volunteer was in complete accord with his earlier nationalistic convictions.

In 1915 Weber requested a discharge from the hospital service as organizational changes had occurred and they were not entirely sure how best to employ him. The intervention of Edgar Jaffé should have brought Weber to Brussels for economic policy investigations on behalf of the German military authority, but a journey there came to nothing. Efforts aimed towards a political project ebbed away, as did his attempt to add his voice to the attempts to solve the Polish question. Thus he concentrated again on his academic work, particularly on his studies on the sociology of religion. His brother, Karl Weber, a professor of architecture, was killed in the war. Weber published the first part of *The Economic Ethic of the World Religions*. His position *vis-à-vis* German war policy meanwhile underwent a fundamental change. He signed the 'Delbrück-Denkschrift',[14] a counter-agreement to the 'Seeberg-Adresse' in which numerous people in public life had placed extensive demands on the objectives of the war. The conquest of Poland and the German invasion of Belgium led him to take up a position against the German policy of annexation. Weber was increasingly disillusioned by the German war policy; he spent much time on letters and appeals, urging a moderate policy in the war objectives. He criticized the attitude of the war-parties as a game of chance played by munitions manufacturers and agrarian capitalists and also reiterated his earlier remarks on the structure of German social policy.

Through the mediation of Friedrich Naumann, Weber joined the Commission on Central Europe in 1916, which examined the requirements for a tariff and economic community among the mid-European countries. Working with this Commission unofficially, Weber travelled to Vienna and Budapest. His extensive journalistic activity, particularly for the *Frankfurter Zeitung*, was characterized by concern for the nation and by a criticism of the unclear objectives of the war. He dealt with the problem of pacifism, fought against the, at first intensified, submarine warfare and espoused the cause of Chancellor Bethmann-Hollweg in particular. In March, together with Felix Somary, he composed a declaration against the intensified submarine war which he sent to public figures. In it he opposed the already widespread unlimited submarine warfare, which in his opinion would undoubtedly bring the USA into the war and would precipitate the German defeat.

In the following year, Weber continued his journalistic activity for the *Frankfurter Zeitung*. In this he frequently came into conflict with the military censor. He attended the Lauenstein Congresses, organized by the Jena publisher and book-dealer Eugen Diederichs, which promoted discussion of Germany's future. Weber's Quixotic characteristics were apparent here too. On his impression of the course of the war, he told Theodor Heuß, a co-participant at the congresses, 'As soon as the war is over, I shall insult the Kaiser until he sues me, and then the responsible statesmen – Bülow, Tirpitz, Bethmann-Hollweg – shall be obliged to make statements under oath.'[15] He tried again for an academic career; he travelled to Vienna and led negotiations over the chair in economics there. During this same period Weber's works on the sociology of religion, on Hinduism and Buddhism (1916) and on Ancient Judaism (1917) appeared. From his dealings with

Wilhelminian foreign policy, he entered increasingly into a critical debate with the internal policy relations of the German Reich. The political failure of the leadership and the alienation between government and people led him to demand a new internal order as a prerequisite for the historical continuity of the state, an order which should create a people's state out of the authoritarian state. He wrote a critique of the Prussian three-class franchise and in the *Frankfurter Zeitung* took issue with the crisis surrounding the Chancellor.

At this time the internal and external situation of Germany threw up the question of a revision of the terms of the constitution, the aim of which Weber regarded as the formation of a parliament. Thus he began work on some sketches of the constitution. These thoughts found their literary expression in a series of articles in the *Frankfurter Zeitung* which were later published separately under the title 'Parliament and government in a newly-reconstituted Germany'. These articles brought him dangerously near to other '*vaterlandslose Gesellen*' as the 'lefties' and pacifists were classified at this time, to the extent that a charge of *lèse-majesté* against Weber was considered by the Prussian Government. Weber must have seen a certain endorsement of his efforts in the Kaiser's famous 'Easter decree' which essentially contained the promise to abolish class franchise. Weber resigned from foreign policy in spring 1917 after the USA had declared its entry into the war which, in Weber's opinion, would pave the way for the USA to become a world-power. His decided opposition to the German policy of annexation was strengthened essentially by the conviction that the German position particularly as a world-power was to be extended not through a policy of occupation, but through a policy of free alliance. Weber began to contemplate the German defeat.

In 1918 Weber accepted on a trial basis the Chair of Political Economy at the University of Vienna. He lectured in the summer term on 'Economy and Society' with the explanatory sub-title 'A positive critique of the materialistic conception of history'. He also pursued his journalistic activities and completed the outline of a federal republican constitution for Germany. As a response to pressure from Alfred Weber, Friedrich Naumann and Erich Koch-Weser, he announced that he was joining the DDP (German Democratic Party). After Germany's defeat, Weber pressed Naumann to motivate the Kaiser into a timely abdication to save the honour of the dynasty. At this time Weber still considered that a constitutional monarchy was still possible for Germany.

In the elections for the National Assembly in January 1919 Weber took an active part in the campaign. He was nominated as Democratic Party candidate in the Frankfurt election district. His application as Reichstag candidate was overturned by party officials and he wound up on a hopeless slate for Hessen–Nassau district. On the Council of the People's Delegates they considered making Weber Secretary of State for the Interior. Konrad Haußmann suggested him as ambassador in Vienna or as committee member of the Democratic Party. In spite of this he was given no position within the framework of the newly constituted political system. However Weber took part as one of thirteen in a non-official function, advising the Ministry of the Interior on the basics of the constitutional outline.

In autumn 1918 Weber was in Munich and he followed with concern and outrage the growing separatist and radical pacifist tendencies in Bavaria. On 4 November 1918 when the revolutionary upheavals were already happening in Kiel and three days before Eisner seized power, Weber spoke at a meeting of the *Fortschrittliche Volkspartei* (Progressive People's Party) against the Bavarian desire for secession: the slogan 'Apart from Prussia', he said, was criminal folly and the pacifist call for 'Peace at any Price' was politically irresponsible. Turning to left-wing politics, he said, 'Playing games with the revolution means that one could take away one's need to *talk*, at the cost of the proletariat. What would the outcome of a revolution be? The enemy on our doorstep and then later a reaction the like of which we have never experienced. And the proletariat will have to pay the price.'[16]

Even Weber's personal contact with Ernst Toller[17] and numerous other revolutionary-minded socialists, and his personal intervention could do nothing to stop the revolutionary upheaval which he had seen coming for a long time, and which he considered to have been provoked by Wilhelm II's personal regiment, his desertion from the capital and his toying with a military *coup*.

In all this it was not only his monarchistic and anti-separatist opinion which made him oppose the revolution. Weber was also embittered because of it and outraged by the outbreak of revolution, as it happened at the moment of Germany's enemies' greatest triumph. It was the major fault of this revolution that it had ultimately knocked the weapons out of Germany's grasp, had made Wilson's role as Justice of World Peace impossible and thus had delivered Germany wholesale into the hands of foreign domination. Wolfgang Mommsen indicates that in this argument Weber came suspiciously close to giving his country a stab in the back and moreover had misjudged the extent of the purely military defeat.[18] And it was not only for nationally motivated, foreign policy reasons that Weber had raged against the 'bloody carnival that does not deserve the honourable name of a revolution',[19] but it was also because of the political effects within Germany, which he feared.

He disapproved sharply of the seizure of power by workers, peasants and soldiers' soviets. Weber expected and diagnosed massive chaos and the senseless waste of the remaining economic potential. In spite of his own vote and his work in the Heidelberg workers' and soldiers' soviet, he frequently publicly condemned the dreadful economic mismanagement of organs of the revolution which were incapable of organized administration. Wolfgang Mommsen suspected, as Weber did, that it was this decisive opposition to the revolution that finally prevented Friedrich Ebert from realizing his plans to make Weber Secretary of the Interior or at least the German emissary in Vienna.[20] Like many of his peers, Weber confessed to having no enthusiasm for the Republic; this was the view of Friedrich Meinecke too, that monarchists of the heart had been changed into republicans of the intellect. In 1919 Weber continued his election campaigning for the Democratic Party. His journalistic utterances made public the question of war guilt in particular.

Following an invitation from the Union of Free Students in Munich, Weber gave his two famous lectures on 'Science as a Vocation' in November 1917, and 'Politics as a Vocation' in January 1919. Marianne Weber, who had taken part in the election campaign together with her husband, was elected as a delegate to the Baden *Landtag*, and in the same year she became leader of the *Bund deutscher Frauenvereine*, the organizing body of the bourgeois women's movement.

In the spring Weber was summoned to be a member of the peace delegation, led by Court Brockdorf-Rantzau, the German Foreign Minister of the Reich. With Count Montgelas, Hans Delbrück and A. Mendelssohn-Bartholdy, he travelled to Versailles to work out in only three days Germany's reply to the Allies' memorandum on war guilt. Largely for personal reasons Weber moved to Munich, where in mid-June 1919 he took over Brentano's chair and gave lectures at the University on 'General categories of social science' (summer term, 1919). He refused offers of a post from Berlin's business school, Frankfurt's *Institut für Gemeinwohl* and from Bonn University. In Munich he witnessed the end of the system of soviet republics. His attempt once again to intervene in the formation of the Reich's constitution did not succeed. He visited Ludendorff to convince him to give himself up voluntarily to the Allies and to clarify objectively the question of war guilt, but in vain. In October Weber's mother, Helene Fallenstein-Weber, died. He worked on the *Grundriss der Sozialökonomik* and on the *Gesammelte Aufsätze zur Religionssoziologie*. Apart from this, his time was filled with his lectures at the University, 'Sketches on universal social and economic history' in the winter term 1919–20; 'General political science and policy' and 'Socialism' in summer 1920. Weber was critical of the Arco-Valley case, the murder of Kurt Eisner.[21] Because of this, right-wing corps students demonstrated against him during his lectures. He declined the democratic party's desire to send him on the first nationalization commission. In June 1920, Lili Schäfer, née Weber, committed suicide. The Webers planned to adopt her four orphaned children, which Marianne would go on to do in April 1927. In June 1920, Weber fell ill with pneumonia; it was treated too late and he died on 14 June of that year.

2

Early writings

Relevant texts

'*Zur Geschichte der Handelsgesellschaften im Mittelalter*' (On the History of Medieval Trading Companies) (1889)
Die römische Agrargeschichte (Roman Agrarian History)
'*Die sozialen Gründe des Untergangs der antiken Kultur*' (The Social Reasons for the Decline of Ancient Civilization) (1896)
The Agrarian Sociology of Ancient Civilizations (1897; 1898; 1909)
General Economic History (1919–20)
'The City' (1920–21)

The origin and effects of modern capitalism

Both the theme of '*Zur Geschichte der Handelsgesellschaften im Mittelalter*' and his treatment of it showed that Weber the lawyer did not intend to work in traditional ways. He approached his legal studies in such a way that at the time of his graduation he was as well-versed in Roman as in German law. This fact incurred not only the disapproval of his teacher and dissertation supervisor Levin Goldschmidt, but also placed him from the start between the warring camps of 'Germanists' and 'Romanists'. Already in this, his first piece of work to be published, Weber concentrated on the theme that was to determine his entire *œuvre*: the origin and effects of 'modern' capitalism. In this dissertation he approached the question of the historical genesis of this specific form of economy from two sides: first, with regard to *content*, by presenting the rise of capitalist trading companies in the late Middle Ages, in particular the enterprises' separation from family communities; and second, with regard to *legal form* by pursuing the controversy of whether it was Germanic or Roman legal contractual elements which exerted a greater influence on Medieval trading companies. His central thesis was that the 'individualistic' Roman law had been displaced by certain assumptions of modern capitalism, which derived from German law.

Weber's presentation of the history of trading companies, which was supported by a comprehensive knowledge of his sources – mainly South European legal principles and digests from the eleventh to the sixteenth century – was aimed in particular at the historical formation of property rights in modern trading companies and limited liability companies. By contrasting the *societas* of Roman law with the modern institutions of commercial law, Weber discovered the most basic difference to be the lack of a separate fund. Under Roman law, a company fund – wealth related to the *societas* as to a juristic personality – was unknown, and Roman institutions were restricted to operations *inter socios*. According to Weber, such a separate fund had 'the closest connection' with the relations of liability, since such a separate fund had to bear the main financial burden in the case of, for example, bankruptcy. He regarded the two factors of joint liability and a separate fund as basic indices of a development towards the modern company. He saw this as the development of a legal institution which appears as an independent subject in relation to a third party as well as to its own members, and which is more than an alliance determined by interests and proportionate to the business concerns of the traders and producers involved. The 'firm' had thus become a central assumption in the capitalist commodity economy.

Weber pursued the legal development of this institution with the aid of the societies of commercial maritime law, the *commenda* – 'a business transaction . . . in which someone takes on the valorization of someone else's commodities, at their own risk, for a share of the profit' (2, p. 17)[1] – and the *societas maris*, the development of a true company as a result of the profit-sharing of the earlier consignee, who carried the risk. The *societas maris* showed a development towards the business with a sleeping partner; but in spite of these approaches to the separate treatment of the society's funds, joint liability could not develop on this basis. Equally, Weber saw in the *societas terrae*, the domestic trading company, some 'essentials' of the later limited liability company (partners who are personally completely liable, associates who are only liable for their own share, and the beginnings of a separate fund); however a personal joint liability of *all* associates was not in evidence. To research their origin, Weber went back to the family community of the Middle Ages, as one of the oldest forms of relationship 'which appears to have led and legally organized the creation of community wealth with the aim of creating community earning power' (2, p. 44).

Weber saw the family community as based on a community of goods and earnings to such an extent that all members of the household are, alongside the father of the house, equally entitled to the household goods, including what is brought in as earnings. The household community, in this instance, included not only relations but also the servants, with all the consequences for property rights that that entailed: it was not the principle of kinship which dominated, but the principle of earning. According to Weber, the development of property rights proceeded to restrict the property-owning community, accounts were kept of the incomings and outgoings from the fund, and the participation of the individual was conceived of more as a share, like an investment in a society. Among municipal artisans, moreover, organizations of working communities arose, which could organize themselves along the lines of the institution of the household community as they adopted its principle of earning.

Out of these relations of community, via family liability for offences committed by a partner, there arose liability for contract guilt, which consisted of two different forms of liability: one, through the wealth of the community, and the other through personal co-liability of the partners. The need to secure the bases of liability led finally to an amicable fixing of even family-based societies; the household community as the usual legal foundation fell into decline and independent institutions like the separate fund and joint liability arose. The 'firm' became the dominant type.

Where Roman law recognized only individual wealth, in the Middle Ages it was the earning community and not the household community which formed the foundation for joint liability. Such liability, however, occurred only where deals were carried out 'on the account of the society', i.e. the firm was already considered separately from its members. Thus the relations of wealth were two-fold; *private* creditors, beyond the private wealth of a businessman, had no claim to the wealth of a society.

Weber discussed this creation of a separate fund in detail in the examples of Pisa, a case of 'the absolute predominance of maritime trading' and of Florence, 'a provincial town, whose outlet to the sea . . . was blocked' (2, p. 128). In Weber's opinion, for Pisa, the *ad hoc* associations of maritime traders seemed essential, as for Florence were the family business undertakings, the foundation of which was the generational continuity of households.

At the end of his investigation, Weber distinguished between two forms of law: a society of several people, who carry on a business under a common name with a joint liability of the associates exclusive of the *creditores societatis*, and with a separate fund, i.e. an open trading company; and a society of several people, of whom one carries on the business in their name while the others participate by way of their capital investment, and are not personally liable, except for their investment, i.e. a limited liability company.

The main theme of this work was an investigation into those forms of community which developed alongside the expansion of maritime and domestic trading and municipal industrial production. The legal institutions which arose organized themselves according to risk- and profit-sharing, according to the respective agreement of commitment and responsibility.

As an answer to the question of, in the widest sense, the *sociological* aspects of this juristic dissertation, the following three points are important:

1   In the contrast between the Roman legal concept of *societas* and the open trading company, Weber's *comparative approach* can clearly be seen, not in any way obviously, but in this case directed against 'narrow-minded patriotism of the field', a frequent target of Weber, particularly against the total separation of Romanists and Germanists.

2   In the course of his investigation Weber made a clear distinction between purely *legal and economic* ways of considering the development of society and he emphasized the possibility of a *disharmonious development* of legal principles and economic events; on the other hand he attempted to work out a *dialectical relationship* between the two areas, according to which economic relations can bring about legal ones, and legal regulations can influence economic consequences. The inadequacy of the jurisprudence of this time, which was oriented towards Roman law, was apparent, according to Weber, in its inability to comprehend in a historically correct manner the legal institutions he was dealing with:

    The entire manner in which lawyers treat and discuss things shows that there is not some economic or even social theory, which they have thought out and consequently implemented, behind their way of considering things; on the contrary it shows that their isolated judgments are merely a result of abstract construction. (2, p. 151)

3   Weber saw in the *social distinctions* a main cause of different *economic and legal developments*:

    If that is the case, then we have here once again proof of the interesting observation that the *commenda* relations and anything attached to them, take

their point of departure from the association between people who are economically and one can even say socially unequal, while joint liability grew out of
communities of equal individuals, and principally those provided with wealth
over which they have equal powers of disposal. (2, pp. 123-4)

Thus, in Weber's first scholarly work, which was written as a dissertation, we can see economic and sociological questions being posed,
questions which revolve around the problem of the evolution of capitalist
society.

Weber's *Habilitation* thesis on 'Roman agrarian history and its importance for constitutional and civil law' set itself the task of investigating
'different manifestations of Roman constitutional and civil law in its
practical importance for the development of agrarian relations (5, p. 1).[2] In
this it is made clear in the introduction that Weber's treatment of Roman
agrarian history was based essentially on an economic, political and
sociological point of view. The history of Roman imperialism was basically
'a continual expansion of the area which was subjected to Roman
occupation and capitalist exploitation' (5, p. 6). The actual object of
contention in domestic policy was the public land, the *ager publicus*, the
distribution of which was of immense social, economic and political importance. Thus alongside the question 'which social strata and economic
interest groups formed the driving force politically?' (5, p. 6) Weber posed
a further one: in the area of agriculture, which economic ideas corresponded to the concept of property, a concept 'which dominates our
legal thought even today, admired by some for its logical consequences and
attacked by others as the root of all things evil in our law of land-owning?'
(5, p. 7). In order to be able to answer this question, that is, in order to be
able to trace the development from original communal property to private
property, Weber turned initially to the different forms of measurement of
the Roman field. He proceeded from the assumption that the method of
surveying Roman land corresponded with the relations of public and civil
law. Weber described three different forms of land distribution:

1   The *ager limitatus, per centurias divisus et assignatus*: this manner of
    distribution, particularly of that land which was allotted to new
    colonialist settlers, was used in cases of full Roman citizenship, the
    taxation resulted from the owner's property tax.

2   The *ager per scamna et strigas divisus et assignatus*: here, state-owned land
    was conferred in return for interest or ground tax and the exact agree-
    ment as to the land's boundaries followed from the mode of taxation.
    Linked to this manner of distribution was the *ager quaestoris*, which
    entailed a transfer of the use of the land in return for capital. In this the

state retained the right to repurchase the land and thus this corresponded to a crude way by which the state could raise loans.

3   The *ager per extremitatem mensura comprehensus*: which concerned those
cases in which the land was neither completely privatized nor
completely under the control of the Roman administration. In these
cases the individual was not directly subject to taxation, but rather the
whole community (*municipium*) guaranteed the amount of taxation to
the tax administration and collected it themselves independently from
the peasants.

Proceeding from these three categories, Weber dealt with the
consequences of land distribution as regards administrative law, in
particular the capability of a census and the access to *mancipation*, i.e. the
form of sale in civil law of the tax-free field, as well as the main controversial forms *de loco* (aimed at a *fixed* plot of land) and *de modo* (aimed at any
amount of land of fixed quality). Connected to this, Weber analysed the
juridical and economic conditions which 'made Rome into the real estate
exchange of the world' (5, p. 99). Weber stated that the general tendency,
which for the functions of ownership and earning amounted to the gradual
disappearance of the *de modo* form, could be summed up thus: 'We have
seen . . . that the Roman *ager privatus* is a product of a conscious tendency
of agrarian policy, which strived by fairly artificial ways to reach
unconditional freedom in the economic and legal disposal of landed
property and its utmost mobilization; and which reached it, not without
putting up with many a social and economic loss' (5, p. 114).

With this 'revolutionary transition' from the *ager publicus* of a field
community to the *ager privatus* of private ownership, namely the freeing of
private landed property, the way was cleared, according to Weber for
large-scale land-ownership:

We shall have to accept that even this economic emancipation bears the character
both of a separation and a union: the victory of the individual economy free from
patrimonial as well as community-economic burdens, and the disintegration of the
field community into private property by being divided up. This was the aim and
result of the same party at the same time. This party created that concept of private
property or rather made use of landed property; the concept which although an
artificial product reflecting the policies of an interested party, has dominated the
ideas of jurisprudence and still dominates it so long as such a thing exists, by virtue
of the refinements of its logical procedure. (5, pp. 117–8)

The last part of the work 'which offers an economic–historical view of
Roman agriculture' (5, p. 3), turned to the age of the Roman Empire as

that episode in Roman history in which the struggle over the *ager publicus*, the public land, led to the most serious internal conflicts. After his investigation into the historical origin and differentiation of the *ager publicus*, Weber described the distribution of the public land by occupation and management which essentially boiled down to 'an unprecedented encouragement of capital'.

For it is often stressed that this free competition proved useful not to the owners of small-holdings but only to the large-scale capitalists, patricians as well as plebeians. In fact it places the most unrestrained capitalism in the area of agriculture, capitalism which has always been listened to throughout history and which will soon be achieved by the encroachments and partitionings of the late Medieval landlords, which we have already described as an analogy. (5, p. 129)

The relations of tenancy at this time tended to simplify large tenancies with sub-tenants which led not only to the 'legal destruction of the community groups' but also to the quantitative increase in large enterprises (5, p. 139). These relations of tenancy were partly hereditary, with the result that the tenant's rent gradually turned into a ground tax and here too private landed property made more headway. The legal forms which had thus developed 'in which land is conferred upon large entrepreneurs' led to the following situation: 'Between the peasants on the one hand and the estate-owners and domain tenants on the other there arose a gulf even in legal status which could not be bridged by any intermediaries' (5, p. 178).

In his conclusion Weber turned to the increasingly dominant position of Roman large-scale land-ownership. This alone was capable of coming up with the capital outlay necessary for profitable wine and oil cultivation or cattle-rearing. While the Roman landed aristocracy became an urban capitalist status group consuming ground-rent, the number of small landowners fell off drastically (5, p. 230) and there was no 'peasant status group of any great significance in society' (5, p. 232) which might have fought against the unjust relations of tenancy. Weber differentiated between the peasants by means of the criterion of their dependence on the landlord: from the small owner via the tenant who served by hand and in harness, and the dependent journeymen down to the slave. Weber specifically linked the decline of the Roman Empire to the increasingly changed and differentiated status of the slaves: because of a dearth in the supply of slaves, the landlords began to differentiate more and more strictly between the slaves (foreman, steward etc.), to give them land to rent and partly to release them from the narrow household of the estate. 'The turning of slaves practically into colonies, i.e. the transformation of rural workers into freeholders is however one of the most important and indubitable facts of the

Roman Imperial era' (5, p. 276). The development of the large estates into private property led, in Weber's view, to a gradual excavation of the community institutions and community property, which gave rise to the following situation:

In fact, however, a network of landlord estates was spread over the entire empire in which the municipalities, without the necessary foci for a productive life or to create capital and also because they were not indispensable market places, were basically nothing but cupping-glasses in the interest of the state tax administration. (5, p. 267)

If we now look at the *sociological* aspects of this work, we can specify a number of approaches which point to both a purely juridical as well as a purely agrarian–historical analysis. Alfred Heuss, one of the few people acquainted with these first works of Weber, seized on this fact with regard to Roman agrarian history when he spoke of Weber's capacity 'to see through juridical institutions, firstly to the economic intention that founded them and, secondly from the juridical form to their social consequences'.[3] This capacity produced the result that Weber's Roman agrarian history 'contains many an observation, which was to gain importance in the later thoughts of Weber the sociologist'.[4] As we have already indicated, the legal and economic evolution of private landed property contained a string of economic, political and social assumptions as well as consequences. Weber's pursuit of these questions placed his investigation above the level of a purely agrarian–historical and juridical monograph; and this is surely the reason for its relatively poor reception in the areas of the science of Antiquity and ancient history.[5]

Even in his *Habilitation* thesis, Weber was moving in a direction which we saw already established in his dissertation: the exploration of the conditions of evolution of capitalist economic management, here in the specific question of the evolution of Roman agrarian capitalism. There are two additional components of this work.

On the one hand this work articulated Weber's recognizably social and political interests when he looked closely at the position of the small peasants, who had fallen into a situation of greater and greater dependency upon the large land-owning aristocracy. Weber provided an approach to the class analysis of Antiquity as a differentiated investigation of the position of the slaves, which contrary to Marxist doctrine he did not see exclusively as an object of exploitation in a 'slave-owning society'. He was concerned with the drift towards an organization based on guilds and the 'work ethos' of these groups, which however did not result in the goal of freedom for which they were striving.

On the other hand, in this early work we can see Weber's lively, if in no way systematic *methodological interest* – his very unusual intention of making a connection between the techniques of land-surveying and the historical evolution of the legal institutions of private property certainly presented a considerable methodological problem. He wrote 'The existence of a connection between two historical phenomena cannot be brought into view such as it is *in abstracto* but only by a presentation of a comprehensive view of the way in which this connection might have been concretely constituted' (5, p. 2). Alongside this emphasis on the importance of empirical-historical research and of a logically consistent formulation of hypotheses, Weber was concerned with the problem of establishing historical 'laws'. In the light of empirically observable contradictions he wrote 'One can establish the law of development as a general one in the sense that such kinds of "laws" present *tendencies* which can be crossed with ones with a stronger local effect' (5, p. 4).

It is worth highlighting one further point. Already in his *Habilitation* thesis Weber had mentioned a concept, which he was later to make into a centrally important element in his methodological deliberations. In explaining the relations of community property and private property, Weber established the rather considerable difference in the respective regions ('It goes without saying that this development was implemented locally to very differing degrees . . .'), in order to assert 'If one wants to formulate the tendencies of the development thus in ideal pictures [sic!], always with the proviso that they are just tendencies and that the degree of their implementation is locally different, and that they will perhaps never appear at all in full purity, then, I believe, one can say without too much audacity . . .' (5, p. 266). It is certainly not over-interpretation if, in this piece from 1891, we can already discern the crude outlines of the later concept of the ideal-typical procedure.

In spite of all these *sociologically relevant* aspects which have as yet been too little discussed, the *Habilitation* thesis, just as much as the dissertation which dealt primarily with commercial law, was primarily a work of agrarian-historical law, which can however be linked with Weber's later specialist sociological works in the way it approached questions as well as in individual methodological aspects.

The decline of the Roman empire

Evidence that Alfred Heuss's theory about Weber was correct ('Weber the "scholar" was formed . . . to an important extent in his work on

Antiquity')[6] can be seen also with reference to the 1896 essay *'Die sozialen Gründe des Untergangs der antiken Kultur'*. In the dissertation and the *Habilitation* thesis Weber dealt in sociologically relevant questions and approaches; in this work we are already in the midst of a genuinely sociological investigation even if here the boundaries of social and economic history (which moreover are objectively scarcely meaningful) might not be unequivocally determinable. It is worth reproducing the course of the argument in outline, as many themes which occupied Weber the sociologist during his lifetime begin to emerge.

Immediately the title indicates what the first section introduced. It was not external causes which brought about the end of Rome's world empire, but essentially *internal* developments. Using his own methods as well as those particular to the sociology of the time, Weber investigated the reasons which could be held responsible for the decay, the 'inner self-liquidation' of a *civilization*. In order to be able to answer this, Weber set himself the task of elaborating the *'characteristics* of the social structure of ancient society' (43, p. 59). In this he named three elements. Ancient civilization was: (1) urban civilization; (2) coastal civilization; and (3) slave civilization. Weber regarded the third aspect in particular as being decisive, since it contained the greatest significance for economic development, and in turn this determined the overall development. A colony-conquering state of agricultural citizens, particularly with conquests overseas, turned into an empire which hunted down people and which needed a continual supply of slaves for its ever-expanding *latifundia* system of agriculture. The rise of a landed aristocracy led to the development which Weber described thus: 'The slave-owner therefore became the economic bearer of ancient civilization, and the organization of slave-labour forms the indispensable infrastructure of Roman society . . . The Roman large-scale land-owning type is not a farmer who runs the enterprise himself, but a man who lives in the city, is politically active and wants more than anything else to receive revenue' (43, pp. 53–4).

Following on from this analysis, Weber turned to the 'social peculiarity' of the slaves from which he draws up an 'ideal schema' (sic!) (43, p. 65) which is of a 'barrack-room existence' – without possessions or family. The slave-barracks, according to Weber's interpretation, were the prerequisite for the political, economic and social system of the Roman empire. And for their part, the barracks were 'dependent on a regular supply of people to the slave-market. What if this were ever to fail? That had to have an effect on the slave-barracks, as the exhaustion of a seam of coal would have an effect on the blast-furnaces. And thus the moment arrived. We are coming to the turning point in the development of ancient civilization' (43, p. 66).

This turning point and with it the decisive cause of the decline of the ancient Roman civilization lay for Weber in the discontinuance of the Roman wars of conquest and its consequences. With this internal and external 'pacification of the ancient circle of civilization', the regular supply to the slave-market dried up too and this resulted in 'the impossibility of progress in production on the basis of the slave-barracks' (43, p. 67). This development led to two further, mutually reinforcing ones. On the one hand it resulted in an ever-stronger rejection of the urban communities in favour of the large estates, which tried to evade inclusion by the communities. On the other it resulted in the gradual evolution of a classification of the people on the estates of the large-scale land-owners, according to their estate: 'The *classification according to estate* had begun as a replacement for the old, simple opposition of the free and the unfree. A development which was almost indetectable in its individual stages led to this since economic relations forced it that way. The development of the *feudal society* was already detectable in the late Roman empire' (43, p. 70). Both these developments led to a more and more concerted move towards a position where the individual needs of the large estates were covered through the division of labour, and thus this led to a gradual disappearance of economic trade with the cities and to an even stronger barter economy. It became increasingly more difficult to maintain and to finance the civil service and the professional army through the state financial policy, which only intensified this development even more.

The decay of the empire was the necessary political consequence of the gradual disappearance of trade and the increase in barter. It meant essentially the abolition of that administrative apparatus and with it the political superstructure of a money economy, which no longer suited the economic infrastructure of barter. (43, p. 75)

In conclusion, Weber produced a résumé of the historical developments of Antiquity, while confirming the disappearance of its decisive elements: the standing army, the salaried civil service, the exchange of goods between localities, the city. His conclusion: 'Civilization has become rural' (43, p. 76).

In Weber's eyes, this development meant the decline of ancient civilization and its 'spiritual work'.

The spectacle moves us to involuntary melancholy, as a development which appears to be reaching for the heights loses its material foundation and collapses in on itself. What is it then that grips us in this violent process? In the depths of the society, organic structural changes were taking place and had to take place, changes which nevertheless indicated a violent restorative process on a major scale. The individual family and private ownership were returned to the masses of the unfree; the masses themselves were slowly raised out of the situation of being 'talking cattle' and restored to the realm of human beings, whose family existence was surrounded by tough moral guarantees from the then nascent Christianity . . . Of course a section of the free population sank immediately into what was in effect bondage, and the highly educated aristocracy of Antiquity fell into barbarism. The barter, which had been driven underground by the increase in unfree labour during the development of civilization in antiquity, at first flourished more and more widely, the more the ownership of slaves differentiated the estates; and after the political emphasis was transferred from the coast inland and the supply of people dried up, barter had forced its structure (which was moving towards feudalism) upon the superstructure which had originally been oriented towards a trade economy. Thus the shrivelled husk of ancient civilization disappeared and the spiritual life of Western humanity sank into a long night. Its decline, however, puts one in mind of the giant of Greek mythology who gained renewed strength when he rested in the bosom of mother earth . . . Not until the *city* had been resurrected in the Middle Ages on the basis of the free division of labour and trade, when the transition to political economy paved the way for bourgeois freedom and broke the constraint under the external and internal authorities of the age of feudalism, only then did the old giant rise up with renewed strength and lift the spiritual legacy of antiquity up to the light of modern, bourgeois civilization. (43, pp. 76–7)

The *sociological* relevance of this 1896 work can be seen clearly in this sketchy outline of the gist of the argument: here Weber was attempting to explain very complex historical processes of transformation (the fall of the Roman empire and its civilization) from changes in the social structure of ancient society. In this the importance of *economic* developments ('economic infrastructure') was strongly emphasized, and Weber went into their effects on the social structure in detail: the evolution of classification according to estate, the disintegration of the professional civil service and professional army, the disintegration of urban civilization. Also of sociological interest is Weber's inclusion of the importance of an ideological, religious system of values as a safeguard ('guarantees') for changes in the social structure.

The *methodological* aspects of the work reinforced the observations from the previous works. Here too Weber was already employing an ideal-typical procedure ('ideal schema') in his description of the slaves, large-scale land-owners, forms of economy etc., and here too he proceeded in an essentially comparative manner (comparing Antiquity with the Middle Ages). Moreover the large amount of normative valuation in the results of his analysis ('decline', 'restorative process') was noticeable, however nothing of his later position as regards 'value-judgements' was recognizable as yet. However we must emphasize that, pretty much as in his *Habilitation* thesis, Weber obviously stood in his valuations on the side of the weakest in society, in this case on the side of the slaves.

East, West and modern capitalism

His intensive occupation with the socio-economic relations of Antiquity in the works we have already discussed brought Weber the reputation of being a specialist in this area. This reputation led to the proposal that he be put in charge of the article in the *Dictionary of State Theory*, 'The Agrarian Sociology of Ancient Civilizations'.[7] This contribution was in three versions,[8] i.e. Weber re-wrote it for each edition of 1897, 1898 and 1909 and each time the scope of the project increased considerably. Alfred Heuss said of the contribution: 'In its content it is the most original, daring and penetrating description that the economic and social development of antiquity has ever undergone. The concept of "agrarian history" has thus been vastly exceeded; much more is dealt with. It is, in fact, a sketch of the entire economic and social history of Antiquity.'[9]

If we look at the 1897 version, we come across most of the arguments we have already discussed. However, an interesting new note turns up in the prefatory comparison between the West and the 'civilizations of East Asia' (48, p. 1), which Weber introduced. In this essay this comparison stood alongside the comparison between Antiquity and the Middle Ages (which until now had returned time and again) and we come across it more and more frequently particularly in Weber's later work. Weber saw the main differences between the West and 'the Asiatics' in the community property of land and the private ownership of cattle ('the primitive origin of all feudalism') in the West. The evolution of Western feudalism was for Weber in this version at any rate the decisive indicator of difference between the two areas of civilization.

In his ideas on Hellenic Antiquity Weber dealt again with farming production methods, the family structure and the manner of colonization. Particularly striking is the strong emphasis on political–military developments and the urban developments. In the section on Roman Antiquity to the end of the republic, we once again come across the arguments from the dissertation and *Habilitation* thesis, in particular the emphasis on the evolution of 'completely mobilized private land-ownership' which resulted in the creation of an 'unprecedented agrarian capitalism' (48, p. 10). Once again Weber was dealing with the 'diametrical opposition of interests' between urban capital, i.e. the slave-owners and the peasants, which he calls the 'struggle between free and unfree labour' (48, p. 11). The triumph of urban capital and the evolution of the large slave-owning enterprises which it made possible, created, in Weber's opinion, the 'political foundation of Caesarism' (48, p. 12). In the section on development in the imperial age, Weber repeated his analysis of the decline of ancient civilization with the stages of the curtailment of the slave-markets, development of classification according to estate, disintegration of the professional civil service and the standing army and a 'crumbling' of the cities. In presenting the evolution of classification according to estate, Weber distinguished between, on the one hand, the status group of those subject to direct taxation, the *possessores*, and on the other the status group of those subject to indirect taxation, the *coloni*. Of the *possessores* he said that it was they who, at the end of the imperial age in the country 'appeared as the exclusive bearer of that measure of bourgeois freedom which the Diocletian epoch still knew' (48, p. 17). The version in the second edition of 1898 was largely the same as that of the first edition, differing however in the inclusion of sketches on the Near East (Egypt, Babylon and Assyria).

This widening of the framework of questioning and general orientation became clearest in the now famous third edition of the *Dictionary* of 1909. Here we come across the Weber of the 'Essay on Objectivity' (62; 10E) and *The Protestant Ethic* (65, 74; 2E), and it is our intention to make clear both in content and methodology the continuities which pervade Weber's works during the entire working phase of his life. The difference between the Weber of the first and the third editions of the dictionary can be found in a *definition of the framework of questioning* and in a *more thorough methodological reflection* of the investigation.

In his introduction to the third edition Weber organized his framework of questioning once again in a comparison of the European Occident with the area of the civilizations of East Asia, but including the Near East. Thus he achieved a considerably more differentiated viewpoint from that of the previous investigations. It was no longer a question of a simple contrast along the lines of 'here we have feudalism, and there we don't'; it was now a precise differentiation of conformities, similarities, analogies and disparities:

Both East Asian and Amerindian civilizations had institutions which, because of their functions, we regard as essentially feudal in character. There is no reason why the concept of feudalism should not be used to characterize all those social institutions whose basis is a ruling class dedicated to war or royal service and is supported by privileged land holdings, rents or the labour services of a dependent, unarmed population. Thus one should call feudal the administrative benefices granted in Egypt and Babylonia as well as the constitution of Sparta. (1E, p. 38)

Weber lifted two specifically Western forms out of such mixed situations: on the one hand the *individualistic form of feudalism* and the specific political form of *urban feudalism*. Of particular importance methodologically are his sceptical and differentiated judgements on the *comparative approach* which we have encountered as a thread running through the works which we have looked at thus far: 'However, such comparisons with Medieval and modern phenomena although seemingly quite plausible, are highly unreliable for the most part, indeed are often an obstacle to clarity and understanding. For the similarities are all too easily deceptive. Ancient civilization had specific characteristics which sharply differentiate it from Medieval and modern civilization' (1E, pp. 39–40). As a particularly significant example we are referred to his ideas on the incomparability of the ancient proletariat with the modern working class (cf. 1E, p. 42). This emphasis on the 'differentiation of forms' and the intention of the research to work out their specific features and characteristics, must be situated within the methodological concept of the 'ideal-typical procedure', which Weber characterized precisely in this *Dictionary* article and which we shall investigate further later.[10]

This much more differentiated standpoint led Weber to correct his previous assessment of the problematic posed by slaves, and he confessed 'to an underestimation of the quantitative importance of free labour' (1E, p. 47), i.e. in particular the importance of the free artisans and the free unskilled wage-labourers of Antiquity.

Here was the question which is central for Weber again and again: 'The question to be considered now, therefore, is this: did a capitalist economy exist in Antiquity, to a degree significant for cultural history?' (1E, p. 48). The answer to this question was naturally dependent on the definition of the concept 'capitalism'. For Weber, 'capital always means wealth used to gain profit in commerce', i.e. goods which serve the production of profit in the trading of goods. 'Therefore we should expect a capitalist economy to be based on commerce' (1E, p. 48). In the light of this, Weber regarded even the land-economy of domain agriculture in Antiquity and the early Middle Ages as 'intermediate in character': 'It is capitalist in so far as goods are produced for the market and the land is an object of trade; it is non-capitalist in so far as the labour force as a means of production cannot be bought or leased in the open market' (1E, p. 49).

With this definition of capitalism, Weber distanced himself from the interpretation which was generally prevalent at that time, and which concentrated exclusively on the form of enterprise of the large capitalist firms run with free (= hired) wage-labour 'because it is this form which is responsible for the characteristic social problems of modern capitalism' (1E, p. 50). For this reason contemporary research into Antiquity had denied the existence and importance of a 'capitalist economy'. If on the one hand, as in Weber's method, 'capitalist economy' was not connected to a single form of valorization of capital, but this term was applied 'where we find that property is an object of trade and is utilized by individuals for profit-making enterprise in a market economy, there we have capitalism. If this be accepted, then it becomes perfectly clear that capitalism shaped whole periods of Antiquity, and indeed precisely those periods we call "golden ages"' (1E, p. 59).

Weber tried to substantiate this hypothesis in detail, by examining the importance of the reserves of precious metals in their relation to the market centres, analysing the economic problematic of slave-labour and stressing the importance of the *political* fates and features of the individual countries with their differing development in bureaucratization. It is only as an example that Weber introduced what he wrote in this context on the monarchical system of government:

Thus monarchical regulation, though beneficial to the great mass of subjects, in fact spelt the end of capitalist development and everything dependent on it. Slavery as a basis of capitalist enterprise regressed and new capital formation expired for the profit margin allowed had sunk below the indispensable minimum needed by ancient capital. Instead the economy became dominated by labour which was formally 'free', but was in fact subject to administrative law and direction. Wherever, in addition, the monarchy assumed a theocratic character, there we always find that religion and law sanction 'protection of the weak' . . . and this set rather precise limits to capitalist exploitation of men. (1E, p. 65)

Again in this context Weber called attention to a further point:

Businessmen, on the other hand, were not sustained by any positive justification of the profit motive. Only among followers of Cynicism and in the lower middle classes of the Hellenistic Near East do we find the beginnings of such an attitude. In early modern times the rationalization and economization of life were furthered by the essentially religious idea of 'vocation' and the ethic derived from it, but nothing similar arose in Antiquity. (1E, p. 67)

In summary, Weber emphasized that the agrarian history of Antiquity was closely involved with the '*peripetien*' of the *city history* of Antiquity, which he attempted to present by means of the development of different types of 'organizational stages' in city development. His interest in the typology and history of city development was resumed extensively in the essay on 'The City' (202; 8E) and we will be dealing with it in our discussion of this work.[11]

After his already strongly methodologically oriented 'introduction', which we have already partly summarized, the main section of the *Dictionary* article on 'The agrarian history of the main areas of ancient civilization' proceeded with extraordinarily detailed presentations of the agrarian history of Mesopotamia (1E, pp. 83-104), Egypt (1E, pp. 105-33), Israel (1E, pp. 134-46), Greece (1E, pp. 147-219) and Rome (1E, pp. 260-335).

In the concluding and summarizing section on the 'Foundations of development in the imperial age' (1E, pp. 336-66), Weber presented once again all those elements, which in his view were causes for the evolution of a *modern* Western capitalism. For one thing, it was the '*triumphant expansion*' of *the* polis through the Western world which was economically, socially, politically and religiously conditioned and effective. Alongside this strand of the development specifically *legal differences* emerged: 'The specific characteristics of modern capitalist development, industrial capitalism, is based on legal institutions which were created in the . . . industrial cities, institutions which did not exist in the ancient *polis*' (1E, p. 340). In comparing the burgher of the ancient *polis* with that of the Medieval city, Weber regarded the Medieval citizen in a greater degree as '*homo oeconomicus*': 'For the citizens of a Medieval town . . . the major aim of policy was and remained peaceful expansion . . . for the sale of their products' (1E, p. 347-8).

The exclusive accumulation of great wealth in the Middle Ages (Medici, Fugger) was however nothing specifically new compared with Antiquity, with its Hammurabis and Crassus. 'It is not here, nor in the manner in which the first great accumulations of money were collected, that we can find the answer to the basic problem: what is the origin of the later Medieval and modern economic system – in a word of modern capitalism?' (1E, p. 348). Weber formulated the two questions he considers to be important (1E, p. 348):

1 'How did consumer demand develop in Medieval times for the industries later organized on capitalist lines?' (development of the market)

2 'How did the endeavour to exploit capital lead to the creation of

organizations of free labour such as never existed in Antiquity?'
(organization of production)

Weber saw the main answer in the development of the *bourgeoisie*. Weber
regarded this development, which was specifically occidental and Medieval
as opposed to ancient as being determined on the one hand by the change of
the geographical arena – from the country to the city, and on the other
hand by two big military–technical revolutions in Antiquity – the introduction of the horse and the use of iron weapons. According to Weber, it
was only in the Middle Ages that armies of knights evolved and this led to
the feudal organization of society as they detached from the army of
yeomen, and to the formation of disciplined modern troops: for Weber, all
these processes led to a triumph of *modern state organization*.

For Antiquity, it was precisely the state organization which had
'throttled' developing capitalism 'slowly but surely' (1E, p. 363). As a
further reason apart from those already mentioned, Weber introduced the
political establishment of 'the exploitation for private profit of the political
conquests of the imperialist city-state' which led to an extensive *bureaucratization* of the life of the state, which for its part had paralysed private
economic initiative. It was precisely this last observation which allowed
Weber to assert a concluding parallel with his own age: 'Whereas in
Antiquity, the policies of the *polis* necessarily set the pace for capitalism,
today capitalism itself sets the pace for bureaucratization of the economy
. . . Thus in all probability some day the bureaucratization of German
society will encompass capitalism too, just as it did in Antiquity' (1E, p.
182).

The *sociological* relevance of Weber's works for the *Dictionary* needs no
further special emphasis: the question we encounter in these works as to the
historical genesis of modern capitalism and its economic, social, political
and normative–ideological assumptions as well as effects is without doubt of
great importance for the social sciences. Weber's presentation, in the
investigations we looked at above, of a 'subtle differential analysis'[12] which
he produced through study and scientific research, set him apart from the
majority of sociologists. The main conclusion his work reached was, as we
have seen, that in Weber's eyes it was just as senseless to deny completely
the existence of capitalist economic procedure in Antiquity, as it was simply
to equate 'ancient capitalism' with 'modern capitalism'. Weber came to the
conclusion that there certainly was a form of capitalist economy in
Antiquity which, however, should only be deemed 'political capitalism',
i.e. a form of economy which was (still) extensively restricted by political,
ethical and ideological conditions.

The *methodological* importance of these works could be seen at its clearest in the 1909 version. In this we saw a considerably differentiated application of the comparative approach, where it was less a question of tracing the conformities, and more one of grasping the 'shifts', in order to discover the specific features of each phenomenon under investigation. Furthermore, we came across the concept of the ideal-typical procedure, which had already been extensively developed, and which we can go into further below.

'Urban sociology'

The essay 'The City' is thematically connected to the works we have already discussed. It was based on material which Weber had developed since 1889, and was probably written between the years 1911-13. This contribution, which in the opinion of the present author must be considered unfinished, was not published in Weber's lifetime. Marianne Weber published it in 1921 in the *Archiv* and included it shortly after in the posthumous 1922 edition of *Economy and Society* which she oversaw, under the same title, 'The City' (8E, pp. 1212-372). After the fourth edition, edited by Johannes Winckelmann, the text can still be found in *Economy and Society*, but now under the title 'Non-legitimate domination (typology of cities)'.

In this work, Weber dealt with a systematic investigation of the historical development and importance of the Western city, with particular reference to Antiquity and the Middle Ages. For a work with such an objective, one of the main difficulties was determining the object of investigation, and here Weber makes use of a multi-dimensional, ideal-typical approach. After a very general, descriptive version - of a relatively closed, large 'settlement' - Weber set out the different aspects of historical and social reality which can only be separated out analytically:

A sociological *perspective* 'The city is a settlement of closely spaced dwellings which form a colony so extensive that the reciprocal personal acquaintance of the inhabitants, elsewhere characteristic of the neighbourhood, is lacking' (8E, p. 1212). Here we could speak of the sociological definition criterion of 'anonymity'.

An economic *perspective* 'We shall speak of a "city" in the economic sense of the word only if the local population satisfies an economically significant part of its everyday requirements in the local market, and if a significant part of the products bought there were acquired or produced specifically for sale on the market by the local population or that of the immediate hinterland.' (8E, p. 1213). Weber described the economic criterion of the 'market centre'. The economic definition led Weber to develop a differentiated typology of 'consumer city' versus 'producer city', 'industry city' versus 'merchant city'. He emphasized that it is not 'our intention here to produce the further casuistic distinctions and specializations of concepts which would be required for a strictly economic theory of the city. Nor do we need to stress that actual cities almost always represent mixed types and hence can be classified only in terms of their respective predominant economic components' (8E, p. 1217).

A political, administrative and legal perspective   Here Weber worked from the assumption that every city – in Antiquity as in the Middle Ages, inside and outside Europe – was a kind of 'fortress' and 'garrison', i.e. a castle or wall belonged to the city and Weber regarded 'the seigneurial castle', and with it castle-seated princes, as a universal phenomenon (8E, pp. 1221-2). According to Weber, in all such settlements the burghers, in the sense of residents of the burg, had to take part regularly in military duties like the building and repair of the wall, keeping watch and defence. 'The problem of the relationship between the garrison, the political citizenry of the fortress, on the one hand, and the civilian, economically active population on the other hand, is frequently exceedingly complex, but it is always of crucial importance for the constitutional history of the city' (8E, p. 1224).

   To limit the endless variety of forms of urban settlement that the criteria of definition have introduced thus far, Weber introduced the concept of the 'city community [commune]' (8E, p. 1226), to which the following five criteria must apply: fortification; market; own court of law and, in part, autonomous law; associational structure; and partial autonomy, i.e. administration by authorities 'in whose appointment the burghers could in some form participate' (8E, p. 1226). Weber commented: 'Hence the characteristic of the city in the political definition was the appearance of a distinct "bourgeois estate"' (the bearer of privileges of an estate) (8E, p. 1226). Such a city commune, according to Weber was only known in the West, at least as a mass phenomenon. Outside the West 'there existed no association which could represent the commune of burghers as such. The very concept of an urban burgher and, in particular, a specific status qualification of the burgher was completely lacking. It can be found neither in China, nor in Japan or India, and only in abortive beginnings in the Near East' (8E, pp. 1228-9).

After a detailed presentation of the respective developments, in particular in Asia, Weber turned to the Western city, chiefly to the city north of the Alps in the Middle Ages, although he continually made comparisons and analogies with Western Antiquity. Weber defined this city type as an 'institutionalized association endowed with special characteristic organs, of people who as "burghers" are subject to a *special law* exclusively applicable to them and who thus form a legally autonomous status group' (8E, p. 1240). The existence of 'burgher rights' according to estate was for Weber the deciding factor which showed that it is not a question of purely juridical determination but much more of *social* effects. For Weber it was crucial whether the inhabitants of such a settlement felt that they were arranged in a 'commune' or not and whether an association in the sense of a 'fraternal association' was formed.

This 'fraternal association' was of central importance to Weber. He saw the Medieval city as, among these characteristics, a 'cultic association' (8E, p. 1247) which was constituted by the burghers' oath and their participation in the Christian Last Supper. 'The Occidental city – and especially the Medieval city . . . was not only economically a seat of trade and the crafts, politically in the normal case a fortress and perhaps a garrison, administratively a court district, but beyond all this also a sworn confraternity' (8E, p. 1248). Along with this went the city church, the city priest, the burghers' participation in the Last Supper, and the official church celebrations of the city – all matters in which Jews for example could not participate (cf. 8E, p. 1247).

Weber emphasized that it is necessary to separate the formal–legal processes from the sociologically and politically important ones: these corporations of the burghers and their authorities have in the formal–legal sense been 'legitimately' constituted. However, in the most important cases of such foundations one was dealing with a 'revolutionary usurpation' (8E, p. 1250). 'In the "spontaneous" case, the commune was the result of a political association of the burghers in spite of, or in defiance of the "legitimate" powers or, more correctly, of a series of such acts . . . The "spontaneous" usurpation through an act of rational association, a sworn confraternization [*Eidverbrüderung; coniuratio*] of the burghers, is found especially in the bigger and older cities, such as Genoa or Cologne' (8E, p. 1250). Weber investigated the processes of the *coniurationes* in detail and stated as a general principle:

The immediate positive aim of the sworn confraternity was the unification of the local landowners for protective and defensive purposes, for the peaceable settlement of internal disputes, and for the securing of an administration of justice in correspondence with the interests of the townsmen. But there were further goals. One was the monopolization of the economic opportunities offered by the city. (8E, p. 1252)

Such purely personal *coniurationes*, which were often only a temporary or short-term agreement, developed in the course of time into permanent political associations the members of which 'were collectively, as urban citizens, subject to a special and autonomous law' (8E, p. 1254). 'The "bourgeois law" was, rather, a status right of the members of the sworn fellowship of burghers; one was subject to it by virtue of membership in a status group which comprised the full citizens and their dependent clients' (8E, p. 1254). In conclusion, Weber turned this relatively briefly presented analysis of the most important elements of urban development in the West to the 'patrician city' in Antiquity and the Middle Ages, where he dealt extensively with Venice (8E, pp. 1268–72), the development in England (8E, pp. 1276–81), the north-European continent (8E, pp. 1281f), and the ancient cities of Greece and Rome (8E, pp. 1282–96). Common to all these investigations was the presence of a 'nobility with family charisma', i.e. 'the patrician domination', a 'patriciate'.

In the last two sections of his essay, on the 'Plebeian City' and 'Ancient and Medieval Democracy' Weber dealt with the breaking of this domination by the old patrician families and the gradual triumph of the *demos*, the *plebs*, the *populo*, the *liveries* and the craft guilds.

Weber turned first to the Italian *populo* at the end of the twelfth and the beginning of the thirteenth century, which were composed partly of the city's entrepreneurs and partly of the artisans. The first of these organizations led the way in the struggle against the knightly families. They created the sworn confraternity of the craft guilds and financed the struggles against the domination of the patricians. In political retrospect, the *populo* formed 'a separate political community within the urban commune with its own officials, its own finances, and its own military organization. In the truest sense of the word it was a "state within the state" – the first *deliberately non-legitimate and revolutionary* political association' (8E, p. 1302). The gradual successes of the *populo* were won in the course of violent and bloody struggles against the nobility, during which it was the 'lower' guilds which brought 'an at least relatively democratic element' (8E, p. 1306) into the city councils. The starting point of such struggles was regularly 'the often far-reaching denial of legal rights to commoners' (8E, p. 1307) which brought the 'status pride' of the knighthood and the 'natural resentment of the bourgeoisie' into conflict. Weber compared this development with that of the ancient *demos* and the *plebs* and points to their great similarity with the *populo* (cf. 8E, pp. 1307–11).

In the ancient as well as the Medieval cities, Weber saw the appearance of the 'city *tyrannis*' as by and large a locally confined phenomenon. Everywhere it was a 'product of the struggle of status groups' (8E, p. 1316). 'What finds expression here is the typical class contrast of the ancient world: between an urban military patriciate as creditors and the peasantry as debtors . . .' (8E, p. 1316). The tyrants perceived themselves and were perceived everywhere, according to Weber as 'specifically "illegitimate" rulers' (8E, p. 1317) and because of this they differed in their political as well as their religious attitude from the old city-kingship. As supporters of 'new emotional cults' they nevertheless sought to preserve the external forms of their commune's constitution in order to make their 'claim to legality'. Particularly important for Weber in this context was the example of the Italian *signoria*, as it was 'the first political power in Western Europe which based its regime on a rational administration with (increasingly) *appointed* officials' (8E, p. 1318). Through the general developments in the direction of an increasing economic indispensability of the producers, the increasing military disqualification of the educated strata of the bourgeoisie, and the increasing rationalization of military techniques in the area of the professional army, these forms of a 'city-tyranny' developed more and more, however, into a hereditary patrimonial princeship: 'Wherever these chances were utilized, the *signoria* thereby entered into the circle of legitimate powers' (8E, p. 1321).

In his attempt to present comprehensively the entire situation of the *Medieval* cities, one comment from Weber made the objective of the entire investigation very clear: 'neither modern capitalism nor the "state" as we know it developed on the basis of the ancient city, whereas the Medieval city, though not the only significant antecedent developmental stage and certainly not itself the carrier of these developments, is inseparably linked as one of the crucial factors with the rise of both phenomena' (8E, p. 1323). Weber arranged the Medieval 'achievements' of the city, graded here according to their importance, along with the following six points:

1 Political autonomy, in some cases independent foreign policy, independent military.
2 Autonomous law creation by the cities and by the (old) guilds and the (later) 'crafts'.
3 Own judicial and administrative agencies ('autocephaly').
4 Power of taxation over its burghers who were free from taxation and other charges by outside powers.

5   The right to hold markets, autonomous trade and craft regulation and monopolistic powers of exclusion.
6   Specific attitude to non-citizen strata, which resulted from the contrast to the specifically non-urban political and feudal–manorial 'structures'. Here Weber established and presented a particularly large number of diverse formations of this sort of contrast.

Weber used this last point in particular in the last section of his investigation as the starting point for a comprehensive comparison of the Medieval with the ancient city type 'in order to get a coherent picture of the basic causes for these differences' (8E, p. 1340). This comparison was made on the one hand between the ancient and the Medieval city type and on the other between the south-European and the north-European city type and each comparison is presented in relation to definite frameworks of questioning. Apparently Weber did not reach a conclusion for the entire investigation, with the result that he effected no systematic contrast. However, his statement that the ancient city was essentially created in a political–military mould and by contrast the Medieval city in an economic one, could be evaluated as a central hypothesis and thus at the 'end result' of his work.

The specifically Medieval city type, the artisan inland city . . . was economically oriented . . . The economic interests of the Medieval townsmen lay in peaceful gain through commerce and the trades, and this was most pronouncedly so for the lower strata of the urban citizenry . . . The political situation of the Medieval townsman determined his path, which was that of a *homo oeconomicus*, whereas in Antiquity the *polis* preserved during its heyday its character as the technically most advanced military association: the ancient townsman was a *homo politicus*. (8E, pp. 1353–4)

This difference, which Weber regarded as basic, is pursued in his various reflections on social stratification, the city constitution, the relationship between peasants and city-burghers, economic policy and the military policy and technique.

The intention of the previous description was to explain the *sociological* importance of Weber's study, 'The City'. It could show that Weber, in his intention to present a systematic investigation of the *historical* development and importance of the Occidental city, thus proceeding from a very general concept, arrived relatively quickly at the *sociological* concept of the 'city commune'. The city commune became Weber's real object of investigation, and it is its importance for the historical development of the *bourgeoisie, modern capitalism, the modern rational and bureaucratic state* and *the Western democracy* that Weber was concerned to analyse. This study, as one of the most important beginnings of what is a strongly specialized 'urban sociology' is taken up again in the section on Weber's influence.[13]

The *methodological* importance of this study is that it can be seen as an example of one of the most convincing applications of the *ideal-typical procedure*, in which the extraordinary historical *differentiation* and the *multidimensionality* of the creation of types can become particularly clear.

Citizenship, competition and capitalism

Turning to Weber's lectures on 'General Economic History' to close this section, we must first justify this inclusion. Under this title we find a lecture given by Weber in the winter term 1919–20 at Munich University under the title 'Draft of universal social and economic history', posthumously reconstructed and published by Siegmund Hellmann in 1923 in collaboration with Melchior Palyi and Marianne Weber. Among Weber's effects there was neither a transcript nor coherent notes of this lecture to be found, 'only a bundle of sheets with notes little more than catchwords set down in a handwriting hardly legible even to those accustomed to it' (16E, p. xvii). The editors compiled the text on the basis of student notes, which they wanted to make clearer by means of a 'fuller organization'. For the third edition of 1958 the text was revised by Johannes Winckelmann, once again on the basis of newly discovered students' notes.

It is not only because of the problems bound up in the editorial history of this text that this work should be dealt with here albeit briefly. The lecture as a whole and in particular the introductory 'Definitions of Concepts' (omitted in the English translation) are thematically, conceptually and temporally closely linked with Weber's work on *Economy and Society*.[14] Both in his lecture and in *Economy and Society* there exist material influences from decades of research in *all* of Weber's fields of study, and it is for this reason that we would rather turn to *Economy and Society*, regardless of similar editorial problems.[15]

However, in connection with this section on Weber's work we must make clear the *continuity* of certain frameworks of questioning and the occurrence of crucial points in the course of Weber's academic *development*. The fourth chapter of Weber's lecture was given the title 'The Origin of Modern Capitalism' (16E, pp. 207–71), the last three paragraphs of which in particular reflect three problem areas, the first being of especial interest to us in this context: 7 – Citizenship; 8 – The Rational State; and 9 – The Evolution of the Capitalist Spirit. His ideas on citizenship drew together much of what we have already encountered in the works looked at thus far, beginning with Weber's dissertation.

Weber approached 'citizenship' from three aspects: first, he meant 'a specific *economic* interest'; second, in the *political* sense the concept comprised for him 'membership in the state, with its connotation as the holder of certain political rights'; and thirdly and lastly in respect of *status groups*, the concept referred to 'those strata which are drawn together, in contrast with the bureaucracy or the proletariat and others outside their circle, as "persons of property and culture", entrepreneurs, recipients of funded incomes, and in general all persons of academic culture, a certain class standard of living, and a certain social prestige' (16E, p. 233).

In each of these three viewpoints, Weber saw the 'citizen' as *peculiar to Western civilization*, in which the social class signification is 'likewise a specifically modern and Western concept, like that of the bourgeoisie' (16E, pp. 233–4). Weber took the definition a step further: 'The citizen in the quality of membership in a class is always a citizen of a particular city, and the city in this sense, has existed only in the Western world, or elsewhere, as in the early period in Mesopotamia, only in an incipient stage' (16E, p. 234). Connected to this are the results of Weber's research into the history of urban development, which we have already described (cf. 16E, pp. 234–49). Again Weber began by emphasizing the *political* character of the ancient city and its economy, when he wrote 'Turning to the question as to the consequences of these relations in connection with the evolution of capitalism, we must emphasize the heterogeneity of industry in Antiquity and in the Middle Ages, and the different species of capitalism itself' (16E, p. 246).

Essentially Weber distinguished between a *non-rational* and a *rational* capitalism. The latter was 'organized with a view to market opportunities, hence to economic objectives in the real sense of the word, and the more rational it is the more closely it relates to mass demand and the provision for mass needs. It was reserved to the modern Western development after the close of the Middle Ages to elevate this capitalism into a system . . .' (16E, p. 247). If, as we have seen, the transition from ancient to Medieval conditions had been effected essentially by the destruction of the cities, which led to the 'throttling of ancient capitalism' (16E, p. 248), then for the development from the late Middle Ages to modern times it was once again *urban development* which plays a central role. Military, judicial and industrial authority in succession were taken away from the cities of the seventeenth and eighteenth centuries. 'In form the old rights were as a rule unchanged, but in fact the modern city was deprived of its freedom as effectively as had

happened in Antiquity with the establishment of the Roman dominion
. . .' (16E, p. 249). However, it was important for the modern development that the cities of the modern age came 'under the power of competing
national states in a condition of perpetual struggle for power in peace or
war' (16E, p. 249).

And it was this national competitive struggle which created 'the largest
opportunities' in modern, Western capitalism.

The separate states had to compete for mobile capital, which dictated to them the
conditions under which it would assist them to power. Out of this alliance of
the state with capital, dictated by necessity, arose the national citizen class, the
bourgeoisie in the modern sense of the word. Hence it is the closed national state
which afforded to capitalism its chance for development – and as long as the national
state does not give place to a world empire capitalism also will endure. (16E, p. 249)

3

Social change in German society

From the numerous works of Weber which can be brought together under the title of this chapter, we shall pick out those which deal with the following sociologically relevant thematic areas, areas which are indispensable for the understanding of Weber's work:

The agricultural workers
The stock exchange
The industrial workers

The agricultural workers

Relevant texts

Works from the enquiry of the Verein für Sozialpolitik

'*Die Verhältnisse der Landarbeiter im ostelbischen Deutschland*' (The Conditions of Agricultural Workers in East Elbian Germany) (1892)

'*Die Erhebung des Vereins für Sozialpolitik über die Lage der Landarbeiter*' (Investigation into the Situation of Agricultural Workers by the *Verein für Sozialpolitik*) (1893)

'*Wie werden einwandfreie Erhebungen über die Lage der Landarbeiter angestellt?*' (How Can we Conduct Incontestable Investigations into the Situation of Agricultural Workers?) (1893)

'*Referat über die ländliche Arbeitsverfassung*' (Report on the Constitution of Agricultural Work) (1893)

'*Entwicklungstendenzen in der Lage der ostelbischen Landarbeiter*' (Developmental Tendencies in the Situation of East Elbian Agricultural Workers) (1894)

Works from the enquiry of the Evangelisch-soziale Kongreß

' *"Privatenquêten" über die Lage der Landarbeiter'* ("Private Enquiries" into
the Situation of Agricultural Workers] (1892)
'*Die Erhebung des Evangelisch-sozialen Kongresses über die Verhältnisse der
Landarbeiter Deutschlands*' (An Investigation by the *Evangelischsoziale
Kongress* into The Conditions of German Agricultural Workers) (1894)
'*Referat über die deutschen Landarbeiter'* (Report on German Agricultural
Workers) (1894)
'*Vorbemerkung des Herausgebers'* (Editor's Preface) (1899)

From the previous chapter Weber's interest in *agrarian history* and the *history
of capitalism* is clear. Both areas and their combined effect were the over-
arching theme of Weber's agricultural-worker studies the origin and
political conclusions of which were described in part in the biographical
section of this presentation.

The agricultural-workers' enquiry of the Verein für Sozialpolitik

In September 1890 the *Verein*[1] commissioned its members Thiel, Conrad
and Sering with the planning and execution of an enquiry into 'The
Conditions of Agricultural Workers in Germany', the results of which
would be presented to the general assembly in 1892. An initial questionnaire was sent in December 1891 to 3,180 farmers, whose addresses had
been provided by the German central agricultural associations, and of
which 2,277 were answered. In February 1892 a second questionnaire was
sent to 562 selected reporters who worked in wholly agricultural areas, of
which 291 were answered. With the help of this wide-reaching survey of
agricultural *employers*, the *Verein* tried to collect information on the position
of the German agricultural workers. The letter of December 1891 which
accompanied the questionnaire stated:

Out of all the questions affecting the farmers at the moment, it is the question of the
workers which heads the list, and for the most diverse reasons of an economic and
social nature this question will not disappear quickly from the order of the day. In
order to be able to rectify the existing damage in the whole worker relationship, to
remedy inadequate conditions, successfully to meet unwarranted demands and have
a timely influence upon public opinion and thus upon the course of legislation too,
the first precondition is a clear and reliable presentation of the actual conditions.[2]

The analysis and interpretation of the questionnaires received was taken
on by seven 'reporters', and the results were published in three volumes of

the *Verein*'s writings (53, 54, 55) in over 2,000 pages. Weber took over the job of evaluating and interpreting the returned questionnaires – which he had helped to compile – in so far as they affected East Elbian Germany (East and West Prussia, Pommerania, Posen, Silesia, Brandenburg, Mecklenburg and Lauenburg). The basis of his work was 77 general reports and 573 special reports which he arranged according to province and administrative district, and ordered and evaluated in tabular form. Under considerable pressure of time – the second questionnaires were returned in February 1892 and the report was to be published for the conference planned for September of the same year – the twenty-eight-year-old Weber presented the results of his work to the *Verein* according to schedule, and they were published as volume 3 of the farm-worker enquiry (8). The results of this 891-page investigation became a leitmotiv through Weber's work, making the knowledge of the results undeniably important for a comprehensive understanding of his work. Neither his inaugural lecture in Freiburg (40) in 1895, nor his lecture on the occasion of the World Exhibition in St Louis (76) in 1904 can be understood without a knowledge of the enquiries. Moreover, this enquiry was a decisive step for the development of a specific methodology in the empirical social sciences in Germany – a fact which until today has hardly ever been taken into consideration.[3]

The work was arranged in three parts: after a short preamble and a cursory sketch of the constitution of work in eastern Germany, there followed the section of about 700 pages on the empirical material, to which was added a critical appreciation and summary of the investigation. By contrast with the two other volumes, Weber included in his investigation two works by Alexander von Lengerke[4] and Theodor von der Goltz,[5] both of which were already available at that time and were comparable works, since Weber intended to go beyond a mere stock-taking of the contemporary status of knowledge in the field to present a *process of change*. 'The changes which have taken place over many decades in the social structure of agriculture in the east, and which we can also recognize from the reports, have the character of *mass phenomena* and rest essentially on the powerful pressure of a general social restratification of the population' (8, p. 4). Weber's professed intention was to make plain the *direction* of these processes of change.

Weber roughly sketched the features of the main elements of the constitution of work in eastern Germany in their historical development. The main problem structurally with every type of rural work is that of *variable need* in agricultural labour powers during the year, in which these fluctuations in different systems of ground use and valorization as well as different production techniques can vary considerably. Large-scale land-ownership in particular, which was Weber's main concern as the typical form in the German eastern regions, always solved this problem through the continuous employment of a *stock* of workers, which could be supplemented according to need by *passing employees*. After the transcendence of serfdom and through the agrarian legislation of the nineteenth century, the possibility of rearing peasants for compulsory service had died out over the ages of tilling the soil and harvesting. Instead, workers were employed by means of *contracts of employment*.

The variable need for agricultural labour led essentially to two main categories of workers: on the one hand, *the contractually bound worker* who lived on the estate and who had to make his/her labour power available at any time; and on the other hand the so-called *'free' worker* who entered into service without contract for different long periods of time. Within the first group Weber distinguishes between three types:

1   The continually required, mostly unmarried, *farmhand*, whose position was comparable with the urban servant.
2   The 'commissioned ranks' of the economic officials, bailiffs, governors, senior shepherds and the like whose regular payment led to their designation as *deputists* (*Deputat* = payment in kind).
3   The *'free contractual labourers'* ('estate journeymen') 'by far the most interesting category socially and economically among the rural workforce in the east' (8, p. 11).

These 'free contractual labourers' (*Instleute*) attracted Weber's particular interest and he outlined their situation in the following way: they lived on the estate in individual cottages or in so-called 'family-houses', i.e. 'rural workers' tenement houses' and were bound to their work mainly through a one-year contract of work which was completed by the *entire family of workers*.[6] By contrast to the *deputists* they received no regular remuneration but a combination of monetary payment and payment in kind, in land for their own use and entitlement to pasture, wherein the relationship of these individual components were strongly differentiated from payment and their respective regulation. The free contractual labourer tendered not only his own labour power and that of his wife and children but also in many cases the labour power of one or two 'corvée workers' or 'day labourers' whom he paid himself. Thus to the lord of the manor the free contractual labourer was an employee, but to the corvée workers he was an employer. This and other reasons made it necessary that only married workers, and workers not completely without possessions, could fill this position.

An additional and extraordinarily important element in the payment of the free contractual labourers was the proportionate share in the entire yield of the threshing, which the labourers were 'allowed' to carry out mainly on their own. A payment on top of the daily wage only took place during the times of sowing and harvest. The rest of the year – up to eight months – was taken up with the work of threshing, the main occupation of the free contractual workers in particular. The yields of the 'threshing amount' – and thus the income of the free contractual worker too – varied naturally according to the result of the harvest.

Weber the lawyer was particularly interested in the legal nature of the relationship between the large-scale land-owner and the free contractual labourer. This relationship appears to us as a mixture of heterogeneous elements. On the one hand it was *not purely a contract of employment* since what was presented was not only a relationship between employer and employee but more than that, a 'relation of domination over the person of the free contractual labourer' (8, p. 18) since the employer/estate-owner held the legal authority at the same time. On the other hand, however, it was *not purely a relation of wage-labour*, since the payment was controlled not only by a fixed wage but by a share in the entire income of the estate economy.

On the one hand the relationship still bore the traces of subservience, the elimination of which had deprived the master of the estate in a material regard of at least as many obligations as rights. It made and makes the worker dependent to a particularly large extent on his or her personal productivity and also on the autocracy of the master. On the other hand, however, it created the foundation for an intensive community of interests between the master of the estate and his free contractual labourers which must be apparent to the latter every day. (8, p. 18)

Thus in spite of its character as a 'strictly monarchical–centralized economic organism', the estate economy became a *community (Gemeinschaft)*[7] of the economic interests of free contractual labourers and master of the estate, despite his 'powerful preponderance'. The free contractual labourer became a partner, a 'small entrepreneur' in the master's business: 'The strictly patriarchal leadership was tolerated because it corresponded to the economic foundations of the relationship. The investigation as to whether this is the case today or will be in the future must be one of the main objects of the following presentation' (8, p. 19). Weber's thesis was that in the case of a divergence of economic interests between free contractual labourers and masters of the estate, the continuance of the old relationship was 'not to be reckoned with absolutely'.

The group of *so-called 'free' workers* was given this designation because they were generally not subject to the policing and legal jurisdiction of the master of the estate, were not bound by a fixed contract together with their families to work for a year on the estate, but worked on the basis of a normal *wage-labour relationship with the individual worker*. As a rule they were paid purely in money. In this group Weber was mainly interested in the question of what chances this circle of people had to rise to the status of independent smallholders. In his opinion these chances depended on several elements: whether and at what age the worker could create financial savings; and whether in each respective area the opportunity of buying or leasing small-holding economies was offered at all. But besides these 'external relationships', the 'subjective disposition' of the worker to become a small entrepreneur seemed to Weber to be at least just as important. By contrast with the free contractual labourers, this circle of people mostly had no opportunity to get the previous experience necessary for running their own business and above all they did not get round to 'adopting the ways of thinking of a professional honour of the agricultural enterprise' (8, p. 34). Payment purely in money

invites comparison with the partially actual, partially (in view of the urban living and market prices) only apparently more favourable wage-conditions of industry and gives him the idea of creating a relationship of ascension, which however prevails only in his imagination, by transferring into the industrial worker status group. Even his material interests, which in relation to the position of product prices, run counter to those of the employer, predisposition him to be caught up in the class consciousness of the modern urban and rural proletariat, which is still in a process of increasing development and above all he has at least in many cases no qualification for running his own business. (8, pp. 34–5)

Besides this type of the so-called 'free' worker there were also workers not bound by contract, who owned their own land or an independent business on leased land. The returns from their own land as a rule did not cover food requirements, which led to a problematic full of consequences:

In fact the peculiar contradiction in the material interests of these people is that on the one hand they are farmers, and on the other, they have to acquire a part of their food requirements by regularly buying more. The price arrangement of their necessary foodstuffs thus affects their interest in completely the opposite way from how it affects the interest of the master of the estate and the peasants. While the latter have an interest in high prices for foodstuffs the farmers on the contrary want low prices. This opposition is partly the emphasized basis of mistrust which occurs in many ways between this category of workers and the land-owners. (8, p. 36)

Among the so-called 'free' workers a particular place is occupied by the predominantly Polish–Russian *migrant workers*, which we shall discuss later.

In a related section of material in the investigation of individual areas, a report is premised on the land conditions, the development of land-ownership and on the division of the cited categories of workers. Alongside this were tabulated extremely detailed presentations of the general working conditions: hours of work, overtime, Sunday working, women's work, child-labour, care for the aged, for the invalid and for sickness, details of educational establishments etc. In spite of undoubted deficiencies – in particular from the standpoint of today's social scientific methodology, for Weber lacked a knowledge of the theory of probability and random samples – this evaluation of the material to hand represented an important stage in the development of social scientific methods and techniques. For this very reason this investigation does not deserve to remain unknown any longer – quite apart from the extraordinary relevance of its results for an understanding of the social and economic reality of Germany at that time.

In his concluding section, Weber went into three aspects of the farm-worker enquiry: *methodological* classification and critique; *legal* questions and his attempt to formulate the direction and the possible, above all political, consequences of the development thus far. In his methodological remarks he restricted himself to the manifestation of basic problems in a questionnaire-survey and indicated a few desiderata. He recognized as an insoluble difficulty the fact that a questionnaire which was tailored to suit the constitution of work in the entire German empire, could not grasp the relevant differences between eastern and western Germany. As a whole, however, he evaluated the material as 'qualitatively quite satisfactory'. We shall not be going into the legal questions here. Suffice it to say that Weber – as in the text – once again drew analogies with the Roman colonies.

In his concluding 'overview' Weber wanted to present neither a summary nor a comprehensive appreciation of the results. He saw the main function of the study as its correction of many popular views, in particular that the position of the agricultural workers was particularly wretched by comparison with the position of the industrial workers. Despite their great dependence on the success and the good will of the master of the estate, Weber designated the position of the farm-hands in particular and the free contractual labourers as such that 'in average relations their material position is more unequally safeguarded even than that of the best-placed industrial worker and under rather favourable conditions virtually cannot be compared with it' (8, p. 775). With this warning, however, Weber indicated developmental tendencies in the rural constitution of work. These tendencies were connected particularly with the changed situation of grain production and changes in consumption. Weber presented these processes exhaustively, in particular the great influence which the consumption of potatoes and more meat exerted on the rural population. On top of this came the effects which strongly fluctuating grain prices produced on the home and the world market as well as the introduction of intensive farming methods and threshing machines. All these elements together had the effect that the traditional foundations of the *community of interests* between employers and workers were gradually eroded. Thus we gradually approach the question of

how the interests of employer [*Arbeitgeber*] and worker [*Arbeitnehmer*] square up to one another, in the *economic position of interests* and the *social* stratification of the workers . . . and of course exclusively . . . if one wants to interpret the signs of the age. The transition from the small farmer and small enterprise at any rate to the proletariat means, when regarded purely materially, a relief at most. A heavy weight of worries is thus removed from the shoulders of the free contractual labourer, whose miserable co-earned harvest yield could be lessened by heaven and the world market . . . But that does not alter the fact that the one-time farmer has become a proletarian, that his interests are those of the consumer, that he completely loses the connection of interests, which are always in mind, to the *individual* good, and becomes a member of the great uniform mass of the propertyless. (8, p. 780)

The destruction of the traditional community of interests and the 'proletarianization' of the agricultural workers made estate-masters and agricultural workers economic opponents, of which, according to Weber, it could be said that 'Between natural economic opponents there can only be struggle, and it is sheer madness to believe that a strengthening of the economic power of one party would benefit the *social* position of the other' (8, p. 790). The common denominator for these processes of development was, according to Weber, the transformation of a *patriarchal* organization into a *capitalist* one. Thus from then it was never the ill-will of individual actors that caused this development and who could thus be 'reproached'.

Both sections, workers and employers operate in the direction indicated and the individual employer acts merely in consequence of the relations presently forming with compulsive force. If he wants to exist under the present relations of competition and with the problem of the work-market, then he cannot proceed in any other way. That is exactly what is threatening about the situation, that the effectiveness of the developmental tendencies contained within it is independent of the action and inaction of the individual. (8, p. 794)

Weber went extensively into the consequences – largely unintentional or rather imprudent – of this development: the effects on military discipline; the displacement of the indigenous, German workforce by the migrant workers; and the gradual loss of the economic position of power from the large-scale land-owners (the 'pillar of the monarchy'). In this context Weber did not consider the 'question of rural workers' to be primarily a problematic of social policy, but rather a political problem which could not be 'unimportant certainly from the standpoint of state interest' (8, p. 295). Thus in Weber's eyes it was primarily a 'rural question', i.e. in his view it was a matter of whether one creates space for the German workers 'up above', whether one offers them the possibilities of rising to an independent existence or prevents this. 'The most important question is whether it can be made possible for them (the workers) to rise to the status group of peasant farmers and thus the question of rural workers in the east turns into the question of *internal colonization*' (8, p. 802). In this context, Weber saw in the importing of Slavic migrant workers an endangering of 'Germanness' in a depopulating eastern area, in which German civilization was placed before the 'question of existence'.

The future of eastern Germany will depend on whether one resolutely accepts the consequences of this situation. The dynasty of Prussian kings was not called to rule over a rural proletariat without fatherland and over Slavic migrants, next to Polish tenant farmers and depopulated latifundia, as the current development in the east could make them if the situation was neglected any longer. It was called to rule over German peasant farmers next to a status group of large-scale land-owners, whose workers retain the consciousness that they can find their future in their homeland by rising to an independent existence. (8, p. 804)

After his intensive task evaluating the enquiry's material, it was Weber's pressing concern to make these results known to a wider circle of those interested in social policy and science. It was important to him that the results he had established became known to a wide public and that the social policy and political recommendations he had suggested he discussed. For these reasons he published several essays (12, 13, 21, 25) in the years 1893–94 in which, apart from his intention of elucidating any misunderstandings which cropped up and countering critical objections, the accent recognizably shifted more and more in the direction of his *political* demands. The address in Freiburg in 1895 (40) represented without doubt a certain 'climax' in this shift of accent. In it, these political convictions, which had arisen from his concern with the question of East Elbian agricultural workers, were presented by Weber in the wider context of an analysis of the historico-political situation of the German Empire at that time, and also the *nation* was raised to the highest value in a policy of political economy. As we have already emphasized, in this presentation we are excluding the *political* aspect and interpretation of Weber's works.[8]

Even in his report (18, 19, 20) to the general assembly of the *Verein* in March 1893 in Berlin, which dealt with the question of the *rural workers*, the *distribution of land property* and the *protection of small-scale land-ownership*, and for which he had prepared his report, Weber planned no report on the results but a 'way into discussion' and above all an expression of 'certain high political questions', which he – as he himself maintained – presented 'somewhat provocatively'. From the very beginning he compared his results with those of the investigations into other areas of Germany, and here once again the 'Polish question', i.e. the problem of the Russo-Polish migrant workers was the most pressing concern in his treatment of the German eastern regions. Weber explained unambiguously the basis for focus: 'Here I am regarding the "question of rural workers" quite exclusively from the viewpoint of *Staatsraison* [reasons of state]; for me it is not a question of agricultural workers, thus *not* the question "are they having a good time or a bad time, how can they be helped?" (18, p. 74). And thus even his practical demands resided exclusively in this context: an absolute exclusion of the Russo-Polish workers from the east of Germany and the encouragement of internal colonization through the state's creation of peasant smallholdings. These measures were intended as such for the 'peaceful defence of Germany's eastern border' (18, p. 85).

The agricultural-worker enquiry of the Evangelisch-soziale Kongreß

In 1892, the same year as he was working on the evaluation of the *Verein*'s enquiry, Weber suggested in the announcements of the *Evangelisch–soziale Kongreß* that these results be supplemented and corrected by carrying out 'private enquiries' (7). In the December of the same year Weber and the general secretary of the Congress, Paul Göhre, carried out a second enquiry on the position of Germany's agricultural workers, on the instructions of the *Kongreß*. Following their own doubts and those expressed by others as to the comprehensiveness and sometimes the credibility of the information the *masters of the estates* provided on the situation of their agricultural workers, Weber and Göhre sought out 'intermediate people, who are as unbiased as possible' (9, p. 536), who could provide further, more correct information. For more technical reasons, they both rejected the suggestion of asking country doctors, and turned instead to the *evangelical priests* in Germany, whose addresses could be obtained very easily through the *Kongreß*. A questionnaire, developed by Weber and Göhre, with twenty-three sometimes extraordinarily detailed questions (in 56, pp. 1–8) was sent to all the evangelical clergy in the German Reich

- around 15,000 of them; by June 1893 about 1,000 had been returned answered. Göhre and Weber divided up the reports, the former working on the west and south of Germany, and Weber on the east.

Also in 1893 Weber reported on the running and aims of this enquiry (9) and acknowledged that he and Göhre were 'almost helpless' in the face of the material, in so far 'as we are not clear up until now how it should be analysed' (9, p. 540). In May 1894, the debates of the fifth *Kongreß* took place in Frankfurt, at which both Göhre and Weber reported on their *provisional* results (31). Part of the results and material was published only in 1899 (cf. 56). In it, Göhre emphasized the investigation's character as a 'supplementary enquiry' (31, p. 46), the intention of which had been to expand and check the *Verein*'s investigation and to supplement in different ways the results already produced. The decision to ask the clergy had been determined by the conviction that they were particularly suited to that sort of thing: 'For the clergyman regards . . . the agricultural worker from a point of view quite different from that of the employer. The latter is biased, like the worker himself; the clergyman is one of the few unbiased people who put themselves purely at the disposal of the country' (31, p. 45). Moreover they intended to oppose the *Verein*'s one-sided preoccupation with purely economic relations in its enquiry with strongly 'social–ethical' frameworks of questioning. They wanted to investigate 'which interactions obtain between on the one hand the economic, and on the other the entire spiritual, moral and religious situation of the different rural strata of workers' (31, p. 45).

In his supplementary report, Weber emphasized that the clergymen had to compile their statements *by interviewing the agricultural workers themselves*, so that the sometimes extraordinarily detailed reports might contain 'a wealth of statements straight from the workers' mouths' (31, p. 62). Besides this, however, the enquiry had a second objective – that of the education of the priests' social–political thinking, i.e. to make easier for them, through the systematic questionnaire, 'the possibility of acquiring in their own and their parish's interest an insight into the economic and social conditions of existence of the members of their parish' (56, p. 101). [9]

According to Weber's statements, the provisional results of the *Kongreß*'s enquiry showed a far-reaching correspondence with the results of the *Verein*'s enquiry; they allowed, however, a very much more convincing refutation of current assertions about supposedly causal connections, for example wage-levels with food-prices, with land-quality or more intensive cultivation techniques.

Through our modern scientific methods we have become used to look upon technical and economic requirements and interests as the basic priority, and to derive the social stratification and political formation of a people from this. Obviously this method is still right for the countryside, but for once we can see here particularly clearly that it is a question of interactions, in which the purely economic moments in no way suit the leading role. (31, p. 66)

Once again, Weber's conclusions ended with essentially *political* remarks, in which his critique of the traditional stratum of large-scale land-owners had sharpened considerably: 'This landed nobleman possessed the naive conviction that Providence had arranged things in such a way that he was called to dominate and the "Others" were called to obey in the country. Why? He does not think about such things. The absence of reflection was of course one of his most essential virtues of domination' (31, p. 70). Weber, who described himself in this context as a 'class-conscious bourgeois' (31, p. 77), saw dominant tendencies of *class formation* both on the side of the large-scale land-owners and on the side of the agricultural workers: the one group became a uniform class of capitalists, the other became a class of proletarians (cf. 31, pp. 70-1). With this development, the previously personal relations of domination were gradually replaced by an 'impersonal class-domination':

Only a class can negotiate with a class; the relations of responsibility between the individual master and the individual worker disappear; the individual entrepreneur becomes, so to speak, capable of being substituted, he is merely a class type. The personal relation of responsibility disappears and something impersonal, which one used to call the domination of capital, takes its place. (31, p. 71)

Through this development, *hatred* of one class for the other arises, a hatred which Weber compared with the 'national hatred' for the 'traditional enemy'. There arises from this hatred, in connection with the objective opposition of interests, the *class struggle*, of which Weber said 'The class struggle exists in and is an integrating component of today's social order' (31, p. 73). In this context we shall exclude Weber's concluding consequences for the church in this situation (cf. 31, pp. 73-82).

Looking at the *sociological importance* of the agricultural worker enquiries, it is to a certain extent obvious. They were careful empirical works analysing relevant aspects of the society in which Weber lived. Of course it must not be forgotten that for instance in 1881, forty-seven per cent of the population of the German Reich capable of gainful employment were still occupied in rural tasks.[10] Weber was investigating here above all the reciprocal effects of the gradual implementation of capitalism in the area of agricultural production – effects in the economic, social, political, psychological and ethical field. In order to be able to show such causes and consequences of general processes, Weber tried to achieve the most comprehensive analysis possible of the social conditions (division of land-ownership, work organization, social facilities etc.) and of the non-socially dependent factors (quality of land, climatic conditions etc.). At the same time he linked *local* realities with *national* ones (grain tariffs, state agricultural policy etc.) and *international* relations (grain price on the world market). He situated these results, which are valid for a restricted territory, in a causal and functional relationship with political and national developments (the 'Polish question') and with 'universal' developments (from traditionalism/patriarchy to capitalism/rationalism), while all the time not losing sight of the historical dimension. We note here in passing that Weber, in connection with his scientific reappraisal of the material, progressed to practical recommendations and a political assessment of these results, and that they were indeed extraordinarily important to him. This observation will be dealt with more systematically in connection with the section on 'freedom from value-judgement'.[11]

Similarly, the methodological importance of these works is obvious: they are historically decisive points in the development of systematic, empirical social research and its methods and techniques. The development, application and testing of the evaluation of statistical data of the most heterogeneous kind (quality of land, population movements, work times, wage charts), of the results of written questionnaires (mostly open questions), through interpretation and the inclusion of the results from – mostly unsupervised – field observations, without doubt do not stand up to today's methodological standards, which, nevertheless, would not have been developed without such preliminary stages. In the presentation of the relations of individual agricultural worker categories, a movement towards an ideal-typical procedure can be discerned, although Weber did not already have this term and the concept behind it at his disposal. We should regard as of basic importance that it was a recognizable concern of Weber to investigate the *interactions* of economic, social, political and psychological contexts – both basic and conditional, and that he endeavoured to avoid any assertion of monocausal explanations and unilinear developments.

The stock exchange

Relevant texts

'*Die Börse I. Zweck und äußere Organisation*' (The stock exchange: I Aims and structural organization) (1894)

'Die Börse II. Der Börsenverkehr' (The stock exchange: II Transactions)
(1896)

Weber's intensive preoccupation with the stock exchange and the literary
expression of this preoccupation in his work were immediately connected
with his agricultural worker studies. At many points in his discussion of the
East Elbian regions, Weber referred to the great importance of the national
and international *grain price* for land-owners *and* agricultural workers. And
since it is at the *stock exchange* where this price was created – according to laws
incomprehensible to the lay public – the impression was frequently formed
at that time not only among industrial workers and social democracy, but
also among large-scale land-owners *and* agricultural workers that what went
on at the stock exchange was 'a kind of conspirators' club to lie and deceive
at the expense of honest working people' (32, p. 17). In Weber's view, such
an opinion had its origins in a 'boundless superficiality, which seeks faults
where only incomprehension or a conflict of interests lies' (32, p. 17).

Weber's preoccupation with the stock exchange led to two kinds of
writings: on the one hand he wrote two booklets on 'The Stock Exchange'
for the *Göttinger Arbeiterbibliothek* edited by Friedrich Naumann (32, 47) and
on the other, in the *Zeitschrift für das Gesammte Handelsrecht* (39, 44), in the
Handwörterbuch der Staatswissenschaften 36, 49) and in the *Deutsche Juristen-
Zeitung* (41) he adopted a firm and extremely critical position towards the
results and suggestions of the stock exchange enquiry commission and the
stock exchange law of 1 November 1897 (184/I; 184/II).

Both booklets on 'The Stock Exchange' are of importance. In them,
Weber was concerned to provide an 'initial orientation' to the aims and
structural organization of the stock exchanges and their transactions for
precisely that circle of people who had 'no connection whatsoever' with the
dealings on the stock exchanges and the capital market. In his opinion,
nothing was more damaging to a labour movement 'than impractical aims,
buried in ignorance of actual relations' (32, p. 17). For Weber the stock
exchange was an institution of modern wholesale trading and just as
indispensable as this kind of trading itself. In didactic and extremely clear
stages, Weber outlined the historical origin of the modern exchange
economy, for which the stock exchange is a modern and very comprehensive *market*, and thus a place where, at regular gatherings, deals for modern
consumer articles in particular are transacted on the basis of demand and
supply. With the aid of examples, Weber described the features of the
commodity market, the stocks and bonds exchange, and the exchange
market. In connection with the presentation of obligations and shares, he
tried to bring out the *impersonality* of the connections between the landlords

and the taxpayers, in order to explain the catchphrase the 'domination of capital' (cf. 32, p. 28). In particular he wanted to relativize the impression that the holders of such bonds are *necessarily* 'a thin stratum of "coupon-cutting layabouts" ' (32, p. 28) or exclusively 'large-scale capitalists' (32, p. 32).

Weber presented in detail the stock exchange's history of origin and its typical functionaries (exchange dealers and brokers). He compared the German stock exchange with those in England, America and France and characterized the then most important German exchanges (in Hamburg and Berlin). In view of their indispensable function, Weber asked whether the group of people who led the contemporary stock exchange organization was qualified to do so. In connection with the second question, Weber made suggestions for a reform of personnel and the establishment of a 'stock exchange tribunal'. 'The stock exchange *is* a monopoly for the rich and nothing is more foolish than to let this fact be hidden by the admission of penniless and therefore powerless speculators, thus giving big capitalist business the possibility of unloading their responsibility on to them' (32, p. 17).

It was precisely the phenomenon of *speculation* which occupied Weber intensively in the second booklet: he outlined the different sorts of uses of local and temporal price differences on the international market for the purpose of making a profit in arbitrage and speculation; and here it was important to Weber to free this kind of economic activity from the stigma of immorality. Each attempt to prevent speculation as such would in his eyes mean a decisive weakening of Germany in the 'relentless' and 'inexorable' *economic* struggle between the nations. 'A strong stock exchange cannot be a club for "ethical culture", and the capital of the large banks is no more a social service than shotguns and canons. For a national economic policy which is aiming at goals in this world, it can be only one thing: *an instrument of power* in that economic struggle' (47, p. 80).

In our context of presenting Weber's works, Weber's preoccupation with the stock exchange is of *sociological importance* in so far as a modification of the viewpoint resulting from his preoccupation with the position of the East Elbian agricultural workers can be discerned. If the agricultural-worker studies showed that the *advance of capitalism* destroyed traditional cultural patterns, then it becomes clear from the investigations and presentations of stock exchange relations that the advance of capitalism also brings with it *new cultural values*. The institutionalization of the stock exchanges made possible the world-wide expansion of the exchange trade in consumer articles, and made it possible to calculate international economic events.

We must stress that Weber assessed these positive functions essentially from the standpoint of 'the political and economic power interests of a nation' (47, pp. 78–9), and his main concern was 'a rational stock exchange policy, which proceeds from the interests of Germany's position of power' (47, p. 79).

The industrial workers

Relevant texts

'*Deutschland als Industriestaat*' (The Industrialization of Germany) (1897)

'*Die Lage der deutschen Buchdrucker*' (The Situation of German Printers) (1900)

'*Erhebungen über Auslese und Anpassung (Berufswahl und Berufsschicksal) der Arbeiterschaft der geschlossenen Großindustrie*' (Investigations into the Vocational Selection and Adaptation of the Workforce in Established Large Industry) (1908)

'*Zur Psychophysik der industriellen Arbeit*' (On the Psychophysics of Industrial Labour) (1908–1909)

'*Zur Methodik sozialpsychologischer Enquêten*' (On the Methodology of Social-Psychological Enquiries) (1909)

'*Probleme der Arbeiterpsychologie*' (Problems of Worker-Psychology) (1912)

Weber's works on the position of the German industrial workers, too, were directly connected to the consequences of the advance of capitalism in Germany's increasing *industrialization*. During the proceedings of the eighth *Kongreß* in Leipzig in 1897 (cf. 52), at which Germany's development into an *industrial state* was discussed, Weber made his basic position clear. That 'secular tendency' through which Germany transformed itself from an agrarian into an industrial state – as an illustration the alteration in the number of those employed in agriculture in the German Reich from 46.7 per cent in 1882 to 39.9 per cent in 1895 (52, p. 65) – was in Weber's eyes an 'inflicted fate' (52, p. 108). Without counting himself among the 'optimists of capitalism', Weber answered his own question of whether the capitalist development of Germany can be prevented: '*no, it cannot be prevented,* it is inevitable for us and only the course it takes can be influenced economically' (52, p. 109). Thus Weber opposed two political developments in particular: the tendency to a 'feudalization of bourgeois capital' and the 'theory of the domestic market', both of which would have led to a conservative domestic capitalism, and might have stood in the way of a 'successful social development' and the development of Germany's political freedom (cf. 52, pp. 110–13).

Stimulated by contemporary discussions about the general effects of, and particularly for the social question of Germany's industrialization, Weber, at the turn of the century, turned increasingly to the problem of the position of the industrial workers. His first act was to collaborate on a private enquiry on the 'situation of German printers' by Walter Abelsdorff (cf. 57). By means of a questionnaire which was distributed via the 'Association of German Printers', Abelsdorff questioned one-sixth to one-seventh of all German compositors and printers (4,815 questionnaires were completed) as to their family status group, its age structure, number of children, marrying age, regional and vocational mobility, intra and inter-generational mobility. In addition he produced a careful investigation and analysis of the household budgets of fifteen selected, four-person printing families in the whole of the German Reich. In his 'preliminary remarks', Weber stressed the necessity of similar analyses of other vocations; he characterized the Abelsdorff study as a 'problematic experiment' and a 'trial beginning'.

A similar investigation of individual strata of the workforce in a *large* industry with particular locations would bring about characteristically diverging results, especially when strong differences in working conditions exist between them. This can equally be said, on the other hand, of investigations within the old guild-organized crafts. It is our intention occasionally to attempt such an investigation by tackling the labour organizations. (57, p. viii)

Weber's intention led ultimately to the large-scale enquiry of the *Verein*, under the title 'Investigations into the selection and adaptation (vocational choice and destiny) of the workers in the different branches of large industry'. The commencement of this enquiry was decided at a committee meeting of the *Verein* in September 1907; the final sub-committee consisted of Heinrich Herkner as chair, and the university professors Schmoller, Sinzheimer, Stein, Zwiedineck-Südenhorst, Alfred and Max Weber. The results of this enquiry, which was finally begun in October 1908, were presented altogether in seven volumes of the *Verein*'s writings (133, 134, 135 I–IV, 153), which were published between 1910 and 1915. They contain the results of investigations on, among other things, the texile industry, the electrical industry, printing, the engineering industry, the automobile industry, leather goods and stoneware. For those working on the enquiry, Weber put together 'working instructions' (in *'Erhebungen über Auslese und Anpassung der Arbeiterschaft* . . .') for the sort of investigations which arose from conversations with his brother Alfred. He sent the text to the chair, Herkner, as a 'stimulus', and Herkner had the document copied and distributed (90).

Weber outlined the research objectives of the enquiry as follows:

The present investigation is attempting to ascertain on the one hand which effect *established large industry* has on the personal characteristics, vocational destiny and extra-vocational lifestyle of the workforce, which physical and psychical qualities it develops in them and how these qualities are expressed in the entire way of life of the workforce. And, on the other hand, to what extent large industry in its developmental capacity and direction is bound to certain qualities; qualities which are generated by ethnic, social and cultural provenance, and by the tradition and living conditions of the workforce. Thus two different questions are coupled together, which the theoretician can and must separate, but which appear almost everywhere combined in the praxis of the investigation, in such a way that in the *last* analysis at least, the one cannot be answered without the other. (90, p. 5)

From this characterization the extraordinary wealth of the course of questioning touched on already becomes clear. Weber emphasized that the investigation was pursuing a *purely social–scientific* aim: 'It is exclusively a question of the material and objective establishing of facts and the tracing of their bases which lie in the conditions of existence of large industry and the characteristics of its workers' (90, p. 6). All the possible *practical* side-effects, as for example social, trade and cultural policy proposals, were not the aim of this investigation. 'With such intentions the scientific impartiality of this investigation would in no way be helped' (90, p. 7).

Weber characterized the individual courses of questioning and formulated detailed questions which result from the general research objective cited above. It was not the exploration of the organization and the internal structuring of enterprises, nor their technical and economic determination which occupied the foreground (i.e. 'morphological' questions), but their *effects on the workforce*. This means, for example, that neither the new, technical developments nor the composition of the required enterprise capital were of interest; for Weber they were 'economic pre-questions' which only led to a clarification of the following questions: 'Now it is to investigate one of the decisive points that first, it is maintained what *kind* of workers with what *kind* of qualities are eliminated on the one side, and which are cultivated on the other; and second, to what extent this is determined by the general economic foundations of the respective industry, which are dependent on the extent and *kind* of capital requirements' (90, pp. 9–10). From this example the general course of questioning becomes clear and we can see the great demands that Weber placed on those working on this investigation. They should possess not only a thorough knowledge of the technology and economy of the respective industry, but moreover should acquire the results of physiological and psychological researches. In order to be able to talk about the vocational destiny of workers, about the social relations of the workers among themselves and about the general 'characterological' qualities of the workforce in the large industries, Weber sketched the frameworks of questioning of these special disciplines and the problems bound up with them for those who will work on these investigations in the future. He went just as much into questions of the physiological effects of making work routines rhythmical (cf. pp. 18–19), of the psychical conditions and consequences of cycles of fatigue (cf. 90, pp. 20–1) and into the consequences of noise in the workplace (cf. 90, p. 23), as into the experimental psychological research into 'recoverability', 'exercise capacity', 'concentration capacity', and 'habituation capacity' (cf. 90, pp. 23–5). Weber took up particularly thoroughly the controversy over 'natural aptitudes' – specifically in the manifestation of 'racial differences' – in their relation to 'acquired qualities' (cf. 90, pp. 28–37).

His position can without doubt be regarded as one which is valid in social scientific discussion even today:

Confronting the material content with a viewpoint which is 'without assumptions' would certainly make it obvious that (1) one *can* understand *any* human expression of life as a certain manner of the 'functioning' of inherited 'dispositions', determined by *present* living conditions, dispositions which for their part have been 'developed' in a certain manner by past living conditions; (2) that, however, the question of whether *in general* the inherited aptitudes or the inherited qualities are originally the decisive factor or predominantly the most important, is already in principle wrongly formulated and thus pointless. It is wrongly formulated because the question of whether something is 'important' as an original factor or not depends upon what it should be 'important' or 'unimportant' *for*; that means from which quite special viewpoint it is regarded *individually* as important. (90, p. 30)

Accordingly, a *social scientific* investigation must not proceed, according to Weber, from an 'inheritance hypothesis', but should have 'the test of the influences of social and cultural provenance, always investigating upbringing and tradition *first* and advancing with this explanatory principle as far as this is at all possible . . . Only after taking into consideration those sorts of influences and their implications would one, in case they were not sufficient as an explanation, come to those questions of psychophysical "predisposition" and *ultimately* to the influence of hereditary qualities' (90, pp. 32–33). Weber expressed an 'energetic warning' against 'the all too unnoticed attribution of complex psychical traits and "character qualities" to "inheritability"' (90, p. 33).

After this general classification, Weber draws up his 'working instructions' for the 'fellow collaborators', in which the investigation's 'methodology' is outlined in detail. The points discussed are: (1) the importance of the working time, of the distribution of breaks, and of the different systems of payment; (2) the inclusion of wages accounting and the use of a roll of permanent workers (workers' log) by the factories. As far as the questioning of the workers themselves is concerned, Weber sees in this – as in the agricultural workers enquiry – 'in principle methodological difficulties' (90, p. 48) in particular because it would be difficult 'to collect material from the workers, which we could combine into a whole with that collected from the entrepreneurs' (90, p. 48). Nevertheless, Weber indicated that such investigations were worthwhile, particularly with 'an at any rate as large as possible number of the sort of workers which appear characteristically differentiated in quantity or quality' (90, p. 48).

Weber formulated the general intention of the enquiries:

We must investigate on the one hand the manner of the 'selection process' carried out by large industry according to its immanent needs on that population which, with its vocational destiny, is chained to it; and on the other hand the manner of 'adaptation' among personnel working 'by hand' or 'by brain' in large industries to the living conditions which such industry has to offer them. In this way the answer to the question should be gradually approached: *What sort of people are moulded* by the modern large industry on the strength of its immanent characteristics, and *what vocational* (and thus indirectly *extra-vocational*) *destiny* is it preparing for them? (90, p. 370)

Weber differentiated between two separate types of *investigation* as the solution to this aim:

1 On the one hand, the form of the *enterprise* or rather the *industrial enquiry*, i.e. the analysis of enterprises according to his 'working instructions'. For this type Weber stressed 'expressly' that besides the 'vocational destiny', the extra-vocational 'life-style' should be the object of the enquiries (cf. 90, p. 53). In this context he spoke of the necessity of researching the 'class-consciousness' of the workforce in large industry (90, p. 55).

2 On the other hand, the form of the *trade union statistics*, i.e. the distribution of the questionnaires by means of the labour organizations.

In conclusion, Weber emphasized that all such enquiries represent 'only an (albeit important) part of a social scientific analysis of modern large industry'. For the completion of these results one must take into account the position of the *technical administrators* in the industry and the *employers*. 'Once all these investigations are brought together, we can produce a picture of the *cultural importance* of the developmental process which large industry is bringing about before our very eyes' (90, p. 57). On the basis of these 'working instructions' from Weber, a 'working plan' was drawn up for the concrete implementation of the enquiry, and on this the *questionnaire* was based. [12]

Even before the *Verein*'s enquiry was tackled, Weber published in the *Archiv* in connection with his 'working instructions' a four-part series of essays 'On the psychophysics of industrial labour' (86, 91). In this, Weber was trying to impart the experiments, discussions and results of the anthropological, physiological, experimental–psychological and psychopathological research of his age. His aim was to inform those working on empirical investigations and to clarify the problems of why there had been no collaboration between these specialist sciences and the social scientific disciplines, and where such possibilities lay for the future. In this 'essay intended as a literary project' (91, p. 523), Weber undertook a 'compilation' of the work and findings of the psychiatrist, Emil Kraepelin and his disciples. [13] Weber was particularly interested in collating the results of the research into the physiological and psychological conditions of *productivity* among the (industrial) workers. The most important themes and concepts are the following: fatigue, recuperation, exercise, habituation and stoppages at work. In extraordinary detail, Weber wrote on the *methodological* problematic of investigations into work-capacity, in particular on the enormous technical difficulties and costs of *labour experiments* (cf. 91, pp. 228–9). As one equally problematic possibility of measuring productivity, Weber suggested the evaluation of wages slips.

Besides this informative part of his 'literary report', Weber introduced in the latter part the results of an *investigation* he carried out himself into the psycho-physical conditions of *labour productivity*. He carried out these studies on the variations in productivity of mill-workers by means of tables and graphs on hourly, daily and weekly productivity in the summer of 1908 in his family-owned textiles factory. It is thus of methodological interest to see the creative imagination with which Weber discussed the most diverse frameworks of questioning and attempted in part to answer them. It was for him a question of investigating those factors which can condition, promote or restrict the *individual* productivity of the worker, as for example, amount of wages, humidity, noise, sexual activities, eating habits, alcohol consumption, lighting, regional origin, religious belief and trade union membership. Weber differentiated between them with the help of the measurable results of time-clocks and the particulars provided by the data of wages accounting on the work-capacity of individual male and female weavers, according to further, job-specific criteria, such as the spinning location being used, the respective technique of the loom and the difference of weaving on one or two looms. In summary, Weber stressed that the results obtained from these data can in no way be generalized, since the enterprise under investigation was not exemplary. It recruited strongly from local workers, it considerably changed its machine stock, and was an untypical branch of industry. He saw as a positive methodological result the observation 'that the sequence of numbers which behave most irrationally . . . produced *averages* which were far less irrational than the sequences of numbers themselves . . .' (91, p. 526). According to Weber, in a practical respect these investigations of his own have made clear the importance of the factor of routine ('practice') and at the same time showed the need for a penetrating concern with the relationship of 'milieu' and 'aptitude' (cf. 91, pp. 531–2). Above all this last framework of questioning, which we see illustrated in the discussion of the heritability of psychic pathologies, was an intense concern and specifically included the position of Freud (cf.91., pp. 532–8). Weber came to the conclusion that precisely for the 'dozens' of such researches being carried out 'for the time being the dispute over *theories* of inheritance must remain completely out of sight' (91, p. 539).

At the proceedings of the *Verein* on 'Problems of worker-psychology' in October 1911 in Nuremberg, Heinrich Herkner reported on the provisional results of the *Verein*'s investigations.[14] It was mainly the Berlin statistician, Ladislaus von Bortkiewicz who spoke on the methodological problematic of the works being presented, in particular that of Marie Bernays. In a sharp response, Weber made it clear that the *Verein* was only *at the beginning* of its investigations and that the provisional 'results' only deserved limited value: 'What has emerged thus far . . . as final results, is still *nothing at all*, at least nothing but a few numbers, which are suited for supporting a few hypotheses, newly formulating other hypotheses, correcting the framework of questioning and . . . *proving* that *from* the material that has been tackled here and with the help of similar material still to be collected, in the course of time – and certainly a very long time – valuable and sweeping results will be obtained, *in all probability*' (115, p. 190).

It seems that after 1911 Weber lost interest to a great extent in his empirical research into the position of the industrial workers. He wrote on this subject on but one further occasion in *'Zur Methodik sozialpsychol-*

ogischer Enquêten und ihrer Bearbeitung' (94) in a discussion of three works by the private researcher, Adolf Levenstein. Between 1907 and 1911, Levenstein had as a private initiative sent around 8,000 questionnaires each with twenty-six questions and had achieved a response of 63 per cent (5,040 receipts).[15] Weber discussed Levenstein's earlier works in the *Archiv* with the intention of making Levenstein's 'material, which is in its way extremely valuable "class-psychologically"' accessible to a *scientific* evaluation. In this he characterized once again which demands he would put on the social scientific research into the position of the industrial workers (cf. 94, pp. 954–5). It is of interest in this that here – without knowing the term, or rather the theory – Weber demanded a kind of 'correlation analysis' when he writes 'In principle it must be demanded that for *all considerable* questions it is established each time that x per cent of those who answered question a with b, have answered question c with d and thus y per cent for the reason g and z per cent for the reason g^2 etc., this being taken, of course, with a pinch of salt. But occasionally the most unexpected connections result from this method' (94, p. 956).

4

The sociology of religion

Relevant texts

The Protestant Ethic and the Spirit of Capitalism (1904–5; 1920)
'The Protestant Sects and the Spirit of Capitalism' (1906; 1920)
'The Economic Ethic of the World Religions' (1911–14)
The Religion of China
The Religion of India
Ancient Judaism (1915–16; 1916–17; 1918–19; 1920)
'*Vorbemerkung*' ('Preface') (1920)
'Religious Groups (The Sociology of Religion)' in *Economy and Society* (1922)

The cultural significance of Protestantism

From the previous sections which dealt with two areas of Weber's academic work, there emerges a recurring motif: his investigation of the causes, forms of appearance and effects of capitalism, the *revolutionizing* force of which Weber looked at from many different angles in all the works we have discussed so far.

His studies in the importance of Protestantism in this context became then, as today, his most popular works. Weber worked on his essay on the Protestant ethic before travelling to the United States in the summer of 1904 and again after his return, and he published his article in the *Archiv für Sozialwissenschaft und Sozialpolitik* (*Archive of Social Science and Social Policy*) in 1904–5. In the following year (1906), he published two drafts of his article on the Protestant sects (69, 70, 74; 5E).

Weber was motivated to produce his own studies in particular by Werner Sombart's two-volume work *Modern Capitalism* (1902) in which Sombart discussed the effects of Calvinism and the Quakers on the development of capitalism.[1] Weber was also inspired by a discussion that had been going on in Germany for some years already[2] – although it was not peculiar to Germany alone[3] – on the connections between religious and economic developments. Thus up to this time Weber's increasing interest in investigating the *roots of modern capitalism* was the motivating factor behind these studies.

Immediately after their publication, Weber's essays on the 'spirit of capitalism' caused a great sensation and led to a series of articles which Weber answered partially in the form of written responses (81, 84, 98, 99). These exchanges, which because of recurrent misunderstandings and insinuations began to irritate Weber, lasted for over five years. Particularly when his friend Ernst Troeltsch published articles on this subject,[4] Weber turned to the more general problem of the relationships between religion, economy and society in an inter-cultural comparative study, the results of which will be discussed in the next section. When in 1919 Weber set to work collating and revising his pieces on the sociology of religion that had appeared up to that time, for the *Gesammelte Aufsätze zur Religionssoziologie*, he was able to include both these discussions and the results of his later research. In this commentary we will stick to the 1919–20 editions, as they illustrate the most recent, valid representation of Weber's own position.[5]

The first article on the Protestant ethic serves to define the problem under discussion. Weber proceeds from an empirical study by his pupil Martin Offenbacher[6] on occupational stratification according to religious denomination in Baden. One result of this investigation revealed that an over-proportional number of Protestants owned capital, were entrepreneurs and made up the higher-qualified technical or sales personnel in modern business. By incorporating similar studies from the historical sciences which had produced a comparable result, particularly regarding the rich towns of the sixteenth century, Weber formulated his first *question*: 'Why were the districts of highest economic development at the same time particularly favourable to a revolution in the Church?' (2E, p. 36). One possible answer, the emancipation from economic traditionalism, was not considered valid by Weber, since the Reformation was not striving to remove the Church's domination over everyday life, but it brought about 'a regulation of the whole of conduct which, penetrating to all departments of private and public life, was infinitely burdensome and earnestly enforced' (2E, p. 36).

This consideration led Weber to his next *question*: 'Now how does it happen that at that time those countries which were most advanced economically (Geneva, Scotland, the Netherlands, New England, England), and within them the rising bourgeois middle class, not only failed to resist this unexampled tyranny of Protestantism, but even developed a heroism in its defence? For bourgeois classes as such have seldom before and never since displayed heroism' (2E, p. 37).

Weber suggested an answer to the first question:

The explanation of these cases is undoubtedly that the mental and spiritual peculiarities acquired from the environment, here the type of education favoured by the religious atmosphere of the home community and the parental home, have determined the choice of occupation, and through it the professional career (2E, p. 39). (The Protestants) both as ruling classes and as ruled, both as majority and as minority, have shown a special tendency to develop economic rationalism . . . Thus the principal explanation of this difference must be sought in the permanent intrinsic character of their religious beliefs, and not only in their temporary external historico-political situations (2E, p. 40).

Proceeding from these observations and inferences, Weber determined the first *task of his investigation*: 'It will be our task to investigate these relations with a view to finding out what peculiarities they have or have had which might have resulted in the behaviour we have described' (2E, p. 40). Weber did not accept another, current answer to these questions – that these manifestations lay in an (alleged) 'other-worldliness' of Catholicism and an (alleged) 'materialistic joy of living' of Protestantism. In his opinion these supposed 'explanations' fail 'where an extraordinary capitalistic business sense is combined in the same persons and groups with the most intensive forms of a piety which penetrates and dominates their whole lives. Such cases are not isolated, but these traits are characteristic of many of the most important Churches and sects in the history of Protestantism. Especially Calvinism, wherever it has appeared, has shown this combination' (2E, p. 43). From this observation Weber drew the *consequence*: 'If any inner relationship between certain expressions of the old Protestant spirit and modern capitalistic culture is to be found, we must attempt to find it, for better or worse, not in its alleged more or less materialistic or at least anti-ascetic joy of living, but in its purely religious characteristics' (2E, p. 45).

Weber stressed that in the attempt to research such an 'inner relationship', a large number of possible relationships can be considered.

It will now be our task to formulate what occurs to us confusedly as clearly as is possible, considering the inexhaustible diversity to be found in all historical material. But in order to do this it is necessary to leave behind the vague and general concepts with which we have dealt up to this point, and attempt to penetrate into the peculiar characteristics of and the differences between those great worlds of religious thought which have existed historically in the various branches of Christianity. (2E, p. 45)

Weber considered it necessary to define more precisely his object of investigation, i.e. in particular his concept of the 'spirit' of capitalism:

If any object can be found to which this term can be applied with any understandable meaning, it can only be an historical individual, i.e. a complex of elements associated in historical reality which we unite into a conceptual whole from the standpoint of their cultural significance. Such an historical concept, however, since it refers in its content to a phenomenon significant for its unique individuality, cannot be defined according to the formula *genus proximum, differentia specifica*, but it must be gradually put together out of the individual parts which are taken from historical reality to make it up. Thus the final and definitive concept cannot stand at the beginning of the investigation, but must come at the end. We must, in other words, work out in the course of the discussion, as its most important result, the best conceptual formulation of what we here understand by the spirit of capitalism, that is the best from the point of view which interests us here . . . This is a necessary result of the nature of historical concepts which attempt for their methodological purposes not to grasp historical reality in abstract general formulae, but in concrete genetic sets of relations which are inevitably of a specifically unique and individual character. (2E, pp. 47–8)

As an 'illustration', Weber quoted from a document by Benjamin Franklin, his instructions to young tradesmen,[7] in which the ideals of the credit-worthy man of honour and the *duty* of the individual were stressed by contrast to his interest in increasing his capital, which is taken for granted as an end in itself. Weber wrote:

Truly what is here preached is not simply a means of making one's way in the world, but a peculiar ethic. The infraction of its rules is treated not as foolishness but as forgetfulness of duty. That is the essence of the matter. It is not mere business astuteness, that sort of thing is common enough, it is an ethos. *This* is the quality which interests us. (2E, p. 51)

What in this document is stressed in a single individual, was in Weber's eyes an 'ethically coloured maxim for the conduct of life', and it is in this sense that he wanted to see the concept of the 'spirit of capitalism' used. 'It is the spirit of modern capitalism. For that we are here dealing only with Western European and American capitalism is obvious from the way in which the problem was stated. Capitalism existed in China, India,

Babylon, in the classic world, and in the Middle Ages. But in all these cases, as we shall see, this particular ethos was lacking' (2E, p. 52).

In particular, being embedded in a *summum bonum* made this 'ethic' into something quite different from merely a veiling of purely eudæmonistic or hedonistic motives. 'Man is dominated by the making of money, by acquisition as the ultimate purpose of his life. Economic acquisition is no longer subordinated to man as the means for the satisfaction of his material needs.' This 'leading principle' of capitalism was for Weber closely connected with the religious ideas of the *actors*, for whom Benjamin Franklin was introduced merely as a representative. In this context, then, the idea of 'duty in a calling' turned up: it was that which is the fundamental basis for the 'social ethic' of 'capitalistic culture'. In this, however, it should not be maintained

that a conscious acceptance of these ethical maxims on the part of the individuals, entrepreneurs or labourers, in modern capitalistic enterprises, is a condition of the further existence of present-day capitalism. The capitalist economy of the present day is an immense cosmos into which the individual is born, and which presents itself to him, at least as an individual, as an unalterable order of things in which he must live. It forces the individual, in so far as he is involved in the system of market relationships, to conform to capitalistic rules of action (2E, p. 54).

Nevertheless, this 'manner of life so well adapted to the peculiarities of capitalism' must have originated historically 'and not in isolated individuals alone, but as a way of life common to whole groups of men. This origin is what really needs explanation' (2E, p. 55).

Weber also discussed the 'opponent' of this 'spirit of capitalism': *traditionalism*. Thus he described that way of behaving and thinking, according to which

a man does not 'by nature' wish to earn more and more money, but simply to live as he is accustomed to live and to earn as much as is necessary for that purpose. Wherever modern capitalism has begun its work of increasing the productivity of human labour by increasing its intensity, it has encountered the immensely stubborn resistance of this leading trait of pre-capitalist labour. (2E, p. 60)

Moreover, Weber spoke of the 'spirit of capitalism' because 'that attitude of mind has on the one hand found its most suitable expression in capitalistic enterprise, while on the other the enterprise has derived its most suitable motive force from the spirit of capitalism' (2E, pp. 64–5). For this attitude of mind, Weber drew up the 'ideal-type' of the *capitalist entrepreneur*, about whom he said:

He avoids ostentation and unnecessary expenditure, as well as conscious enjoyment of his power, and is embarrassed by the outward signs of the social recognition which he receives. His manner of life is, in other words, often, and we shall have to investigate the historical significance of just this important fact, distinguished by a certain ascetic tendency . . . It is, namely, by no means exceptional, but rather the rule, for him to have a sort of modesty . . . He gets nothing out of his wealth for himself, except the irrational sense of having done his job well.

But it is just that which seems to the pre-capitalistic man so incomprehensible and mysterious, so unworthy and contemptible. That anyone should be able to make it the sole purpose of his life-work, to sink into the grave weighed down with a great material load of money and goods, seems to him explicable only as the product of a perverse instinct, the *auri sacra fames*. (2E, pp. 71-2)

Weber then asked, as if following his own demand for more precision in the aim of his investigation:

Now, how could activity, which was at best ethically tolerated, turn into a calling in the sense of Benjamin Franklin? The fact to be explained historically is that in the most highly capitalistic centre of that time, in Florence of the fourteenth and fifteenth centuries, the money and capital market of all the great political Powers, this attitude was considered ethically unjustifiable, or at best to be tolerated. But in the backwoods small bourgeois circumstances of Pennsylvania in the eighteenth century, where business threatened for simple lack of money to fall back into barter, where there was hardly a sign of large enterprise, where only the earliest beginnings of banking were to be found, the same thing was considered the essence of moral conduct, even commanded in the name of duty. To speak here of a reflection of material conditions in the ideal superstructure would be patent nonsense. What was the background of ideas which could account for the sort of activity apparently directed toward profit alone as a calling toward which the individual feels himself to have an ethical obligation? For it was this idea which gave the way of life of the new entrepreneur its ethical foundation and justification. (2E, pp. 74–5)

In this context Weber took from Werner Sombart the hypothesis that the basic motive of the modern economy was an 'economic rationalism'.[8] Weber expanded this concept considerably and suggested:

It might thus seem that the development of the spirit of capitalism is best understood as part of the development of rationalism as a whole, and could be deduced from the fundamental position of rationalism on the basic problems of life. In the process Protestantism would only have to be considered in so far as it had formed a stage prior to the development of a purely rationalistic philosophy. But any serious attempt to carry this thesis through makes it evident that such a simple way of putting the question will not work, simply because of the fact that the history of rationalism shows a development which by no means follows parallel lines in the various departments of life . . . Rationalism is an historical concept which covers a whole world of different things. It will be our task to find out whose intellectual child the particular form of rational thought was, from which the idea of a calling and the devotion to labour in the calling has grown . . . which has been and still is one of the most characteristic elements of our capitalistic culture. We are here particularly interested in the origin of precisely the irrational element which lies in this, as every conception of a calling. (2E, pp. 76–8)

Weber maintained that this religiously determined idea of the 'calling' in the sense of 'vocation' is a 'product of the Reformation' (2E, p. 80), in which at any rate one thing was new – 'the valuation of the fulfilment of duty in worldly affairs as the highest form which the moral activity of the individual could assume. This it was which inevitably gave every-day worldly activity a religious significance, and which first created the conception of a calling in this sense' (2E, p. 80). However, this idea was capable of assuming many different forms, and this led to a variety of inferences:

The effect of the Reformation as such was only that, as compared with the Catholic attitude, the moral emphasis on and the religious sanction on, organized worldly labour in a calling was mightily increased. The way in which the concept of the calling, which expressed this change, should develop further depended upon the religious evolution which now took place in the different Protestant Churches. (2E, p. 83)

After a highly detailed investigation of this idea in Martin Luther, Weber came to the conclusion, 'Thus for Luther the concept of the calling remained traditionalistic. His calling is something which man has to accept as a divine ordinance, to which he must adapt himself. This aspect outweighed the other idea which was also present, that the work in the calling was a, or rather *the*, task set by God' (2E, p. 85). The Lutheran version of the idea of the calling was therefore for Weber 'at best of questionable importance for the problems in which we are interested . . . It is thus well for us next to look into those forms in which a relation between practical life and a religious motivation can be more easily perceived than in Lutheranism' (2E, pp. 86–7). Thus he turned to Calvinism and other Protestant sects, in particular in England. In this Weber felt it was important to stress the following aspect:

We thus take as our starting-point in the investigation of the relationship between the old Protestant ethic and the spirit of capitalism the works of Calvin, of Calvinism, and the other Puritan sects. But it is not to be understood that we expect to find any of the founders or representatives of these religious movements considering the promotion of what we have called the spirit of capitalism as in any sense the end of his life-work . . . We shall thus have to admit that the cultural consequences of the Reformation were to a great extent, perhaps in the particular aspects with which we are dealing predominantly, unforeseen and even unwished-for results of the labours of the reformers. They were often far removed from or even in contradiction to all that they themselves thought to attain. (2E, pp. 89–90)

The aim of such an investigation should be to 'form a contribution to the understanding of the manner in which ideas become effective forces in history' (2E, p. 90). However, in order to grasp precisely the *limitations* of the research's object, and in order to prevent any criticism which may arise from misunderstandings and assumptions, Weber took great pains in the exact definition of his goals.

In such a study . . . no attempt is made to evaluate the ideas of the Reformation in any sense, whether it concern their social or their religious worth. We have continually to deal with aspects of the Reformation which must appear to the truly religious consciousness as incidental and even superficial. For we are merely attempting to clarify the part which religious forces have played in forming the developing web of our specifically worldly modern culture, in the complex interaction of innumerable different historical factors. We are thus enquiring only to what extent certain characteristic features of this culture can be imputed to the influence of the Reformation. At the same time we must free ourselves from the idea that it is possible to deduce the Reformation, as a historically necessary result, from certain economic changes. Countless historical circumstances, which cannot be reduced to any economic law, and are not susceptible of economic explanation of any sort, especially purely political processes, had to concur in order that the newly created Churches should survive at all.

On the other hand, however, we have no intention whatever of maintaining such a foolish and doctrinaire thesis as that the spirit of capitalism (in the provisional sense of the term explained above) could only have arisen as the result of certain effects of the Reformation, or even that capitalism as an economic system is a creation of the Reformation. In itself, the fact that certain important forms of capitalistic business organization are known to be considerably older than the Reformation is a sufficient refutation of such a claim. On the contrary, we only wish to ascertain whether and to what extent religious forces have taken part in the qualitative formation and the quantitative expansion of that spirit over the world. Furthermore, what concrete aspects of our capitalistic culture can be traced to them. In view of the tremendous confusion of interdependent influences between the material basis, the forms of social and political organization, and the ideas current in the time of the Reformation, we can only proceed by investigating whether and at what points certain correlations between forms of religious belief and practical ethics can be worked out. At the same time we shall as far as possible clarify the manner and the general *direction* in which, by virtue of those relationships, the religious movements have influenced the development of material culture. Only when this has been determined with reasonable accuracy can the attempt be made to estimate to what extent the historical development of modern culture can be attributed to those religious forces and to what extent to others. (2E, pp. 90–2)

The second article on the Protestant ethic served to investigate and prepare an 'explanation' of those problems and relations which were presented and defined in the first article. As has already become clear, Weber was concerned to research the historical roots of the ethical maxims which produced the religiously constructed idea of 'calling', which possessed a 'certain ascetic tendency'. If Weber had confirmed the extensive latent traditionalism in the Lutheran moulding of Protestantism, he now turned to other manifestations of Protestantism, which stress these specific ideas more strongly in a form more suited to 'economic rationalism'. The research into this 'irrational moment' of the Protestant sects, which was to attain as an 'unwished-for result' such a huge importance for the 'history of rationalism', stood for Weber as a model for the historical effectiveness of ideas.

The way in which the framework of the problem is made more precise becomes clear in the title of the second article, the Practical Ethics of the Ascetic Branches of Protestantism. Weber investigated Calvinism, Pietism, Methodism and 'the sects growing out of the Baptist movement' as the historical bearers of this special form of Protestantism. Weber stressed that it would not be enough to look purely at the 'moral practice', but that it was imperative to deal with the different *dogmatic* roots.

But the original connection with those dogmas has left behind important traces in the later undogmatic ethics; moreover, only the knowledge of the original body of ideas can help us to understand the connection of that morality with the idea of the after-life which absolutely dominated the most spiritual men of that time. Without its power, overshadowing everything else, no moral awakening which seriously influenced practical life came into being in that period. (2E, p. 97)

Thus it was not so much a question of the content of the official *doctrine* 'rather [of] something entirely different: the influence of those psychological *sanctions* which, originating in religious belief and the practice of religion, gave a direction to practical conduct and held the individual to it. Now these sanctions were to a large extent derived from the peculiarities of the religious ideas behind them' (2E, pp. 97–8).

Weber turned firstly to Calvinism, as that faith 'over which the great political and cultural struggles of the sixteenth and seventeenth centuries were fought in the most highly developed countries, the Netherlands, England, and France' (2E, p. 98), and in particular he discussed the 'dogma of election', the heart of the so-called 'doctrine of predestination'. In an extraordinarily careful and detailed argument, Weber spread out the theological and dogmatic basis of this doctrine, according to which people exist for the sake of God and human life has no other meaning than that of glorifying God. Equally, a part of humanity is predetermined as blessed and another part damned by God, and no human credit or debt can change anything in God's absolutely free decisions. The 'extreme inhumanity' of such a doctrine had in Weber's opinion one consequence in particular, 'a feeling of unprecedented inner loneliness of the single individual' (2E, p. 104). With this doctrine and its radical repercussions (no priest, no sacrament, no church, and as a final consequence, no God) (cf. 2E, p. 104) Weber considered the conclusion to have been reached of 'that great historic process in the development of religions, the elimination of magic from the world which had begun with the old Hebrew prophets and, in conjunction with Hellenistic scientific thought, had repudiated all magical means to salvation as superstition and sin' (2E, p. 105). This passage was written in 1919–20, after Weber's works on *Die Wirtschaftsethik der Welt-religionen*.

There was no magical or any other means of attaining grace for those to whom God had decided to deny it. Thus this doctrine formed 'one of the roots of that disillusioned and pessimistically inclined individualism which can even today be identified in the national characters and the institutions of the peoples with a Puritan past' (2E, p. 105). And here Weber came across a paradox.

It seems at first a mystery how the undoubted superiority of Calvinism in social organization can be connected with this tendency to tear the individual away from the closed ties with which he is bound to this world. But, however strange it may seem, it follows from the peculiar form which the Christian brotherly love was forced to take under the pressure of the inner isolation of the individual through the Calvinistic faith. In the first place it follows dogmatically. The world exists to serve the glorification of God and for that purpose alone. The elected Christian is in the world only to increase this glory of God by fulfilling His commandments to the best of his ability. But God requires social achievement of the Christian because He wills that social life shall be organized according to His commandments, in accordance with that purpose. The social activity of the Christian in the world is solely activity *in majorem gloriam Dei*. This character is hence shared by labour in a calling which serves the mundane life of the community. Even in Luther we found specialized labour in callings justified in terms of brotherly love. But what for him remained an uncertain, purely intellectual suggestion became for the Calvinists a characteristic element in their ethical system. Brotherly love, since it may only be practised for the glory of God and not in the service of the flesh, is expressed in the first place in the fulfilment of the daily tasks given by the *lex naturae*; and in the process this fulfilment assumes a peculiarly objective and impersonal character, that of service in the interest of the rational organization of our social environment. (2E, pp. 108–9)

From this dogmatically founded doctrine, Weber saw the emergence of a problem and its wide-reaching 'solution'.

For us the decisive problem is: How was this doctrine borne in an age to which the after-life was not only more important, but in many ways also more certain, than all the interests of life in this world? The question, Am I one of the elect? must sooner or later have arisen for every believer and have forced all other interests into the background. And how can I be sure of this state of grace? . . . He [Calvin] rejects in principle the assumption that one can learn from the conduct of others whether they are chosen or damned. It is an unjustifiable attempt to force God's secrets. The elect differ externally in this life in no way from the damned; and even all the subjective experiences of the chosen are . . . possible for the damned with the single exception of that *finaliter* expectant, trusting faith. The elect thus are and remain God's invisible Church. (2E, pp. 109–10)

Calvin's uncompromising position brought greater and greater difficulties, in particular for pastoral praxis, with the result that essentially two strategies formed for the *epigones* and the broad stratum of ordinary people to deal with this problem. On the one hand it was postulated as a 'duty' to consider onself chosen and to reject any doubt as a temptation of the devil, and 'on the other hand, in order to attain that self-confidence intense worldly activity is recommended as the most suitable means. It and it alone disperses religious doubts and gives the certainty of grace' (2E, p. 112).

In this doctrine it was not a question of a reproduction of the doctrine of the 'holiness of work'; here the question of which *sign* the elect can take to be his or her 'effectual calling' remained in the background. 'Thus, however useless good works might be as a means of attaining salvation, for even the elect remain beings of the flesh, and everything they do falls infinitely short of divine standards, nevertheless, they are indispensable as a sign of election' (2E, p. 115).

Weber compared this attitude with that of Catholicism and Lutheran Protestantism where atonement, grace of the sacraments and the certainty of forgiveness was a 'release' from that tremendous *tension* under which it was the Calvinist's inexorable fate to live, admitting of no mitigation. 'For him such friendly and human comforts did not exist. He could not hope to atone for hours of weakness of or thoughtlessness by increased good will at other times, as the Catholic or even the Lutheran could. The God of Calvinism demanded of his believers not single good works, but a life of good works combined into a unified system' (2E, p. 117). This systematization of ethical conduct and its 'rational character', which led to the sanctifying of life as a whole (and which almost took on 'the character of a business enterprise' (2E, p. 124), led to constant self-control and a planned regulation of life. Weber summarized this 'systematic method of rational conduct' (2E, p. 118) under the concept of 'worldly asceticism' (2E, p. 120). In contrast, rather, with monastic asceticism, which 'the more strongly it gripped an individual, simply served to drive him farther away from everyday life' (2E, p. 121), added a 'positive' idea to Calvinism, 'the idea of the necessity of proving one's faith in worldly activity' (2E, p. 121).

It gave the broader groups of religiously inclined people a positive incentive to asceticism. By founding its ethic in the doctrine of predestination, it substituted for the spiritual aristocracy of monks outside of and above the world the spiritual aristocracy of the predestined saints of God within the world. It was an aristocracy which, with its *character indelebilis*, was divided from the eternally damned remainder of humanity by a more impassable and, in its invisibility, more terrifying gulf than separated the monk of the Middle Ages from the rest of the world about him, a gulf which penetrated all social relations in its brutality. This consciousness of divine grace of the elect and holy was accompanied by an attitude toward the sin of one's neighbour, not of sympathetic understanding based on consciousness of one's own weakness, but of hatred and contempt for him as an enemy of God bearing the signs of eternal damnation. (2E, pp. 121–2)

After this presentation of the dogmatic conception of Calvinism and its repercussions, Weber investigated in a similar but no longer as detailed way 'Pietism' (2E, pp. 128–39) with particular reference to its German expression (2E, pp. 132–8); and Anglo-American 'Methodism' (2E, pp. 139–43), which for the purposes of his investigation he saw as resting on a 'foundation of uncertainty' (2E, p. 142).

Following on from this, as the second independent bearer of Protestant asceticism besides Calvinism, Weber investigated the *Baptist movement* with its sectional expressions in the Baptists, the Mennonites and, above all, the Quakers. Weber saw the radicalization of the 'radical devaluation of . . . the world', through which, stronger again than in Calvinism, 'the intensity of interest in economic occupations was considerably increased by various factors' (2E, p. 150). Weber regarded as the most essential of these 'factors' the strict refusal to accept political office and the invincible antagonism to any sort of aristocratic way of life.

After this journey through the different Protestant religious sects, in which the idea of 'calling' had gained a specifically 'ascetic' character, Weber summarized and explained the continuing aim of the investigation.

It is our next task to follow out the results of the Puritan idea of the calling in the business world, now that the above sketch has attempted to show its religious foundations. With all the differences of detail and emphasis which these different ascetic movements show in the aspects with which we have been concerned, much the same characteristics are present and important in all of them. But for our purposes the decisive point was . . . the conception of the state of religious grace, common to all the denominations, as a status which marks off its possessor from the degradation of the flesh, from the world.

. . . though the means by which it was attained differed for different doctrines, it could not be guaranteed by any magical sacraments, by relief in the confession, nor by individual good works. That was only possible by proof in a specific type of conduct unmistakably different from the way of life of the natural man. From that followed for the individual an incentive methodically to supervise his own state of grace in his own conduct, and thus to penetrate it with asceticism. But . . . this ascetic conduct meant a rational planning of the whole of one's life in accordance with God's will. And this asceticism was no longer an *opus supererogationis*, but something which could be required of everyone who would be certain of salvation. The religious life of the saints, as distinguished from the natural life, was – the most important point – no longer lived outside the world in monastic communities, but within the world and its institutions. This rationalization of conduct within this world, but for the sake of the world beyond, was the consequence of the concept of calling of ascetic Protestantism.

Christian asceticism, at first fleeing from the world into solitude, had already ruled the world which it had renounced from the monastery and through the Church. But it had, on the whole, left the naturally spontaneous character of daily life in the world untouched. Now it strode into the market-place of life, slammed the door of the monastery behind it, and undertook to penetrate just that daily routine of life with its methodicalness, to fashion it into a life in the world, but neither of nor for this world. With what result, we shall try to make clear in the following discussion. (2E, pp. 153–4)

In this undoubtedly extremely methodologically difficult task of researching the 'connections' between fundamental religious ideas (the Puritan idea of calling, asceticism) and the maxims for everyday economic life ('capitalist spirit'), Weber turned to selected theological writings which have an explicit relation to pastoral *praxis*. As a major representative of this Puritan ethic, Weber selected Richard Baxter (1615–91), the famous priest to the Anglican community in Kidderminster and the founder of the 'Worcester Association'.[9] With the aid of a thorough interpretation of his works, in particular in *A Christian Directory: or a Sum of Practical Theology and Cases of Conscience* (London 1673), Weber emphasized all those elements of ascetic Protestantism, which appeared to him to be relevant for the development of modern capitalism.

This worldly Protestant asceticism . . . acted powerfully against the spontaneous enjoyment of possessions; it restricted consumption, especially of luxuries. On the other hand, it had the psychological effect of freeing the acquisition of goods from the inhibitions of traditionalistic ethics. It broke the bonds of the impulse of acquisition in that it not only legalized it, but . . . looked upon it as directly willed by God . . .

On the side of the production of private wealth, asceticism condemned both dishonesty and impulsive avarice. What was condemned as covetousness, Mammonism etc., was the pursuit of riches for their own sake. For wealth in itself was a temptation . . . the religious valuation of restless, continuous, systematic work in a worldly calling, as the highest means to asceticism, and at the same time the surest and most evident proof of rebirth and genuine faith, must have been the most powerful conceivable lever for the expansion of that attitude toward life which we have here called the spirit of capitalism.

When the limitation of consumption is combined with this release of acquisitive activity, the inevitable practical result is obvious: accumulation of capital through ascetic compulsion to save. (2E, pp. 170–2)

Characterized thus, this Puritan conception of life 'favoured the development of a rational bourgeois economic life; it was the most important, and above all the only consistent influence in the development of that life. It stood at the cradle of the modern economic man' (2E, p. 174).

The decisive turning point in this development took place, however, only if the thus *prepared* formation of an altered evaluation of economic action was freed from its religious origins.

[T]he full economic effect of those great religious movements, whose significance for economic development lay above all in their ascetic educative influence, generally came only after the peak of the purely religious enthusiasm was past. Then the intensity of the search for the Kingdom of God commenced gradually to pass over into sober economic virtue; the religious roots died out slowly, giving way to utilitarian worldliness. Then . . . the isolated economic man who carries on missionary activities on the side takes the place of the lonely spiritual search for the Kingdom of Heaven of Bunyan's pilgrim, hurrying through the market-place of Vanity.

When later the principle 'to make the most of both worlds' became dominant in the end . . . a good conscience simply became one of the means of enjoying a comfortable bourgeois life, as is well expressed in the German proverb about the soft pillow. What the great religious epoch of the seventeenth century bequeathed to its utilitarian successor was, however, above all an amazingly good, we may even say a pharisaically good, conscience in the acquisition of money, so long as it took place legally . . . A specifically bourgeois economic ethic had grown up. With the consciousness of standing in the fullness of God's grace and being visibly blessed by Him, the bourgeois business man, as long as he remained within the bounds of formal correctness, as long as his moral conduct was spotless and the use to which he put his wealth was not objectionable, could follow his pecuniary interests as he would and feel that he was fulfilling a duty in doing so. The power of religious asceticism provided him in addition with sober, conscientious and usually industrious workmen, who clung to their work as to a life purpose willed by God. Finally, it gave him the comforting assurance that the unequal distribution of the goods of this world was a special dispensation of Divine Providence, which in these differences, as in particular grace, pursued secret ends unknown to men. (2E, pp. 176–7)

Thus the main effect of this Puritan ethic, at least in the context dealt with by Weber, was the evolution of a *rational way of life* based on the *idea of calling* which had arisen from the spirit of *worldly asceticism*. And it was this idea which became a constitutive component of the modern capitalist spirit and modern civilization.

For when asceticism was carried out of monastic cells into everyday life, and began to dominate worldly morality, it did its part in building the tremendous cosmos of the modern economic order. This order is now bound to the technical and economic conditions of machine production which today determine the lives of all the individuals who are born into this mechanism, not only those directly concerned with economic acquisition, with irresistible force. Perhaps it will so determine them until the last ton of fossilized coal is burnt. In Baxter's view the care for external goods should only lie on the shoulders of the 'saint like a light cloak, which can be thrown aside at any moment'. But fate decreed that the cloak should become an iron cage.

Since asceticism undertook to remodel the world and to work out its ideals in the world, material goods have gained an increasing and finally an inexorable power over the lives of men as at no previous period in history. Today the spirit of religious asceticism – whether finally, who knows? – has escaped from the cage. But victorious capitalism, since it rests on mechanical foundations, needs its support no longer . . .

No one knows who will live in this cage in the future, or whether at the end of this tremendous development entirely new prophets will arise, or there will be a great rebirth of old ideas and ideals, or, if neither, mechanized petrification, embellished with a sort of convulsive self-importance. For of the last stage of this cultural development, it might well be truly said: 'Specialists without spirit, sensualists without heart; this nullity imagines that it has attained a level of civilization never before achieved.' (2E, pp. 181–2)

In summarizing the results of his investigation, Weber once again took great pains in the *classification* of his study both methodologically and in its content. Weber was fully aware of the problematical appeal of theological tracts on the moral praxis of conduct as he wrote, 'we are here naturally not so much concerned with what concepts the theological moralists developed in their ethical theories, but, rather, what was the effective morality in the life of believers – that is, how the religious background of economic ethics affected practice' (2E, p. 267, note 42). However, Weber reflected thoroughly the enormous methodological problematic of the economic connection of religious ideas with material, economic developments. At the start he stressed that the intention of his research was to provide a contribution to the illustration of the historical effect of *ideas*, [10] and thus he referred to the fact 'that I consider the influence of economic development on the fate of religious ideas to be very important and shall later attempt to show how in our case the process of mutual adaptation of the two took place' (2E, p. 277, note 84).

The clear recognition of the *one-sidedness* of his questioning was also what made Weber, in conclusion, formulate the necessary aims of any future research.

The next task would be rather to show the significance of ascetic rationalism, which has been only touched on in the foregoing sketch, for the content of practical social ethics, thus for the types of organization and the functions of social groups from the conventicle to the State. Then its relations to humanistic rationalism, its ideals of life and cultural influence; further to the development of philosophical and scientific empiricism, to technical development and to spiritual ideas would have to be analysed. Then its historical development from the Medieval beginnings of worldly asceticism to its dissolution into pure utilitarianism would have to be traced out historically [my insertion – omitted by Parsons] through all the areas of ascetic religion. Only then could the quantitative cultural significance of ascetic Protestantism in its relation to other plastic elements of modern culture be estimated.

Here we have only attempted to trace the fact and the direction of its influence to their motives in one, though a very important point. But it would also further be necessary to investigate how Protestant Asceticism was in turn influenced in its development and its character by the totality of social conditions, especially economic. The modern man is in general, even with the best will, unable to give religious ideas a significance for culture and national character which they deserve. But it is, of course, not my aim to substitute for a one-sided materialistic an equally one-sided spiritualistic causal interpretation of culture and of history. Each is equally possible, but each, if it does not serve as the preparation, but as the conclusion of an investigation, accomplishes equally little in the interest of historical truth. (2E, pp. 182–3)

Before we present a short summary of the sociological and methodological relevance of this famous study, we shall look briefly at the essay 'The Protestant Sects and the Spirit of Capitalism'. Weber wrote this on the basis of impressions he gained travelling in the United States and he published it in 1906 in two parts in the *Frankfurter Zeitung* (69, 70). This article was republished, in somewhat expanded form, the same year in the *Christliche Welt* (74). For its inclusion in the *Gesammelte Aufsätze zur Religionssoziologie*, Weber reworked this text once again in 1919–1920, indicating that the reworking had been motivated by the fact that the *concept of sects* which he had developed in this study had been taken over in the meantime by his friend, Ernst Troeltsch. [11]

Once again Weber proceeded from a sociographical observation. In spite of the widespread ignorance of religious groupings in the American State, the number of persons not affiliated to a church in Weber's time proved to be around six per cent of the entire population, and this was despite the considerable particularly material burdens entailed by belonging to a church or sect in the United States. Starting from the impressions he collected on his journeys, Weber identified the *question* which emerges from this observation: why is it that the question of religious affiliation was almost always posed 'in social life and in business life which depended on permanent and credit relations?' (5E, p. 303).

On the basis of rather coincidental personal observations, Weber made the general assertion that only those citizens who belong to Methodist or Baptist or other *sects* can show any economic success. That these people 'found credit everywhere' Weber put down to the fact 'that a fully reputable sect would only accept for membership one whose "conduct" made him appear to be morally *qualified* beyond doubt' (5E, p. 305). Thus the question of which creed one belonged to was of no importance whatsoever, so long as the membership was linked to an ethical, particularly economically ethical 'certificate of moral qualification' (5E, p. 305).

In this context, Weber introduced the distinction between 'church' and 'sect', which was to be of great consequence in his later work.

A church is a corporation which organizes grace and administers religious gifts of grace, like an endowed foundation. Affiliation with the church is, in principle, obligatory and hence proves nothing with regard to the member's qualities. A sect, however, is a voluntary association of only those who, according to the principle, are religiously and morally qualified. If one finds voluntary reception of his membership, by virtue of religious *probation*, he joins the sect voluntarily. (5E, p. 305-6)

This appearance, which comes from religious conceptions and had decisive economic relevance, underlay, as Weber confirmed, a process of 'secularization'. The methods of researching and ascertaining one's ethical qualifications were taken over by a multitude of organizations and 'associations'. They all pursued the same goal – the test of *credit*worthiness. Once again, specific religious concepts were distanced from their original theological contexts and were thereby turned to very general use. 'Yet one must never overlook that without the universal diffusion of these qualities and principles of a methodical way of life, qualities which were maintained through these religious communities, capitalism today, even in America, would not be what it is' (5E, p. 309).

Weber looked into how it was particularly the bourgeois middle class who had these conceptions as 'the typical vehicles of social ascent into the circle of the entrepreneurial middle class' (5E, p. 308). This development led to 'tendencies leading toward aristocratic status groups', and to the development of a definite ideal of the (American) 'gentleman'.

The investigation of the *sociological relevance* of Weber's studies in the cultural importance of Protestantism means adopting a position in a scientific discourse that has been going on for over eighty years. The possible 'ways of reading' these works are oriented towards different epistemological interests and theoretical contexts, and the literary results are enough to fill libraries.[12] One particular problem emerges. If one reads the studies on Protestantism on the basis of their arrangement in the *Gesammelte Aufsätze zur Religionssoziologie* of 1919–1920, what emerges are interpretative approaches which are essentially other than those which would come from an 'isolated' consideration of the texts. Here we shall firstly follow the original chronology, that is, consider the Protestantism studies alone and shall, in conclusion, once again place them in a comprehensive context.

From the two previous sections on Weber's work it is clear that the main attention of Weber's scientific interest up to the beginning of the *Protestant Ethic* was the *cultural importance of capitalism* both in the past and in the present. Weber turned to Protestantism as one of the historical *sources* of this economic order. He was primarily interested in a specific constitution of the socio-economic structures of Western civilization, and it was through this that Weber was diverted into researching the religious order.

In the research of these relations, the analysis operates on three levels. [13]

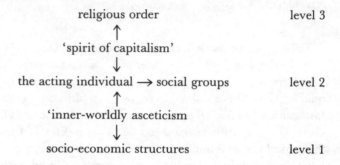

Mediations take place between the three levels, and these are indicated by the two ideal-typical constructs 'spirit of capitalism' and 'worldly asceticism'. Weber did *not* maintain a causal adequacy (*kausale Adäquanz*), but an *adequacy 'on the level of meaning'* (*sinnhafte Adäquanz*) i.e. he did *not* say, if A (= Puritanism) then B (= capitalism) but rather, if A (= capitalism) and B (= ethos of calling, worldly asceticism) coincide, then modern capitalism *can* (*Chance*) succeed as the dominant economic form and it has done this in the historical cases Weber investigated.

This *mediation* between levels 1 and 3 takes places by means of processes which start from level 2 and which affect it through the behaviour of *acting individuals*. These actors are not abstract constructions, but rather Weber based them on concrete persons who attach a *subjective meaning* to their action. Thus he started by referring to Benjamin Franklin and only then to the 'spirit of capitalism'; the beginning of the processes out of which such a complex historical figure as capitalism 'himself' arose, necessarily needed *bearers*. Neither Protestantism, Puritanism, nor Calvinism were the beginning; it was individuals who adopted certain religious convictions and converted them into action. However, this did not remain with individuals, but the interest of Weber, the sociologist, turned to collectives of people, to *social groups*. It did not remain like this for Benjamin Franklin, but Weber passed on to the 'bourgeois middle class' as the 'bearers' of the interpretations of meaning he investigated. In the course of time, these interpretations of meaning manifest an 'attitude' (*Gesinnung*), which was presented by Weber as 'the product of a long and arduous process of education' (2E, p. 62).

For Weber, the most gripping aspect of this development, was, however, the processes of the unintended detachment of these subjective interpretations of meaning from the actors and their fixture to the binding (economic) norms of everyday action. Only this emerging *dialectic* of the forces of spiritual drives ('subjectively intended meaning') and the organized socioeconomic structures ('modern capitalism') allowed the 'cultural importance' of (religious) ideas to penetrate the field of vision. The *subjectively intended meaning* was related to the use of means of attaining salvation, or rather for the documentation of its being granted. It became an *objective complex of meaning* through its encounter with the evolving forms of organization of the modern capitalist economy. On this basis, the aggregates of subjective meaning could evolve into general norms of social action, which from then on could detach themselves from their original religious contexts. Modern capitalism, once it had achieved the dominant economic form, no longer needed the vehicle of religious convictions to legitimize itself, and it could even turn against them. Under certain conditions, such ideas could provoke effects, which in turn could become causes of the destruction of these very ideas.

These processes of the historical effect of ideas on the action of individuals and groups are thus *not* controlled by any form of 'material forces', rather it was primarily actors, i.e. individuals acting intentionally and capable of reflection, who set these processes in motion. On the other hand, these subjective interpretations of meaning were not phenomena which arose unconditionally; they arose against the background of concrete, materially conditioned contexts. A modern capitalism could not develop without a corresponding ethic, and neither could this ethic become established without being supported by capitalism. In these investigations, historical reality was regarded as a reality which can be influenced by and constructed by the actor, and at the same time it confronted him/her, conditioning and restricting his/her possibilities of action.

Doubtless as much material – and controversial material – has been written about the *methodological* importance of Weber's studies on Protestantism as on its sociological relevance which is inseparable from it. In these works, Weber based his analysis on the concept of a comparative and ideal-typical procedure.[14] Moreover, his attempt to reconstruct the extraordinarily intricate *complex of meaning of 'ideas' and 'material' reality*, is of the greatest importance methodologically. However we should in no way even attempt to take up a position in this wide-reaching debate on the problem of 'base-superstructure'.[15]

We have described above what Weber wanted. Equally we have stressed that he was clearly aware of the *one-sidedness* of his questioning. And a third element of these works is of lasting methodological importance: the premise that the subjectively intended *meaning* of single, acting individuals, via the aggregation in social groups, is a centrally important component of socio-economic reality, and thus is of even greater importance for scientific understanding (*Verstehen*). The social action of people becomes the point of departure for a methodology of 'interpretive sociology' (*verstehende Soziologie*).[16]

'The Economic Ethic of the World Religions'

From 1911 to 1914, Weber worked on the 'sketches in the sociology of religion' for 'The Economic Ethic of the World Religions'. From 1915–16, he published them in the *Archiv*, reasoning that it would be impossible to resume this 'chain of thought' after the end of the war. 'Incidentally the essays were also intended to appear at the same time as the discussions on 'Economy and Society' contained in the *Grundriß der Sozialökonomik*, and to interpret and supplement the section on the sociology of religion – or at any rate to be interpreted by it in many cases' (127, p. 1, note 1). On the publication of this previously incomplete version, Weber added at the beginning an 'Introduction' which he wrote in 1915 and in which he undertakes a kind of initial and provisional summary of the main results. He made a very modest claim when he wrote, 'In their present form, they (the discussions) can perhaps be useful to supplement in some places the presentation of problems in the sociology of religion and perhaps even occasionally in economic sociology' (127, p. 1, n. 1). For reasons which we shall go into below, in the case of the Introduction, we are relying on the 1914 version (127), but for the discussions on the world religions we shall use the reworked 1919–1920 editions, which were cleared of 'major imperfections' (184, 203, 204, 205).

In this 'Introduction', Weber defined the basic concepts and the goal of research of his investigations into the sociology of religion on the 'economic ethic' of the 'world religions' and also formulated some of their provisional results. By 'world religions', Weber understood 'the five religions or religiously determined systems of life-regulation which have known how to gather multitudes of confessors around them . . . The Confucian, Hinduist, Buddhist, Christian, and Islamist religious ethics' (3E, p. 267). As the sixth, Weber mentioned Judaism and for a treatment of Christianity he referred us to his discussions of the Protestant ethic, knowledge of which he assumed. By 'economic ethic', Weber did *not* mean 'the ethical theories of economic compendia (it) points to the practical impulses for action which are found in the psychological and pragmatic contexts of religions . . . An economic ethic is not a simple 'function' of a form of economic organization; and just as little does the reverse hold, namely, that economic ethics unambiguously stamp the form of the economic organization' (3E, pp. 267–8).

In order to be able to define the determinants of the economic ethic, Weber turned to the religious certainty of the *directive elements in the life conduct* of those *social strata* 'which have most strongly influenced the practical ethic of their respective religions. These elements have stamped the most characteristic features upon practical ethics' (3E, p. 268). Thus it was *not* Weber's assumption 'that the specific nature of a religion is a simple "function" of the social situation of the stratum which appears as its characteristic bearer, or that it represents the stratum's "ideology", or that it is a "reflection" of a stratum's material or ideal interest-situation' (3E, pp. 269–70). On the contrary, however, his theory was that 'for every religion we shall find that a change in the socially decisive strata has usually been of profound importance. On the other hand, the type of religion, once stamped, has usually exerted a rather far-reaching influence upon the life-conduct of very heterogeneous strata' (3E, p. 270).

Turning to the criterion of the evaluation of *suffering* in each religious ethic and the eventual changes in these evaluations, Weber differentiated between a 'theodicy of good fortune' and a 'theodicy of suffering' (cf. 3E, p. 271). The 'religions of salvation' in particular, which were stamped by the latter theodicy, were primarily oriented not towards the fortunate, the propertied, the ruling strata, who did not need a redeemer and prophets, but towards the oppressed, or those threatened by distress. Weber saw a 'rational conception of the world' contained potentially in the 'myth of the redeemer', which developed on this basis, i.e. a 'rational theodicy of misfortune' (3E, p. 274). In addition, this idea underwent a widespread dissemination as 'the need for an ethical interpretation of the "meaning" of the distribution of fortunes among men increased with the growing rationality of conceptions of the world. As the religious and ethical reflections upon the world were increasingly rationalized and primitive, and magical notions were eliminated, the theodicy of suffering encountered increasing difficulties' (3E, p. 275). Weber saw in the 'religions of salvation' a fundamental mistrust of wealth and power, which became the point of departure for a rational religious ethic, which began in the less socially valued strata and had considerable repercussions on their 'inner conditions'. The conception of 'redemption' in particular 'where it (is) a systematic and rationalized "image of the world" ' (3E, p. 280), was in an important sense dependent on the answers to the questions 'from what' and 'for what' one wanted to be redeemed. Weber took account of the different answers and summarized, 'Behind them always lies a stand towards something in the actual world which is experienced as specifically "senseless". Thus the demand has been implied: that the world order in its totality is, could, and should somehow be a meaningful "cosmos" ' (3E, p. 281). *Which* of these possibilities become socially and historically important 'is historically and socially determined, at least to a very large extent, through the peculiarity of those strata that have been the carriers of the ways of life during its formative and decisive period. The *interest* situation of these strata, as determined socially and psychologically, has made for their peculiarity, as we here understand it' (3E, p. 281). Starting with the *results* of his individual analyses, Weber distinguished between such different social bearers as political officials, warriors, peasants, citizens and intellectuals. He stressed, however,

that the nature of the desired sacred values has been strongly influenced by the nature of the external interest-situation and the corresponding way of life of the ruling strata and thus by the social stratification itself. But the reverse also holds: wherever the direction of the whole way of life has been methodically rationalized, it has been profoundly determined by the ultimate values towards which this rationalization has been directed. (3E, pp. 286–7)

These 'ultimate' values, according to Weber were wholly *religiously determined values*. Weber introduced a further differentiation which is becoming important. These 'supreme', 'ultimate' values and gifts of grace were now *not* universally distributed and valid, but had to be linked with the 'empirical fact . . . that men are *differently qualified* in a religious way' (3E, p. 287). From this fact there emerged a 'status stratification, in accordance with differences in the charismatic qualifications' (3E, p. 287). Weber meant here essentially the differences between a 'virtuoso' religiosity and a mass religiosity (3E, p. 287) and he was particularly interested in the prevailing relationship to everyday life as the 'locus of the economy' (3E, p. 289). These connections took on highly differentiated forms in the different religious designs and systems, and it was they who were the actual theme of Weber's studies in the economic ethic of the world religions. It was *not* his intention to develop a 'systematic "typology" of religion', but

They [the following presentations] are 'typological' in the sense that they consider what is typically important in the historical realizations of the religious ethics . . .

Other aspects will be neglected . . . The feature of religions that are important for economic ethics shall interest us primarily from a definite point of view: we shall be interested in the way in which they are related to economic rationalism. More precisely . . . the economic rationalism of the type which, since the sixteenth and seventeenth centuries, has come to dominate the Occident as part of the peculiar rationalization of civic life . . . (3E, pp. 292-3)

With such a goal to his investigation, Weber accepted an 'unhistorical' procedure, in the sense

that the ethics of individual religions are presented systematically and essentially in greater unity that has ever been the case in the flux of their actual development. Rich contrasts which have been alive in individual religions, as well as incipient developments and ramifications, must be left aside; and the features that to the author are important must often be presented in greater logical consistency and less historical development than was actually the case. If it were done arbitrarily, this simplification would be a historical 'falsification'. This, however, is not the case, at least not intentionally. The author has always underscored those features in the total picture of a religion which have been decisive for the fashioning of the *practical* way of life, as well as those which distinguish one religion from another. (3E, p. 294).

China

As the first world religions in his 'comparative essays in the sociology of religion' Weber turned to *Confucianism* and *Taoism*, the two great religious orders of old China. Unlike the studies on Protestantism, Weber used half of his investigation to sketch, in four sections, the 'sociological foundations' of Chinese society.

The first section dealt with the conceptual triad City, Prince and God. According to Weber, China was a land of large walled cities, the lord of which was the prince and this development was essentially favoured by the prevailing taxation policy. Moreover, China was a land of *inland trade* with paramount importance in agrarian production. In this context, Weber spent time presenting the Chinese *money economy*.

From these basic premises, in Weber's view, two 'peculiar facts' (4E, p. 12) resulted.

The strong increase of wealth in precious metals led unmistakably to a 'certain' stronger development of the money economy, which in no way favoured a capitalist development, but rather an increase in *traditionalism*.

The 'enormous' growth of population equally formed *no* stimulation for a capitalist formation of the economy.

In Weber's eyes, this confirmation of 'stationary forms of economy' required an explanation. In order to be able to provide this, he first traced the historical genesis of the *Chinese city*. Primarily, according to Weber, it was the 'residence of the viceroy' which was linked to the lack of an 'urban market monopoly'. In particular, in China there lacked the 'political autonomy' of the city, i.e. it was not a 'commune' with political privileges of its own, as Weber had observed in the Occidental city.[17] These assessments produced the most important result that the Chinese city was not the home of a 'citizenry', whose great historical importance Weber had seen in the West. In China 'the fetters of the sib were never shattered', it lacked 'the oath-bound political association formed by an armed citizenry' and there were 'actually . . . fewer formal guarantees of self-government' in the Chinese cities (cf. 4E, pp. 14–15).

Weber gave the following as reasons for this difference in urban developments (4E, pp. 15–20).

China was predominantly an inland area.

The Chinese imperial bureaucracy was very ancient. The city was predominantly a product of rational administration.

The existing guild monopolies were primarily determined by sibs and tribes.

Lack of maturation of a systematic city policy for guilds.

Lack of legal foundations.

Lack of own politico-military power for cities and guilds.

As a precondition for the development of an imperial *central authority* and the *patrimonial officialdom* bound up with it, Weber claimed that 'the need to control rivers was prerequisite to a rational economy' (4E, p. 20), which meant mainly the protection against floods by dykes and canal construction for inland water transport. The groups of river administrators and the police 'formed the nucleus of the pre-literary and purely patrimonial bureaucracy' (4E, p. 21).

Completely unrelated to this sketch of historical processes of development, Weber commented, 'It may be asked to what extent these conditions were consequential not only . . . for politics, but also for religion' (4E, p. 21). To answer this question, Weber compared the Chinese developments with development in the Near East, using their different conceptions of God as a way of differentiating their development. Since a number of geographical and economic conditions in both areas are relatively similar, Weber concluded that these different religious ideas cannot be derived from economic conditions alone, but have their origin in 'foreign political areas'.

In a comparison of the politico-military situation of Mesopotamia and China, the latter was presented as a *pacified world empire*, which on the basis of this pacification, brought about a considerable change in its norms. From the ideal of the 'bachelor house' via the ideal of the 'highly trained individual hero, equipped with costly arms' to the 'rule of the literati', a dominant 'pacifist turn of ideologies' emerged (4E, pp. 21–5).

Weber turned his research interest to the historical position of the Chinese emperor and the military and religious changes in this position. For the first time, here a *politically* coloured application of the concept of 'charisma' appeared[18] which Weber defined in detail in his Introduction (cf. 3E, p. 295). In this context, Weber dealt with the central problem of the *corroboration* of charismatic qualities in the 'sociological' sense of 'extraordinariness' (4E, p. 26, note 58). The foundations of charismatic domination and their corroboration could thus be of different kinds. 'For cultural evolution the decisive question was whether or not the *military* charisma of the warlord and the *pacifist* charisma of the . . . sorceror were united in the same hand' (4E, p. 30).

In China, 'co-determined' by the great significance of river regulation, imperial authority emerged from *magical* charisma. 'The Chinese monarch remained primarily a pontifex' (4E, p. 31), i.e. 'a monarch by divine right' (4E, p. 31). However, this domination was dependent upon the criterion of *corroboration*, i.e. of *success*. If this was lacking, in the extreme case the emperor was permitted to be killed by the great *officials* (4E, p. 32).

In the second section Weber attempted a comparison of the feudal state in the West and the prebendal state (prebendal economy) in China. Political feudalism was not primarily connected with landlordism in China, but emerged from the 'state organization of the *gentes*', i.e. was a case of 'political feudalization' (4E, p. 34). In filling the positions of domination, the sibs who were already in power were taken exclusively into consideration, i.e. the 'charisma' necessary for these positions was not attached to the single individual but to his sib. The 'great families' which were formed were thus 'charismatic sibs whose position was financed largely through political incomes and hereditary landed wealth' (4E, p. 35). For Weber the result was that in China, by contrast with the West, the 'hereditary charisma' of the *sib* was always primary to and the basis for a 'hereditary charismatic feudalism'.

Weber depicted in detail the position of the imperial sib within the system of social stratification in Chinese society, and the processes which triggered the competitive struggle between the princes, the officials and the literati. The main result of these complex processes was the gradual dissolution of feudalism, and here Weber, again in a relatively unrelated move, emphasized the *religious dimensions* to these processes when he wrote, 'Feudal elements in the social order gradually receded and patrimonialism became the structural form fundamental to the Confucian spirit' (4E, p. 47). In connection with this, Weber discussed the origin and the rules of Chinese patrimonialism and the bureaucracy which resulted from it. The 'patrimonial bureaucracy' as in the West, was 'the firmly growing nucleus to which the formation of the great state was bound. In both cases collegiate authorities and "departments" typically emerged, but the spirit of bureau-cratic work differed widely in the East and in the West' (4E, p. 50).

Weber based the dissimilarity of this 'spirit' on numerous factors. One he saw as caused by the varying system of public burdens, i.e. the taxation system as it had formed on the basis of the Chinese money economy. This taxation system, in connection with the pacification of the empire, had another consequence in Weber's view: a huge population growth. And here he came across his 'central problem' once again (4E, p. 55); the lack of even the least inclination towards 'modern capitalist developments'.

As an explanation, Weber argued that both 'economic and intellectual factors' had to be mentioned. Both complexes of factors, however, had a common element in that they 'resulted from the peculiarity of the leading stratum of China, the estate of officials and candidates for office, the mandarins' (4E, p. 55). Weber described their material position as one in which even officialdom *as a whole* had access to a huge income from prebends, but the individual official was compelled 'to make the most of' his short term of office (4E, p. 59). Weber saw in this material dependence on a highly differentiated system of prebends an essential reason for the extreme administrative and economic-policy *traditionalism* of the Chinese officialdom.

The third section on the sociological foundations of Chinese society was concerned essentially with the agrarian structure of China. Furthermore, in the forefront of Weber's interest is the question of the causes for capitalist development's failure to materialize. Weber added another precondition to those already included, which were relatively favourable ones (growth in population, increase in reserves of precious metals, beginnings of a rational economy and administration), namely the unsurpassed industry and capacity for work of the Chinese, which led to an 'intense *acquisitiveness* (which) has undoubtedly been highly developed' (4E, p. 63).

In his search for the causes of the non-appearance of a Chinese capital-ism, Weber came across another, in his opinion decisive, contrast between Chinese and Western development; the enormous *growth* in the peasant population in China since the beginning of the eighteenth century. The changes in agrarian structure which lay behind this led Weber back once again to a fundamental re-organization of the military and fiscal policies of the Chinese government. As the specialist in agrarian history, for which we have already come to know him, Weber went into extraordinary detail in the historical developments in the Chinese agrarian structure, and in particular the evolution of private property in land (cf. 4E, pp. 67–8). It is important to note here that, according to Weber, there was no evolution of large, agricultural 'rational' units of production and that the old peasant sibs were bearers of the land-holding as 'self-help communities'.

The fourth section summarized the observations introduced thus far on the sociological foundations of the Chinese development, and Weber tried to clear up the problem of how in China there was only a 'rudimentary' development of a market capitalism, seeking free-trading opportunities, in spite of the many preconditions and processes in its favour. Weber stated once again what he considers to be *lacking* for such a development – burghers conscious of their interests, as well as 'legal forms and societal foundations for capitalist "enterprise" [with its] rational depersonalization of business' (4E, p. 85). On the other hand, as a result of the prebend system, 'through political accumulation of property, there had developed a stratum of land magnates who leased lots. This (albeit) unstable patriciate bore neither a feudal nor a bourgeois stamp, but speculated in opportunities for the purely political exploitation of office . . . a system of internal booty capitalism prevailed' (4E, p. 86).

Weber regarded the institution of the *sib associations* and the importance of the *ancestor cult*, which lay behind them, as responsible for this turn in the historical development. Both these moments prevented a development of the *city* comparable to the West, and made the *village* the point of departure and of reference for China's developmental processes. The *patrimonial state structure* which was closely bound up with the sib ideas prevented the development of a rational, calculable functioning of administration and the judiciary – both necessary preconditions for a developing trade. The 'irrationalities' of these forms of government prevented the emergence of the political groundwork for a 'rational entrepreneurial capitalism'. But it was not only this lack of a formally guaranteed *law*, of a rational administration and judiciary and the ramifications of a system of prebends which prevented a capitalist development. If thus far Weber dealt essentially with the economic, political and socio-structural conditions, he then turned to the 'peculiar mentality'. He is concerned 'above all . . . by the attitude rooted in the Chinese "ethos" and peculiar to a stratum of officials and aspirants to office' (4E, p. 104). And it is this 'particular mentality' which Weber designated as his 'central theme'.

The fifth section is concerned with the *bearers* of this peculiar mentality, the *literati*. This status group owes its social position to a specific Chinese tradition. 'For twelve centuries social rank in China has been determined more by qualification for office than by wealth' (4E, p. 107). The fact that literary qualification was made into a measure of social value in China led to a position where the 'literati' were the ruling stratum in China. This leading stratum of intellectuals, which had grown out of ritual training, was essentially a genteel 'laymanship'. It was neither hereditary nor exclusive to belong to this stratum of literati, membership depended merely on the number of exams and the mastery of the abilities which the Chinese education demanded for this stratum. The literati as a *status group* regarded themselves as a unity, both in their professional honour as well as being the sole bearers of Chinese culture.

Generally in Chinese history, the literati had a particularly intimate connection with the patrimonial princes, particularly with the emperor. The ritually trained literati 'politicians' were primarily oriented towards the problems of internal administration and towards the problems of the current 'order' of administration. This orientation led to a practical political rationalism, which became evident in its specification of the concept of 'office' (*Amt*), in the creation of an ethos of 'official duty', and the conception of the 'public weal'. With the pacification of the empire which led to the creation of a unified state, the princes' competition for the literati came to a halt. 'The literati and their disciples then came to compete for the existing offices, and this development could not fail to result in a unified orthodox doctrine adjusted to the situation. This doctrine was to be *Confucianism*' (4E, p. 112). At the same time this was the decisive point in the turn toward *pacifism* and *traditionalism*. 'Tradition displaced charisma' (4E, p. 113).

At the nucleus of the literati status group were the mandarins, from whom all classes of Chinese civil servants were recruited. It was

a status group [*Schicht*] of certified claimants to office prebends . . . and their qualification for office and rank depended on the number of examinations they had successfully passed . . . The question usually put to a stranger of unknown rank was how many examinations he had passed. Thus, in spite of the ancestor cult, how many ancestors one had was not decisive for social rank (4E, p. 115).

In order to be able to understand this specifically Chinese development, Weber sketched the 'great types of education'. He distinguished between the two 'polar opposites in the field of educational ends', on the one hand to inculcate charisma, and on the other to impart specialized expert qualifications. The Chinese ideal of education with its system of examinations meant that no one could be assigned to both poles; it was not a question of imparting both specialist qualifications and charismatic abilities. Amid all the skills of writing, stylistics and the mastery of classical literature there was the imparting of a prescribed 'mentality' (*Gesinnung*), 'the *ways of thought* suitable to a cultured man' in which the literary, bookish character of this education was the decisive element. For Weber, it was precisely the literary character of this education which is of great importance, with as a consequence its emphasis on writing, as opposed to those traditions of education in which speech occupied a privileged position. 'Writing and reading were valued artistically and considered as worthy of a gentleman, for they were receptive of the artful products of script. Speech remained truly an affair of the plebs' (4E, p. 124). This peculiarity had wide-reaching consequences, in particular the loss of education in language, in defining and reasoning, and the lack of training in logic.

With the greatest practical matter-of-factness, the intellectual tools remained in the form . . . reminding us of the means of expression of Indian chieftains rather than of rational arguments. The absence of speech is palpable, that is speech as a rational means for attaining political and forensic effects, speech as it was first cultivated in the Hellenic *polis*. Such speech could not be developed in a bureaucratic patrimonial state which had no formalized justice. (4E, p. 127)

The supposed contradiction in this tradition was that this purely literary intellectuality as the conversational ideal of genteel men and the emphasis on excluding all practical-political questions was compulsory for a stratum of officials who had to administrate a huge empire. 'One did not manage the administration with mere poetry even in China' (4E, p. 132). For Weber it was basically a question of determining the *mentality* which lay behind the system and the personnel in the Chinese bureaucracy. This *mentality* was applicable not only to the actual status group of literati with the emperor at the top, but in exactly the same way to the whole population. Only the *level* of education was different but not the educational ideal. 'For only classic education existed' (4E, p. 134). Thus this conception of Chinese education had first to establish itself in the course of a long historical trial against powerful groups and ideas – the 'great families' of the feudal period, the purchasers of office, sultanism and the eunuch economy which supported it and the military powers. 'But in the long run and again and again the literati won out. Every drought, inundation, eclipse of the sun, defeat in arms, and every generally threatening event at once placed power in the hands of the literati. For such events were considered the result of a breach of tradition and a desertion of the classic way of life, which the literati guarded' (4E, p. 139).

In order to explain this triumphal march of a specific stratum and its ways of thinking, Weber asked 'What was the *material* content of the orthodox ethic of this status group which set the standard for the spirit of the state administration and the ruling strata?' The sixth section, under the heading 'The Confucian Life Orientation' was dedicated to answering this question of the material content of the orthodox ethic of Confucianism. According to Weber, the Chinese patrimonial bureaucracy had never been threatened by an autonomous hierarchy. By contrast with Western, Middle Eastern and Indian development, China had never had any socially powerful prophets, nor a powerful priesthood, nor its own doctrine of salvation, ethics or education provided by autonomous religious powers. 'Hence, the intellectualistic rationalism of a stratum of officials could freely unfold itself; here as elsewhere this intellectualism inwardly despised religions unless they were needed for the taming of the masses' (4E, pp. 142–3). One 'lay religion' alone, prescribed by the state, the belief in the power of ancestral spirits and its cult was allowed and the charismatic character of this religion 'suited officialdom's interest in self-preservation' (4E, p. 143). What was important was this 'religion's' primary orientation toward this world, and its main interest in long life, children and (moderate) wealth. There was no hint of an eschatology or doctrine of salvation.

This resulted in a lack of interest in the problem of the inequality of people's *religious* qualifications. Any idea of differentiating according to each person's 'state of grace' was unknown to Confucianism. On the other hand, classical Confucian doctrine contained the idea of a principled *equality* of people as a constitutive element. Here again, the same idea emerged, that it is not birth but the *degree of education* which was decisive for social position. The educated class was the ruling class as were those who possessed the necessary material prosperity, where an 'interest in maintaining social tranquility (leading) to the predilection for the most equal distribution of property possible' was an 'ultimate' goal of this society (4E, p. 148).

Another moment in Confucian life orientation was the lack of a development of natural law in the modern Western mould and the associated lack of China's own estate of jurists. The absence of a development in the area of the rationalization of law, in the Roman legal sense, did not lead to the formation of a codified law, but to a system of welfare justice which was oriented toward tradition and concrete situations. Thus, a 'modern' legal system did not emerge and like theological and philosophical 'logic', juristic 'logic' also failed to develop.

Weber summarized these individual aspects:

Consequently, practical rationalism, the intrinsic attitude of bureaucracy to life, free of all competition, could work itself out fully. There was no rational science, no rational practice of art, no rational theology, jurisprudence, medicine, natural science or technology; there was neither divine nor human authority which could contest the bureaucracy. Only an ethic congruent with bureaucracy could be created and this was limited solely by consideration of the forces of tradition in the sibs and by the belief in spirits. Unlike Western civilization, there were no other specifically modern elements of rationalism standing either in competition or in support of bureaucracy. Western culture in China was grafted upon a base which, in the West, had been essentially overcome with the development of the ancient *polis*. Hence, the culture of this bureaucracy can be considered an experiment which approximately tests the practical rationalism of government by office prebendaries and its effects. Orthodox Confucianism resulted from this situation. The rule of orthodoxy followed from the unity of the theocratic world empire and its authoritative regulation of doctrine. (4E, pp. 150f)

Thus, for Weber, Confucianism was essentially an 'innerworldly morality of laymen', which meant 'adjustment to the world, to its orders and conventions' and finally 'a tremendous code of political maxims and rules of social propriety for cultured men of the world' (4E, p. 152). All society's problems were, in the last instance, problems of education, the goal being the self-development of the individual. There was no 'evil' as such, for example in the Christian sense, but only *faults* particularly as a result of deficient education. 'Certainly the world, the social world in particular, was, as it were, just as imperfect as man . . . but, given respectively the educational level of man and the charismatic quality of the ruler, the world was as good as could be' (4E, p. 153).

The educational ideal of this morality was 'propriety', politeness and grace. 'Controlled ease and correct composure, grace and dignity in the sense of a ceremonially ordered court-salon characterize' the Confucian gentleman (4E, p. 157). The *repression of passion* in particular, as the disruptive source of the desired harmonious equilibrium, was to be attained. In addition to this there was the 'one basic social duty', the cardinal virtue, *piety*. What honour had been to feudalism, piety (hsaio) was to patrimonialism, understood as a subordination to parents, teachers, superiors in the official hierarchy, and the emperor. The goal of this ethic was the inculcation of unconditional discipline which was believed to be omnipotent. 'Insubordination is worse than low thinking' (4E, p. 158).

A further component of this 'bureaucratic morality' was the proscription of the *profit motive* which was despised as a source of social unrest: 'the poise and harmony of the soul are shaken by the risks of acquisitiveness' (4E, p. 160). The status ideal of cultivation of the all-round educated Confucian gentleman aimed at 'self-perfection' in the sense of universality and turned against the riches to be gained merely by one-sidedness. 'Not even in the most influential position could one achieve anything in the world without the virtue derived from education. And vice versa, one could achieve nothing, no matter what one's virtue, without influential position. Hence, the "superior" man coveted such a position, not profit' (4E, p. 161). These educational ideals could only be reached along one path: by incessant learning, i.e. a life-long literary study of the old classics. 'The "princely" man reflects and "studies" everything incessantly and anew' (4E, p. 163).

Thus we see piety as the source of discipline and literary education as the universal and inexorable means to perfection. Weber called Confucianism a 'rationalism of order' (4E, p. 169). A quotation ('Rather be dog and live in peace than be man and live in anarchy', Chen Ki Tong) served as Weber's proof for this interpretation and also for the pacifist character of Confucianism, which he described briefly as 'pacifist, inner-worldly, and solely oriented to the fear of the spirits' (4E, p. 169).

After his discussion of orthodox Confucianism, Weber used the seventh section of his analysis to consider heterodox *Taoism*. The point of departure for this continuation of the analysis was sociological: the Chinese state cult described thus far was presented as the work of a genteelly educated stratum of intellectuals. It was this fact which, according to Weber, left 'entirely aside the typical religious needs of the masses' (4E, p. 173) and this resulted in a 'gap' between the doctrine of the mandarins and the religious conceptions of the masses of non-mandarins, i.e. between classic Confucianism and a 'non-classical popular religion'. In this context Weber was interested essentially in whether this popular religion possibly 'could have or has been the source of a methodical way of life differing from the official cult in orientation' (4E, p. 174).

In Weber's answer to this question, it emerged that the canonical, Confucian doctrine and the religiously sanctioned state rites certainly *tolerated* the existing folk cults but put limits on them as a 'private affair'. Such 'private cults' found themselves facing resistance from the Confucian bureaucracy and its mercantilist and currency interests. 'The individual's mystic or ascetic quest for salvation was an interest entirely alien to (classical) Confucianism . . . The quest for individual salvation had, of course, just as little place in Chinese bureaucratic rationalism as it had in the way of life of any bureaucracy' (4E, p. 177–8).

Weber now turned to the doctrine of Lao-tzu and stressed, 'Here we are not concerned with [him] as a philosopher but with his sociological position and his influence' (4E, p. 180). Weber attempted to explain the similarities and differences between Taoism, as Lao-tzu's heterodoxy, and Confucianism. He considered as essential to his investigation the consequences of both religious conceptions for *political* ideals. If, in Confucianism, he noted a trend towards centralism of the rationally and bureaucratically governed welfare-state, in Taoism and the mystics he saw 'the greatest possible autonomy and self-sufficiency for the individual parts of the state, those small communities which might form a locus of plain peasant or civic virtue. The mystics upheld the slogan: as little bureaucracy as possible' (4E, p. 184). An essential part of Taoism is a principled '*apoliticism*'.

Another crucial difference for Weber was the *aliterary* and *antiliterary* character of the later Taoism. In Weber's opinion, this was the reason which 'accounts for the interesting fact that it took strong (though not exclusive) root among the circles of traders. This is a very distinct example of a fact which we shall learn repeatedly: the nature of a stratum's religiosity has nowhere been solely determined by economic conditions. But *vice versa* the peculiar nature of Taoism could not be irrelevant for the way of life of the merchants' (4E, p. 196). However, in China there was *never* the evolution of a 'bourgeois ethic' in the Western sense.

Both orthodoxy and heterodoxy tolerated or rather positively cultivated *magic*, which pushed the development of that kind of rationalization in the direction of a *magic image of the world*. Weber confirmed this thesis by presenting the history of science in China and enormous importance of, for example, astrology, pharmacology and geomancy. Thus, beyond all differences, we find a *common* effect of Taoism and orthodox Confucianism, that is the reinforcement of *traditionalism*.

In any case not only was there no path leading from Taoism to a rational method of life, be it inner or other-worldly, but Taoist magic necessarily became one of the most serious obstacles to such a development. For laymen the genuine ethical imperatives in later Taoism were substantially the same as those in Confucianism; while the Taoist expected personal advantages the Confucian expected rather the good conscience of the gentleman from their fulfilment. While the Confucian operated with the polar opposites 'right' and 'wrong' the Taoist, like all magicians, operated rather with 'clean–unclean'. Despite the interest in immortality and in rewards and punishments in the beyond the Taoist retained a worldly orientation like the Confucian. (4E, p. 205)

As a conclusion to his investigation into the economic ethic of Confucianism and Taoism, Weber formulated his 'result'. He used as a yardstick a category the importance of which increased noticeably in the course of the discussion, the category of *rationality*. For Weber, religion represented a stage in the prevailing process of rationalization and he noted two criteria in this process. 'One is the degree to which the religion has divested itself of magic; the other is the degree to which it has systematically unified the relation between God and the world and therewith its own ethical relationship to the world' (4E, p. 226).

In order to be able to classify 'Confucian rationalism', Weber drew a comparison with the 'rationalism of Protestantism' as the form which is 'geographically and historically closest to us': Weber discovered, in connection with the importance of magic, that it was only in Protestantism that 'the complete *disenchantment* of the world' was implemented in all its consequences, whereas Confucianism left untouched 'the significance of magic for redemption'. Thus for Weber 'it should be perfectly clear that in the magic garden of heterodox doctrine (Taoism) a rational economy and technology of modern occidental character was simply out of the question' (4E, p. 277).

Furthermore, as we have seen, Weber considered the *earthly* 'affirmation of and adjustment to the world' of this purely magical religiosity to be important. Any kind of 'redemption' apart from lack of education, was not desired by the Confucian and there was an absence of any transcendent anchorage of ethics.

Tension toward the 'world' had never arisen, because, as far as known, there had never been an ethical prophecy of a supramundane God who raised ethical demands . . . The leading intellectual stratum, officials and candidates for office, had consistently supported the retention of ancestor worship as absolutely necessary for the undisturbed preservation of bureaucratic authority. They suppressed all upheavals arising from religions of redemption. (4E, pp. 229–30)

This lack of 'prophecy' in China was for Weber of great importance: prophecy created for him a systematic orientation of one's conduct toward one internal *measure of value*. By contrast to this, Confucianism meant 'adjustment to the outside, to the conditions of the "world"' (4E, p. 235). This attitude to the 'world' stands in complete opposition to a Western religious ethic. 'The Confucian system of radical world-optimism succeeded in removing the basic pessimistic tension between the world and the supra-mundane destination of the individual. But no Christian ethic, however entangled in mundane compromises, could attain this' (4E, p. 235).

With this characterization of the social ethic, Weber arrived at the real object of his research: the economic ethic. In classifying Confucianism, Weber, as we have seen, emphasized the tradition of the cult of the *sib*.

It is of considerable economic consequence whether or not confidence, which is basic to business, rests on purely personal, familial, or semi-familial relationships as was largely the case in China. The great achievement of ethical religions, above all of the ethical and asceticist sects of Protestantism, was to shatter the fetters of the sib. These religions established the superior community of faith and a common ethical way of life in opposition to the family. (4E, p. 237)

Despite existing measures and rules of economic *policy*, an economic *mentality* (*Gesinnung*) comparable to that in the West did not develop. 'Still economic policy did not create the economic mentality of capitalism' (4E, pp. 237–8). And in particular it was the lack of evolution of a 'civic and methodical way of life' which distinguished the Confucian from the Puritan–Christian economic mentality.

The contrast [of Puritanism] to Confucianism is clear: both ethics had their irrational anchorages, the one in magic, the other in the ultimately inscrutable resolves of a purely supra-mundane God. But from magic there followed the inviolability of tradition . . . From the relation between the supra-mundane God and the creaturally wicked, ethically irrational world there resulted, however, the absolute unholiness of tradition and the truly endless task of ethically and rationally subduing and mastering the given world, i.e., rational, objective 'progress'. Here, the task of the rational transformation of the world stood opposed to the Confucian adjustment to the world. (4E, p. 240)

On the other hand, Weber showed, there is another important factor missing in China: the principle of a *calculating mentality* in modern capitalism. Despite intensive business and a crass 'materialism', China did not evolve the 'great and methodical business conceptions which are rational in nature':

In this typical land of profiteering, one may well see that by themselves neither 'acquisitiveness', nor high or even exclusive esteem for wealth, nor utilitarian 'rationalism' have any connection as yet with modern capitalism . . . The Chinese [businessman] lacked the central, religiously determined and rational method of life which came from within and which was characteristic of the classical Puritan. For the latter, economic success was not an ultimate goal or end in itself but a means of proving one's self. (4E, p. 243-4)

This lack of a rational methodical life was, as we have seen, the result of a specific educational ideal.

For the Confucian, the specialist expert could not be raised to truly positive dignity, no matter what his social usefulness . . . the 'cultured man' (gentleman) was 'not a tool'; that is, in his adjustment to the world and in his self-perfection he was an end unto himself, not a means for any functional end. (4E, p. 246)

In conclusion, Weber drew up a summary:

'Rationalism' . . . was embodied in the spirit of both ethics. But only the Puritan rational ethic with its supra-mundane orientation brought economic rationalism to its consistent conclusion. This happened because nothing was further from the conscious Puritan intention. It happened because inner-worldly work was simply expressive of the striving for a transcendental goal . . . Confucian rationalism meant rational adjustment to the world; Puritan rationalism meant rational mastery of the world. (4E, pp. 247-8)

The *importance* Weber attributed to the roots of this *mentality* of economic order was apparent in his concluding remarks.

To be sure the basic characteristics of the 'mentality', in this case the practical attitudes toward the world, were deeply co-determined by political and economic destinies. Yet, in view of their autonomous laws, one can hardly fail to ascribe to these attitudes effects strongly counteractive to capitalist development. (4E, p. 249)

Before Weber turned to the religious systems of thought of India (Hinduism and Buddhism), and after including his investigation into the Chinese economic ethic, he inserted in the November 1915 edition of the *Archiv* some 'Interim Observations' (*Zwischenbetrachtung*) which he took up later in the *Gesammelte Aufsätze zur Religionssoziologie*. If we remarked above that the Introduction represented a preliminary and provisional summary of the results of the entire investigations into the sociology of religion, then we can say the same of the 'Interim Observations'. The latter pursued a specific line of investigation. In it, Weber attempted to develop a 'Theory of the stages and directions of religious abnegation of the world'.

Through an ideal-typical procedure, Weber tried to clarify the question of 'the motives from which religious ethics of world abnegation have originated, and the directions they have taken. In this way we may clarify their possible "meaning"' (5E, p. 323). Through 'expediently constructed rational types', Weber intended in his essay on the sociology of religion, to produce a contribution 'to the typology and sociology of rationalism' (5E, p. 324). Weber developed a typology of 'world abnegation' in particular with the aid of the two pole categories 'asceticism' and 'mysticism'. Thus he came to differentiate between an inner-worldly and an escapist asceticism, and between an escapist contemplation and an inner-worldly mysticism. Basically, the different 'relations of tension' were as follows:

Religion versus 'the world'
Religion versus 'the economic sphere'
Religion versus 'the political sphere'
Religion versus 'the erotic sphere'
Religion versus 'the intellectual sphere'

Since the important results of these typologies were taken up again and completed by Weber when he wrote his 'Preliminary Remarks' (1920) to the collection of works on the sociology of religion in the *Gesammelte Aufsätze zur Religionssoziologie*, and that he formulated his theory of 'rationalization' there, we shall dispense with a presentation of the 'Interim Observations'.

India

Weber's investigations into the economic ethic of *Hinduism and Buddhism*, which he published in the *Archiv* in 1916–17 and which were taken up as an unaltered reprint in the second volume (1921) of the *Gesammelte Aufsätze zur Religionssoziologie*, were arranged to the same principle as Weber's works on China: in the first section Weber dealt with the social system of India, in the second he was concerned with orthodox Hinduism and heterodox Buddhism, and in the third on the Asiatic sects and the redemption religions, he investigated their effects on the day-to-day ethic of Indian society.

In presenting India's social system, Weber outlined its characteristics concisely. India was a land of villages and of absolute organization according to birth, a land of domestic trade, particularly of foreign trade and of credit usury. The princely methods of warfare, politics and finance were rational, politics was theoretically based ('made subject to . . . quite Machiavellian theorizing'), urban development paralleled Western Medieval phenomena (the West is also indebted to India for the rational number system). There were numerous philosophical schools and religious sects. Indian law showed 'numerous forms which could have served capitalistic purposes as easily and well as corresponding institutions in our own Medieval law' (6E, p. 4). In addition to this 'the acquisitiveness of Indians of all strata left little to be desired' (6E, p. 4) and there was a high social 'evaluation' of wealth.

But, in spite of these favourable economic, political and spiritual pre-conditions Weber maintained the one fact to which he links the aims of his investigation. 'Yet modern capitalism did not develop indigenously before or during the English rule. It was taken over as a finished artifact without autonomous beginnings. Here we shall enquire as to the manner in which Indian religion, as one factor among many, may have prevented capitalistic development (in the occidental sense)' (6E, p. 4).

The dominant form of Indian religion is *Hinduism*. In his classification, Weber made use of the pair of concepts already developed in the context of his work on Protestantism – 'sect' and 'church',[19] according to which in the sociological sense a *sect* 'is an exclusive association of religious virtuosi or of especially qualified religious persons, recruited through individual admission after establishment of qualification'; and *church* is 'a universal-istic establishment for the salvation of the masses' which claims 'that everyone, at least each child of a member, must belong by birth' (6E, p. 6). Weber classified Hinduism as 'a strictly birth-religion'.

In order to present this moment of exclusivity precisely, Weber looked at those processes by which populations of non-Hindu origin, particularly the 'guest peoples' ('pariahs'), were subjected to a process of 'Hinduization'. Weber questioned the reasons behind the spread of Hinduism both among the 'missionaries' as well as among the 'converted'. The 'missionaries' were essentially the *Brahmans*, the caste which was the institutional bearer of Hindu religious belief. Their motives were 'primarily [of] material interest', i.e. for them it was a matter of

Expanding income, ranging from service fees for the casting of horoscopes to prebends and the gifts due to house and sacrificial priests. Rich gifts of cattle, money, jewelry, and, above all, land and land rent (pepper-rent) were the compensations for Brahmans who provided the necessary 'proofs' of genteel descent for the Hinduized ruling stratum of an area undergoing assimilation. (6E, p. 16)

The motive of the tribes which took on the 'enslaving yoke' of Hindu rituals for doing so, was essentially the desire to *legitimize* their social position, and in particular the interests of the *ruling strata* of these new castes were of prime importance here. Thus integration into the Hindu community had a double function. 'It not only endowed the ruling stratum of the barbarians with recognized rank in the cultural world of Hinduism, but, through their transformation into castes, secured their superiority over the subject classes' (6E, p. 16).

Weber explained the 'unusually quick victory of Hinduism' particularly against the specifically anti-Brahmanical salvation religions, Jainism and Buddhism, in 'the fact that Hinduism could provide an incomparable religious support for the legitimation interest of the ruling strata as determined by the social conditions of India. The salvation religions . . . were unable to supply such support' (6E, p. 18).

Although Weber expressly emphasized that he was interested in the assimilative power of the Hindu way of life only in so far as it could produce these specific achievements of legitimizing social rank and the economic advantages bound up with this, he examined the typology of the *goals of salvation* and the *roads* towards it in relatively great detail. Thus it appears that Hinduism is certainly something other than a 'religion' in the Western sense. This emerged in particular from the observation that a pious Hindu is essentially a member of a Hindu *sect* and that Hinduism itself is primarily a *ritualism* the nucleus of which forms the ritualistic duty or 'Dharma'. This 'Dharma' is not of a constant importance, but varies greatly according to *social position* and historical *changes*. Out of this variability and the ensuing lack of a codified 'ethic', results the huge power and importance of a certain caste. 'To acknowledge the authority of the Veda . . . means simply the acknowledgment of the authority of Hindu tradition resting on the Veda and the continued interpretation of its world image; it means acknowledgment of the rank station of its leaders, the Brahmans' (6E, pp. 28–9).[20]

Before Weber turned specifically to the Brahmans, he directed his attention to that important element and structural principle of the Indian social constitution, the *castes*. "Caste" (shares) the central position of the Brahmans in Hinduism' (6E, p. 30). To determine what a caste is, Weber asked what distinguishes it from the other associations which are apparently related to it. He distinguished caste from 'tribe', from occupational association (merchant and craft guilds), from 'status group', from 'class' and from 'sib'. In summary Weber does define *caste* as a social, ultimately occupational association within a social community, in which *hereditary* membership is of the utmost importance. In particular the extremely rigid rules about commensalism (particularly dining communities) and connubium (ban on intermarriage) made the caste into a *'closed status group'* in the extreme.

The complete impossibility of 'fraternization', which we came to see as important in the Medieval urban development in the West, had important *political* consequences.

For the castes excluded every solidarity and every politically powerful fraternization of the citizenry and of the trades. If the prince observed the ritual traditions and the social pretensions based upon them, which existed among those castes most important for him, he could not only play off the castes against one another – which he did – but he had nothing whatever to fear from them, especially if the Brahmams stood by his side. Accordingly, it is not difficult even at this point to guess the political interests which had a hand in the game during the transformation to monopoly rule of the caste system. This shift steered India's social structure – which for a time apparently stood close to the threshold of European urban development – into a course that led far away from any possibility of such development. (6E, pp. 38–9)

Weber looked at a peculiarity of the Indian social constitution in detail, the principle of 'clan charisma'. By 'charisma' in general he understood 'that an extraordinary, at least not generally available, quality adheres to a person. Originally charisma was thought of as a magical quality. "Clan charisma" means that this extraordinary quality adheres to sib members *per se* and not, as originally, to a single person.' (6E, p. 49). This development, as a consequence of a 'routinization' of the originally purely personal charisma, was in Weber's opinion of great importance for the development of *commercial law*. 'The unusual importance of trade in India would lead one to believe that a rational law of trade, trading companies, and enterprise might well have developed' (6E, p. 52). Weber explained the fact that it did *not* develop because of the emergence of 'clan charisma', the *sib fetters* of credit. By contrast with Western development, where the evolution of a citizenry and the establishment of free-trade contracts was an important advantage for the origin of capitalism, the clan charisma of the caste system prevented a comparable development.

Linked to this, Weber describes in detail the four large groups of about 2,000 to 3,000 Hindu castes.

The Brahmans (priests)
The Kshatriyas (warriors)
The Vaishyas (merchants)
The Shudras (village craftspeople; artisans; farm-workers)

Weber adopted the division between 'tribal castes' and 'professional castes' and investigated closely the processes of caste schism and its consequences. He was mainly interested in the original economic contexts: differentiation of properties, changes in occupation and technical skill (see 6E, p. 103). Besides these economic origins of the caste system, Weber was particularly interested in the economic *effects*, and his main thesis was 'that this order by its nature is completely traditionalistic and anti-rational in its effects' (6E, p. 111). In explicit opposition to Marx, whom he literally addressed in this context, Weber looked for the economic consequences of the caste system not in the particular position of the Indian village artisan, but rather he saw the 'bearer of stability' in the caste order in general. 'The core of the obstacle did not lie' in specific individual difficulties, 'which every one of the great religious systems in its way has placed, or has seemed to place, in the way of the modern economy' (6E, p. 112). What was important for the prevention or rather the obstruction of the emergence of a modern capitalist economy, was much more the 'spirit' of the whole system (see 6E, p. 112) with the result that 'it must still be considered extremely unlikely that the modern organization of industrial capitalism would ever have *originated* on the basis of the caste system' (6E, p. 112).

This 'spirit' of the Indian caste system was what prevented the development of a rational enterprise of modern capitalism before its introduction by English colonial lords. 'This was in spite of the presence of those who were 'in part, virtuosi in unscrupulous profiteering', and despite the favourable socio-structural preconditions we sketched initially. And even *after* its introduction by the English nothing changed fundamentally in the attitude of, for example, the Indian factory labour-force which 'shows exactly those traditionalistic traits which also characterized labour in Europe during the early period of capitalism' (6E, p. 114). Thus the increase in wage rate did not have the effect of an incentive to more work, but rather caused a reduction in working time and an increase in expenditure on luxury goods. Weber characterized the Indian worker as a 'casual labourer', who did not know the concept of 'discipline'.

As we have seen, Weber regarded the caste order of Indian society as the decisive precondition for the extreme traditionalism of the Indian economy and society. We have already described how the ritualism of Hinduism in particular demands the most correct fulfilment of caste duty. In this context, Weber was concerned with the religious 'dogmatic' foundations for these ideas. He distinguished essentially between two basic principles of Hindu religiosity: the belief in the transmigration of souls (samsara) and the doctrine of compensation (karman). With great precision and clarity he described those religious ideas according to which the individual, and in particular his or her never-ending fate of rebirth and 'second death', is solely dependent upon the 'credits' and 'debts' of their earlier life, and these in turn determine the present life. This too, however, is the decisive link with the caste order. It is no 'accident' which caste the individual is born into but solely the consequence of his or her own deeds and failures in the previous life. 'An orthodox Hindu confronted with the deplorable situation of a member of an impure caste would only think that he has a

great many sins to redeem from his prior existence . . . In this life there is
no escape from the caste, at least no way to move up in the caste order' (6E,
p. 121). Precisely the conviction that on the one hand he has 'served' his
present life through his previous existences, and on the other hand, that the
strict fulfilment of his present caste duties constitute the undeniable
preconditions for rebirth in a higher caste – including the possibility of
rebirth as a god! – makes 'devotion to caste', for the orthodox Hindu, into
a very personal interest in salvation. Any attempt to revolutionize the world
order appears senseless, not only because the world was regarded as
eternally valid, but also because a revolution would have taken away the
possibility that 'next time' they might not be born as 'a worm in the
intestine of a dog' but from the womb of a queen and Brahman's daughter.
'So long as the *karma* doctrine was unshaken, revolutionary ideas or
progressivism were inconceivable . . . It was impossible to shatter
traditionalism, based on caste ritualism anchored in *karma* doctrine, by
rationalizing the economy' (6E, p. 123).

Precisely this exceptionally strong effect of religious conceptions on the
economic and social constitution of Indian society led Weber to question
the *causes* behind the origin of the caste order which is 'found nowhere [else]
or only incipiently elsewhere' (6E, p. 123). Weber investigated the different
origins of caste and, apart from status and economic conditional contexts,
he looked in particular at ethnic ones. Weber's presentation of the
'developmental conditions' can be summarized as follows: the interaction
of an increasingly powerful 'dominant priesthood' of the Brahmans, whose
position of *material* interests we have already discussed, with the patrimonial
Hindu princes, who pursued a strong interest in legitimacy and domesti-
cation, and this led to the establishment of the caste system.

This well-integrated, unique social system could not have originated or at least
could not have conquered and lasted without the pervasive and all-powerful
influence of the Brahmans . . . The combination of caste legitimacy with *karma*
doctrine, thus with the specific Brahmanical theodicy – in its way a stroke of genius
– plainly is the construction of rational ethical thought and not the product of any
economic 'conditions'. Only the wedding of this thought product with the empirical
social order through the promise of rebirth gave this order the irresistible power over
thought and hope of members . . . (6E, p. 131)

If in the first section of his investigations into the Indian economic ethic
Weber dealt with the general social conditions and effects of Hinduism, in
the second section he turned more to the *contents* and the *bearers* of *orthodox*
and *heterodox holy teaching* in India.

The institutional bearers of orthodox official Indian religiosity consists of, as we saw, the caste of Brahmans, the stratum of priestly nobility and genteel literati. Following the yardstick of the relation of religion to mysticism and asceticism, which he had already introduced,[21] Weber characterized Brahmanical religiosity as one which did not take over the orgiastic and emotionally ecstatic elements of the old magic rites and at best tolerated them in the form of an unofficial folk magic. Broadly, Weber compared the Indian Brahmans with the Chinese literati and frequently with the ancient Hellenic priests in order to be able to highlight the similarities and differences as sharply as possible. Like the Confucian mandarins, the Brahmans too were a status group of genteel literati, whose magic charisma rested primarily on 'knowledge' and whose 'rationalism' consisted essentially in the rejection of all irrational forms of holy seeking.

Nevertheless there were considerable differences between the Chinese and the Indian situations, which Weber attempted to make clear through the 'different social structures of the respective intellectual status groups'. 'In China the Mandarins form a stratum of officials and candidates for office; in India the Brahmans represent a status group of literati partly comprising princely chaplains, partly counsellors, theological teachers, and jurists, priests and pastors' (6E, pp. 139–40). The Brahmans were essentially *advisors* to individual princes and nobility on private and political questions; they were organizers of states – always on the basis of the correct doctrine of Hinduism. They financed their material living, unlike the Mandarins, not from a state salary but from fixed land and tribute rent, which were granted to them *permanently*.

Weber saw the decisive difference between India and China in the historical fact that in India there was no institution of imperial supreme pontifex, but rather the stratum of literati faced a multitude of petty princes in their respective statelets. By contrast with the Chinese relationships, the individual princes did not derive their *legitimacy* from a paramount imperial pontifex, but 'the concept of legitimacy was rather simply that the single prince was ritualistically correct when and to the extent to which his behaviour, especially toward the Brahmans, conformed with the holy tradition' (6E, p. 141). One of the main causes for this establishment of legitimation, which is very different from the Chinese form, Weber saw as based on the fact that the Indian princehood had developed purely from the war-like traits of 'charismatic warrior chieftains'. We have already discussed the decisive importance of the unity or duality of politico-military charisma.[22] In India, the *separation* of both sources of the charismatic foundation of domination had wide-reaching consequences, in particular the establishment of an *independent priesthood* as a gentile charismatic guild, i.e. as a caste with fixed lineage and educational qualifications as prerequisites for holding office, as well as the fact that no Hindu prince or great king was ever able to claim pontifical power. The independence and status-group superiority of the Brahmans, moreover, prevented the development of a universally valid ethic and led to a coexistence of status group ethics, which differed from and partially contradicted each other.

Weber's enquiries into the ideational–normative prerequisites for this division and the status-group restriction of 'ethics', brought him to a central axiom of Hindu doctrine:

Men were not – as for classical Confucianism – in principle equal, but forever unequal. They were as unlike as man and animal. All men, however, had equal opportunities, but not in this life. Through rebirth they could either achieve heaven or descend to the animal kingdom or to hell . . .

. . . no 'absolute sin' could exist. There could only be a ritual offense against the particular *Dharma* of the caste. In this world of eternal rank orders there was no place for a blissful original state of man and no blissful final kingdom . . . There was no sort of 'natural law'. But there was, in theory at least, only holy, status-compartmentalized positive law in areas which remained unregulated as indifferent. There were positive statutes of princes, castes, guilds, sibs and agreements of individuals.

. . . There simply was no 'natural' equality of man before any authority, least of all before a super-worldly god . . .

This is the negative side of the case. Most important, it excluded forever the rise of social criticism, of rationalistic speculation, and abstractions of natural law type, and hindered the development of any sort of idea of 'human rights'. (6E, p. 144)

Such views effected not only the division of 'worldly' and 'spiritual' power and the formation of special ethics for status groups, but also brought about a number of other developments. In India there were no concepts such as 'state' and 'citizen' and there was no formation of a 'political ethic', which Weber made clear by means of his views on the political and military behaviour of the princes. However, in this, the specialization of the status group ethics, once again in contrast to the Confucian rejection of the 'expert', led to the development of *special sciences*, particularly the development of a *formal logic* as a technology of rational proof. Precisely because there was no universal ethic, which was generally valid for life in the world, there developed in India techniques for special callings and 'spheres of life, from construction technique to logic as the technology of proof and disproof to the technology of eroticism' (6E, p. 147).

Once again Weber investigated the *causes* of this specific Indian development. 'The fact of these ideational developments as well as their form are correlated with social peculiarities of the Indian literati stratum, their vehicle' (6E, p. 147). Thus Weber turned to the organization and 'techniques' of the Brahmans, who according to their background are to be interpreted as 'priests', i.e. in these circumstances 'magicians'. Because of this, Weber renewed his interest in the specific relationship of Brahmanic Hinduism to *asceticism* and *mysticism*. According to Weber, Brahmanhood was 'never able completely to shake off the historical relation to ancient magical asceticism out of which it had grown' (6E, p. 148). This Indian asceticism was thus 'the most rationally developed in the world' and became 'rationalized into a theoretical technology'. The Brahmanhood was that status group of ritual experts, whose social claims rested on *knowledge* and genteel *cultivation*. It was this knowledge in particular which rejected everything 'irrational', in the sense of emotionally ecstatic practices of asceticism and mysticism, as being 'unclassical' and 'barbarian'. It was precisely this strongly ascetically regulated worldly way of life of the classical Brahman which made him first into an 'Arva' (gentleman), which one could become exclusively through *culture* and a 'rational' methodology for achieving holy states outside everyday life. Such 'rational' methods were an ascetic flight from the world or contemplation. Through such ways of personal mystic holy seeking the Brahmans attempted, with varying degrees of success, to implement and maintain their monopolistic power.

Weber described in detail the organization of the Indian hermits ('yatis') and the schools of the isolated 'professional ascetic' ('gurus'). The schools or monastical organizations ('math') served the purpose of preserving and carrying on the Brahmans knowledge without the Brahmans having to worry about the maintenance. In the course of historical development, the *hereditary* allotment to an ancient school or group of monastic prebendaries became the prerequisite to being a caste member of full Brahmanhood, i.e. to that stratum of Brahmans who were, on the other hand, qualified for performing rites and on the other for accepting gifts and foundation grants ('dakshina') (see 6E, p. 156). Life in these Hindu monasteries was almost totally dissimilar from Western cloister rules; Hindu monkdom developed out of wandering magicians, there remained largely an 'itinerant mendicancy', complete withdrawal was always available to the individual, discipline was lax, and according to the doctrine of the holy ways there were hardly any chores to be done.

As in the case of Confucianism, Weber investigated the position of Hinduism towards 'classical' literature. Although the Brahmans too saw themselves as 'scholarly scribes', the Hindu culture was essentially less a written culture than the Chinese. By contrast, in India the holy doctrine could only be transmitted orally, and this had wide-reaching consequences: court procedure was oral, speech played an important role as a means to power, Indian oral culture was essentially oriented towards acoustic memory, and oral transmission and recitation had a widespread importance. All this led to the peculiarities of 'Indian rationalism' (6E, p. 160), for example the 'luxuriant growth of incredible bombast' in the religious and ethical literature and the development of a 'pseudo-systematization'. In spite of excellent scientific achievements in the fields of algebra, grammar, anatomy and musicology, Weber declared the contemporary natural sciences, for example, in India to be on a level 'about (our) fourteenth century', since it 'did not even (achieve) the beginnings of rational experimentation' (6E, p. 161). In general, Indian thought was 'in the last analysis . . . indifferent to the actualities of the world' and was formally determined, according to Weber, 'by the techniques of contemplation of the intellectual strata' (6E, p. 162).

In his investigation of such contemplation techniques Weber dealt extensively with the 'most typical form of intellectualized holy technique', 'yoga', which he interpreted as 'the rationalization of ecstatic practice (of ancient sorcerors)'. This and other techniques all had the same goal: 'The purpose is always to free one's self from the world of the senses, from anxieties, passions, drives and striving, and the purposeful considerations of everyday life, thereby preparing one's self for a final state signifying eternal rest (that is, the salvation (*moksha, mukti*) from these pressures) and unison with the godly' (6E, p. 166). It was always a matter of rejecting everyday life and being delivered from the world as such. It was not the suffering, the sins, the lovelessness nor the imperfection of the world, which the believer wished to escape, but its *transitory nature*. This world appeared as an eternal, meaningless 'wheel' of recurrent births and deaths, steadily rolling through an eternity of ages – and it was valid to escape this, as an *individual*. 'Apart from the belief in predestination the religious solitude of the single soul has never been placed on such a sounding-board as in this conclusion from Brahmanical doctrine. In polar opposition to the belief in election by divine grace, this doctrine left it entirely to the individual soul to work out its own fate' (6E, p. 169).

Weber devoted great detail to the content of the great Indian teaching system, which he presents as 'rational conceptions of thinkers who were consistent in their ways' (6E, p. 177). He examined in particular the Veda schools of the Samkhya and the Vendanta and investigated their ideas on the different *holy paths* (ritual works, asceticism and wisdom). Precisely the differing caste and profession-specific demands of the 'Dharma' as the individual's binding path of social–ethical behaviour, led to a relationship of considerable tension between everyday Dharma and religious holy striving. What appeared to the Brahmanical intellectual to be Dharma, thus essentially flight from the world, could never meet the needs of the educated laity, and of the knighthood in particular. Common to all, however, was the belief in the decisive importance of 'constancy' in the state of grace. Whoever follows his or her own Dharma without regard to success and without personal interest in their actions, he or she will partake of the grace of salvation (see 6E, p. 189).

After his in-depth concern with the classical Indian literatis' ideas, as created by the intellectual strata of the ancient epoch of nobility and petty princes, Weber turned to two other religious frameworks in India 'which in all essentials had grown on the soil of the ancient intellectual stratum, but which were regarded by the Brahmans not only as unclassical, but were fought, cursed and hated as most base and objectionable heresies' (6E, p. 192–3), *Buddhism* and *Jainism*.

In its general teachings, Jainism was based on classical Hinduism, and in particular it shared the interpretation that 'salvation' consisted in being freed from the wheel of rebirth and that this was only to be achieved through detachment from this world of transitoriness, from inner-worldly action and from the *karma* which is linked to this action. This doctrine was heterodox mainly because of its rejection of the Veda education in ritual, and particularly because of its rejection of Brahmanhood. In Jainism, *asceticism* as the means to salvation, besides study and meditation, was taken to extremes. 'He achieves supreme holiness who starves himself to death' (6E, p. 195). In order to prevent any involvement in personal or local relationships, the classical Jain rules prescribed for the monk the duty of wandering restlessly from place to place; this duty brought about, with a powerful missionary force, this order of 'professional monks'. The Jain laity, who were regarded as disenfranchised, were subject to conflicting rules, as for example a form of travel prohibition. In general, possessions were limited to what was 'necessary'; it was not the *acquisition* of wealth which was forbidden, but the striving to 'be' rich. This doctrine, bound up with the strict prohibition on saying anything false or exaggerated, caused 'absolute honesty in business life', so that the Jains, who had nearly all become *traders*, became famous for their honesty (6E, p. 200). They dedicated themselves primarily to banking and money-lending, as a result of which Weber frequently compared them with the Jews. The Jains, who felt themselves to be a specifically *ascetic* sect, did not escape the process of

Hinduization, and became a numerically insignificant group, interesting to Weber only as a quite specific sect of merchants.

Buddhism, which Weber turned to in great detail, presented a completely different picture. The specific ideal of ancient Buddhism was to enjoy the bliss of the escapist life already in this world. To achieve this goal, one had to divest oneself of all distractions, under which were included both asceticism and speculation on any problems (be they worldly, other-worldly, social or metaphysical). Ancient Buddhism was the 'religious "technology" of wandering and of intellectually schooled mendicant monks' (6E, p. 206). It was (and here it is comparable to Hinduism) a 'salvation religion', which must *not* be understood as salvation into an eternal life, but salvation from the cycle of life and death, motivated by a ' "satiety" with "death" ' (see 6E, p. 207). This salvation was thus exclusively the action of the single individual, who received no help whatsoever from a god or saviour in this. There was neither 'grace' nor 'predestination' – 'inspiration' alone was the reward for continual, meditative contemplation. Essentially the aim of this meditation was a 'truth', the 'thirst' (trishna) for the world and people, which must be counted along with suffering, and recognized as meaningless. Only he or she who was free from the longing for the world and a life beyond had escaped the endless wheel of rebirths. This salvation, as an absolutely individual achievement of one's own endeavour, needed *no* confirmation or proof from any inner or extra-worldly *action*; it entailed no consequences in terms of social behaviour, since, of course no social community could help the individual in this: 'the specific asocial character of all genuine mysticism is here carried to its maximum' (6E, p. 213). Such an 'ethic of non-action' naturally could not develop 'a rational economic ethic' (see 6E, p. 216). 'Any sort of religious premium for a specific economic behaviour was lacking completely' (6E, p. 219).

From the doctrine that the basis of all life and thus of all suffering is the meaningless 'thirst' for life and conduct in life, even beyond death, there emerged a demand for the total elimination of any form of inner-worldly motivation in conduct. 'Thus, there is lacking an element which in occidental monkhood increasingly developed and signified so much, namely, the strain toward rational method in life conduct in all spheres except that of the pure intellectual systematization of concentrated mediation and pure contemplation' (6E, p. 222).

Once again Weber was interested in what was the dominant medium of presentation and how the religion was passed on. In Buddhism it was 'the *Socratic dialogue*, by which the opponent is led through a considerable argument to a *reductio ad absurdum* and then forced into submission' (6E,

p. 225). The understanding of and participation in such dialogues, Weber emphasized, required 'an excellent upbringing', which is the main reason why Buddhism was not linked to any ' "social" movement' and did not establish any ' "social–political" goal'. This 'absolutely unpolitical move-ment' as a whole was 'the product not of the underprivileged but of very positively privileged strata' who did not seek to change the social order (see 6E, p. 227).

In this context, Weber came across a paradox. As an extremely individu-alistic salvation religion, which emerged from the immutable charismatic qualities of people, Buddhism became one of the greatest missionary religions on earth. Weber indicated that the 'actual practical motives' for this were the *material interests* of the monks. 'Decisive for the success of the (Buddhist) propaganda as with the Jains was the appearance of the "professional monks" in the form of communities. The decisive motive for the propaganda activities was naturally given by the material interests of the monks in the increase of the givers of subsistence' (6E, p. 229).

Further favourable circumstances added to the great success of the Buddhist missionary work. One particular demand which this doctrine made on the laity was the duty of providing maintenance for the monks, or rather for one particular monk. This 'purely parasitical character of Buddhistic income seeking' led to 'an overflow onto the land of missionary disciples and monks' which spread into the burgeoning cities and the larger towns. However, we must emphasize that Weber did not attribute any great significance to this aspect of the historical developments. 'Yet Buddhism would hardly have been able to embark at least upon its career of international conquest without the historical accident that one of the first great kings, ruling almost over the entire Indian cultural area became its ardent adherent' (6E, p. 230).

From what we have already said, it has become clear that both Hinduism and Buddhism were essentially soteriologies for and by genteel intellec-tuals. We have already introduced a number of causes and effects of this strata-specific restriction, which is common to both of the great religious movements in India. It was decisive that the content and doctrines were tailored specifically to that tiny group which consequently became *monks*, and which ignored the religious needs of the rest of the members of society. Weber turned to this problem and its consequences in the third section, in which he deals with 'The Asiatic sects and the redemption religions'.

Within Buddhism, however, there were processes of transformation, for which 'alongside the unavoidable accommodation to actual conditions of the world' the *interest* of the laity was made responsible (see 6E, p. 234).

After the establishment of a great Indian kingdom under the Dynasty of the Maurya, a standing army, a kingly bureaucracy, a large group of kingly tax farmers and a kingly police developed. From now on in place of the ancient petty kingdoms there emerged the patrimonialism of the great king, and with this the position of the nobility as well as the bourgeois patricians was changed. With the accession of Ashoka, the first great king of the Maurya Dynasty, who ruled over a unified Indian empire, Buddhism reached an epoch which 'aimed at satisfying plebeian religious needs' (6E, p. 236).

Weber made it clear that the petty bourgeois and peasant could do nothing with the soteriologies of the educated gentility, on the one hand because the aims of *nirvana* and unity with the Brahman appeared unattractive to them, and on the other hand because they did not have the means to achieve this at their disposal, particularly the leisure time necessary for this. And they lacked one thing in particular:

It in no way satisfied the specifically religious need for emotional experience of the superworldly and for emergency aid in external and internal distress. Such unsatisfied emotional needs were and are always decisive for the psychological character of religion for the masses, in contrast to the rational character of all soteriologies of intellectuals. (6E, p. 237)

The adjustment to these 'specific plebeian religious needs' proceeded, according to Weber, all over the world, via two types of possibility, *magic* or a *saviour*. Weber described in detail the transformation processes of ancient Buddhism, the effects of which were, for example, the development of a charitable ideal of a welfare state, the development of a literary tradition and in particular a 'process of deification', i.e. the reinterpretation of the Buddha from being an exemplary person into a 'saviour'. Weber saw the main causes of these 'far-reaching transformations' as the adaptation to the religious needs of the laity, as well as 'adaptation to economic conditions' (6E, p. 250).

After his in-depth investigations of Buddhism and its ramifications, Weber returned once more to its historical point of departure, the establishment of the great Indian kingdom, and turned to a second line of development – the *Hindu sects*, which existed prior to Buddhism and continued to do so, rejected both by the Hindu teaching of the orthodox genteel Brahmans, as well as by Buddhism. These sects too formed the basis for changes which were essentially determined by the opposition towards the intellectuals' doctrine and by the religious needs of the unliterary strata.

The ancient, cultivated, intellectual soteriology, as we saw, ignored and banned all orgiastic–ecstatic and emotional elements together with the correlated magical practices belonging to original folk belief. Below the level of those seeking Brahmanical gnosis there was a scorned substratum of disreputable magicians preoccupied with the problem of folk religiosity. (6E, p. 295)

Weber described these magical, orgiastic doctrines and practices of *Tantra*-magic, the 'Sakta' sects, Shivaism, Vishnuism, Krishna-orgiasticism, and the Rama-cult. He afforded particular attention in all these presentations to the role and significance of each respective *guru*, whose power became vast in the mass sects, and whose partly princely income 'led to the sharp resistance of the Brahmans to the usurpation of these positions' (6E, p. 319). Weber compared the enormous social, economic and political power of the guru, power which was greatly encouraged by the capitalist development imported by the English (see 6E, p. 323), with the developments of the established Catholic church, and he observed important differences which he explained alongside the Western development of the papacy (see 6E, p. 325). In the case of India he states

It is quite evident that no community dominated by inner powers of this sort could out of its substance arrive at the 'spirit of capitalism'. It was also unable to take over the economically and technically finished form as an artifact, as occurred in Japan. There appeared here clearly and undoubtedly greater difficulties than in Japan, despite the English domination. When, today . . . the penetration of Indian society by capitalistic interests is already so extensive that they can no longer be eliminated, it is still possible for some eminent English students of the land to argue on good grounds that the removal of the thin conquering strata of Europeans and the *Pax Britannica* enforced by them would open wide the life and death struggle of inimical castes, confessions, and tribes; the old feudal robber romanticism of the Indian Middle Ages would again break forth. (6E, p. 325)

Weber deemed the caste ties, the *guru* domination over the masses and the dogma of the unalterability of the world particularly responsible for the 'economic and social traditionalism of Hinduism' which prevailed in India.

The devaluation of the world which each salvation religion brought with it could here only become absolute flight from the world. Its highest means could be nothing other than mystic contemplation, not active ascetic conduct . . . Always the extraordinary quality and irrationality of the holy means remained . . . At any rate, it would occur to no Hindu to see in the course of his economic professional integrity the signs of his state of grace or – what is more important – to evaluate and undertake the rational constitution of the world according to empirical principles as a realization of God's will. (6E, p. 326)

To conclude his 'extremely superficial tour of the Asiatic cultural world', Weber attempted to *summarize his findings*, beginning with a comparison with Western development. For Weber, Asia is the land of free competition among religions, of 'toleration', with the juxtaposition of all sorts of cults, schools, sects and orders. The separation of the orthodox from the heterodox was thus essentially a *social*, strata-specific matter. In particular the 'cleft' between the literary educated intellectuals and the aliterary masses of 'philistines', and, moreover, the brief that it was *knowledge* which facilitated the absolute way to the highest salvation, characterized the Asiatic religions. The 'knowledge' is thus 'not a rational implement of empirical science such as made possible the rational domination of nature and man as in the West. Rather it is the means of mystical and magical domination over the self and the world: gnosis. It is attained by an intensive training of body and spirit, either through asceticism or, and as a rule, through strict, methodologically ruled meditation' (6E, p. 331). From these ideas there emerged both the 'redemption aristocracy' in Asiatic soteriology as well as its 'asocial and apolitical character'. 'Given its [the soteriology's] world indifference, it could now assume the form of a flight from the world or, indeed, in an inner-worldly manner, with however, world-indifferent behavior: a protection against the world and one's own acts, not in and through both' (6E, pp. 332–3).

In spite of the enormous social gulf between the bearers of intellectual religiosity and the plebeian religiosity of the masses it was, however, the mostly hereditary bearers of charisma who determined the *practical* life conduct of the masses and afforded them magical salvation. And even the everyday economic world came under their influence, preventing the formation of a rational, practical ethic and life methodology which could have emerged from this 'magic garden'.

It was these 'psychological historical causes' which, in spite of the prevalence of an 'unrestricted lust for gain of the Asiatics', made a development towards capitalism impossible.

It was lacking in precisely that which was decisive for the economics of the Occident: the refraction and rational immersion of the drive character of economic striving and its accompaniments in a system of rational, inner-worldly ethic of behavior, e.g., the 'inner-worldly asceticism' of Protestantism in the West. Asiatic religion could not supply the presuppositions of inner-worldly asceticism. (6E, p. 337)

On top of these causes of the 'lack of economic rationalism', which Weber regarded as decisive, there were others; for example, the geographical position and the restriction on foreign trade which was co-determined by this, feudalism (especially in Japan), and finally the lack of a speech community.

But Weber regarded as most important the *ideational ordering*, linked to the *material interests* of its bearers in specific social structures and historical situations, and he wrote in conclusion

The social world was divided into the strata of the wise and educated and the uncultivated plebeian masses. The factual, inner order of the real world of nature as of art, ethics, and of economics remained concealed to the distinguished strata because this was so barren for its particular interests. Their life conduct was oriented to striving for the extraordinary, for example, in finding throughout its point of gravity in exemplary prophecy or wisdom. However, for the plebeian strata no ethic of everyday life derived from its rationally formed missionary prophecy. The appearance of such in the Occident, however – above all, in the Near East – with the extensive consequences borne with it, was conditioned by highly particular historical constellations without which, despite differences of natural conditions, development there could easily have taken the course typical of Asia, particularly of India. (6E, p. 343)

Ancient Judaism

Weber's investigations into the economic ethic of *ancient Judaism*, which he published in the 1917–18 and 1918–19 *Archiv* (150 and 166), and which were published posthumously unaltered as the third volume of the *Gesammelte Aufsätze zur Religionssoziologie*, diverge from his previous investigations both in their structure and in style. The work was constructed chronologically and the style is much more strongly narrative in nature. In his works on Judaism, Weber concentrated more intensively on the historical and theological developments and rarely reached the question of the *economic* preconditions and effects of this world religion.

In classifying Judaism sociologically, Weber generally used the concept 'pariah people', which he understood to be 'a guest people who were ritually separated, formally or *de facto*, from their social surroundings' (7E, p. 3). By contrast with the Indian pariah tribes he had already dealt with, Judaism became a pariah people in a caste-free environment, and its religious expectations differed considerably from those of Indian castes. In Weber's basic question 'how did Jewry develop into a pariah people with highly specific peculiarities?' (7E, p. 5), it becomes clear both that this framework of questioning was different from examining the *economic ethic* of Judaism, as well as that this constitutes basically a *historical–sociological* framework of questioning.

Once again, Weber described in extraordinary detail the position of the inhabitants of the Syrian–Palestinian mountainland between Mesopotamia (Babylon) and Egypt, and in this he was concerned above all with the cultural, climatic, geographical and economic conditions. He reconstructed the social structure out of the conflict between the desert Bedouins and an urban patriciate – in cities which were frequently the seat of an armed group, the local deity and his priests and of the political power bearer, for which, however, the sib organizations were of considerable importance. Weber dealt comprehensively with the political development of Israel, in particular with the origin of an aristocracy and kingship. In the Israelite cities too there arose a typical, ancient class stratification; the city-dwelling patrician sibs dominated the flat land economically and the peasants were their debtors (see 7E, p. 21). The artisans and merchants were categorized as 'gerim' (*Beisassen* or metics), and formed, at least the 'royal artisans' (goldsmiths, shopkeepers and vendors of ointments), a specifically urban *demos* which was organized mostly in guilds.

Besides the free camel-breeding Bedouins and the settled population – urban patriciate and peasants – Weber turned his interest to a third group, which is of prime importance for his presentation, the semi-nomadic smallstock breeders, who bred sheep and goats. As a result of radical historical developments – alternating war and peace, population growth, origin of large land-ownership – there occurred stronger and stronger attachment to fixed, small grazing districts, to a large reduction in the number of these groups and to a *demilitarization* of the herdspeople (cf. 7E, pp. 39–46). For Weber, these tribes of herdspeople were of great importance for one reason: in the formation of the prophetic Yahwe-religion they played 'an important historical role'. From them arose the 'patriarchs', who are described as a quite specifically pacifist phenomenon. The small-stock breeders were 'powerless . . . caught' between three groups, equally hostile to one another – the settled farmers, the nomadic Bedouins and the urban patriciate (see 7E, pp. 49–52). Only the creation of a unified military monarchy with a contingent of chariot fighting knights and the foundation of the city of Jerusalem brought about the fact that 'social formations hitherto essentially . . . standing side by side as stock-breeding tribes, peasant tribes, cities, now became fused; the capital and its ruling sibs became politically paramount' (7E, p. 56).

Weber pursued the reflection of these social structural relationships in the Jewish legal collections (7E, pp. 61–75) and came across here what he considered to be the important concept of the 'berith', the name for the *oathbound league*, the important precondition for the 'theocratizing of the

Israelite social order' (7E, p. 75). The 'berith' became an important pre-condition for numerous legal and social relations within Israelite society, and Weber concluded 'In historical times the inner political history of Israel developed through ever repeated ritualistic confederate resolutions' (7E, p. 77). The peculiarity of Israel's history, bound up with this concept of 'berith', was based, according to Weber, on the fact that 'the ancient social structure of Israel in part rested essentially upon a contractually regulated, permanent relationship of landed warrior sibs with guest tribes as legally protected metics: itinerant herdsmen and . . . priests . . . That the covenant with the god, Yahwe himself, became a fundamental conception for Israel's own judgment of its place among nations was bound up with the following circumstances' (7E, p. 79). Weber referred here to the great weakness of all *political* organizations and the extreme stability of the *religious orders*, as for example the Rechabites. Why these orders had such foundations and what determined their great stability becomes a method-ologically important point:

Now, the point at issue is not that the life conditions of the Bedouins and semi-nomads had 'produced' an order whose establishment could be considered as something like the 'ideological exponent' of its economic conditions. This form of historical materialist construction is here, as elsewhere, inadequate. The point is, rather, that once such an order was established the life conditions of these strata gave it by far the greater opportunity to survive in the selective struggle for existence against the other, less stable political organizations. The question, however, why such an order emerged at all, was determined by quite concrete religious–historical and often highly personal circumstances and vicissitudes . . . Mohammed's as well as Jonadeb ben Rechab's religious promises are not to be 'explained' as products of population phenomena or economic conditions, though their content was co-determined thereby. They were, rather, the expression of personal experiences and intentions. However, the intellectual and social means which they utilized and further the great success of creations of this very type are indeed to be understood in terms of such life conditions. (7E, pp. 79–80)

Weber was deeply concerned with the foundational history and the structure of the tribe of Judah, a specifically religious fraternization, as the basis of a fixed tribal cohesion, and in this Weber presented the Israelite confederacy as a *cultic war confederation* which had entered into a 'berith' with Yahwe, as the war god of this union. Weber was particularly interested in the foundations of 'law-speaking' within this union and the concept of the 'holy war' which was particular to this union. Weber considered that certain religious traits, for example circumcision, can be explained on the basis of warrior asceticism, which is linked with this concept.

Only under King Solomon did a tightly organized political construction emerge from the loose confederacy of peasants, herdssibs and small mountain towns – a city-dwelling monarchy with twelve royal administrative districts, a chariot fighting army of knights, royal officials, officers and judges. This development had many social consequences, above all the increase in power of the schooled priests in place of the charismatic ecstatics, and the demilitarization of the peasant strata.

At this point in his presentation of the historical development of Judaism, Weber came across a figure, which he will no longer lose sight of as his presentation of ancient Judaism progresses, the *prophet*. In ancient Judaism, as everywhere in the world, there emerged seers and magicians, who played a varyingly influential role particularly through oracular prophecy and interpretation. However, Weber saw in Israel the appearance of a particular variant on this original type, distinguished from the worldwide general run of soothsayers and magicians, in that it rejects the usual techniques of orgiastic intoxicants, sexual orgiasticism and mass ecstasy, and, moreover, propounds specifically *political prophecies*. Prophets emerge in particular from the groupings of the stock-breeding tribes, and their proclamations were not primarily directed at the constitutional powers, but primarily at the politically interested *public*. They did not supply these prophecies on request, but appear *unasked* and impart above all the threat of *doom*. The history of such prophets began for Weber with the prophet Elijah, of whom Weber wrote

Elijah received his commands from Yahwe in solitude and announced them personally as the emissary of his God . . . His incomparable prestige rested on this and upon his hitherto unheard of lack of discretion in standing up to the political power holders. Historically he is important as the first fairly ascertainable prophet of doom. In this he is the forerunner of a series of grand figures which for our present day literary sources began with Amos and end with Ezekiel.

They became the intellectual leaders of the opposition against kingship . . . (7E, pp. 108–9)

The sociologically important criterion which differentiates between these prophets from ultimately comparable phenomena, was the fact that such a prophecy of doom could not be taught as a profession – by contrast with a 'prophecy of salvation' – and that such a prophecy was not exploitable as a source of earnings.

It was precisely this last idea, bound up with the impressive mixture of limitless *solitude* and just as limitless *lack of discretion* in these 'greatest ideologists of Yahwism', which was obviously so fascinating for Weber about the Israelite prophets. He never tired of describing extensively the individual representatives of this type – particularly striking are his psychological characterizations of Amos, Hosea, Joshua, Jeremiah and Ezekiel (7E, p. 297) – and of propounding their teachings in detail. Their orientation towards the 'time-honoured "law"' of the ancient Israelite confederacy, their uncompromising criticism of the social injustice and the kings of their corrupt way of life, their passionate opposition to bureaucracy which for them was merely the horrific vision of the 'Egyptian house of bondage', these and other moments were what Weber went into so thoroughly in this stratum of literary educated political ideologues, which he described as the 'troublesome democratic crusaders' (7E, p. 112). Exactly at the time in which kingship and the urban patriciate began to adopt 'haughty sultanistic airs' (horses, chariots and harems), these powerful figures appeared, concerned more for the 'brotherly equality and simplicity of the comrades in the desert' and they demanded that the king and patriciate turn back to the old traditions. 'Then Yahwe, the old god of the covenant, would be with him [a charismatic *primus inter pares* as king] as once with the peasant army, against enemies regardless of how seemingly overwhelming, if only – this was the prerequisite of all else – he were to renounce the pretensions to world politics which were responsible for all these innovations' (7E, pp. 115–16).

For Weber, what was important about this god Yahwe, whose prestige derived from the destruction of the Egyptian army (see 7E, pp. 124–5) is that it was not a question of an old-trusted local or tribal god, but of a foreign and mysterious form which consecrated the Israelite confederacy and formed the 'berith' with them. This god was always a God of *salvation* and *promise*, above all of salvation from present *political* circumstances. 'The god offered salvation from Egyptian bondage, not from a senseless world out of joint. He promised not transcendent values but dominion over Canaan which one was out to conquer and a good life' (7E, p. 126). Weber discussed the extremely anthropomorphic conception of this *war god*, who was essentially an unpredictable and capricious god of *natural catastrophes*, and not of eternal natural order. This god entered a 'berith' with a union of free confederate people, which stood in a relationship of joint liability of the members of the union for the sins of all individuals.

Weber went into the competing religious conception of the *Baal cult* and particularly into the respective 'cult managers', both of the Baal cult and of Yahwist religiosity. In the latter case there was obviously no generally recognized status group of priests originally, which might have had a monopoly of sacrifice in the name of the union, and equally there were no communities in the contemporary sense of the word. In both cases the old sib order was still functioning. Only since the ninth century BC, against a background of political distress, was a hereditary charismatic qualified stratum of Yahwe priests who know the *law* and ritual developed, whose sacrificial rituals should *expiate* the guilt of Israel.

With increasing rationalization of life, the demand for means of determining and expiating sins increased everywhere, including Mesopotamia, and under the pressure of its political fate this need gained an especially great momentum in Israel. Thus, with the increasing importance of the expiatory sacrifice and instruction concerning Yahwe's will the demand increased for persons having knowledge of Yahwe and His commandments. (7E, p. 165)

According to the religious conception of ancient Judaism, there was actually only one reason for Yahwe's anger, the violation of the 'berith' entered into with Him.

Hence, it was necessary for the authorities as well as for the individual from the outset to ask which commandment had been violated? Irrational divination means could not answer this question, only knowledge of the very commandments and soul searching. Thus, the idea of *berith* flourishing in the truly Yahwistic circles pushed all scrutiny of the divine will toward an at least relatively rational mode of raising and answering the question. (7E, p. 167)

Weber turned to the *bearers* of this rational questioning, and described the long struggle between the different Levitical priestly sibs, above all the Elides, Zadokites and Aaronites, over the position of monopoly. This controversy came to an end with the victory of the Zadokites, the priesthood of Jerusalem and with the establishment of Jerusalem as the sole adequate place for sacrifice (see 7E, pp. 169–93).

In connection with the rationalization of the Israelite world of ideas, Weber investigated the increase in the *literary* intellectual culture. Out of the need to dissociate itself from the religious and cultural conceptions of Egypt and Babylon 'the existence of an independent, cultured stratum (was required) which received and rationally refashioned the old oracles and promises of the surrounding world' (7E, pp. 205–6). And here a serious difference from the world religions discussed earlier – Confucianism, Taoism, Hinduism and Buddhism – becomes clear: those *intellectual* soteriologies were always stratum-specific religions of literati, which could not and did not want to meet the religious needs of the 'plebs'. It was a similar case – according to Weber's presentation – for the religious conceptions of Egypt, Mesopotamia, ancient Greece and the late Roman states.

In contrast to this, the pre-exilic plebeian was at first in fact, later, in memory and aspiration, a free militia man of the confederacy, who had defeated the knighthood of the culture areas. To be sure he could never have created the rational conception of the Scriptures on his own. Others had to do this for him. But he was receptive to most of the Scriptures. One of the secrets of the development of Yahwism lies, indeed, in the interaction between an enthused stratum of intellectuals and this public composed of demilitarized and socially declassed strata under the impact of social change during the time of the kings.

Rarely have entirely new religious conceptions originated in the respective centers of rational cultures. Rational prophetic or reformist innovations were first conceived, not in Babylon, Athens, Alexandria, Rome, Paris, London, Cologne, Hamburg, Vienna, but in Jerusalem of pre-exilic, in Galilea of late Jewish times, in the late Roman province of Africa, in Assisi, in Wittenberg, Zurich, Geneva and in the marginal regions of the Dutch, lower-German, and English cultural areas, like Frisia and New England. To be sure this never occurred without the influence and impact of a neighbouring rational civilization. The research for this is always the same: prerequisite to new religious conceptions is that man must not yet have unlearned how to face the course of the world with questions of his own. Precisely the man distant from the great culture centers has cause to do so when their influence begins to affect or threaten his central interests. Man living in the midst of the culturally satiated areas and enmeshed in their technique addresses such questions just as little to the environment as, for instance, the child used to daily tramway rides would chance to question how the tramway actually manages to start moving.

The possibility of questioning the meaning of the world presupposes the capacity to be astonished about the course of events. Now, the experiences which the Israelites had before the Exile and which gave them cause to ask such questions were the great wars of liberation and the rise of kingship, the development of the corvée state and of urban culture, the threat of great powers. Particularly, the collapse of the Northern Kingdom and the same fateful threat to the Southern Kingdom, the last remnant of unforgotten grandeur, stood before everybody's eyes. Then came the Exile. The wars of liberation established Yahwe's prestige as war god. The social degradation and demilitarization of the exponents of the old Yahwe militia created the Yahwistic history legend. The paramount questions of theodicy, however, were raised only with the threatened collapse of the kingdom. (7E, pp. 206–7)

Weber firmly emphasized the great importance which *knowledge* possessed for the origin of a Yahwistic, rational ethical absolutism (*Gesinnungsethik*): 'Magic did not have its usual dominance in Israel . . . The fate of magic in Old Testament religion was determined by the systematic opposition of the Torah teachers' (7E, p. 219). Particularly because it is a 'rational providence' of the personal god Yahwe which determines Israel's destiny (see 7E, p. 223), the knowledge of the Levites and the Torah interpreters was required to read God's commandments. Precisely because this god was not only a 'god of plebeians' but just as much a 'god of history', of political–military history in particular, one could enquire into his divine purposes, the reasons for his wrath and the conditions of his mercy, just as with a great king. (see 7E, p. 225). Thus Weber was concerned with the origins, content and effects of *Torah teaching* (see 7E, pp. 235–63), which in his interpretation brought about a 'theologizing . . . of law' as well as a 'rationalization of religious ethics' (7E, p. 243).

In a second section on 'The Establishment of the Jewish Pariah People' Weber took up again his concern with Yahwistic prophecy and its representatives. He was interested in the history and effects of the great prophets of the age from the ninth century, the beginning of a renewed policy of expansion in Babylon and Egypt, until post-exilic times. Now Jerusalem had become the great stage for prophets like Hosea, Joshua, Jeremiah and Ezekiel, who, of their own accord, addressed the public in the marketplace like demagogues. But these occurrences were in no way party political. On the contrary, the prophets were never primarily oriented towards political interests: their sole concerns and standards were the fulfilment of Yahwe's commandments. Weber investigated the social origin of these prophets, their material situation, their position regarding the king and the priesthood, their psychological disposition, and above all the content of their largely ecstatic oracular prophecies. These long sections were written in such an extraordinarily fascinating and gripping style that we must not forget that here Weber let himself be carried away by his own impressions and he became deeply embroiled in the narratives. Our prime concern with *sociological* relevance means that we must omit large parts of these passages. It is only towards the end of his presentation that Weber re-examined the question of the influence of this pre-exilic prophecy on the development of an ethic, but we note that even here he dealt with the specific *economic ethic* only peripherally. Weber saw the Yahwistic ethic as the result of a 'collaboration' of the *prophets*, oriented toward political catastrophes and apocalyptic expectations, with the rationalization of the Levitical *Torah teachers*. However, Weber undoubtedly attributed greater importance to the prophets.

The entire inner construction of the Old Testament is inconceivable without its orientation in terms of the oracles of the prophets. These giants cast their shadows through the millennia into the present, since this holy book of the Jews became a holy book of the Christians too, and since the entire interpretation of the mission of the Nazarene was primarily determined by the old promises to Israel . . .

Prophecy together with traditional ritualism of Israel, brought forth the elements that gave to Jewry its pariah place in the world. (7E, pp. 334 and 336)

This pariah situation was especially exacerbated during the period of exile; only now did the strict exclusivity of Judaism develop into a group the base of which was essentially religion, a group which was, however, already prepared by the influence of the Torah and of prophecy before the exile. But, with the loss of an actual area base, the religious segregation of a now internationally resident 'guest people' increased, for example with the uncompromising increase in the duties of circumcision and observation of the Sabbath, and in the prohibition of connubium and commensalism with non-Jews. In the area of economics in particular there arose an important division between in-group and out-group morality, with especial reference to the 'prohibition of usury' (see 7E, p. 342), which led to a 'dualism of economic ethic'. Weber formulated the decisive result thus: 'In any case, there was no soteriological motive whatever for ethically rationalizing out-group economic relations. No religious premium existed for it' (7E, p. 345). There thus formed a 'Jewish pariah capitalism' the normative foundations of which were diametrically opposed to the economic ethic of the Puritan capitalists.

Thus, economic pursuits could never furnish the setting for 'proving' one's self religiously. If God 'blessed' his own with economic success, it was not because they had 'proven' themselves to be pious Jews in business conduct, but because he had lived a god-fearing life outside his economic pursuits . . . The area of proving one's piety in practice, for the Jew, lay in quite a different area than that of rationally mastering the 'world' and especially the economy . . . In any case, the oriental and South and East European regions where the Jews were most and longest at home have failed to develop the specific traits of modern capitalism. This is true of Antiquity as well as of the Middle Ages and modern times. Their actual part in the development of the Occident rested essentially on their character as a guest people, which their voluntary segregation imposed on them. (7E, p. 345)

In the section on 'The Pharisees' (7E), which was published only posthumously, Weber emphasized certain characteristics; even the processes of transformation in Judaism since Maccabean times only increased developmental tendencies towards segregation (which according to Weber was essentially *voluntary*) from non-Jews and which led ultimately to the division according to sect through the Pharisaic movement (7E, pp. 385-6)

It was the Phariseehood which effected the dominant development into a Judaism with an urban, bourgeois character, the 'product' of which was above all the rise to power of the *rabbis* (7E, p. 391). But this 'stratum of plebeian intellectuals' was the one which pressed solely for the correct fulfilment of the law as the only way to salvation and prevented 'any point of departure for an economically ordered methodic or inner-worldly asceticism' (7E, p. 401).

We referred above to the unity, both temporal and in content, of Weber's works on 'The Economic Ethic of the World Religions', which we dealt with previously, and of the passages on 'Religious Groups (The Sociology of Religion)' in *Economy and Society* (8E, pp. 399–634). Here we shall dispense with a discussion of the section on the sociology of religion in *Economy and Society*: in both texts Weber worked with the same material which he merely arranged differently. The investigative purpose of the works on the sociology of religion dealt with thus far were each presented; the aim of the passages from *Economy and Society* was – as in the character of a dictionary – overwhelmingly that of *systematization* and *generalization*. Here Weber discussed the origin of 'the' religions, of 'the' religious action, of 'the' magician, 'the' priests and 'the' prophets, of 'the' idea of God, 'the' religious ethic, 'the' taboo, 'the' community, 'the' pastoral care, 'the' religiosity of certain classes and estates, the problem of 'the' theodicy, and of 'the' salvation. In this context we are interested in that section of *Economy and Society* in which Weber wrote about another world religion, a religion which he no longer dealt with in his essays: *Islam* (8E, p. 623)

Weber described Islam as a religion which ' "accommodated" itself to the world', a 'comparatively late product of Near Eastern monotheism' which transformed itself into a 'national Arabic warrior religion'. Typical of this 'religion of masters' was the acceptability of slavery, obedience, polygamy and the disesteem for women, a predominantly ritualistic conception of religious duties and few ethical demands made on adherents. The individual quest for salvation and mysticism are alien to Islam; it promises wealth, power and glory – all typical 'martial promises' and also the world beyond is pictured as 'a soldier's sensual paradise'. Even the economic ethic of Islam is primarily feudal in form, valuing highly the pursuit of wealth and the enjoyment of riches.

This type of religion, with its orgiastic and mystical elements, with its essentially irrational and extraordinary character, and with its official and thoroughly traditionalistic ethic of everyday life, became influential in Islam's missionary enterprise because of its great simplicity. It directed the conduct of life into paths whose effect was plainly opposite to the methodical control of life found among

Puritans, and indeed, found in every type of asceticism oriented toward the control of the world. (8E, p. 626)

We know from Marianne Weber (Foreword to 204, p.v) that Weber intended to pursue his investigations into the sociology of religion. He was going to deal with the Psalms and the Book of Job, Talmudic Judaism, early Christianity, Medieval orders and sects in pre-Reformation times and – extensively – Islam. In spite of apparently isolated preliminary writings, the execution of this plan by which he had set so much store, remained incomplete. We have previously emphasized the importance of the Introduction (1915) and now to conclude this presentation of Weber's works in the sociology of religion, we turn to his famous Preface (181), which he composed for the publication in book form of the *Gesammelte Aufsätze zur Religionssoziologie*. This text has implications which reach far beyond the actual works in the sociology of religion: it acts to focus the results of Weber's activity as a researcher over the decades. Thus it is a kind of 'key' – a retrospectively formulated 'programme' of *all* his writings in the sociology of religion. Nevertheless, it must be treated as the conclusion to his religious–sociological writings, as they represent the most important starting point for an overall interpretation of Weber's work.

In this text Weber appears as the *universal historian* concerned with one question above all others: 'What chain of events in the West and only here led to the appearance of cultural phenomena which nevertheless – as we at least like to believe – developed in a way which was of universal importance and value?' (181 p. 1) Linked to this question, Weber cited those major social areas in which – in his opinion – considerable differences between the West and the other cultural regions can be perceived:

1   The *sciences*: Weber considered as peculiar to the West the foundations of mathematics, rational 'argument', rational experiment, the biological/ biochemical basis of the natural sciences, a rational chemistry, the 'Theucydidean Pragma' of writing history, the systematization and rational concepts of the doctrine of the state, the strict schemata and ideational forms of the law.

2   *Art*: according to Weber only the West had a rational, harmonic music, the basic instruments of organ, piano and violin being the means to this transformation; only the West had a rational use for the Gothic vault or a press designed only for printing.

3   *Administration*: it was only in the West that Weber observed that rational and systematic specialized area of science which takes on the education of

trained 'experts'. It was to the 'expert advisors' in particular as the 'cornerstones of the modern state and modern economy' that Weber attributed the greatest importance in the specific development of the West.

But the absolutely ineluctable domination of our entire existence, the basic political, technical and economic conditions of our being, in the body of a specially trained *organization* of officials, the technically, commercially and above all the juristically trained state official as the bearer of the most important day-to-day functions of social life, has known no land and no era in the same way as the modern Occident. (181, p. 3)

4   The *state*: Weber already regarded the feudal state (*Ständestaat*) as the specific characteristic of the West, just as much as the institution of parliaments. But the 'state' as a 'political institution' with a rationally legislated 'constitution', with a rationally legislated legal system, and an administration of civil servants which was oriented towards rationally legislated rules ('laws') – this combination of characteristics and their unity in this institution was, according to Weber, known only to the West.

5   The *economy*: Weber devoted particular attention to this social sub-system. He reiterated the West's speciality: *capitalism*. If in the previous social areas Weber was keen in each case to make it clear which approaches developed in a similar direction in other cultural regions and where the specific Western development diverged from this, this aim was even stronger in his characterization of Western capitalism. In a 'circuitous' fashion, Weber described the specifics of the 'most fateful power of our modern life' (181, p. 4): it was not the striving for maximum profit which distinguished Western capitalism.

The 'drive to earn', the 'striving for profit', to profit in money has in itself nothing to do with capitalism. This striving was and is to be found in waiters, doctors, drivers, artists, prostitute women, corruptible officials, soldiers, robbers, crusaders, gamblers and beggars; indeed in 'all sorts and conditions of men' in all ages in all countries of the world where there was and is the objective possibility for doing it in any way. One should have given up this naive conceptualization once and for all back in the nursery of history and culture. The rampant desire to acquire does not in the least equate to capitalism, and even less to its 'spirit'. But capitalism *can* directly equate to the *taming*, at least to the rational tempering of this irrational instinct. At any rate, capitalism is identical with the striving for profit in continuable, rational capitalist business, for a profit which is continually renewed, for '*profitability*'. (181, p. 4)

To avoid misunderstandings over this last aspect, Weber stated unambiguously:

A 'capitalist' business transaction should mean firstly one which resides on the expectation of profit through the exploitation of possibilities of *exchange*, i.e. on the possibilities of (formally) *peaceful* gain. Gain which is (formally and actually) violent behaves according to its own laws and it is not reasonable to put it in the same category with business which is (ultimately) oriented to possibilities of gain through exchange. (181, p. 4)

Other characteristics of the trend towards capital accounting and dealing in money are not yet peculiar to the West:

In this sense, 'capitalism' and 'capitalistic enterprises', even with the rationalisation of capital accounting, have existed in *all* civilized countries in the world since economic documentation began . . . capitalist enterprises, and even the capitalist entrepreneur, not only the opportunist but also the long-term entrepreneur, are as old as the hills and spread all over the world. (181, p. 6)

At this point of transition in the argument, we come across Max Weber the 'sociologist'. If, thus far, it had been socially relevant facts which had helped define the economic form of 'capitalism', now Weber introduces *societal* elements in order to understand the specific universal historical position of Western capitalism. These elements are as follows:

The rational capitalistic organization of (formally) *free work*
Rational business forms which are oriented towards the possibilities of the
  consumer market
The *separation of household and business*
Rational *bookkeeping*

These peculiarities of Western capitalism, however, first became important through their connection with the capitalist organization of labour which brought about the essential moment of calculability. In this connection, Weber interpreted the origin and functioning of the stock exchange as the development of a 'rational socialism', the emergence of the 'burgher' as the formation of the 'bourgeoisie', and of the 'proletariat' as 'classes'.

In a universal history of civilization, the central problem for us, purely economically, is in the last analysis *not* the emergence of capitalist activity (changing merely in form) as such . . . Rather it is the origin of *bourgeois enterprise* capitalism with its rational organization of *free labour*. Or speaking in cultural–historical terms, the origin of the Western bourgeoisie and its individuality, which of course is closely connected with the origin of the capitalist organization of labour, is not simply identical with it. (181, p. 10)

Weber concluded his stock-taking of the essential specifics of Western development with his exhaustive treatment of capitalism, and then turned to the different dimensions of the possible explanation for this uniquely Western development, again using a 'circuitous' procedure. Because of this and also because of the general dialectical link of possible, causal connections, these passages are extremely well suited to explaining the procedure and aims of Weber's sociology.

Specifically modern Western capitalism is in the first place evidently determined to a large extent by the developments in *technical* possibilities. Today its rationality is determined by the *calculability* of technically decisive factors: the proof of exact calculation. In reality, however, this means determined by the individuality of Western science, particularly the natural sciences, which were mathematically and experimentally exact and rational. The development of these sciences and the technology which was based on them contained and contains on the other hand decisive impulses of capitalistic possibilities, which are linked like rewards to their economic valorizability. The development of Western science was certainly not determined by such possibilities . . . Even the origin of mathematics and mechanics was not determined by such possibilities. This was not the case with the technical use of scientific knowledge, however: this important factor for the ordering of the masses was determined by economic rewards which in the West were placed on it. These rewards, however, were derived from the peculiarity of the *social* order in the West. We must also ask *which* components of this peculiarity they were derived from as doubtlessly not all were of equal importance. Among those which were certainly important numbered the rational structure of the *law* and the administration. For modern rational enterprise capitalism also requires, like calculable technical means of labour, a calculable legal system and administration according to formal laws, without which adventure capitalism and speculative merchant capitalism and all possible forms of politically determined capitalism are possible, but no rational private economic enterprise with fixed capital and a certain *calculation* is possible. Such a legal system and administration in such an accomplished legal, technical and formalistic form is only available to the economic leadership of the West. Where does it derive this law from, we ask. As any investigation would show, *even* capitalist interests, among other conditions, have undoubtedly smoothed the way for the domination of the status group of lawyers (schooled in rational law) in the administration of justice, although in no way only or primarily for them. And it was not they who *created* this legal system themselves, but completely different forces were at work in this development. Why did capitalist interests not act similarly in China or India? In these countries, why did neither scientific, artistic, state, nor scientific development follow those lines of *rationalization* which are peculiar to the West? (181, pp. 10f.)

At this point the original question is obviously turned around: it is no longer the question of the origins of specifically Western *capitalism* which occupies centre stage, but the question of the characteristics of a 'specifically constructed "rationalism" in Western culture' (181, p. 11), and the question of its causes and effects.

Next we come again to the question of recognizing the particular *characteristics* of Western rationalism and of explaining its origin. Any such attempt at explanation must, according to the fundamental importance of the economy, take account above all of the economic conditions. In doing this, however, we must not disregard the inverted causal relationship. For economic rationalism in its origin is in the final analysis dependent (as it is upon rational technology and rational law) upon the capability and disposition of people to *lead their lives* in certain ways practically and rationally. Where this was obstructed by spiritual inhibitions, even the development of an *economically* rational way of life came across serious inner resistances. The most important elements which made up the way of life belonged everywhere in the past to magical and religious powers and to the ethical ideas of duty which were anchored in their belief. *This* is what we shall discuss in the following collected and expanded essays. (181, p. 12)

Weber said of the reprinted Protestantism investigations that they attempt 'in *one* important single point to come closer to the side of the problem which is most difficult to grasp: the determination of the origin of an "economic mentality" – of an "ethos", an economic form derived from certain religious beliefs and certainly from the example of the connection of the modern economic ethic with the rational ethic of ascetic Protestantism. Here we shall pursue only *one* side of the causal relationship' (181, p. 12).

On the other hand, the essays on the 'economic ethic of the world religions' attempted

to investigate *both* causal relationships, in an overview of the relations of the most important cultural religions to the economy and the social stratification of their environment, in so far as it is necessary to find the point of *comparison* with the Western development we are analysing. For only in this way can we tackle the to some degree causal *addition* of those elements of the Western religious economic ethic, which are, by contrast to others, peculiar to the West. (181, pp. 12f)

Weber expressly emphasized the 'limited aim' of these works and their 'completely provisional character' which should in no way be regarded as comprehensive cultural analyses. Rather 'in every cultural region they emphasize quite intentionally what is and was in opposition to Western cultural development. Thus they are completely oriented to what appears important from *this* point of view in the presentation of Western development' (181, p. 13).

5

Economy and Society

Relevant texts:

'*Vorwort*' *zu Bd. 1, Grundriss der Sozialökonomik* ('Preface' to volume 1 of
Social Economics) (1914)
Economy and Society (1922)
The Rational and Social Foundations of Music (1921)

In the biographical section we briefly mentioned the history of the origin of
Economy and Society. In 1909, the *Archiv*'s publisher, Paul Siebeck, brought
in Weber to edit the major collection, *Grundriss der Sozialökonomik*. This was
originally intended to replace the *Handbuch der Politischen Oekonomie*, which
was edited by Gustav von Schönberg (first edition in 1882, fourth in
1896–8) and published by H. Laupp. After the publishers were taken over
by J. C. B. Mohr (Paul Siebeck), and Weber took over as the main editor,
this plan was abandoned as 'unrealizable' (123, p. ix). Weber developed an
entirely new plan for the whole project, chose the new title and looked
around for contributors, among whom were Herkner, Jaffé, Michels,
Oldenberg, von Schulze-Gaevernitz, Schumpeter, Sombart, Alfred Weber
and von Zwiedineck-Südenhorst. Many delays in the submission of the
commissioned contributions and some disappointing results led Weber to
the idea of considerably expanding his own contribution.

Since, in the case of some contributions, a replacement could not be arranged,
I thought of providing a comprehensive sociological statement in the section
'Economy and Society'. This would mean coming up with an equivalent, thus to
increase its originality, and sacrificing other works which were far more important
to me – this was a project which I would in other circumstances never have taken
on.[1]

The first volume of the *Grundriss* appeared in 1914 and the last of altogether
twelve volumes, after the interruption of the war, appeared in 1930.

Two parts were planned for section III, 'Economy and Society': one by

Weber on 'The economy and the social orders and powers' and one by Eugen von Philippovich on 'The development of economic, social and political systems and ideals'. Weber commented on his own contribution in the 'Foreword': 'The connections between the economy and the social orders are dealt with more fully than is usually the case. This is done deliberately so that the autonomy of these spheres *vis-à-vis* the economy are made manifest. We proceed from the idea that the development of the economy in particular must be understood as a specific epiphenomenon of the general rationalization of life' (123, p. vii).

Weber worked on his contribution from 1909–20; the bibliography shows how many other works he was writing during this period. By the time of his death, Weber had only prepared the first draft for publication (210). All 'complete' editions (215 a-f) appeared *posthumously* and were reworked by their respective editors, Marianne Weber on the 1922, 1925 and 1947 editions, and Johannes Winckelmann on the 1956, 1972 and 1976 editions.

The undoubtedly difficult editorial situation of this ultimately unfinished text makes any presentation and interpretation of it a tricky exercise. [2] It is a known fact, however, that Weber wrote the present part II of *Economy and Society* in the years leading up to 1913. He did not get round to a final polishing of all individual sections, but he only put together the present part I in 1918–20 and worked on it up to the stage of the edited galley proofs.

In its last version (8E) *Economy and Society* Part II is made up of sixteen chapters which have roughly the following customary titles today:

Economic sociology (chapters I, II)
Sociology of social and political communities: race, kin, people, nation
(chapters III, IV, V, IX)
Sociology of religion (chapter VI)
Sociology of law (chapter VIII)
Sociology of domination/political sociology (chapters X to XVI)
Sociology of markets (chapter VII)

In general, Weber tried to use and arrange in *Economy and Society* the great mass of material he had worked on up to that point. For this very reason, it seems neither possible nor necessary to go into all sections of *Economy and Society* with the same depth that we applied to previous sections of Weber's work. In its coverage of the material, *Economy and Society* feeds off *all* the areas of Weber's work that we have looked at so far, and thus it is not accessible without knowledge of what has gone before.

On the other hand, the main content and arguments of certain thematic areas have already partially been covered – for example sociology of religion,[3] and urban sociology,[4] which are texts incorporated into the sociology of domination (chapters XIV to XVI). Moreover, we shall deal with 'economic sociology' and 'sociology of domination' on the basis of the later texts from part I of *Economy and Society*. For these reasons we shall deal with just the relevant passages from part II in which Weber presents his 'sociology of law'.

Sociology of law

We can see from the areas of Weber's work we have looked at so far that Weber is continually dealing with the *reciprocal* relationship between law and the social order. The inclusion of law as *one* medium in the organization of social order became particularly clear in his dissertation, his *Habilitation* thesis, his treatment of the constitution of agriculture in Antiquity and in his writings on agricultural workers. Also in this category are several strictly juristic works which we will not deal with here.[5] In each case Weber treated the law as an area of historical and social reality, and he analysed the reciprocal, legal relationships between society, law, religion, economy and domination.

In producing a systematic sociology of law, Weber saw his first task as giving a *sociological* meaning to the concept of law, and thus to distinguish it from its purely juristic content. The most important sociological question for Weber was thus

What *actually* happens in a group owing to the probability that persons engaged in social action (*Gemeinschaftshandeln*), especially those exerting a socially relevant amount of power, subjectively consider certain norms as valid and practically act according to them, in other words, orient their own conduct towards these norms? (8E, p. 311)

Thus Weber emphasized the *empirical validity* of legal norms and to a large extent left aside the differentiation of motives which can lead to such a validity in the sense of *conformity*. ' "Law", as understood by us, is simply an "order" endowed with certain specific guarantees of the probability of its empirical validity' (8E, p. 313) Weber stressed the importance of a 'coercive apparatus' according to which a (legitimate) order becomes law

wherever coercive means, of a physical or psychological kind, are available; i.e. wherever they are at the disposal of one or more persons who hold themselves ready to use them for this purpose in the case of certain events; in other words, wherever we find a consociation specifically dedicated to the purpose of 'legal coercion'. (8E, p. 317)

Law in the sociological context is thus defined as 'a complex of actual determinants (*Bestimmungsgründe*) of human conduct' (8E, p. 312) which has been enforced by an apparatus specially designed for it and in this sense, therefore, can be said to be 'valid'. This sociological interpretation of 'validity' means just the *possibility*, i.e. the *probability* of compliance in an individual case, independent of the 'motives' for the compliance. The introduction of the concept of 'probability' (*Chance*) is of great sociological importance as it can be used to show that sociologists are not trying to make the validity of a legal norm dependent upon the fact that it is generally observed. The sociological validity, which can really only be represented as a percentage stands out against the *possibility* of the orientation and, according to Weber, is co-determined by the possibility of the application of mental or physical coercion by the apparatus which is created to do just that (cf. 8E, p. 314). In the course of historical development, this legal coercion has become a 'monopoly of the state', that is 'law guaranteed by the state, only when legal coercion is exercised through the specific, i.e. normally directly *physical*, means of coercion through the political community' (8E, p. 314). However, Weber made it clear that the 'validity' of a law or a legal norm is in no way established merely because this coercive apparatus exists. In the majority of cases it is more likely to be utilitarian, ethical or subjectively conventional motives ('consisting of the fear of disapproval by the environment' (cf. 8E, p. 134), which are decisive.

The functional relationship between the legal norm and the economic norm becomes clear when Weber discusses the effects of a valid legal system. For the individual, one of its main effects is the fact that it produces 'certain calculable chances of having economic goods available or of acquiring them under certain conditions in the future' (8E, p. 315). This moment when the legal norm – which is secured not only by the coercive political apparatus but also by other socially relevant institutions such as organizations and churches – becomes calculable and reliable is very important for any economy that wants to plan for the future.

Weber saw the law as 'a complex of actual determinants . . . of human conduct' and stressed that the legal norm belongs 'to the same continuum' (8E, p. 319) as the areas of *convention* and *custom*, which led from one to the other 'with imperceptible transitions' (cf. 8E, pp. 319–25). Following the aim of the *socio-economic* approach, Weber took his time in explaining the relationships between law and the economy. He picked out six particularly important aspects which serve to elucidate both the relative independence as well as the interdependence of both areas.

1   Law (in the sociological sense) guarantees by no means only economic interests but rather the most diverse interests. . . . Above all, it guarantees political, ecclesiastical, familial, and other positions of authority as well as positions of social pre-eminence of any kind which may indeed be economically conditioned or economically relevant . . . but which are (not) economic in themselves . . .

2   Under certain conditions a 'legal order' can remain unchanged while economic relations are undergoing a radical transformation . . . Should such a situation ever come about . . . the legal order would still be bound to apply its coercive machinery
. . .

3   The legal status of a matter may be basically different according to the point of view of the legal system from which it is considered. But such differences (of legal classification) need not have any relevant economic consequences . . .

4   Obviously, legal guaranties are directly at the service of economic interests to a very large extent. Even where this does not seem to be . . . economic interests are among the strongest factors influencing the creation of law . . .

5   . . . Yet, the power of law over economic conduct has in many respects grown weaker rather than stronger as compared with earlier conditions . . . the measure of possible influence on economic activity is not simply a function of the general level of acquiescence towards legal coercion.

6   From the purely theoretical point of view, legal guaranty *by the state* is not indispensable to any basic economic phenomenon . . . But an economic system, especially of the modern type, could certainly not exist without a legal order with very special features which could not develop except in the frame of a public legal order . . . modern business communication requires a promptly and predictably functioning legal system, i.e., one which is guaranteed by the strongest coercive power . . . The universal predominance of the market consociation requires on the one hand a legal system the functioning of which is *calculable* in accordance with rational rules. On the other hand, the constant expansion of the market . . . has favored the monopolization and regulation of all 'legitimate' coercive power by *one* universalist coercive institution . . . (8E, pp. 333–7)

Chapter VIII of *Economy and Society*, formally entitled 'Economy and Law (The Sociology of Law)' systematizes the dimensions of the complex relationship between the individual areas of society which we have dealt with in these basic remarks, areas which have been enriched and made clearer by many historical presentations. After a discussion of the division between public and private law, Weber turned to analysing the historical roots of *lawmaking* and *lawfinding*. He distinguished between irrational and rational legal technical means, investigating both their formal and their material side. This differentiation of 'legal rationality', for example through the logical generalization of abstract interpretations of meaning, and 'legal irrationality', through magical acts like prophecy and oraculism, not only helps as a historical systematization, but also as the point of departure for the comparative presentation of legal systems, social systems and systems of domination. For the 'rationality' of each legal system is dependent upon the structure of each political organization and the degree to which the respective economy is rational (cf. 8E, p. 655).

Weber's study particularly aimed at the monopolization process of the coercive apparatus by the state, focusing especially on the political community as the dominant source of 'legitimate' law (cf. 8E, p. 657). To a certain extent, this historical development finished off the principle of 'freedom of contract' (cf. 8E, pp. 668f.) and the formation of 'special laws' for limited sectors of the population (cf. 8E, p. 694). Both historical processes have a direct connection with the formation of an exchange and a market economy.

The ever-increasing integration of all individuals and all fact situations into one . . . institution which today, at least, rests in principle on formal 'legal equality' has been achieved by two great rationalizing forces, i.e., first, by the extension of the market economy and, second, by the bureaucratization of the activities of the organs of the consensual groups. (8E, p. 698)

Even these over-arching processes, which we come across continually in Weber's work, each discover a stratum-specific formation and significance. For example, the fact that 'everyone "without respect of person" may establish a business corporation, (nevertheless) the *propertied* classes *as such* obtain a sort of factual "autonomy", since they alone are able to utilize or take advantage of these powers' (8E, p. 699).

Thus we can see the four themes which dominate Weber's sociology of law:

[T]he ways and the destiny of *rationalizing* the law': this is his *historical* presentation of the development of *new* laws from out of the irrationality of magic to the rationality of technology. The historical process of rationalizing the law encompasses the process of 'secularizing' the elaboration of law (8E, p. 755), legal thought (8E, p. 784) and the administration of justice (8E, p. 770).

The *social bearers* of this development from the legal doctrine of the guilds to the 'rational' juristic formation of the universities.

The social groups whose (material) interests are, in a particular way, taken into consideration by this development.

The 'influence of the form of political authority on the formal aspects of the law' (8E, p. 809), in particular the influence of the patrimonial sovereign's legal elaboration over the creation of laws and the administration of justice by status groups and patriarchy, which turned the law into a revolutionary law of nature. Weber sees all this as the preparations for the formation of the modern institution of the state with its 'modern' law.

Weber included all his previous material in his discussion of these four themes. It is precisely the inter-cultural and diachronic comparison which clarifies even the narrow relationship of this development to the *religious conceptions* of the different ages and cultures. All these dimensions – 'legal', social, economic, political and religious were brought together in Weber's final words:

From a theoretical point of view, the general development of law and procedure may be viewed as passing through the following stages: first, charismatic legal revelation through 'law prophets'; second, empirical creation and finding of law by legal *honorationes*; third, imposition of law by secular or theocratic powers; fourthly and finally, systematic elaboration of law and professionalized administration of justice by persons who have received their legal training in a learned and formally logical manner. From this perspective, the formal qualities of the law emerge as follows: arising in primitive legal procedure from a combination of magically conditioned formalism and irrationality conditioned by revelation, they proceed to increasingly specialized juridical and logical rationality and systematization . . . Finally, they assume . . . an increasingly logical sublimation and deductive rigor and develop an increasingly rational technique in procedure.

Since we are here only concerned with the most general lines of development, we shall ignore the fact that in historical reality the theoretically constructed stages of rationalization have not everywhere followed in the sequence which we have just outlined, even if we ignore the world outside the Occident. We shall not be troubled either by the multiplicity of causes for the particular type and degree of rationalization that a given law has actually assumed . . . (8E, pp. 882–3)

'General Sociology'

In an attempt to collate the results of his investigations – which had piled up over the years – into universal history, which were thematically very wide-reaching, Weber wrote part I of *Economy and Society* in the years 1918–20. Marianne Weber characterized the relationship between the two parts as follows:

The systematic part (part I), which Weber presumably would have continued, presupposed for the *researcher* mastery of the empirical material which he [Weber] wanted to form into the most significant sociological conceptual doctrine possible. On the other hand, the reader's understanding of this doctrine and its reception is helped considerably by the more detailed description of sociological phenomena in part II. Even in the sections which could be described as 'concrete' sociology by contrast with the 'abstract' sociology of the first part, the vast historical material is already 'systematic', i.e. by contrast with a merely descriptive presentation, it is ordered according to 'ideal-typical' concepts . . . However, while in the first, abstract part the history which Weber referred to everywhere served essentially as an illustration of the concepts, the ideal-typical concepts appear from now on, vice versa, to serve the interpretive interpenetration of world-historical events, institutions and developments. (215f, p. xxxii)

The title *'Soziologische Kategorienlehre'* (Conceptual Exposition) for part I did not come from Weber himself, who would have preferred the title *'Allgemeine Soziologie'* (General Sociology), but from Marianne Weber.[6] Doubtless, during the creation of part I there emerged the problem of the presentation of Weber's sociology, which was bound up with the history of this text, the problem that Weber did not manage to co-ordinate the concepts and definitions he developed later with the expositions in part II. We can see clearly the decisive change of concepts, as for example, the exchange of the previously used concept *Gemeinschaftshandeln* (community action) for the concept *soziales Handeln* (social action), or the replacement of the concept *Gemeinschaft* (community) by *Verband* (organized group). Within the framework of our investigation, we should, however, disregard these important modifications, and rely on the late version of 1918–20. On this textual basis, if we want to deal with Weber's economic sociology, with his sociology of domination and – only peripherally – with his sociology of music, it will be necessary for reasons of internal context, to deal with his 'General Sociology' first.

In chapter 1 of the so-called 'Conceptual Exposition' Weber expanded the 'Basic Sociological Terms' in their systematic context. In this text which is a continuation of the article which appeared in 1913, 'On Some Categories of Interpretive Sociology' (116), Weber developed his concept of sociology, its organization in content as well as methodology, its central concepts and its delimitation from other scientific disciplines. The seventeen paragraphs which are a 'discussion of concepts' are 'unavoidably abstract and hence give the impression of remoteness from reality' (8E, p. 3). They present *no theory*, neither the theory of an 'interpretive sociology' nor a 'theory of

social action'. Rather, they form the conceptual instrumentarium of
Weber's sociology. Consequently Weber proceeded from his basic assertion
'Sociology . . . is a science concerning itself with the interpretive understanding of social action and thereby with a causal explanation of its course
and consequences' (8E, p. 4) in order to arrive at the concepts which are
centrally important for all his scientific investigations. We shall deal with
their content and their 'architectonic' context in what follows.

First, Weber determined the object domain of his sociology. His *point of
departure* was the concept of 'social action' as shown in figure 1:

Human behaviour (menschliches Verhalten), as he called his most general
definition, is 'behaviour – be it overt or covert, omission or acquiescence' (8E, p. 4).

Action (Handeln), as a sub-domain of this, exists 'in so far as the acting
individual attaches a subjective *meaning* to his behaviour' (8E, p. 4).

Social action (soziales Handeln) exists 'in so far as its subjective meaning takes
account of the behaviour of others and is thereby oriented in its course'
(8E, p. 4).

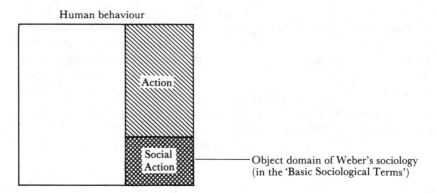

Figure 1

Following this basic determination, which aims at an experiential,
scientific, interpretive sociology, within the 'Basic Sociological Terms'
there are two excursions on the 'Methodological Foundations' of this
understanding of sociology and on 'social action'.

For the 'Methodological Foundations' Weber pinned down his concept
of an 'interpretive sociology', for which the concept of 'meaning' is central.

In his sociology as an *empirical* science, meaning signifies first

the actual existing meaning in the given concrete case of a particular actor, or . . . the average of approximate meaning attributable to a given plurality of actors; or secondly . . . the theoretically conceived *pure type* of subjective meaning attributed to the hypothetical actor or actors in a given type of action. (8E, p. 4)

Weber expressly emphasized the constructedness of meaning established in this way, in which it is neither a question of any 'objectively "correct"' meaning nor of 'one which is "true" in some metaphysical sense'. For a 'typological scientific analysis', Weber demanded the investigation of the rationally comprehensible, i.e. the 'immediately and unambiguously intellectually meaningful' graspable elements of the action to be investigated. In this, a constructed, purely instrumental course of action is assumed, i.e. the question is asked

what the course of action would have been if it had not been influenced by irrational affects; it is then possible to introduce the irrational components as accounting for the observed deviations from this hypothetical course . . . Only in this way is it possible to assess the causal significance of irrational factors as accounting for the deviations from this type. The construction of a purely rational course of action . . . serves the sociologist as a type (ideal type) . . . to understand the ways in which actual action is influenced by irrational factors of all sorts, such as affects and errors, in that they account for the deviation from the line of conduct which would be expected on the hypothesis that the action were purely rational. (8E, p. 6)

For these 'reasons of methodological convenience', Weber acknowledged a 'rationalistic' method, which he did not want to be understood as 'rationalistic bias', 'but only as a methodological device' which should 'not involve a belief in the actual predominance of rational elements in human life' (8E, p. 7).

If the concept of 'meaning' represents the decisive category in Weber's concept of action, then the concept of *Verstehen* (understanding) is at the centre of his methodology. Since the 'intended meaning' of an action should be 'understood', the differentiation of the understanding corresponds to that of the meaning. Accordingly, understanding means the 'interpretive grasp of' '(a) . . . the actually intended meaning for concrete individual action; or (b) . . . the average of, or an approximation to the actually intended meaning; or (c) the meaning appropriate to a scientifically formulated pure type (an ideal type) of a common phenomenon' (8E, p. 9).

Once again it is the *constructedness* of this understanding which Weber referred to emphatically.

[Such ideal-typical constructions] state what course a given type of human action would take if it were strictly rational, unaffected by errors or emotional factors and if, furthermore, it were completely and unequivocally directed to a single end . . . In reality, action takes exactly this course only in unusual cases . . . and even then there is usually only an approximation to the ideal type. (8E, p. 9)

This procedure, in which a concrete, observable, human action is under-pinned by an ideal-typical constructed 'meaning', which is established with the help of an instrumentally equipped 'understanding' does not lead to a 'causally valid interpretation' but solely to a 'peculiarly plausible hypothesis'. It is not only that the actor or actors are themselves often not conscious of the motives of their action or rather are 'repressed' by others, but also the fact that behind actions, which from the outside may be judged as the same or similar, very different complexes of meaning can lie, both these reasons make the construction of a certain complex of meaning only the 'uncertain procedure of the "imaginary experiment"' (8E, p. 10).

As the motive of an action, Weber described a 'complex of subjective meaning which seems to the actor himself or to the observer an adequate ground for the conduct in question' (8E, p. 11). Weber's differentiation between *subjective adequacy or 'adequacy on the level of meaning' (Sinnadäqanz)* and *'causal adequacy' (Kausaladäquanz)* emerged from this definition:

The interpretation of a coherent course of conduct is 'subjectively adequate' (or 'adequate on the level of meaning'), in so far as, according to our habitual modes of thought and feeling, its component parts taken in their mutual relation are recognized to constitute a 'typical' complex of meaning . . . The interpretation of a sequence of events will on the other hand be called *causally* adequate in so far as, according to established generalizations from experience, there is a probability that it will always actually occur in the same way . . . Thus causal explanation depends on being able to determine that there is a probability, which . . . as always in some sense calculable, that a given observable event . . . will be followed or accompanied by another event. (8E, pp. 11–12)

The aim of Weber's sociology is to link subjective and causal adequacy together, in order to achieve 'interpretive' *and* 'explanatory' statements, which could be given more precision though statements of probability:

Statistical uniformities constitute understandable types of action, and thus constitute sociological generalizations, only when they can be regarded as manifes-tations of the understandable subjective meaning of a course of social action. Conversely, formulations of a rational course of subjectively understandable action constitute sociological types of empirical processes only when they can be empirically observed with a significant degree of approximation. (8E, p. 12)

Already we can see the object domain of Weber's 'interpretive sociology' being limited to 'social action'. The primary agent of 'action' is always for Weber the individual person. 'Action in the sense of subjectively under-standable orientation of behavior exists only as the behavior of one or more *individual* human beings' (8E, p. 13). If it is useful and necessary for other cognitive purposes to proceed from other objects of investigation, in the case of interpretive sociology, even in the investigation of 'social collectivities', such as the 'state', an 'association' or 'business corporation', it is a specifically different matter: 'But for the subjective interpretation of action in sociological work these collectivities must be treated as *solely* the resultants and modes of organization of the particular acts of individual persons, since these alone can be treated as agents in a course of subjectively understandable action' (8E, p. 13).

Through this sharp dissociation both from anything to do with collective concepts, as well as from purely functionalistic disciplines which ignore the meaning attributed by actors, Weber described the task of his sociology:

In the case of social collectivities . . . we are in a position to go beyond merely demonstrating functional relationships and uniformities. We can accomplish something which is never attainable in the natural sciences, namely the subjective understanding of the action of the component individuals . . . This additional achievement of explanation by interpretive understanding, as distinguished from external observation, is of course attained only at a price – the more hypothetical and fragmentary character of its results. Nevertheless, subjective understanding is the specific characteristic of sociological knowledge. (8E, p. 15)

In these decisionistic and apodictic approaches, Weber attempted a dissociation from other scientific disciplines such as research into animal behaviour, psychology and history. Central to this is his methodological concept of *ideal type*, which we shall look into in the next section.[7]

In his excursion into 'social action', Weber defined this concept more closely and distinguished it from other forms of action such as symmetrical action, action influenced by others, mass-conditioned action and imitative action, and he emphasized the 'fluidity' of the transitions and differences. Beyond the definition he had already given, Weber emphasized the *historical dimension* of this category, when he wrote: 'Social action, which includes both failure to act and passive acquiescence, may be oriented to the past, present or expected future behavior of others' (8E, p. 22). Weber's sociology is in no way *only* about 'social action', but it forms 'its central subject matter, that which may be said to be decisive for its status as a science' (8E, p. 24).

Thus Weber elaborated on the foundations of his initial definition of sociology, and proceeded further with the systematic context of his categories. Here he introduces his ideal-typical division of social action into four sections, which emerged from the typically possible *orientations* of social action. Accordingly social action can be determined as

1 *instrumentally* rational [*zweckrational*] that is determined by expectations as to the behavior of objects in the environment and of other human beings; these expectations are used as 'conditions' or 'means' for the attainment of the actor's own rationally pursued and calculated tools;
2 *value-rational* [*wertrational*] that is determined by a conscious belief in the value for its own sake of some . . . form of behavior, independently of its prospects of success;
3 *affectual* (especially emotional), that is, determined by the actor's specific affects and feeling states;
4 *traditional*, that is, determined by ingrained habituation. (8E, pp. 24–5)

With this typology of the possible orientations of social action, Weber wanted neither to undertake a classification which is 'meant to exhaust the possibilities of the field', nor to assume that there might be concrete social action which would correspond only to one or another type. He described an absolute instrumental rationality as above all 'a limiting case' (8E, p. 26).

In the two paragraphs we have discussed already, Weber presented this definition of sociology (paragraph 1) and a typology of the orientations of social action (paragraph 2); in the following fifteen paragraphs he introduces the conceptual systematics of his sociology. In paragraph 3 he introduced the category of 'social relationship'. 'The term "social relationship" will be used to denote the behavior of a plurality of actors in so far as, in its meaningful content, the action of each takes account of that of the others and is oriented in these terms' (8E, p. 26). Here *Weber the specialist sociologist* becomes clearly recognizable, at any rate from today's viewpoint. The category of 'social relationship' means action related one to another, independently of whether it is action of 'solidarity' or not. As the *contents* of such relations Weber gave as examples conflict, hostility, sexual attraction, friendship, piety, economic exchange and competition. As his conception of sociology is oriented to subjective *meaning*, Weber emphasized that the category of 'social relationship' means that 'the subjective meaning need not necessarily be the same for all the parties who are mutually oriented in a given social relationship; there need not in this sense be "reciprocity"' (8E, p. 27).

Emphasizing the varying degrees of permanence of social relationships,

Weber once again underlined the *constructedness* of this category. 'Thus that a "friendship" or a "state" exists or has existed means this and only this: that we, the observers, judge that there is or has been a probability (*Chance*) that on the basis of certain kinds of known subjective attitude of certain individuals there will result in the average sense a certain specific type of action' (8E, p. 28).

Although the subjective meaning of social relationships can change, uniformities can nevertheless be observed, i.e. 'courses of action that are repeated by the actor or . . . occur among numerous actors since the subjective meaning is meant to be the same' (8E, p. 29). Weber differentiated such types as 'usage' (*Brauch*) – which includes 'fashion' (*Mode*) – and 'custom' (*Sitte*) which he distinguished from 'convention' (*Konvention*) and 'law' (*Recht*).[8]

In paragraph 5 Weber concluded the 'framework' of his sociology by introducing 'legitimate order'. This is Weber's own categorization: 'Action, especially social action which involves a social relationship, may be guided by the belief in the existence of a legitimate order. The probability that action will actually be so governed will be called the "validity" [*Geltung*] of the order in question' (8E, p. 3). Weber then discussed 'order', 'if the conduct is, approximately or on the average, oriented toward determinable "maxims"' (8E, p. 31). The 'validity' of such an order occurs when these 'maxims' – which are certainly comparable with today's sociological understanding of 'norms' – '[are] in some appreciable way regarded by the actor as in some way obligatory or exemplary for him' (8E, p. 31). The 'orientation' to such an 'order' in no way exclusively means 'conformity'. 'Even in the case of evasion or disobedience, the probability of their being recognized as valid norms may have an effect on action. A thief orients his action to the validity of the criminal law in that he acts surreptitiously. The fact that the order is recognized as valid within his society is made evident by the fact that he cannot violate it openly without punishment' (8E, p. 32).

Of an order which is valid purely in its actuality – in the sense of its *conformity* – based on purely 'instrumental' motives Weber said that these are far less convincing than an orientation of acting individuals which results from their *belief* in the order's 'legitimacy'. Such a legitimacy can be *ascribed* to an order for four – ideal-typical – reasons:

(a) *tradition*: valid is that which has always been;
(b) *affectual*, especially emotional, *faith*: valid is that which is newly revealed or exemplary;

(c)   *value-rational faith*: valid is that which has been deduced as an absolute;

(d)   positive enactment which is believed to be *legal*. (8E, p. 36)

Weber distinguished between two kinds of order: 'convention' the validity of which is guaranteed by the probability of social 'disapproval', and 'law' which is guaranteed by 'the probability that physical or psychological coercion will be applied by a staff of people' (8E, p. 34).[9] Added to these 'external' guarantees can be 'internal' ones, in particular by the *ethical* safeguarding of norms.[10]

In the concepts of 'social action', 'social relationship' and '(legitimate) order', we have set out the three most important 'building blocks' and their internal relationships to Weber's sociology. This relationship can be illustrated as shown in figure 2.

These sketches should make it clear how the three concepts *can* relate to one another; these schemata do not do justice to the complexity of Weber's approach. For example they lack Weber's emphasis on the *historical dimension*, both in the 'social relationship' and in the 'legitimate order', which can lead to an 'unsimultaneity' of 'social action'. Moreover it is not shown that each mutual orientation can have very *different contents* and ultimately opposing motives – for example a mixture of sympathy and antipathy.

The remaining ten paragraphs of the 'Basic Sociological Terms' deal on the one hand with different mouldings of *social relationships*: para. 8: 'Conflict, Competition, Selection', para. 9: 'Communal and Associative Relationships', para. 10: 'Open and Closed Relationships', para. 16: 'Power and Domination'; and on the other hand with their different *forms of organization*: para. 12: 'The Organization', para. 14: 'Administrative and Regulative Order', para. 15: 'Enterprise, Formal Organization, Voluntary and Compulsory Association', para. 17: 'Political and Hierocratic Organizations'.

Since our aim was merely to sketch the *centrally* important concepts of Weber's 'General Sociology', we must leave out these definitions and concepts. In any case we shall come across some of them in the following sections on Weber's 'economic sociology' and his 'sociology of domination'.

Economic sociology

If one looks at Weber's economic sociology on the textual basis of part I of *Economy and Society*, as we intend to do here, the relationship with his 'General Sociology' which we have just dealt with becomes strikingly clear.

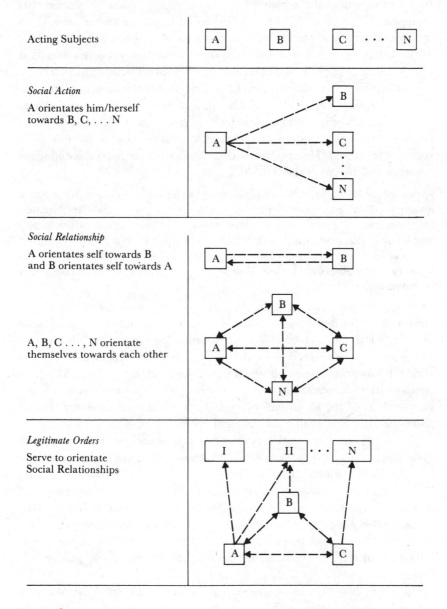

Acting Subjects A B C · · · N

Social Action

A orientates him/herself
towards B, C, . . . N

Social Relationship

A orientates self towards B
and B orientates self towards A

A, B, C . . . , N orientate
themselves towards each other

Legitimate Orders

Serve to orientate
Social Relationships

Figure 2

In his explanation of the concept of 'social action' Weber indicated that economic action does not have to be social action from the outset; an individual's economic action only becomes social action 'if it takes account of the behavior of someone else . . . in so far as the actor assumes that others will respect his actual control over economic goods' (8E, p. 22).

Thus in chapter II, 'Sociological Categories of Economic Action', Weber did not intend to propound some 'economic theory', but 'it consists only in an attempt to define certain concepts which are frequently used and to analyze certain of the simplest sociological relationships in the economic sphere' (8E, p. 63). He made immediate links with his general sociological concepts when he gave this definition:

Action will be said to be 'economically oriented' so far as, according to its subjective meaning, it is concerned with the satisfaction of a desire for 'utilities' (*Nutzleistungen*). 'Economic action' (*Wirtschaften*) is a peaceful use of the actor's control over resources, which is rationally oriented, by deliberate planning, to economic ends. An 'economy' (*Wirtschaft*) is autocephalous economic action. An 'economic establishment' (*Wirtschaftsbetrieb*) is an organized system of continuous economic action. (8E, p. 63)

In his detailed explanations, Weber once again made it clear that according to his definition, a *sociological* view of the economic field must proceed from the fact 'that all "economic" processes and objects are characterized as such entirely by the *meaning* they have for human action in such roles as ends, means, obstacles, and by-products' (8E, p. 64). In a similar way to his sociology of law, Weber constantly presented the inter-relationships of the social sectors, here between economics and politics[11] and between the economy and the legal order.[12]

This sociological orientation is clear too in his conceptual determination of 'utilities', which Weber defined as 'advantages (*Chancen*) or opportunities for present or future use . . . by one or more economically acting individuals [whose] action . . . is oriented to the estimated importance of such utilities as means for the ends of their economic action' (8E, p. 68). Weber called material utilities 'goods' and human ones 'services'. Their advantages in disposal he called 'economic advantages', which are determined by custom, interest and by the traditionally or legally guaranteed order.

Up until now the recognizable similarity in structure of Weber's concepts of economic sociology with the structure of his 'General Sociology', is continued when Weber addressed the ideal-typical possibilities of the orientation of economic action. He distinguished between a *traditional* and a *goal-oriented* economic orientation (8E, p. 69), in which for him the rational even dominates the managerial action. Only the pervasive transcendence of the traditionalistic determinations of economic action enabled 'the further development to the specifically modern type of capitalistic economy' (8E, p. 71)

Exchange as *an*, if not one of the most important, economic media, was defined by Weber as 'a compromise of interests on the part of the parties in the course of which goods or other advantages are passed as reciprocal compensation' (8E, p. 72). Once again Weber distinguished between traditionally and rationally oriented forms of exchange. As 'means of exchange' Weber differentiated two forms of 'means of payment': 'chartal' i.e. artificially created means of exchange, like *money*, and 'natural' means (8E, p. 76).

By way of a subtle analysis of different forms of money and credit, Weber reached the concept of the 'market situation' as the entirety of *recognizable* exchange opportunities in the competitive price struggle,[13] by which he means predominantly *monetary exchange*. For him, money was 'the most "perfect" means of economic calculation. That is, it is formally the most rational means of orienting economic activity' (8E, p. 86). Thus *calculation* in terms of money and not its actual *use* is 'the specific means of rational, economic provision'.

If we distinguish between budgetary management and profit-making as two typical forms of economic action, Weber defined *profit-making* as an 'activity which is oriented to opportunities for seeking new powers of control over goods' (8E, p. 90). Weber added to this rational economic profit-making a particular form of monetary calculation: 'capital accounting'. This is

the valuation and verification of opportunities for profit and of the success of profit-making activity by means of a valuation of the total assets . . . of the enterprise at the beginning of a profit-making venture, and the comparison of this with a similar valuation of the assets still present and newly acquired, at the end of the process. (8E, p. 91)

The orientation of capital accounting towards *profitability*, i.e. towards expectations of prices which are formed by the conflict and compromise of interests contains an important societal premise for the sociologist: 'Capital accounting in its formally most rational shape . . . presupposes the *battle of man with man*' (8E, p. 93). For Weber the concept of '*the power of capital*' which is important in this context is that

the possessors of control over the means of production and over economic advantages which can be used as capital *goods* in a profit-making enterprise enjoy, by virtue of this control and of the orientation of economic action to the principles of capitalistic business calculation, a specific position of power in relation to others. (8E, p. 95)

Linked to capital accounting and economic 'position of power' is also the formation of *capital interest*, which Weber looked at in detail.[14]

The stressed 'formal rationality' of monetary calculation is linked in Weber's presentation to two specific 'material' conditions:

1 Market struggle of economic units which are . . . autonomous. Money prices are the product of conflicts of interest and of compromises; they thus result from power constellations. Money is not a mere 'voucher for unspecified utilities', which could be altered at will without any fundamental effect on the character of the price system as a struggle of man against man. 'Money' is, rather, primarily a weapon in this struggle, and prices are expressions of the struggle; they are instruments of calculation only as estimated quantifications of relative chances in this struggle of interests.

2 Strict capital accounting is further associated with the social phenomena of 'shop discipline' and appropriation of the means of production, and that means: with the existence of a 'system of domination' (*Herrschaftsverhältnis*). (8E, p. 108)

In order to be able to present the sociological side of the economy, Weber turned to the modes of 'division and organization of human services in the interest of production' (8E, p. 114) where he distinguished between two – managerial services, and services oriented to the instructions of a managerial agency, which he calls 'labour'. He differentiated each according to the technical and social side of service and labour.[15] It is of considerable sociological importance to investigate how the relations of appropriation, i.e. the relations of domination, are each constituted,[16] and here Weber discussed in detail the appropriation (*Expropriation*) of the workers.[17]

Stylistically extremely blunt, Weber's 'Principal Forms of Appropriation and of Market Relationship' (8E, pp. 144–50) undertook not only to present the different organizational forms, but also to sketch universally-historically and schematically the development of capitalism. He came to the conclusion – as we have already discovered from previous works – that the development of the 'free handicraft organization' had its classical formation as the dominant type in the Western Middle Ages. However, this development, which took place exclusively in the Occident, 'cannot be explained entirely in purely economic terms', according to Weber (8E, p. 150).

In order to obtain the best circumstances for calculating the performance of 'labor engaged in carrying out specifications', Weber cited three essential premises: '(a) The optimum of aptitude for the function; (b) the optimum of skill acquired through practice; (c) the optimum of inclination for the work' (8E, p. 150). Similarly Weber names eight reasons for obtaining a maximum of 'formal rationality' of capital acounting in production enterprises:

1 Market freedom,
2 Freedom of management,
3 Free labour, freedom of the labour market and freedom in the selection of workers,
4 Substantive freedom of contract,
5 Mechanically rational technology,
6 Formally rational administration and law,
7 Division between enterprise and household,
8 Formally rational order of the monetary system. (See 8E, p. 161-2)

Weber was looking in particular at the modern capitalistic economy, and dealing extensively in this context with the functional relationships between the *modern state* and the *nature of money*. [18] In conclusion Weber returned once again to his sociological determination of economic action, saying of the 'motives' of this particular form of action

All economic activity in a market economy is undertaken and carried through by individuals acting to provide for their own ideal or material interests . . . In a market economy the striving for *income* is necessarily the ultimate driving force of all economic activity. (8E, pp. 202-3)

Sociology of domination

In our presentation of the basic concepts and main arguments of Weber's economic sociology it became clear how much Weber oriented himself to the structure of argument in his 'General Sociology'. Even in his sociology of domination he talks about a *special form of social action and social relationships*. [19] Here it is a question of those social relationships in which an individual or group imposes their will *upon* another individual of a group and in such a way that the partners in this action 'obey' this will. The fact, verifiable throughout human history, that all conceivable qualities of one or several people and all conceivable constellations put someone in a position to impose his/her will in a given situation, was Weber's concern and so he formulated these questions:

Which *personal qualities* in he, she or they that give the orders and he, she or they that obey orders make such a social relationship possible?

Which historical, cultural, political, social and economic *preconditions* facilitate or hinder such a social relationship?

What *consequences* has such a social relationship on the different levels of social reality?

In order to approach these questions conceptually, Weber developed a three-pronged system: power–domination–discipline.

A. 'Power' (*Macht*) is the probability that one actor within a social relationship will be in a position to carry out his own will despite resistance, regardless of the basis on which this probability rests.

B. 'Domination' (*Herrschaft*) is the probability that a command with a given specific content will be obeyed by a given group of persons. 'Discipline' is the probability that by virtue of habituation a command will receive prompt and automatic obedience in stereotyped forms, on the part of a given group of persons. (8E, p. 53)

We can reach no final verdict on the inter-relationship of the three concepts, and particularly on whether Weber actually accepted a three-pronged conceptual system as well as an equality of importance among the definitions. The fact is that Weber only briefly dealt with the two concepts of 'power' and 'discipline',[20] against which he was concerned with the phenomenon of 'domination' scientifically and in practical politics during his whole life. The main reason was that 'domination' represented a category which was considerably fruitful in sociology – because of the (relative) reciprocity of the social relationship: the desire to dominate on the one hand and the desire to obey on the other. In this sense 'domination' is the result of a sociologically more precise definition of 'power'.

In the third chapter of the 'Conceptual Exposition' Weber attempted under the title 'The Types of Legitimate Domination' to differentiate analytically and make more precise the conceptual field of 'domination'. Linked to the purely defining form of the 'Basic Sociological Terms', Weber emphasised that the motives for obedience in the fact of domination can cover a wide spectrum that reaches from 'simple habituation' to a purely rational calculation of advantage. However, common to all forms is that 'a minimum of voluntary compliance, that is, an *interest* (based on ulterior motives or genuine acceptance) in obedience' belongs to every 'genuine' relationship of domination (8E, p. 212).

This internal structure presents a more precise version of Weber's position in the 'Basic Sociological Terms', which however is tantamount to a restriction. Obviously this became necessary in the face of his self-created task: Weber's problem in assembling his categories was continually his effort to find a distinction between the *forms* of certain social relationships and their *contents* without tying himself down totally to one or the other component through his methodology. His starting point – exemplified here in the category of 'domination' – is the following methodological postulate.

It should be self-evident that the sociologist is guided exclusively by the factual existence of such a power of command, in contrast to the lawyer's interest in the theoretical content of a legal norm. As far as sociology is concerned, power of command does not exist unless the authority which is claimed by somebody is actually heeded to a socially relevant degree. (8E, p. 948)

We can see here positions which oppose those of normative dogmatism and thus it emerges that according to Weber, every actual compliance with orders would have to be designated as 'domination'. By contrast however, Weber is convinced that 'the merely external fact of the order being obeyed' (8E, p. 946) was *not* enough to grasp the different variations in the causal chain from an order to its being carried out. To elucidate this causal chain 'purely psychologically', Weber named two 'principal types of influence of one person over another', 'empathy' and 'inspiration' (8E, p. 946; see also 8E, pp. 321–2). However, such distinctions, for a type-formation of domination which should be investigated as a *sociological* phenomenon, were in Weber's view 'not decisive' (8E, p. 214).

To safeguard his chances of implementation, the person who possesses domination 'normally', according to Weber, needs an *administrative staff* whose connection to the dominator can vary according to the type of social action. Purely material, instrumental motives for the link between chief and administrative staff effect merely a relatively unstable situation of domination. Because of this, 'normally' and in particular in 'exceptional' cases, affectual or ideal [*wertrational*] motives come into play. But even the linkage of material and instrumental motives with affectual and ideal motives still does not form a 'reliable' basis for domination: 'In addition there is normally a further element, the belief in *legitimacy*' (8E, p. 213).

Experience shows that in no instance does domination voluntarily limit itself to the appeal to material or affectual or ideal motives as a basis for its continuance. In addition every such system attempts to establish and to cultivate the belief in its legitimacy. But according to the kind of legitimacy which is claimed, the type of obedience, the kind of administrative staff developed to guarantee it, and the mode of exercising authority, will all differ fundamentally. Equally fundamental is the variation in effect. Hence, it is useful to classify the types of domination according to the kind of claim to legitimacy made by each. (8E, p. 213)

Here too we can see the similarity of structure in the argumentation of Weber's sociology of domination with his 'General Sociology': 'domination' appears as a particular form of social action and social relationships. A typology of different forms of domination results from different *orientations* of this action and these relationships towards different legitimate orders. Thus his three 'pure' types of *legitimate* domination are distinguished purely and simply by their respective claims to legitimacy. These may be based on

1 *Rational* grounds resting on a belief in the legality of enacted rules and the right of those elevated to authority under such rules to issue commands (legal authority).
2 *Traditional* grounds resting on an established belief in the sanctity of immemorial traditions and the legitimacy of those exercising authority under them (traditional authority); or finally,
3 *Charismatic* grounds resting on devotion to the exceptional sanctity, heroism or exemplary character of an individual person, and of the normative patterns or order revealed or ordained by him (charismatic authority).

In the case of legal authority, obedience is owed to the legally established impersonal order. It extends to the persons exercising the authority of office under it by virtue of the formal legality of their commands and only within the scope of authority of the office. In the case of traditional authority, obedience is owed to the *person* of the chief who occupies the traditionally sanctioned position of authority and who is (within its sphere) bound by tradition. But here the obligation of obedience is a matter of personal loyalty within the area of accustomed obligations. In the case of charismatic authority, it is the charismatically qualified leader as such who is obeyed by virtue of personal trust in his revelation, his heroism or his exemplary qualities so far as they fall within the scope of the individual's belief in his charisma. (8E, pp. 215–16)

We must point out that this 'legitimacy' of form of domination – like the 'validity' of an order – was determined by Weber merely as 'the probability (*Chance*) that to a relevant degree the appropriate attitudes will exist, and the corresponding practical conduct ensue' (8E, p. 214). It is moreover very important that Weber extended considerably the forms of appearance and the effects of 'determination . . . by virtue of domination'. Weber equally included phenomena in the cultural sphere like forms of speech and of written language in this context (8E, p. 215)

After sketching the basic concepts, Weber dealt with the three types of domination in detail in the following sections, investigating:

The valid *ideas of the character of domination* on the side of the dominating *and* of the dominated.

The *structure* and *rules of conduct* of the *administrative staff*.
The *personnel* and the *recruiting mechanisms* of the *administrative staff*.
The *relationship* of domination to the *law*.
The *relationship* of domination to the *economy*.

Alongside his treatment of the type of charismatic domination, Weber developed his thesis of the 'routinization of charisma' the main points of which can be summarized thus: if the social relationship of 'charismatic domination' between the possessor of domination ('charismatic leader') plus his/her administrative staff and those subject to domination lasts for a length of time longer than a moment, then the character of this social relationship is changed essentially.

The possible directions of this change were for Weber either a process of traditionalization or of legalization ('rationalization') in the social relationships.

As possible causes for such changes, Weber listed

The ideal and also the material interests of the *followers* in the continuation and the continual reactivation of the community;
The still stronger ideal and also stronger material interests of the *members of the administrative staff* in continuing their relationship of domination, and not only this but continuing it in such a way that both from an ideal and a material point of view, their own position is put on a stable *everyday basis*;
The removal of charisma's '*anti-economic character*', i.e. it now participates in fiscal forms of finance to satisfy needs – and thus in economic conditions concerning tax and duties. (cf. 8E, p. 246)

A possible immediate *cause* for these changes might be the disappearance of the personal charismatic leader and the resulting *problem of succession* and Weber discussed six typical possibilities of solution (cf. 8E, pp. 246–7) in which the two conceptions of an 'hereditary charisma' and a 'charisma of office' are of particular importance. When the charismatic leader disappears, the interests of the administrative staff – the ideal and to a greater extent the material interests which we have already looked at – are mobilized with greater strength. 'The great majority of disciples and followers will in the long run "make their living" out of their "calling" in a material sense as well. Indeed, this must be the case if the movement is not to disintegrate' (8E, p. 249).

This striving ideally and materially to secure the administrative staff leads to the exact regulation of the *recruiting* of the administrative staff and of the *opportunities of earning* of its members. In this new regulating of recruitment Weber dealt with several possibilities of which only the establishment of educational and testing norms can be identified as leading easily to the entrenchment of traditional *status-group*, and thus 'hereditary charismatic' structures. To regulate the possibilities of earning of the administrative staff in the course of this routinization, Weber distinguished between the possibilities of solving this problem of the prebends, the administrative offices and the fiefs. Common to all three forms is that they all help to get rid of the once constitutive 'anti-economic character') of charisma and aid participation in fiscal forms of finance to satisfy needs, to which end economic conditions are created which include taxation.

Alongside this economic 'routinization', Weber documented a further development, which he considered to be of at least equal importance, namely the transition from purely charismatic administrative staffs and the corresponding principles of administration to an 'everyday' one, i.e. traditional or legal ('rational'). Weber characterized this – unavoidable – development as 'the most fundamental problem' (8E, p. 253) more important than the problem of succession or at least independent of the solution to this problem.

To summarize, Weber named the three central causes in the process of routinizing charisma:

The striving for security, i.e. for the legitimization of the social 'positions of authority' and of the economic advantages enjoyed by the followers and sympathizers of the charismatic leader;

The – for Weber – 'objective' necessity of adapting the order and the staff organization to the normal, everyday needs and conditions of carrying on administration, particularly in cases of judicial decision;

The necessity and unavoidability of the administrative staff and all its 'administrative practices' being adapted to everyday economic conditions.

In an equally exhaustive manner, Weber was concerned with what he regarded as an historically important form of domination – *feudalism* – which must be distinguished both from traditional patrimonialism as well as from the forms of charismatic domination. Both the form of *feudalism based on fiefs* as well as *feudalism based on benefices* had considerable political influence (the struggle of the enfieffed administrative staff with the feudal lord), social influence (the foundation of distinctions on the basis of status group) and economic influence (the possession of land).

From section 7 onwards, Weber's sociology of domination could be headed 'Types of Democracy'. Precisely because it was *not* Weber's intention to 'exhaust' (8E, p. 216) the *historical* reality in his conceptual schema, but rather through them to investigate historically *mixed situations* and *processes of transformation*, he turned once again to 'The Transformation of Charisma in a Democratic Direction' (*Herrschaftsfremde Umdeutung des Charisma*) (8E, pp. 266–71) as a point of departure. If the charismatic legitimation principle was – 'basically' – subject to an authoritarian interpretation, it could in the course of historical development equally be subject to an anti-authoritarian interpretation,

for the validity of charismatic authority rests entirely on recognition by the ruled . . . But when the charismatic organization undergoes progressive rationalization, it is readily possible that, instead of recognition being treated as a consequence of legitimacy, it is treated as the basis of legitimacy: *democratic legitimacy* . . . The personally legitimated charismatic leader becomes leader by the grace of those who follow him since the latter are formally free to elect and even depose him . . . Now he is the freely elected leader. (8E, pp. 266–7)

Proceeding from these basic ideas, Weber investigated the different stages of historical development in the evolution of *democratic* forms of domination, dealing in particular with two series of types: the types of 'plebiscitary leadership' and the types of leaderless democracy which are 'characterized by the attempt to minimize the domination of man over man' (8E, p. 269). In the same context Weber gave detailed determinations of the different forms of the means to *limit domination*, i.e. collegiality and the division of powers. [21]

Here Weber returned to discuss the development of *bureaucracy*, which he had already dealt with extensively within the framework of his presentation of 'Legal Authority with a Bureaucratic Administrative Staff). [22] Appearing in the same context were Weber's discussions of *parties* which he defined as

associations, membership in which rests on formally free recruitment. The end to which its activity is devoted is to secure power within an organization for its leaders in order to attain ideal or material advantages for its active members. (8E, p. 284)

Since, in the system of plebiscitary democracies with political leaders, the parties form a decisive instrument for the conquest of leading positions, Weber, in his classification of different types of 'direct democracies' dealt particularly with different forms of the *representation* of those subject to domination. Weber understood by representation 'that the action of certain members of an organization, the "representatives", is considered binding on the others or accepted by them as legitimate and obligatory' (8E,

p. 292). In his concluding summary we come across an argument which on the one hand connects different categories of Weber's sociology of domination with each other and on the other situates them in an historical context, a context which has been entrusted to us throughout his entire oeuvre:

Genuine parliamentary representation with the voluntaristic play of interests in the political sphere, the resulting plebiscitary party organization with its consequences, and the modern idea of *rational* representation by interest groups, are all peculiar to the Western World. None of these is understandable apart from the peculiar Western development of status groups and classes. Even in the Middle Ages the seeds of these phenomena were present in the Western World, and *only* there. (8E, p. 299)

The last chapter of the 'Conceptual Exposition', on 'Status Groups and Classes'[23] presents a basic sketch of Weber's 'theory of social inequality'. Making an explicit connection with Marx, Weber developed a two-pronged conceptual schema, formed from the two categories of 'class' (*Klasse*) and 'status group' (*Stand*). The main aim of this sketch is to get away from a one-sided judgement of the social position of individuals and groups exclusively from the viewpoint of their material, economic condition (defined as 'class') and to reach at least a two-dimensional standpoint by *joining up* with a view according to which lifestyle and social 'estimation' are also of categorical importance (defined as 'status group').

Sociology of music

Marianne Weber reports that her husband had a plan that 'at some time in the future he was going to write a sociology embracing all the arts'.[24] The only part of this plan that Weber carried out was the *preliminary work* to *The Rational and Social Foundations of Music*, which we shall discuss here shortly. This was probably written between 1910–11, published in 1921 after Weber's death and was printed as an appendix to *Economy and Society* until the fourth edition, when it recently appeared as a separate work once again.[25]

Weber referred to the *conclusions* of this fragment at several points which are important for his entire oeuvre, particularly in the Preliminary Remarks to the *Gesammelte Aufsätze zur Religionssoziologie* (181, p. 2) in his famous lecture 'Science as a Vocation' (*Gesammelte Aufsätze zur Wissenschaftslehre*,

p. 596) and in his essay 'The Meaning of "Ethical Neutrality" in Sociology and Economics' (in 10E, pp. 30–2).

This preliminary work in the sociology of music is above all a *collection of material* with individual questions which are sometimes tackled without an obvious link being made. As a result of its extensive treatment of problems in the theory of music, particularly in the area of harmony, this work was in the main not taken up sociologically. Alphons Silbermann divided the study into twenty-five parts – points of view, themes, considerations – and only writes on point twenty-one (on the development of string instruments). 'From about this point onwards Weber begins to place the emphasis of his train of thought more on the sociological foundations of music than on the rational ones.'[26] After all that we have discussed thus far about all Weber's writings, such a distinction cannot be maintained: the universal historical process of 'rationalization' is one of the central themes of Weber's work and thus of eminent sociological importance. Weber investigated this process in the fields of economics, science, law, domination and religion. He was attracted by the question of how far this process could be detected even in the area of 'culture', precisely because of the alleged 'irrationality' of this area. This hypothesis is the basic theme of his fragments on the sociology of music.

All the assertions which Weber made about harmony in 'ancient' and 'modern' music, about the origin of musical notation and on the development of instrument construction, all tend in the direction of a gradual elimination of the mystical and 'irrational' qualities in art, or rather in the practice of art and its gradual replacement by rational models. Weber pursued this argument comparatively and historically, by looking at the primitive and ancient stages in social development, just as much as the development of the modern era. The main conclusion of this investigation was that the principle of the simple distance between tones was replaced by the 'rational' principle of chordal harmony. Weber interpreted this development as the sign of a rational mentality in Western society.

To support his argument, Weber made reference to the most disparate social developments: the origin of Western monasticism; the domination of feudal structures in the Middle Ages; the participation of women in choral singing; and the influence of language on the development of melody. There are in particular two moments which Weber regarded as responsible for the 'rational' development of Western music, the development of modern *notation* and the development of modern *instruments*. Weber brought a socio-economic approach to the development of instruments – an approach we have encountered throughout his work.

Professional organization secured the musical influence of the bards. This in turn was a basic factor in the continuous improvement and typification of their instruments. These instruments were indispensable for the advancement of music.

Furthermore, technical improvements in the construction of string instruments were connected, towards the end of the Middle Ages, with the musical guild organizations of instrumentalists which in the Sachsenspiegel were still treated as having no legal rights. This guild organization appeared in the thirteenth century, providing a fixed market for the manufactured instruments, helping standardize their types.

Still other social factors are represented in the gradual acceptance of instrumentalists beside the singers in the bands of the hierarchy, of princes and of communities . . . This gave to the production of instruments an even more productive economic foundation . . . In connection with the demands of court orchestras the ascension of string instruments to their perfection began in the sixteenth century . . . The new instruments were soon employed in the orchestra of the operas . . . This is due to the traditional social ranking of the instruments.

Since the lute was a court instrument, the lutenist was inside the pale of society. His salary in the orchestra of Queen Elizabeth was three times as much as that of the violinist, five times as much as that of the bagpipe-player. The organist was considered to be a complete artist.

Only by great efforts did the violinists first manage to gain recognition and only after this . . . did an extensive literature for string instruments begin to develop. (9E, pp. 107ff)

The degree to which Weber linked cultural, economic, social, technical and even climatic factors in his sketch in the sociology of music, becomes most obvious when he comes to discuss the development of the *piano* as the 'specifically modern keyboard instrument'.

[T]he particular sonorous effects of its expressive tone oscillations permitted it [the clavichord] to yield before the hammer piano only when a small stratum of musicians and amateurs with delicate ears no longer decided over the fate of musical instruments, but when situations prevailed and the production of instruments had become capitalistic . . .

Only the internationally famous virtuosity of Mozart and the increasing need of music publishers and of concert managers to satisfy the large music consumption of the mass market brought the final victory of the hammer piano . . . Machine-made mass production of the piano occurred first in England (Broadwood) then in America (Steinway) where first-rate iron could be pressed into construction of the frame. Moreover, iron helped overcome the numerous purely climatic difficulties that could affect adoption of the piano. Incidentally, climatic difficulties also stood in the way of adoption of the piano in the tropics . . . The building of the piano is conditioned by the mass market. It is the peculiar nature of the piano to be a middle-class home instrument . . .

Therefore it is no accident that the representatives of pianistic culture are Nordic peoples, climatically house-bound and home-centered in contrast to the South. In southern Europe the cultivation of middle-class home comforts was restricted by climatic and historical factors. The piano was invented there but did not diffuse quickly as in the North. Nor did it rise to an equivalent position as a significant piece of middle-class furniture. (9E, pp. 118ff)

It would be superfluous to stress the sociological importance of *Economy and Society*. Alongside Weber's works on the sociology of religion, this work belongs to the constitutive international public property of this science, even if its reception was and is in part extremely selective and arbitrary.[27] For all the named 'specialist sociologies' – economic sociology, the sociology of religion, the sociology of law, the sociology of domination, the sociology of music, and even for many subsections within these areas, for example a sociology of bureaucracy, of political parties, and research into stratification and mobility – this great work serves repeatedly as a nursery for the establishment or confirmation of present-day research.

In conclusion we will draw up neither a schematic reproduction of the results nor provide an overall estimation of the work, rather we will refer to a few points which seem crucial.

1 *Economy and Society* is concerned with the *mutual* and *developmental* relations between society, law, religion, economy and domination. This is based on a *socio-economic* approach.

2 Weber attempts to introduce the conceptual category schema which he developed in his 'General Sociology' as the foundation for a sociology based on the *study of experience*. To reduce this sociology to abbreviated formulae like 'interpretive sociology' or 'sociology of social action' does not do justice to the *multifacetedness* of Weber's approach. Certainly he proceeds from the social action of single, acting individuals and the social relations which proceed from that. However he pursues their effects into the areas of *structures* and *orders*. It is here that the focal points of Weber's presentation lie.

3 The general emphasis on the functioning of *ideal* and *material* interests does *not* mean that one can place Weber on the side of a normatively oriented sociology. He attempts to escape the one-sidenesses of purely functionalistic approaches just as much as those of purely 'materialistic' approaches. His theme is the multiple, often contradictory and unintentional effects of the interaction of 'ideal', 'social' and 'material' factors.

4   In *Economy and Society* Weber classifies the sub-categories and lateral communications he is investigating as *component phenomena* in a general historical development of the *rationalization* of life. We come across this thesis in *all* the sub-sections of Weber's work we have discussed – it is not to be drawn from *Economy and Society* alone. During his investigative preoccupation (which equally appears in his entire oeuvre) with the origins and effects of *capitalism*, Weber comes across a general, encroaching development – rationalization. In his investigations into the preconditions and the 'cultural meaning' of this universal–historical phenomena, Weber pursues its manifestations – interculturally and diachronically – in all subsections of society, like economy, politics, law, religion and culture. Rationalization, as the 'fate of our age', was the common formula for those *component processes* which he, in turn, calls bureaucratization, industrialization, capitalist development, specialization, secularization, objectivization, demystification and dehumanization. Weber's research into the 'validity' of his hypotheses led him both into areas of historical reality, for which a rational approach was expected (like technology, science, economy and law), but also (and here we detect his special interests) into areas which would otherwise be perceived as 'irrational' – such as religion, ethics, music, art and culture.

5   These processes of the march of rationalization, which Weber outlined and investigated, are *not* presented by him as *unilinear, regularly behaving developments*. Both his assertion that historical reality can only be described analytically as hybrid relationship of ideal-typical constructions, as well as his repeated emphasis on counteracting developments –for example the 'pendulum movements' of 'ratio' and 'charisma' in the field of domination – should be enough to prevent Weber being cast as a propagandist with a blind enthusiasm for progress. A 'theory of evolution' which would present world history as a continual ascension towards the accomplishment of rational world domination, would be a grotesque *misunderstanding* of Weber's work. It was precisely the incredible, the 'haphazard' in this process which he called rationalization, and at the same time its constant disruption by 'non-rational' developments which fascinated Weber all his life and which made him move his questioning constantly into fresh areas.

6   In working out his thesis of the rationalization of life, there were four questions in particular which always remained essentially the same:

Why was it only the West which had a specifically 'rational' culture with universal–historical significance?

Why was it only in modern Western Europe that a 'rational' science and technology, a 'rational' industrial capitalism, and a 'rational' bureaucratic state organization developed?

Why was there no similar process of 'rationalization' in the world outside Europe, particularly in Asia, where far older and more differentiated cultures existed?

What advantages did this 'rationalization' bring to each society and to groups within it, and what price was demanded from the society, from social groups and from single individuals for this development?

It becomes particularly clear from Weber's answers to the last question that the insinuation that he was presenting the development of rationalization merely as something extremely positive and worth fighting for, thus presenting an 'apologia for the bourgeois age', misunderstands his deep *scepticism* and his fears for the effects of this development. His own excursions into the possible *irrationality* of these processes of rationalization, which bring with them, alongside an increase in productivity, a wide-reaching *dehumanization*, place Weber above the accusation that he had become an apologist for such developments.

6

Methodological writings

In the Introduction to this book we indicated that a separation of 'content' and 'method' would misrepresent Weber's project. However, if we speak of Weber's methodology today, we mean for the most part those methodological observations which originally appeared separately in periodicals and which were published posthumously in 1922 by Marianne Weber under the title *Gesammelte Aufsätze zur Wissenschaftslehre* (*Collected Essays on Scientific Methodology*). We must realize that these collected texts consisted of casual projects and commissioned work, which for the most part remained fragmentary.

The condition of this source material is in part reasonable for the controversy that divides previous interpretations into two camps; one promotes unity in Weber's scientific doctrine,[1] the other argues for diversity.[2] Both positions were able to put forward good arguments. Doubtless Weber's methodological position itself was defined in the course of decades of research, which for him always took top priority, and as a result his own changes in position must be discussed. On the other hand, many cogent arguments can be settled without necessarily reducing the consequent discussion to one, uniform scientific doctrine.

Moreover, we must realize that Weber's own works on the methodology of the social sciences are connected very closely to their historical background. One set of texts were critical discussions of other contemporary authors,[3] and thus a comprehensive understanding is impossible without knowledge of the writings under discussion. Equally all these contemporary debates and controversies took place within a philosophical context handed down by tradition and amid current social changes, particularly in the contemporary politics of the sciences. The formation and gradual institutionalization of the social sciences – sociology among others – provides an important backdrop to Weber's methodological project. In this condensed sketch of Weber's statements on sociological method, we can only include the historical background in an incomplete form. Equally we will not have the space to discuss both the continuities *and* the breaks in Weber's sketches.

Weber's work was organized in a way which befitted an important theorist in the methodology of modern sociology, thanks basically to three methodological concepts which we shall discuss below. These are:

1 The concept of *Verstehen*, or 'understanding'.
2 The concept of the 'ideal-type'.
3 The postulate of 'freedom from value-judgement' (*Werturteilsfreiheit*).

The concept of *Verstehen* or 'understanding'

Seen from the perspective of today's scientific sociology, the formation of 'interpretive sociology' (*verstehende Soziologie*) appears as an extremely important development which has had wide-reaching effects up to the present day. If we look back at the previous different manifestations and stages of this development, it is possible to recognize the division (albeit relatively arbitrary) of all existing sociological theories into three tendencies – interpretive, functionalist and reductionist.[4] A similar analytical structure is thus made possible for the contents of all research areas in sociology: for action theory and systems theory as well as for all 'intermediary' concepts as, for example, role theory, reference group theory and theories of institutionalization.

It is remarkable that after a lengthy period of relative insignificance in the face of functionalist approaches, the interpretive orientation has at the present time regained considerable international importance. Trends like symbolic interactionism, ethnomethodology, ethnosociology, phenomenology, etc., have recaptured an important role in international sociological discourse.[5] And as part of this, the persistent references to Weber, albeit frequently critical, are noticeable even when his work generally only constitutes their historical point of departure.[6]

In view of today's extremely wide-reaching scientific and theoretical discussion, above all on the relationship between 'understanding' (*Verstehen*) and 'explanation' (*Erklären*), it becomes particularly necessary to comprehend Weber's original position. It is here in particular that clichés and misunderstandings have taken root; for one thing they attempt to tie Weber down exclusively to the interpretive method by presenting him as the 'father of interpretive sociology', and for another they misconstrue 'interpretation' as a method which involves empathy or intuition, both somewhat vague and arbitrary qualities.

In our presentation of Weber's position, we will refer to his later texts (1913–19), in particular to the 'Conceptual Exposition' and the 'Basic Concepts in Sociology' in *Economy and Society*, in spite of the fact that he had already tackled the problem of the interpretive approach much earlier.[7]

In our previous discussion of his 'General Sociology'[8] we were proceeding from Weber's definition of empirical sociology, according to which it is the science 'concerning itself with the interpretive understanding of social action and thereby with a causal explanation of its course and consequences'. The interpretive understanding of 'social action' as the object domain of Weber's sociology leads to an investigation into the determining effects of *meaning*. Weber defines his interpretive sociology as an empirical sociology of the understanding of meaning (*Sinn-Verstehen*). Its methodological procedure cannot be separated from a causal analytical procedure. Moreover Weber makes explicit an internal connection between the two heuristic strategies. It is precisely this relationship which, according to Weber, establishes the character of sociology as a discipline orientated towards reality.

Thus as we have already explained, 'meaning' is not intended as some pre-formed ideality but as one real, determining factor in human action. At this point the central premise of every interpretive approach emerges: the actor attaches a 'meaning' to his or her action and this 'meaning' acts at the very least as a contributory determinant to the action. Thus any scientific attempt to analyse human action requires the inclusion of meaning in an *explanation* of social phenomena.

From this basis Weber distinguishes terminologically between 'direct observational understanding' (*aktuelles Verstehen*) and 'explanatory understanding' (*Motivationsverstehen*).

Accordingly 'direct observational understanding' is

'direct rational understanding of ideas';
'direct observational understanding of irrational emotional reactions'; and
'rational observational understanding of actions'. (See 8E, pp. 8–9.)

Motivational or 'explanatory understanding' similarly enquires into the symbolic quality of observable action, but goes one stage further by aiming beyond the understanding of the intended meaning towards an explanation of the manifest action. This is achieved by situating the action within a 'context', i.e. 'rational understanding of motivation, which consists in placing the act in an intelligible and more inclusive context of meaning' (8E, p. 8). Weber arrives at his definition of 'explanation': 'Thus for a science which is concerned with the subjective meaning of action, explanation [*Erklären*] requires a grasp of the complex of meanings in which an actual course of understandable action thus interpreted belongs' (8E, p. 9).

The introduction of the concept of a 'context of meaning' sheds light on that problematic which has frequently led to misunderstandings. Weber proceeds from the 'subjective' meaning of individual actors, but the relativizing formula of the subjectively 'intended' meaning makes it clear that Weber recognizes that this meaning does not have to be the meaning which *actually* determines the relevant action, and that the individual does not have to be *conscious* of his/her 'real', *actually* effective motives for his/her action.

The differentiation we have discussed above between different method-ological ways of grasping meaning[9] made it clear that Weber tends particularly towards conceptually constructed, pure types ('ideal types') of different meanings. Just as Weber, in his 'general sociology' had reached the category of '(legitimate) order', from the individual acting subjects via the concepts of 'social action' and 'social relations'[10] he moves up from the construct of a 'subjectively intended meaning' to socially mediated 'contexts of meaning'. Lurking within these are all *intersubjectively* compulsory (i.e. according to his definition) 'valid' measures of meaning and value within a society, measures towards which individual actors and social groups are oriented. In other words even the (supposedly) subjective meaning is a *social* meaning, i.e. a meaning which is reciprocal, and oriented towards and mediated by order. 'Action which is specifically important for interpretive sociology is behaviour which

1   in terms of the subjectively intended meaning of the actor refers to the *behaviour of others*.
2   is in its course *in part determined* by this meaningful reference, and thus
3   can be *explained* by the interpretation of this (subjectively) intended meaning. (213b, p. 429)

Even if this position were not formulated unambiguously in the 'Basic Concepts in Sociology', it can still be seen in Weber's entire material work. His investigations into the social order of Antiquity or those on the sociology of religion leave no doubt that the concept of socially constructed meaning is one of Weber's basic conceptions. Weber is always concerned to present meaning as being *communicable*. However, communicability is always already social and intersubjective and is expressed in changeable, symbolic forms.

To summarize, we can distinguish three variations on the interpretation of the concept of meaning in Weber's work, all of which can be grasped by the method of *Verstehen*:

1 Meaning as *cultural significance*, i.e. as 'objectified' meaning in a 'world of meanings'.
2 Meaning as *subjectively intended meaning* which is intersubjectively comprehensible and communicable.
3 Meaning as *functional meaning* which is influenced by objective contexts, is intersubjectively mediated and is of functional significance for social processes of change.

If we look, for example, at Weber's investigations into the cultural significance of Protestantism,[11] all these variations can be seen. In these studies, Protestantism can be grasped as the 'world of meanings' under investigation, in which acting individuals and groups interacting with one another seek to realize subjective frameworks of meaning and projects for action. This action, thus defined as 'meaningful', had in turn a function in the origin of capitalism. Only through this could a certain religious meaning influence capitalism so strongly that it had a functionally adequate ('adequate on the level of meaning') effect on this economic form. The religious world of meanings was functional to the capitalist order and vice versa; the level of mediation was, as we have seen, the social, 'meaningful' action of individuals and groups.

Overlying Weber's differentiation of the concept of meaning and the method of *Verstehen*, there is another factor: Weber expressly stresses the *complementarity* of *Verstehen* and 'causal explanations'. 'The "understanding" of a context must always still be monitored as far as possible by the otherwise usual methods of causal inclusion, before an interpretation – however obvious – becomes the valid "understandable explanation"' (213b, p. 428). Weber fought vehemently against those contemporary attempts, particularly by Wilhelm Dilthey and his followers, to create a specific method of the 'human sciences' (*Geisteswissenschaften*) out of a concept of *Verstehen* which comes from individual experience, intuition and empathy. On the contrary, Weber seeks neither a natural–scientific nor a human–scientific foundation or method for his sociology, but a *social scientific* one. In this method, 'meaningful' interpretations of a concrete relationship are despite all the 'evidence' only 'hypotheses by imputation' which require 'verification'.

Causal chains into which instrumentally (*zweckrational*) oriented motivations are inserted by interpretive (*deutend*) hypotheses are directly . . . accessible by statistical inspection and . . . are thus accessible via (relatively) acceptable proof of their validity as 'explanations' (*Erklärungen*). Conversely, statistical data . . . wherever they suggest the result or consequences of behaviour . . . are only 'explained' to us when they are also meaningfully interpreted in a concrete instance. (213b, p. 437)

Here we arrive at a substantive definition of Weber's methodological linkage between *Verstehen* and *Erklären*. Following his demand for an explanatory control on *Verstehen*, he asserts, 'Thus interpretation in terms of rational purpose possesses the greatest degree of certainty (*Evidenz*). By a purposively rational disposition we mean one which is exclusively oriented towards means conceived (subjectively) as adequate for attaining goals which are unambiguously understood' (213b, p. 428). Although, as we have seen,[12] Weber expressly emphasizes that such an instrumentality of social action is a 'limiting case', he introduces as a kind of yardstick the concept of a 'rationality of correctness' (*Richtigkeitsrationalität*) in the sense of a rationality of means and ends.

This apparent discrepancy between 'subjective' intention and 'objective' verification disappears if one looks at the pragmatic research justification Weber gives. For his *empirical* sociology, whatever degree of 'rationality of correctness' an action has is an 'empirical question' (213b, p. 437) But Weber is in no way insinuating that actual human social behaviour can be determined predominantly instrumentally: 'Looking at the role which "non-instrumental" (*zweckirrational*) affects and "emotional situations" play in human action . . . one could equally well assert the exact opposite' (213b, p. 429). However to be able to achieve understanding (*Verstehen*) and explanation (*Erklären*) which can be controlled, Weber introduces the ideal-typical borderline case of the *supposed* validity, i.e. the hypothetical validity of absolute instrumentality and of a 'rationality of correctness'. In other words, he asks how the action would have taken place, *supposing* this rationality had actually operated. Such a *Verstehen* means not only investigating the subjectively intended meaning of the actor or actors, but at the same time measures the degree of deviation from a constructed 'type of correctness' (*Richtigkeitstyp*). Weber confirms this kind of typification in instrumental complexes of meaning in his aim of reaching a maximum of non-ambiguity and conceptual precision. With this strategy, Weber wants to rid the 'interpretive' method of its 'intuitionist' character. He wants to create an intersubjectively verifiable method, with the aid of which the social relations of people and groups, both with regard to their (supposed) subjective creation of meaning, and including socially and culturally imparted and determined orders of value and structural conditions can be both 'understood' *and* 'explained'.

The concept of the 'ideal-type'

In our presentation of Weber's work we encounter *throughout* one methodological concept with which Weber is inextricably linked – the concept of the *ideal-typical procedure*. No other theme in Weber's works on the methodology of the social sciences has aroused such a widespread discussion – a discussion which has lasted until today. In this, as in any *isolated* discussion of Weber's methodological writings, the *instrumental* significance of this concept is, for the most part, not acknowledged, and this has led to considerable misunderstandings.

In fact, however, the concept of the ideal-typical procedure is inextricably linked to the material part of Weber's work: we have shown that crude outlines of this concept are already recognizable in his *Habilitation* thesis of 1891.[13] As late as 1904, Weber made use of a defined methodological concept of the ideal-typical method, although we shall not go into the inconsistencies between the earlier and the later formulations here.[14]

When he took over the *Archiv* in 1904, Weber defined the main exercise of the journal as 'breathing scientific synthesis' into the extensive subject matter of scientific analyses. In tackling this exercise, Weber sees one procedure in particular as being suitable:

We shall have to consider the expression of social problems from *philosophical* viewpoints to a much greater extent, as in the form of research – called *theory* in a more narrow sense – of our special area: the formation of clear concepts. Although we are far from thinking that it is valid to squash the riches of historical life into formulae, we are still overwhelmingly convinced that only clear, unambiguous concepts can smooth the way for any research that wishes to discover the specific importance of social and cultural phenomena. (61, p. vi)

This intention to form 'unambiguous concepts' is the driving idea behind Weber's formulation of the ideal-typical procedure. The development of this method evolved against the background of several scientific and theoretical – and also frequently scientific and political – discourses and developments. Both the so-called *Methodenstreit*[15] between the historical and the theoretical tendencies in political economy (Gustav Schmoller versus Carl Menger) as well as the controversy within the framework of the schools of 'neo-idealism' (Wilhelm Dilthey, Edmund Husserl, Georg Simmel) and 'neo-Kantianism' (Heinrich Rickert, Rudolf Stammler, Wilhelm Windelband) are the contexts from which Weber formulated his own concept.[16] It is clear from this that neither the concept of 'ideal-type' nor the ideal-typical method were Weber's 'invention'.[17] The idea of a certain methodological procedure linked to the ideal-typical method emerged from a broad discussion which had begun long before Weber's contributions and which carried on after his death – partly without regard to his suggestions. This discussion, which can be characterized through the names of its main participants – Droysen, Lamprecht, von Below, Dilthey, Windelband, Rickert, Schmoller and Hintze – centred around the determination of the scientific character of *historical writing*.

And as in controversies like political history versus cultural history, individual history versus circumstantial history etc., this discussion was about the conflict between the 'natural sciences' which were becoming ever more important, and the established 'human sciences' (*Geisteswissenschaften*), which were beginning to feel threatened. The controversies of the time were made all the more violent and uncompromising by the fact that political and economic power positions played a role alongside theoretical and methodological problems.

In this intellectual controversy in Germany at the turn of the century, Dilthey, Windelband and Rickert, among others, made the concept of *Verstehen* the starting point for the division between natural and human sciences. *Verstehen* was to designate that specific method by means of which one could seek out knowledge of the particular, the individual and the unique, i.e. the alleged sphere of the human and cultural sciences, in which no *laws* could operate as in the natural sciences.

Weber's essay of 1904 on ' "Objectivity" in Social Science and Social Policy' (in 10E), was to represent the fulfilment of Weber's intention in taking over the *Archiv*, and it appeared in the same first volume of the new series as the 'Preface'. It came up against the fixed positions which stemmed from the idea of a constitutive and unchangeable division of problem areas and of the relevant sciences. In his interpretation both of *Verstehen* and the ideal-typical method in the context of this debate, Weber wanted to correct those historians who thought that the multiplicity and perpetual modification of historical circumstances did not permit the application of fixed and precise concepts. As he totally agrees with the view of reality as an unordered 'chaos', he pushes the demand for 'sharp' concepts all the more forcibly.

But the unstructured multiplicity of the *facta* in no way proves that we should construct woolly *concepts*, but the reverse: that *sharp* ('ideal-typical') concepts must be *applied* correctly, not as schemata to assault the historical given, but to be able to determine the . . . character of a phenomenon with its help: i.e. to indicate *to what extent* the phenomenon approximates to one or another 'ideal-type'. (217, p. 280)

Weber's overriding concern was to explain the 'cultural meaning' of historical facts in order to establish some conceptual order in the 'chaos', not to undertake a reconstruction of the past with the help of lists of facts and data. His programmatic demand was as follows: 'We seek knowledge of an historical phenomenon, meaning by historical: significant *in its individuality (Eigenart)*' (10E, p. 78). The point of reference for Weber's own essay on the scientific analysis of the cultural importance of the 'unstructured multiplicity of the *facta*' was, as we saw from the presentation of his work, that Western process of rationalization, whose various manifestations, causes and effects he pursued.

Thus it is the prime task of the ideal-type to incorporate hypothetically the chaotic multiplicity of individual phenomena into an 'ideal' i.e. an *ideational* course of events. Ideal-types for Weber, are 'ideal' in two respects: on the one hand, they are always based on a concept of logical and ideational perfection and they pursue this through many considerations to a conceivable extreme; on the other hand, they are also related to 'ideas' i.e. they are 'analytical constructs' (*Gedankenbilder*), thus are plans for thought (*Gedanken*). The accentuation and synthesis of certain elements and moments of observable reality orients itself towards 'ideas', which are interpreted as crucial for the behaviour of people and groups.

Again and again Weber refuses to see the 'true content' of history or its 'essence' in the ideal-types he develops. He warns repeatedly of the danger of hypostatizing ideal-types as the real, driving forces in history (10E, p. 94). When he speaks of the 'analytical accentuation of certain elements of reality' (10E, p. 90) he means on the one hand that the ideal-types must be extracted from historical reality, and on the other, that a cosmos of ideational contexts, internally lacking in contradiction, is created by accentuation, to the point of creating a utopian situation. The fact that for ideal-types reality is never taken into consideration, makes them into an exclusively formal instrument for the intersubjective, discursive understanding of historical reality, while this instrument must have the attributes of logical consistency and inner non-contradiction.

At least on the textual basis of the 'objectivity' essay, ideal-types present this heuristic aid to understanding historical phenomena from the viewpoint of its cultural significance. In Weber's last phase, in his work on the first part of *Economy and Society*, we can see his efforts to found a universal historical sociology with the aid of ideal-typical concepts which would be valid across time. We encounter this intention, and particularly the strategy he put forward of a 'procedure of measuring distance' away from the absolute ends–means–rationality of *Richtigkeitsrationalität* when Weber first propounds the concept of *Verstehen*.[18]

Both these positions – chronologically and in content separable from one another – led to the distinction between 'historical' and 'sociological' ideal-types.[19] The former aimed more at the cultural determination of certain historical phenomena, and the latter had an atemporal, systematic character. From his own suggested 'model' of ideal-typical variants (10E, p. 103), Weber suggests a tripartite[20] and four-part[21] structure. The only clear point to emerge from this is that Weber in no way envisaged the concept of 'ideal-types' as unitary and this caused numerous contradictions in the interpretation controversy.

To summarize our discussion we can draw up the following five points:

1   The ideal-type is a *genetic concept*, i.e. it releases from a collection of attributes those that are regarded as originally essential for certain 'cultural meanings'. As such its context should be reconstructed in a 'pure' way.

2   The ideal-type is itself *not a hypothesis*, but it can indicate the direction for the formation of hypotheses. Thus it is not 'falsifiable' by checking-up on historical reality: a too restricted 'adequacy' to empirical circumstances and for a particular line of enquiry, however, compel the continual development of *new* ideal-typical constructions.

3   The ideal-type serves as a *heuristic means* to guide empirical research, while it formulates possible viewpoints for the interpretation of social action by oneself and others. A strategy should thereby be made possible which classifies the interminable, meaningless multiplicity of empirical data by reference to an ideational ('ideal') context. The usefulness of an ideal-typical construction is measured by its 'success' in helping understanding.

4   The ideal-type is used in the *systematization* of empirical–historical reality, in that its distance from the typified construction is 'measured' interpretatively. The ideal-type is a *construction* – but this construction is derived from reality and is constantly examined against reality, by using the 'imagination' and the nomological knowledge of the researcher. The continual reconstruction and new development of ideal-types should enable an approach to purely nomothetical and

ideographical methods, and to purely causally explanatory and purely individualizing interpretive methods. It should also *mediate* one method via the other.

5   The results which are produced with the aid of the ideal-typical procedure for the explanation and interpretation of historical phenomena underpin a *process of re-interpretation* which is never-ending. The social sciences belong to those disciplines 'to which eternal youth is granted . . . to which the eternally onward flowing stream of culture perpetually brings new problems. At the very heart of their task lies not only the transciency of *all* ideal types *but* also at the same time the inevitability of *new* ones' (10E, p. 104). Here we must point out a principal hypothesis of this procedure: the success of the ideal-typical ordering of historical reality depends on the degree of concordance between the formation of types and concepts of the actors in the given social context, and the formation of types and concepts of the scientists who are investigating these contexts. [22]

The postulate of 'freedom from value-judgement' (*Werturteilsfreiheit*)

The so-called 'value-judgement dispute' is an extremely difficult phenomenon to define in the history of science and cannot be reduced to a controversy in a special discipline about a specific, unambiguously localizable problem. The multiple problems which were fought over in this 'dispute' are not merely related to certain sciences like political economy or sociology but they engage with the *basic determination of any scientific knowledge*. As difficult as it is to determine the actual 'beginning' of this controversy, it is easy to assert that Weber's relevant works were the decisive points of contact for the discussion which has lasted until today[23] particularly his essays ' "Objectivity" in Social Science and Social Policy', 1904 (in 10E), 'The Meaning of "Ethical Neutrality" in Sociology and Economics', 1917 (in 10E) and the text of his lecture 'Science as a Vocation', 1919 (in 10E).

If the reception of *The Protestant Ethic* and the methodological concepts of *Verstehen* and the ideal-type were frequently the occasion for the creation and perpetuation of misunderstandings, Weber's conception of 'freedom from value-judgement' underwent the most thorough distortion through misunderstanding and trivialization. But this fact cannot be traced back merely to different 'interests', but equally to the extremely complex structure of the situation in which Weber formulated his position. For a comprehensive understanding, and thus for an exhaustive discussion, we must examine at least four contextual areas which partly intersect, namely

1 The philosophical background
2 The theoretical background
3 The organizational background
4 The position and political self-consciousness of German science at the turn of the century

Within the scope of this book we can only give a very cursory survey of each area.

1 To reconstruct the philosophical background, what is important is the deep crisis in Europe's historical and social consciousness which took place during the twenty-five years before the First World War.[24] In shorthand, this crisis is known as the 'crisis of historicism'. Despite considerable differences in position among the main participants in the argument at that time, particularly Hermann Cohen, Wilhelm Dilthey, Wilhelm Windelband, Heinrich Rickert, Max Weber, Ernst Troeltsch and Friedrich Meinecke, they shared a common denominator in their *critique of positivism*. Initiated by a variety of shake-ups in the positivist conception of the world and of humanity in general – for example by Freud, Jung, Nietzsche, Bergson, Baudelaire, Dostoevski and Proust – the fiction of a rationally ordered world was plunged into confusion, and the gulf between the world of being and the world of meaning was seen increasingly as unbridgeable. From this viewpoint, which was frequently clothed in the garb of *Kulturkritik* and cultural pessimism, the question emerged of whether a science of history or society would ever be possible. A few historians and sociologists were inclined to think that human subjectivity and irrationality would considerably restrict any science in its explanatory and prognostic value.

Some participants in the discussion of method at the turn of the century, particularly Dilthey, Windelband, Rickert, Meinecke and Troeltsch, who believed in a *meaning of history*, directed their efforts against this 'relativism' and pessimism. Moreover, this belief was frequently linked to a conviction in the basic rightness of the German *political* development since 1870-1.

Precisely in order to avert relativism in all areas, these scientists sought an examination of the methodological and epistemo-theoretical foundations of the science of history. To understand Weber's position in *this* context, we need to understand two very different positions in this epistemological and theoretical discussion. First, the south-west German school of neo-Kantianism represented by Windelband and Rickert, and second, the position of Dilthey.[25] Weber was fundamentally influenced by both groups, personally and theoretically. In part he took over their frameworks of questioning and reached, via an *attempt at mediation* between the opposing positions, his own orientation, which would become of considerable importance for the following debates – in spite of or even because of the many misunderstandings and foreshortenings. A comprehensive understanding of Weber's position is not possible without knowledge of how these arguments progressed.

2   The theoretical background means those contexts of argument which dealt with the *orientation of the German political economy* in the last third of the nineteenth century. The representatives of 'classical' political economy, in particular Wilhelm Roscher, Bruno Hildebrand and Karl Knies as the so-called 'older historical school', had already, around 1850, tried to establish the basis for a historically oriented political economy, which was directed towards empirical science, in order to check the contemporary influence of the prevailing naturalistic and positivistic currents.

As a consequence of changes caused by political influences, particularly through an increased state intervention in economic policy, these concepts of the 'younger historical school' were taken up once again by their acknowledged leader, Gustav Schmoller. In particular the idea of having to include the historical dimension of economic processes was of crucial importance. The close connection of the 'younger school' with practical economic policy led to the institutionalization of the dialogue of science and politics in the *Verein* in 1872. We will be investigating this briefly in the next section.

During the dispute with the 'younger school', the eighties brought that discussion which has gone down in the history of German economic policy as the *Methodenstreit* and which can be classified by the two names of Gustav Schmoller and Carl Menger.

In his 1883 work *Untersuchungen über die Methode der Sozialwissenschaften and der politischen Ökonomie insbesondere*, Menger differentiates the sciences into three groups: historical, theoretical and practical. Accordingly, the historical disciplines are directed towards the understanding of the individual, the theoretical disciplines towards extracting generalities from phenomena, and the practical disciplines are concerned with what should be, with what one must do to attain certain goals for people. In the *theoretical* mode of research that Menger ascribes to himself, he distinguishes between two variants: the *empirical–realistic direction* that wants to establish real types; and an *exact direction* that wants to set up strict laws, comparable to 'laws of nature'.

In the same year, Schmoller responded with an article entitled '*Zur Methodologie der Staats- und Sozialwissenschaften*'.[26] In it he emphasized the intrinsic value of the *descriptive* procedure, because with the aid of 'the descriptive experiences of all kinds, the classification of phenomena which improves the formation of concepts, the typical rows of phenomena and their context of causes can be more clearly recognized in their entire scope'.[27] According to Schmoller, the progress of science did not lie in a further distillation of the precepts of the old dogmatism which have been investigated again and again. Whoever proceeded from hypotheses would only get hypothetical sentences to which one would then try to give the appearance of strict scientific method by using the adjective 'exact'.

Carl Menger felt personally attacked by Schmoller's critique and responded violently to it the same year.[28] In all this it was largely ignored that from the beginning Menger had suggested a mediating position which amounted to acknowledging *both* positions, the theoretical *and* the historical. However, the contemporary controversies between 'positivism' and 'historicism', between 'natural sciences' and 'cultural, or rather, human sciences' forced the adoption of frequently simple, dichotomized polarizations. In any case, they effected a systematic reflection on the methodological foundations in *all* sciences, and particularly in disciplines which were not organized like the natural sciences.

Weber, who engaged with the *Methodenstreit* in the most intensive way (40, 60, 62, 68, 71, 80, 88, 92) once again took up his position as a *mediator*. He wanted to detach the controversy from its connection with problems of political economy alone, and to place it in the context of the discussion which we have described as the 'philosophical background'. Weber was influenced greatly by the debate over the relationship between the 'human sciences' and the 'natural sciences', as led by Windelband[29] and Rickert,[30] and this brought him to formulate his concept of a 'science of reality' (*Wirklichkeitswissenschaft*)[31].

3   Both the philosophical as well as the theoretical background to Weber's concept of freedom from value-judgement meant discussions which were carried out largely in a literary way. Those discussions which were and are described as the actual 'value-judgement dispute' nevertheless found *organizational* 'stages' on which these debates were performed – especially the *Verein*, and for Weber in particular the *Deutsche Gesellschaft für Soziologie*.

After the turn of the century three 'fractions' of the *Verein*'s membership, who were made up predominantly of academics, high-ranking civil servants, journalists, trade-unionists, bankers and entrepreneurs became roughly distinguishable. These were a 'left wing', the so-called 'academic socialists' (*Kathedersozialisten*), comprising Brentano, Sombart, Naumann, Harms and Max and Alfred Weber among others; a 'centre' of Schmoller, Gneist, Nasse and others; and a 'right wing' of Wagner, von Philippovich and others. At the Mannheim conference of 1905 on 'The relationship of the cartels to the state', the discussions became very heated at some of Schmoller's demands for the control of the cartels. These discussions provoked Schmoller to the point of threatening resignation, if the left wing – Naumann in particular – persisted in pursuing its 'materialistic demagogy'. In these initiatory, highly polemical arguments over the understanding of theory and method in the *Verein*, and indeed of the *Verein* itself, the left wing demanded that theory and method be made the objects of discussion, while the right wing wanted to prevent such discussions and saw the main task of the *Verein* as influencing practical social policy – because of which, the themes had to be of a 'practical nature'. Schmoller, in his role as integrator and mediator, strove to keep the *Verein* as a forum for the discussion and publicizing of *science*, which could, however, also influence practical social policy. Weber, meanwhile, still very much kept his distance from these affairs (77, 78).

The 'value-judgement dispute' broke out in its totality at the Vienna conference of 1909, at which Eugen von Philippovich, Weber's predecessor in the Freiburg chair, and as representative of the 'Austrian School' gave the first purely scientific–theoretical paper in the history of the *Verein*, on 'The Essence of National Economic Productivity'. He presented a survey which charted the history of ideologies and raised the challenges which lie in the concept of national economic productivity. Sombart, Max Weber and Gottl von Ottlilienfeld criticized the scientific uselessness of the concept of productivity as it might hide proper evaluations, and particularly since it was increasingly mixed with the concept of 'national prosperity'. Weber began his vehement campaign against 'a mixture of science and value-judgement' (102, p. 584) and saw 'the work of the devil in the inter-mingling of prescriptive notions in scientific questions . . . work which has frequently richly provided for the *Verein*' (102, p. 584). Von Zwiedineck-Südenhorst, Spann, Goldscheid and Neurath spoke out against Weber's position (Tönnies being on his side) in the course of the lively debates. For reasons of *Verein* policy, they demanded, a *fundamental discussion*, both on the problematics of 'value-judgements' in the *Verein*'s proceedings, as well as on the economic character of the political economy, should be postponed until the 1911 sitting in Nuremburg. However, at this sitting, Weber's initial proposal was as follows: 'I would like to suggest that the question of whether we have to exclude value-judgements here or not, or whether they are justifiable in principle, and of how far their exclusion is practicable, be presented once by the *Verein* committee as a special issue on the agenda' (115, p. 163).

In preparation for this special conference, a circular letter was sent out in 1912 at Weber's instigation to the committee members asking them to take up positions. Out of the fourteen authors of the published paper (117), Epstein, Eulenburg, Rohrbeck and Neurath adopted Weber's position; Hartmann, Wilbrandt, Schumpeter, Spann and Oldenberg turned out to be reconcilable with Weber's position, and only Goldscheid, Hesse, Oncken, Spranger and von Wiese took up more or less overt opposition. The committee meeting on 5 January 1914 from which the publicized positions took the lead and which fifty-two members attended, produced no result and brought the standpoints no closer together. Apart from Sombart, Weber could scarcely find any other advocates for his approach among the younger and middle generations.

The outbreak of the First World War did not completely interrupt the work of the *Verein*, but it did put an end to the value-judgement discussion. Weber revised his written position in 1912 and published the new version in 1917 in the journal *Logos* with the title 'The Meaning of "Ethical Neutrality" in Sociology and Economics' (in 10E). That Weber was still willing to continue working in the *Verein* in spite of what had happened, is shown by his election to deputy chairman in September 1919.

The second organizational 'stage' on which the 'value-judgement dispute' was played out, and which we need to know about to understand Weber's position in more than a fragmentary way, was the *Deutsche Gesellschaft für Soziologie* (German Society for Sociology), in the foundation of which Weber took a considerable, initiatory part in 1909. Precisely because of his experiences in the *Verein*, Weber tried to avoid the possible repetition of what were in his opinion unprofitable disagreements. To do this, he suggested on the occasion of his 'invitation' to found the *Gesellschaft*

The *Gesellschaft* should . . . have a purely objective, scientific character. It follows from this that *any* kind of political, socio-political, socio-ethical, or any other kind of propaganda for *practical* aims or ideals within or under the name of the *Gesellschaft* must be *excluded*. The *Gesellschaft* may only serve the research of facts and their contexts. (185, p. 1)

Weber's demand was preserved in paragraph one of the Society's statute, which said:

The aim [of the *Deutsche Gesellschaft für Soziologie*] is to promote sociological knowledge by the arrangement of purely scientific investigations and enquiries, by the publication and support of purely scientific works and by the organization of German sociology conferences to take place periodically. It will give equal space to all scientific directions and methods of sociology and will reject the representation of any practical (ethical, religious, political, aesthetic etc.) goals. (108, p. v).[32]

The embittered controversies at the two initial sociology conferences in 1910 and 1912 (108–13; 118–21), particularly the arguments with Rudolf Goldscheid on the principle of freedom from value-judgement led to Weber's disappointment and resignation, and to his ultimately leaving the *Gesellschaft* in 1913. Weber saw himself as 'a Don Quixote of an allegedly unfeasible principle'.[33]

4   These three backdrops to the so-called 'value-judgement debate' must be connected to the general position and the – particularly political – self-consciousness of German science in the years before the First World War, if we are to reach a comprehensive understanding from which to derive any adequate evaluation of Weber's position. Such a discussion can, in this book, only serve to highlight certain details.

If the Bismarck years brought stormy developments in the natural sciences to the German university system, these processes nevertheless did not effect any far-reaching identity-crisis in the human sciences. The dominant position of the historians was maintained and the established disciplines and their representatives, basically because of a prevailing liberal–nationalist attitude, kept a fundamental consensus with the political system. However, in time, currents emerged which were called *Kulturkritik* (critique of civilization) and 'cultural pessimism', which began to doubt the legitimacy of the political and social order, from the perspective of the 'social question'. The extremely popular writings of Paul de Lagarde and Julius Langbehn, in particular, began to give space to a fundamental critique of the kind of 'false science' that could only confirm the facts, when by contrast the 'ultimate goal' of 'true science' was to formulate value-judgements.[34] They saw something equally untrue in the 'objectivity' of science, 'like that modern humanism, which says that all human beings are of equal value.'[35] Such demands for an *evaluative science* were thus not only 'a matter taken up by German youth – and a youth that was not spoiled, not badly educated, and not prejudiced'[36] but between 1890 and 1914, such views spread more and more widely. George Hinzpeter, Wilhelm II's tutor, complained at the German state school conference in 1890 that 'personal, spiritual development' had once been considered as 'the highest goal worth aiming at'. Meanwhile, however, education was merely regarded as 'the means to successful participation in the wild struggle for existence'.[37] In 1902, Friedrich Paulsen stated that the task for German universities was to represent 'in their entirety something like the public conscience of the people with a view to good and evil in politics'.[38]

Such statements, which amounted to demands to create, with the support of the German universities, a conflict-free, ideologically identical society out of German Wilhelminian life were not only taken from instances of (educational) policy, but fell on fertile ground in the universities themselves as can be seen in the activities of the *Euken-Bund*.[39]

The four contextual areas we have sketched outline the background against which Weber tried to determine his own position. Since these debates stretched across the period from 1890 to 1920, a knowledge of all relevant works in which he discussed the problem of 'values' and 'evaluations' is vital for an *exact* representation of Weber's position (60, 62, 68, 71, 75, 117, 155, 177). We shall leave out the modifications of his position in the course of discussion and will try to elaborate the general arguments.

As a way in, we can look at the *interpretations* of Weber's approach which have been current until today. Accordingly, Weber's demand attests to a 'freedom from value-judgement' for the (social) sciences:[40]

Social scientists must refrain from all evaluating statements, either all the time, or in the practice of their profession, or when they publish the results of their work.

Social scientists must not take on any kind of aesthetic or moral evaluations; 'evaluations' in the sense of distinguishing between true and false are allowed.

Social scientists must not be politically active.

All conceivable ethical and political absolute values, like freedom, equality, and justice are of equal value; science must therefore not accord a higher rank to one over another.

Values and evaluations of social actors are not the subject of the social sciences.

Weber's approach is covered by *none* of these interpretations. Basically it is divided into two mutually detachable arguments: (1) the demand for 'freedom from value-judgement' (*Werturteilsfreiheit*) in the narrow sense; and (2) the problem of 'relevance to values' (*Wertbeziehung*).

The demand for 'freedom from value-judgement' in the narrow sense

On the first level, Weber's demand for freedom from value-judgement meant

the intrinsically simple demand that the investigator and teacher should keep unconditionally separate the establishment of empirical facts (including the 'value oriented' conduct of the empirical individual whom he is investigating) and *his* own practical evaluations, i.e. his evaluation of these facts as satisfactory or unsatisfactory . . . These two things are logically different and to deal with them as though they were the same represents a confusion of entirely heterogeneous problems. (10E, p. 11)

This 'postulate . . . which they often misunderstand so gravely' (10E, p. 6) and which caused 'unending misunderstanding' and the 'completely sterile dispute', was set up by Weber as a reference to the 'professorial prophecy' which was not uncommon in his time. With explicit reference to university teachers like Treitschke, Theodor Mommsen and Schmoller, Weber condemns the propagation of practical–political ideals in the lecture hall from the lectern, and demands as the 'absolute minimum', as 'a precept of intellectual honesty', the suppression of personal prophecy and the announcement of a '*Weltanschauung*'.

Today the student should obtain, from his teacher in the lecture hall, the capacity: (1) to fulfill a given task in a workmanlike fashion; (2) definitely to recognize facts, even those which may be personally uncomfortable, and to distinguish them from his own evaluations; (3) to subordinate himself to his task and to repress the impulse to exhibit his personal tastes or other sentiments unnecessarily. (10E, p. 5)

Only in this way could the 'self-importance', the 'fashionable "cult of the personality" [in] the throne, public office or the professorial chair' which could prejudice the matter, be combatted.

An unprecedented situation exists when a large number of officially accredited prophets do not do their preaching on the streets, or in churches or other public places or in sectarian conventicles, but rather feel themselves competent to enunciate their evaluations on ultimate questions 'in the name of science' in governmentally privileged lecture halls in which they are neither controlled, checked by discussion, nor subject to contradiction. (10E, p. 4)

Weber expressly emphasizes that the 'distinction between empirical statements of fact and value-judgements' which he demands, is *difficult* and even that he himself has offended against this distinction (10E, p. 9). Even so, Weber does not dispute the fact that the choice of theme and the selection of subject matter already involves 'evaluations'. Moreover, he stresses that this does *not* imply 'that empirical science cannot treat "subjective" evaluations as the subject matter of its analysis – (although sociology depend[s] on the contrary assumption)' (10E, p. 11).

Thus on the 'first level' of Weber's postulate of 'freedom from value-judgement' *in science*, he asserts that 'evaluations', in the sense of assessments as 'objectionable' or 'approvable', must be *separated* from statements of empirical facts and circumstances. If a scientist cannot or will not forgo such an evaluation, he must separate his personal standpoint, for which he may not claim any *scientific* legitimation, from the description of facts, both with respect to his discourse partners and with respect to *himself*. Science for Weber is a '*professionally* run "vocation" . . . in the service of the self-consciousness and awareness of factual contexts, and not a gift of grace for seers and prophets, bestowing cures and revelations, or an element of the thoughts of sages and philosophers on the *meaning* of the world' (213b, p. 609).

The problem of 'relevance to values'

Weber's essential, deep concern goes far beyond what we have just looked at and touches a basic problematic in all sciences, but particularly in all social sciences. This is a question of the 'relevance' and relation of the results of scientific research to the 'values' of the researcher.

Because Weber stresses that the evaluations that lie at the heart of the actions of the individual – whether scientist or the observed acting subject – must not be accepted as 'fact', but can be treated 'as the object of scientific criticism' (10E, p. 12), the question emerges of *how* empirical disciplines based on the science of experience can settle this task. It is thus a matter of investigating each 'evaluation' with respect to its 'individual social [and historical] conditions', which for Weber can only be possible through an *understanding explanation (verstehendes Erklären)*. This has

high scientific importance: (1) for purposes of an empirical causal analysis which attempts to establish the really decisive motives of human actions; and (2) for the communication of really divergent evaluations when one is discussing with a person who really or apparently has different evaluations from one's self. (10E, p. 14)

In determining this task Weber sees that

the real significance of a discussion of evaluations lies in its contribution to the understanding of what one's opponent – or one's self – really means – i.e., in understanding the evaluations which really and not merely allegedly separate the discussants and consequently in enabling one to take up a position with reference to this value. (10E, p. 14)

Because the 'understanding' (*Verstehen*) of another's evaluations does *not* mean its approval, a scientific investigation of each value which might possibly collide with another becomes both possible *and* necessary.

Although Weber inclines towards and proceeds from an acknowledgement of a 'polytheism' of ultimate values, and that between values 'it is really a question not only of alternatives between values but of an irreconcilable death-struggle, like that between "God" and the "Devil" ' (10E, p. 17) (and here there can be no relative measures or compromises), Weber, representing the viewpoint of a 'collision of values', resists the insinuation of 'relativism' (10E, p. 18) with great resolve.

To be able to deal with values and evaluations in an empirical way, Weber puts forward four functions for a scientifically productive 'discussion of value-judgements':

(a)   The elaboration and explication of the ultimate, internally 'consistent' value-axioms, from which the divergent attitudes are derived . . .

(b)   The deduction of 'implications' (for those accepting certain value-judgements) which follow from certain irreducible value-axioms, when the practical evaluation of factual situations is based on these axioms alone . . .

(c)   The determination of the factual consequences which the realization of a certain practical evaluation must have . . . Finally:

(d)   the uncovering of new axioms (and the postulates to be drawn from them) which the proponent of a practical postulate did not take into consideration . . . (10E, pp. 20–1)

Such a method of researching 'value-judgements' which constructs *ideal-types*, in which the analysis of ideas of value, the specification of suitable means and combinations of means for chosen purposes ('values'), the assessment of prospects for success, the assertion of the secondary effects of the available means, the estimation of the 'costs' of the sought-after values and the estimation of the compatibility (in a logical as well as a practical sense) of different values which lie at its centre – such a method displays its 'relevance' to values. With reference to Rickert, Weber uses the concept of 'relevance to values', meaning 'the philosophical interpretation of that specifically scientific "interest" which determines the selection of a given subject matter and the problems of an empirical analysis' (10E, p. 22). This concept, which is extremely important for the sociology of science, points to the fact that 'cultural (i.e., evaluative) interests give purely scientific work its direction' (10E, p. 22).

Here, Weber uses again the concept which he formulated in 1904: 'epistemological interest' (*Erkenntnisinteresse*). Then, he was concerned to emphasize the *constructedness* of a certain perspective from which one could approach the particular object under investigation. He wrote on his own 'socio-economic' perspective:

The quality of an event as a socio-economic phenomenon is not something which is 'objectively' attached to the event. Rather it is determined by the direction of our epistemological *interest*, as it emerges from the specific cultural meaning which we attribute to the event concerned in the individual case. (213b, p. 161)

If the (social) scientist wants to approach his or her object of investigation, he or she must do it from the perspective of certain values which the surrounding culture offers. Without such a value-loaded perspective, reality remains an unordered chaos of the multiplicity and contradiction of facts and phenomena. Already, the infinite complexity of reality makes a simple 'description' of events impossible. If, in scientific knowledge, it is a question of discovering the contexts of causation, one needs a knowledge-motivated interest from which one can derive a desire to 'understand' and 'explain' social and historical reality. The task of the cultural sciences, among which sociology numbers, is, according to Weber, to research the reality and operation of 'meaning' and 'significance'. There is no possibility of 'objective' treatment for this task, but merely a research selection by means of 'value-ideas', in which 'culture' is regarded as a particular case.

From the standpoint of the *human being*, 'culture' is a finite section of the senseless infinity of world events, furnished with meaning and sense . . . A transcendental precondition of any *cultural science* is *not* that we find a certain 'culture', or even any 'culture' *valuable*, but that we are cultural *beings*, gifted with the capacity and the will to take up a conscious *position* with regard to the world and to give it a *meaning*. Whatever this meaning may be, it will lead us to *judge* certain phenomena of human interaction in life on the basis of this meaning, and to take up a position in the face of it which is (positively or negatively) *significant*. (213b, pp. 180–1)

'Epistemological interest' and 'value ideas' establish the 'relevance to values' between the researcher and the object of research, and are of great importance for the results of the research. *Which* 'value ideas' are selected as determining research and knowledge is not a subjective, arbitrary matter for the individual scientist.

What becomes the object of the investigation and how far this investigation stretches into the infinity of causal relationships is determined by the value-ideas which govern the researcher and his epoch . . . For scientific truth is only that which *desires* to be valid for everyone who *wants* the truth. (213b, p. 184)

This *intersubjectively* determined and controlled choice of research ideas and interests is the basis for a continuing *process of change*. With the change in 'cultural problems', i.e. in the 'dominant value-ideas', the points of view by which research is carried out are also changing. This amounts to the 'eternal youth' of all historical disciplines 'to which the eternally progressing stream of culture supplies continually new problems' (213b, p. 206).

If the 'starting points' of the cultural sciences remain 'variable far into the boundless future' (213b, p. 184), there is however, *'progress'* in scientific-cultural research. It lies in a continual process of formation and re-formation in scientific *concepts*, i.e. the 'ideal-types' with which the inexhaustible reality must be grasped.

The history of the sciences of social life is and remains a continual fluctuation between the attempt to order facts ideationally through the formation of concepts . . . and the formation of concepts from scratch . . . It is not the incorrectness of the attempt to form conceptual systems *in the first place* which is expressed here, but the fact that in the sciences of human culture the formation of concepts depends on the posing of the problems, and that the latter is altered alongside the content of culture itself. The relationship of concept and conceptualized in the cultural sciences makes the transitoriness of every such synthesis unavoidable. (213b, p. 207)

To emphasize intersubjective restraint and the control of social-scientific research and to postulate an accumulation of conceptual knowledge changes nothing in the basic transitoriness and fluctuation of all social-scientific 'epistemology'. Decades before the formulation of the concept of 'paradigmatic change' in the sociology of science, Weber recognized the fundamental importance of fixing knowledge to 'value-ideas' and 'epistemological interests', and of their permanent 'revolutionizing'.

But at some time or another the complexion changes: the significance of unreflectedly realized viewpoints becomes uncertain, and one loses one's way in the growing darkness. The light of the great cultural problems has moved on. Then science too prepares itself to change its position and its conceptual apparatus and to look down from the heights of ideation on to the stream of activity. (213b, p. 214)

7

The reception of Weber's work during his lifetime

In spite of international research which has been going on for decades, *no comprehensive account* of the reception and effect of Weber's work has hitherto been presented.[1] In order to get beyond the usual, extremely fragmentary and selective kind of study, which deals only with stereotypical 'instructive pieces', such as the thesis on Protestantism and capitalism, the typology of domination, the concept of *Verstehen* or the notion of 'freedom from value-judgement', it is necessary to start from a comprehensive knowledge both of Weber's life as well as of his entire oeuvre, and to arrange this according to the social history and the sociology of science in their traditional contexts and schools of thought.

One of the most important reasons for the lack of such an account is the fact that until now no historical and sociological analysis of the development of early German sociology has existed. It is only against the background of the processes of institutionalization and professionalization as 'sociology' was gradually formed as an academic subject within the German university system that we could escape the sterility of these typical seminar topics. Discussions and accounts of 'connections' between Weber and Marx, Weber and Simmel, Weber and Schütz, Weber and Parsons etc., must be separated from a *systematic* investigation into the influence and reception of Weber's work. In this way we would not only avoid the dangers of 'comparing the incomparable', but equally our attention would be freed for the first time to be devoted to Weber's *actual* influence, beyond any hero-worshipping and/or ideological distortion.[2]

The aim of such a systematic investigation into Weber's reception and influence would thus be to work out typical 'patterns of reception and groups of recipients' i.e. the analysis of typical 'Weber images'.[3] In this it would initially be necessary to formulate 'a kind of infrastructure of reception'[4] which is oriented both towards the basic social functions of science, for example according to Max Scheler's categories: knowledge of work/achievement, knowledge of domination, knowledge of education, knowledge of salvation/redemption,[5] as well as towards the 'role field' of science, for example, technical advisors, technological leaders and experts, inventors, discoverers, systematizers, reformers, polemicists, historians and theoreticians of science, researchers, fact-finders and problem-finders, disseminators, popularizers and scientific administrators.[6] The following exposition on the reception of Weber's writings should be regarded as merely the first sketch in such a systematic history of his reception and influence.

The studies in the agrarian, economic and social history of Antiquity and the Middle Ages attained by comparison the least resonance of all of Weber's works.[7]

His *dissertation* on trading companies was reviewed positively by Eduard Heyck[8] and Leopold Menzinger[9] soon after its publication, and underwent very thorough treatment from Max Pappenheim[10] in the *Zeitschrift für das Gesamte Handelsrecht*. Pappenheim emphasized the necessity of the work and generally agreed with its results. However he fundamentally disagreed with one of the major theses, and maintained that it was not the working community of all members of the household, but 'the family relationship of the brothers managing the work together [which] has formed the basis of their community of property'.[11] Weber's doctoral supervisor, Levin Goldschmidt, endorsed Pappenheim's objections as he too regarded Weber's basic idea as over-interpretation. Nevertheless he incorporated the results of Weber's work in the third edition of his *Handbuch des Handelrechts*[12] and makes reference to them in his *System des Handelsrechts*.[13] Alongside these direct reactions we must also mention the evaluation of Weber's disser-tation by Lujo Brentano, his predecessor in the Munich professorship (Brentano called it an 'unusual achievement'),[14] Werner Sombart's positive appreciation[15] and the reception by the economic historian Sir William J. Ashley.[16]

Discussion of Weber's *Habilitation* thesis, *Die römische Agrargeschichte* of 1891 began in 1889 with the famous dispute with Theodor Mommsen at Weber's graduation, which we mentioned above.[17] In his second thesis Weber maintained a principal difference between the forms of settlement of the *colonia* and the *municipium*, and Weber linked the latter to the manner of field arrangement and map-work (1, p. 57). When Weber resumes this basic idea in his *Habilitation* thesis, Mommsen takes a detailed look at

Weber's theses in a longer article.[18] He describes Weber's work as stimulating and refers in particular to its economic perspective. However, with his differentiation of colonia and municipium, Mommsen again disagrees. As well as this, for Weber, very honourable recognition by the famous historian, we must mention a longer review by Paul Krüger,[19] who accused Weber of arbitrarily interpreting his sources at important points. Mommsen's pupil, L. M. Hartmann,[20] while principally praising the work, sharply criticized individual points and likewise remained sceptical regarding Weber's basic thesis. Hermann Schiller's judgement on the work was more positive[21] and Robert Pöhlmann[22] in his review referred in particular to the productiveness of the Meitzen frame of reference. Weber himself, however, who later, in connection with this work spoke of 'the sins of my youth', regarded this frame of reference as inappropriate, and held on to his main results as still being applicable.[23] Werner Sombart's extensive review in 1893[24] was certainly an important basis of his friendship with Weber: Sombart brought out the central points and indicated the specific representation of capitalism. He emphasized this point as being central for works even later than the *Habilitation*.[25] If we look at these specialist, competent reactions to *Die römische Agrargeschichte*, and if we further add the review of this work by Benedictus Niese[26] and Otto Hintze[27] then we *cannot* agree with Alfred Heuss's evaluation that this work has been 'ignored' by the science of Antiquity and that its influence, in the end, is not ascertainable.[28] 'Even if Weber's theses have turned out to be false, or rather speculative, they nevertheless provoked an extensive discussion.'[29]

When Marianne Weber, writing about the influence of the three *Handwörterbuch* articles on the agrarian sociology of ancient civilizations (48, 54, 95-7), says that this text 'also remained inaccessible to a wider audience',[30] then even this evaluation can 'only partly be sustained'.[31] One of those who from the very beginning regarded this article as very important was the ancient historian, who was later to become extremely famous, Michael Rostowzew. Rostowzew took over the article in the *Handwörterbuch* on the *colonat* (estate fee farm)[32] from Weber, who originally wanted to compile it himself. In his monograph on the Roman *colonat* which appeared in 1910,[33] Rostowzew described Weber's *Handwörterbuch* article as 'path-breaking' and he quotes Weber frequently.[34] Although it appears that they did not establish personal contact, the material points of contact between Weber and Rostowzew, who had become famous in the USA, became so great that Wollheim concludes 'Taken as a whole, Rostovtzeff's work is designed to supplement Max Weber's interpretations of ancient capitalism considerably, and perhaps even largely to replace them.'[35] According to a letter from Weber to Georg von Below, pupils of the ancient historian and papyrus-expert Wilcken had been stimulated by Weber's article.[36] In 1914, von Below himself sent Weber his work on the German state in the Middle Ages, later quoted Weber's positive letter, and frequently referred to the *Handwörterbuch* article.[37] Already from these indications it becomes clear that the experts followed Weber's work attentively and respectfully. And not only the close circle of the brotherhood of ancient historians did this: Ernst Troeltsch worked the article into his '*Soziallehren der christlichen Kirchen und Gruppen*' of 1912,[38] Erich Fechner[39] and Fritz Heichelheim[40] make it clear that they were inspired by Weber's analysis. And not least, Marianne Weber's investigation '*Ehefrau und Mutter in der Rechtsentwicklung*'[41] is based on her husband's scientific researches into Antiquity.

The study 'The City' (8E, pp. 1212ff.) was given its greatest contemporary attention by Werner Sombart, who called it 'by far the most important treatise on the city and its historical development'.[42] The transcript of lectures on '*Wirtschaftsgeschichte*' (216) was taken on board by Franz Oppenheimer, who occupied the first chair in sociology at Frankfurt. The second volume of his *System der Soziologie* particularly, called '*Der Staat*', is based on Weber's material.[43] In it, Oppenheimer takes on Weber's differentiation between internal and external morality, his characterization of the civilization of Antiquity as a coastal civilization, his formulation of the concept of citizenship, and his investigations into the origin of money, of the ancient and Medieval city and of the slave economy. This posthumous publication was also noticed by Werner Sombart[44] and Waldemar Mitscherlich.[45] Among foreign recipients were Henri Pirenne[46] who expressed Weber's basic thesis in the formula 'the victory of rationalism over traditionalism', and also Pitirim Sorokin.[47]

If we examine the above data on the contemporary reception and influence of Weber's works on the agrarian, economic and social history of Antiquity and the Middle Ages, it is clear that Alfred Heuss's thesis does not completely stand up: 'To sum up, we might well say that the specialist study of Antiquity carried on as if Max Weber had not lived.'[48] This statement must however be modified in the sense that the reception of these works did not, essentially at that time, go beyond this small circle of immediate *specialists*. However, it seems appropriate to apply to this circle itself what Karl Christ wrote on Weber's influence: 'Through Max Weber, agrarian history and beyond that the areas of social and economic history [have] been placed in a new light.'[49] We cannot report with certainty, however, on the wider reception, for example by the lay public. For this,

Weber's dry style and his mainly juridical and historical concepts must be held responsible.

The contemporary reception and influence of the studies in the social and economic constitution of Wilhelminian Germany appears to be not very much different.[50] The enquiry and report on the *Lage der ostelbischen Landarbeiter* found wide recognition throughout the academic world. The renowned agrarian historian Georg Friedrich Knapp in particular praised Weber's work and was of the opinion 'that our expertise is at an end and we must begin to learn from the beginning again'.[51] This approval found another expression in the inclusion of Weber on the inner committee of the *Verein* in 1894. Apart from this, the reception was a more (socio-)political one, and one which will not occupy us any further here. Even Weber himself regarded the political consequences of his works as the most important result for him and this can be deduced from his Freiburg address of 1895 (40).

Weber's works on the stock exchange too led to a more economic and political reception and influence. Since he had taken part in the discussions of the provisional stock exchange committee, he knew the material and the outlines for the planned stock-exchange legislation in detail, even if he remained relatively ineffectual regarding his own objections. A discussion of the scientific reception of this work is, however, not possible here.

It was a similar story for the reception and influence of Weber's works on the position of German industrial workers. Although Heinrich Herkner, in his address to the *Verein* in September 1920 on Weber's death, praised the 'classicism' of Weber's exposé method[52] (90) and von Zwiedineck-Südenhorst in 1948 described the entire enquiry as the *Verein*'s most valuable piece of work in the second quarter-century of its existence,[53] nevertheless these works had no wide-reaching scientific influence. One possible effect, which was indirectly intended by Weber did not appear: this was the accelerated promotion of empirical social research in Germany. Doubtlessly the break caused by the First World War was just as responsible for this development as the fact that Weber himself did not pursue these researches and concentrated solely on the political application of his results. A few, rather unimportant dissertations (by Salli Goldschmidt,[54] Andreas Grunenberg,[55] Alfred Klee,[56] Felix Gerhardt,[57] Karl B. Breinlinger,[58] Eugen Katz,[59]) emerged from the agricultural worker enquiries, and a few further studies were derived from or at least were inspired by Weber's empirical investigations into industrial labour.[60]

Nevertheless, a possible initial spark for modern industrial and factory sociology in Germany remained absent, and it was only at the end of the twenties that research caught up with Weber's position again,[61] some of it, however, without the slightest acquaintance with Weber's groundwork.

If we now turn to the scientific influence of Weber's writings on the sociology of religion we encounter a somewhat different picture.[62] His studies in the cultural significance of Protestantism in particular experienced the widest, most lasting and best documented reception of all his works. Precisely because the theme of a 'connection' between 'capitalism' and 'Protestantism', whether causal, functional, or arbitrary, was a current theme at that time, and was frequently discussed by religious historians and national economists, Weber's essays encountered a well-prepared and receptive 'terrain'. Weber's position, generally speaking, found wide agreement among contemporary theologians, but among historians and national economists, by contrast, it was overwhelmingly criticized.

The first criticisms with which Weber took issue came from the historical philosopher H. Karl Fischer and the historian Felix Rachfahl. Fischer[63] judged Weber's work to be commendable and reviewed it extensively, but on the whole adopted a critical stance towards it. He commented that Weber's attempt at forming an 'idealistic interpretation of history' could not overwhelmingly prove a religious basis to the idea of vocation, and equally the conjuncture of Protestantism and capitalism was not historically provable everywhere. Fischer himself offered a supposedly 'psychological' explanation for the connections. In his second essay, Fischer attempted to prove that in this case, Weber's theses could only claim validity, if they could exclude all other factors in the origin of capitalism. In both his responses (81 and 84), Weber restricted himself to only a few clarifications, corrections and rejections. Rachfahl, a pupil under Lenz and Schmoller, similarly misunderstood Weber's intentions.[64] Rachfahl himself was the editor of a comprehensive work on reforming influences on William of Orange[65] and thus was familiar with the material. His dislike of categories and concepts which were empirically insufficiently grounded had set him against the nascent sociology from the very start. From his critique, only a few central points need be stressed: first, the concept of the 'spirit of capitalism' seemed to him to be unsuited to grasping the *economic* motivation behind capitalism; and second, in his opinion, capitalism still appeared in places where a 'spirit', with the religious origin that Weber imputed to it, was not detectable. This critique indicates a general characteristic of these early readings of Weber's studies – and not only of these: namely the lack of knowledge and understanding of Weber's concept of the 'ideal type', which he had presented at the same time in his 'Essay on Objectivity' (10E). Thus it is only under these circumstances that we must regard Rachfahl's accusation that Weber had investigated only *one* factor in the development of modern capitalism, or that his types could not be found in historical reality, etc. Weber's responses to Rachfahl (98 and 99) leave nothing to be desired in terms of sharpness and annoyance, when he writes of 'the gross mistakes caused through superficial reading' (99, p. 554). Weber regarded this reaction as nothing more than 'sterile polemics'.

The political economists and economic historians Lujo Brentano and Werner Sombart also pointed out the neglect of other aspects, which were more important for capitalism. Brentano[66] regarded Rachfahl's objections as 'quite considerable', while on the whole agreeing with Weber's work. His own critique may be reduced to the following points: Weber's concept of the 'spirit of capitalism' is a *petitio principii*, since he already presupposes what he aims to investigate in his definition – once again a criticism that misunderstands the concept of 'ideal-type'. Furthermore, Brentano claims, 'capitalism' in its beginnings does not date merely from Protestantism, but can be seen much earlier, for example in the Italian cities of the Middle Ages (with the Medici) and in Germany (Fugger). Brentano's critique of Weber's concept of vocation revolves around the argument that it was not only under Protestantism that vocational work attained a religious reverence, and that this alone would not determine capitalism. Both capitalism and the capitalist 'spirit', Brentano claims, are bound up with the origin of trade. It was a similar case in Sombart's reception.[67] He too was acquainted with the connection between Calvinism and capitalist development, nevertheless he was hostile to Weber's treatment of the theme. In exact opposition to Weber, he tried to investigate the anti-capitalist features of Protestantism, in the process of which, he had to research *all* the factors that had contributed to the formation of capitalism. Like Brentano, he did not want to tie himself down to modern Western capitalism. Thus, in his book on *Die Juden und das Wirtschaftsleben*[68] he emphasized the fundamental importance of the Jews in the formation of capitalism, especially in finance capitalism and 'political' capitalism. In his reply to this, Weber restricted himself to extended footnotes in the re-worked edition (2E, pp. 185ff) and to the immanent defence of his approach.

The reception of Weber's work on the *Protestant Sects* (5E) was important in the main for Weber's differentiation between 'church' and 'sect', a distinction which was taken up by his friend Ernst Troeltsch.[69]

We have only introduced here those contemporary experts whose reception Weber answered or gave his attention to directly. Over and above this, these works were acknowleged by further influence which was extremely long and continuous – and which carried on even after Weber himself had grown weary of this controversy. Weber became well known for the first time beyond the disciplines of agrarian history and political economy through these writings which were widely distributed. And here once again, the problems which accompanied this fame must be emphasized. It was partly a question of considerable misunderstandings and misinterpretations. For one thing, Weber's scrupulous circumscriptions and relativizations were not taken into consideration. The interpretation of Weber's work as a monocausal view of history stubbornly persisted. For another, Weber's works were turned extremely quickly into 'counter-evidence' for any materialist, Marxist interpretation, at least of the history of capitalism.[70] Added to this were misunderstandings regarding the methodological procedure, in particular the ideal-typical approach, as well as 'misunderstandings regarding Weber's conceptual apparatus'.[71] Altogether, we must agree with a comment by Ephraim Fischoff when he concludes his *Geschichte einer Kontroverse*, 'By and large the majority of his critics did not understand the direction of his interest, the limitations of the aim of his investigation, and the carefulness of his procedure.'[72]

In yet another respect, the reception of the 'Protestant Ethic' became important – above all for the creation and handing down of misunderstandings. The reception of these works introduced the process of Weber-interpretation in the USA and has for a long time until today remained the determining factor in it. From 1910 onwards the work was read in America, for example by P. T. Forsyth, William J. Ashley (one of R. H. Tawney's teachers), H. D. Foster, Hermann Levy, Charles Robinson, and Preserved Smith among others.[73] In the twenties, the economic historian R. H. Tawney[74] and H. H. Maurer from Chicago, who had graduated in Marburg, looked after the dissemination of the 'Weberian thesis'. Talcott Parsons, who had come to Heidelberg in 1925, had graduated under Edgar Salin on the subject of Weber's, Marx's and Sombart's theories of capitalism[75] and who in 1930 translated the 'Protestant Ethic' into English,[76] was to become particularly important. This translation and its translator occupy a central position in the first phase of the American reception of Weber. That Parsons too considered *The Protestant Ethic* to be a refutation of Marxist theory in one particular historical instance, has had a lasting effect to this day.

The studies in 'The Economic Ethic of the World Religions' which were in their scope and in Weber's own evaluation of them very much 'more weighty', did not achieve anywhere near the popularity of the works on Protestantism until today. There are few summarizing contemporary judgements on this work. In the 1931 *Handwörterbuch der Soziologie*, Joachim Wach characterized the *Gesammelte Aufsätze zur Religionssoziologie* and the chapter on the sociology of religion in *Economy and Society* as a first attempt at determining the area and tasks of the sociology of religion: 'With this, Weber became with his friends Sombart and Troeltsch the original founder of the sociology of religion . . . Thus far Weber has not found any actual successors especially for his efforts at systematization.'[77] Hermann Kantorowicz emphasized the systematic and theoretical aspects of Weber's sociology of religion, apart from the socio-historical ones, and highlighted the investigations into the nature of Indian castes as the 'model for research into group theory'.[78]

Out of the few competent reactions to the individual studies, we can sketch the following five. Alois Dempf characterized the *work on China* as the most comprehensive presentation he knew. Certainly, he wrote, Weber had underestimated the importance of Buddhism for India, nevertheless it was 'by far the best' German investigation, and the third volume constituted 'a quite extraordinary' scientific achievement.[79] In his review, Erich Rothacker recommended the third volume as 'a socio-historical commentary of the Old Testament'.[80] Paul Barth described the essays as 'an important, valuable contribution to sociology';[81] Andreas Walther interpreted the investigations more as 'a cross-check' on *The Protestant Ethic*;[82] and even Ernst Troeltsch interpreted the analyses as an attempt to do justice to the 'base-superstructure' problem.[83]

Arthur von Rosthorn took issue particularly critically with the studies on China, accusing Weber of regarding the political, economic, social and religious relations of China too statically and of not differentiating enough between the different phases of development.[84] On the other hand, Julius Braunthal described this essay as 'far and away the most important and instructive out of all the available literature on Chinese economic history'.[85] Otto Franke refers to Weber's works in connection with the mobility of the ancient Chinese city, but equally accuses Weber of a lack of differentiation; in Weber's writings 'the circumstances and conditions of different centuries are run colourfully together'.[86] Stefan Balázs, one of the founders of German Sinology, himself admitted to having been inspired by Weber. The very question of the character, importance and development of the nature of the Chinese city was, according to Balázs, 'to my knowledge, scarcely or never posed, let alone answered, except by Max Weber'. However, Balázs writes 'Weber's very enlightening expositions remain lacking in historical evidence, and are in the first place inspired guesswork, which turn out however – probably through historical researches – to be completely correct.'[87]

In the case of the second volume of the *Gesammelte Aufsätze zur Religionssoziologie*, with the investigations into *Hinduism and Buddhism*, we know of no other reactions except for those already described. Paul Honigsheim reports that not even Weber's Heidelberg colleague, Karl Rathgen, had taken note of, for example, the remarks on Japan.[88]

The influence of Weber's investigations into *Ancient Judaism*, of which Gerhart von Schulze-Gävernitz said that they came closer 'to the genesis of the "Jewish spirit" . . . than a whole library of current literature which was campaigning for and against the Jews',[89] was largely confined to mostly critical reviews. Certainly, H. Meinhold judged the study to be a 'great success', but labelled Weber as a well-read amateur, who did not stand up to a detailed critique.[90] Erwin Kohn criticized the category of the pariah-people for the Jews, and particularly attacked Weber's thesis of a division between internal and external morality.[91] The most fundamental review of this study was provided by Julius Guttmann, who emphasized the sociological perspective in particular. He too criticized a lack of mediation in the derivation of religious ideas from social causes, and he regarded the concept of the pariah as misleading.[92] In his dispute with Weber, Wilhelm Caspari demanded a more extensive control, correction and expansion of Weber's results.[93]

In summary, we must emphasize that an extreme imbalance in the reception of *The Protestant Ethic* and the works on the '*Wirtschaftsethik der Weltreligionen*' – an imbalance which is certainly not justified – must without doubt be seen as the main characteristic of the early reception and influence of Weber's works on the sociology of religion.

The contemporary reception of *Economy and Society*[94] is on the one hand quantitatively relatively unimportant and on the other hand strongly *selective* from the outset. There are few complete evaluations of Weber's work: in his concise overview, Erich Rothacker indicates that part I can be read as a 'glossary' to part II, and describes both volumes as Weber's 'major work'.[95] Hans Freyer called the work 'the greatest system in recent German sociology' and emphasized its unification of formal systematics and material presentation.[96] Eduard Spranger characterized the work as 'the most important produced by German sociology to this day'.[97]

Friedrich Gottl von Ottlilienfeld regarded the publication of *Economy and Society* as the possibility of producing a more precise definition of the relationship between political economy and sociology. Although he considered Weber's concept of a 'social economy' (*Sozialökonomik*) to be a 'sickly neologism', he took Weber's system on board. He classifies part I as a 'systematic sociology' in a specialist discipline and compared it to Simmel's '*Formen der Vergesellschaftung*' and to Leopold von Wiese's '*Beziehungslehre*'.[98] Andreas Walther emphasized the 'structural and functional view of history', which had been worked out by Weber in *Economy and Society* in the analysis of the 'external conditions of action'.[99] The most extensive review of *Economy and Society* was written by the constitutional historian Otto Hintze: he characterized the work as a 'system of sociology' which represented 'an epoch in sociological science'. The 'Basic Sociological Terms' especially were 'a magnificent attempt to encapsulate the entire wealth of the universal historical life of the state and society in few typical concepts'.[100] In 1937, Karl Mannheim characterized the importance of *Economy and Society* in the following way:

> It is not an easy read, but whoever has worked their way through it will see the world with new eyes and understand history in a new sense. Marx's great achievement in having formulated the social process as a theoretical problem is converted here into a detailed piece of independent research. However, it avoids suggesting any political standpoint through science. Unfortunately, Weber's work does not extend to the present day. What we can gain from him are tools for understanding society; their application to solve our problems must be worked out for ourselves.[101]

From early on, Weber's sociology of domination was regarded as the centre of the work. In his already mentioned review, Otto Hintze concentrated on this area of *Economy and Society* in particular and described Weber's approach – of illuminating the cultural circle of universal history with the 'magic-lantern' of the three ideal-types of legitimate domination – as 'epoch-making'.[102] Weber's sociology of domination was acknowledged extensively by Richard Thoma[103] and Herbert Sultan.[104] But this part of Weber's work without doubt exerted the greatest influence on the works of Robert Michels. For Michels, it was in particular the concept of charismatic domination and Weber's sketches of a sociology of political parties and elections which had the greatest influence on his works.[105] When, in 1911, Michels published his work which was quickly to become famous, '*Zur Soziologie des Parteiwesens in der modernen Demokratie*',[106] he dedicated it to Weber. However, we must not overlook considerable differences both in content and methodology between Weber and Michels.[107] In particular, Michels' consequence of the 'iron law of oligarchy', namely the radical denial of the possibilities of democratic forms of organization and the 'solution' through a fascistic, charismatic figure are diametrically opposed to Weber's position.

Next to Weber's sociology of domination, it was his 'Conceptual Exposition' and its concern with the founding of an 'interpretive sociology' which was 'taken heed of the most'.[108] Since Hermann Kantorowicz's attempt in 1923 to found an original sociology in the '*Erinnerungsgabe für Max Weber*',[109] there resulted discussions over Weber's establishment of sociology as a science which would interpret social action and explain it from its origins. Those taking part in these discussions were Eduard Spranger,[110] Othmar Spann,[111] Hans Lorenz Stoltenberg,[112] Hans Freyer,[113] Andreas Walther,[114] Max Scheler[115] and Franz Oppenheimer.[116] If there is a common denominator in these debates, it would be the *rejection* of Weber's conception: all these authors criticized Weber for conceiving of sociology too narrowly. They thought that sociology must be more than a theory of social action and that action could not be abbreviated merely to subjective, particularly instrumental action. Correspondingly the accusation of psychological reductionism appeared.[117] This criticism which, as probably became clear from the previous chapters on Weber's work and his method, rests essentially on gross *misunderstandings* and *foreshortenings*, was however of decisive importance in the early phase of the institutionalization of German sociology. When Eduard Spranger, in his ironic analysis of the contributions to the Max Weber commemoration of 1923, maintained that the only thing the positions had in common was 'the beautiful piety for the deceased', or else each of the authors understood something different by sociology,[118] we can today in retrospect say that on the contrary it was precisely the debate with *Weber's* work out of which each position could crystallize. These positions were important for the further development of this discipline in Germany, and abroad, for they were positions which answered the question of whether sociology was merely a certain method, a special science or a universal science. However, so long as this development is not subjected to even a basic analysis from a historical–sociological point of view, it will be impossible to work out the actual importance of Weber for the development of German and international sociology.

The section 'The economy and social norms' in *Economy and Society* experienced no contemporary reception worth mentioning; apart from references in Kantorowicz,[119] Scheler,[120] Heichelheim,[121] Oppenheim,[122] Gottl von Ottlilienfeld,[123] Wilbrandt,[124] and Mannheim,[125] this extremely dry section has exerted no extensive influence. It is a similar story with the contemporary reception of Weber's sociology of law. Even if today Weber, next to Eugen Ehrlich, is regarded as the 'second great founder of the sociology of law'[126] his sketches for a sociology of law for his age remain as good as unknown both to sociologists and to lawyers.[127] Apart from an essay by Fritz Sander,[128] and a contribution by Carl Schmitt in the commemorative volume edited by Palyi,[129] there is no extensive evaluation. Even for Weber's sociology of music there is only a contemporary essay by Otto Benesch[130] who evaluated the concept of a 'rationalization' of music extensively and positively, and an exposition by Arnold Schering in the 1931 *Handwörterbuch der Soziologie*.[131]

To summarize, we must stress that Weber's so-called 'magnum opus' at the time encountered an echo, which is rather too small to mention. Apart from very few exceptions it fell prey immediately to a strong 'influence which was segmented according to disciplines'.[132] The influence of Weber's formulation of a programme and a methodology of scientific, empirical and interpretive sociology appears not to have reached beyond its influence on Sombart, Simmel and later Alfred Schütz. They, however, were in their time all 'outsiders' to the academic and professional institutionalization of the young university discipline of sociology. The single fact that in the period 1922 to 1947 less than 2,000 copies of *Economy and Society* were sold[133] makes this situation clearer – if one compares this figure with for example the 12,000 copies of Schmoller's '*Grundriß der allgemeinen Volkswirtschaftslehre*' which were sold in the period 1900 to 1920.[134]

As far as Weber's works on the methodology of the social sciences[135] were concerned, we have already emphasized in our description how much his position, particularly in the concepts of 'understanding', the 'ideal-type' and of the 'freedom from value-judgement' were bound up with discussions which were going on at that time. That might lead to the assumption that Weber's work on methodology might have received greater contemporary attention than his research works. However, we must stress that the *significance* of Weber's works in this context was presented as considerably greater, particularly in view of the latter interpretations, than it actually was. For example, in the value-judgment dispute in particular, it was historically *not* the case that Weber was the *central figure*. Alfred Weber deals with precisely this fact when, in retrospect, he bewails the lack of reception of his brother's 'great methodology which united theory and history'.[136] Both Weber's subject matter as well as, and above all, the manner in which he presented it, alienated more people than it convinced. Weber's 'failure' in the *Verein für Sozialpolitik* and in particular in the *Deutsche Gesellschaft für Soziologie* serves to underline this fact. Even here, trivializations and misunderstandings once again played a part, when for example Weber's call for 'freedom from value-judgement' in the sense described above was turned into an unspecified 'value-freedom' which was then 'refuted' for its senselessness and unworkability.

The effect of Weber's position is perhaps clearest in the reception of his famous lecture of 1919, 'Science as a Vocation' (in 10E). As a printed text, this lecture became widely popular and soon took its place among the 'classic' texts of self-determination among social scientists.[137] However much Weber could be misused here as a mere 'point of comparison' for the propagation of one's own postulations is made clear by the equally famous 1920 piece by Erich von Kahler, a leading member of the Stefan George circle, on 'The Vocation of Science' (*Der Beruf der Wissenschaft*). Here Weber is seen as a representative of 'relativism' whose 'narrowly rational belief in progress . . . has not penetrated the entire true progress of the living'.[138] On the other hand, it was maintained that 'organic feeling', 'instinct' a 'healthy human understanding' and 'wisdom' were all based on 'inner directives'.[139] Similarly, Ernst Robert Curtius[140] makes use of Weber's position of an 'extremely relative concept of science' in order to call for 'the experiential duty of the entire personality' as opposed to sober knowledge 'purely for the sake of the subject matter'. Already in this contemporary reception, the cliché of Weber as the neo-Kantian positivist was beginning to be created – and his colleagues, friends and pupils, Ernst Troeltsch,[141] Max Scheler,[142] and Heinrich Rickert[143] collaborated in this formulation and in its perpetuation.

In conclusion, we must remember that the early reception of Weber's writings, both of the material and of the methodological, was extremely *selective*. It concentrated above all on the Protestant ethic writings and the printed versions of the lectures 'Science as a Vocation' (1919, 1921, 1930) and 'Politics as a Vocation' (1919, 1926). Even Marianne Weber's attempts to bring some of the scattered texts to a wider readership in her four collected volumes *Gesammelte Politische Schriften* (206) of 1921; *Gesammelte Aufsätze zur Wissenschaftslehre* (213) of 1922; *Gesammelte Aufsätze zur Sozial- und Wirtschaftsgeschichte* (217) of 1924; and *Gesammelte Aufsätze zur Soziologie und Sozialpolitik* (218) of 1924, too, did not much alter the basically *weak* reception and influence of Weber's writings during the period leading up to the Second World War.[144]

8

Weber's importance for sociology today and in the future

Weber has become regarded throughout the world as an undisputed 'classic' of sociology. Every lexicon or 'history' of this discipline mentions his name as central and emphasizes his authoritative influence on its development. This stands in obvious contrast to Weber's reception and influence during his lifetime, as we have documented it. There are two main causes for this development, which came about largely during the post-war period:

1   The American development of structural functionalism in sociology was, from about 1950 to 1965, the internationally dominant theoretical orientation of sociology. One of the 'leaders' of this development, Talcott Parsons, brought about an awareness of Weber and an interest in the German sociologist's work through his own writings and his translations of the *Protestant Ethic*[1] and *Economy and Society*.[2] Regardless of one's position *vis-à-vis* Parsons's interpretation of Weber, it must be stressed that it was his work which first of all aroused broad *international* interest in Weber. Although Parsons's translations have scope for improvement and his interpretation of Weber has necessitated a 'de-Parsonization' of Weber,[3] this changes nothing of the historical importance of Parsons in promoting Weber, the 'classic'. Even in Germany, the re-discovery of Weber after the Second World War was only set in motion by the reception of American structural functionalism.

2   In the course of the re-discovery of Weber after the Second World War, interpretations of Weber's life and work which directly or indirectly derived from persons and groups that were – more or less – *directly* influenced by Max Weber during his lifetime, became important. These groups involved Marianne Weber, Jaspers, Hellmann, Palyi, Loewenstein, Baumgarten, Brinkmann, Honigsheim, von Schelting, Lukács, Plessner, Troeltsch, Heuss, Michels, Gerth, Shils, Rheinstein, Fischoff and Winckelmann, among others.

Through the direct or indirect 'influencedness' of these thinkers, most of whom were under the spell of Max Weber, 'the man' or rather 'the myth of Heidelberg', a glorification and stylization of Max Weber the 'intellectual aristocrat', the 'Titan', 'the demon', 'the genius' arose which made a distanced and critical view somewhat difficult. An introductory judgment such as 'Max Weber was the greatest German of our era'[4] hinders an unbiased approach to Weber's work rather than facilitates it. Moreover, the majority of these editors, translators and interpreters were or are not specialist sociologists. The interest in Weber's universal historical framework frequently turns one's attention away from the *sociological* content of the work.

This brings us to a further characteristic of today's picture of Weber, the 'classic'. While noting the contrast between the relative lack of effectiveness and the 'failure' of Weber during his lifetime and his eminent international prominence and 'classicism' since the Second World War, it is nevertheless remarkable that this reception today is characterized by a surprisingly high degree of *selectivity*. It was only after 1904, i.e. with the *The Protestant Ethic* and the 'Essay on Objectivity', that Weber's work became recognized as sociologically important. It is because of this that our intention was to indicate the inadequacy of this viewpoint through the presentation of his entire *oeuvre*. The division of Weber's life into periods as lawyer, agrarian historian, political economist, religious expert, cultural historian, sociologist, philosopher, politician, social researcher, academic theoretician etc., denies its demonstrable continuities and consequently makes a comprehensive understanding impossible. This pattern of reception is particularly effective in two different ways: (1) Weber's plan for an 'interpretive sociology', as documented in the 'Conceptual Exposition' and the 'Basic Sociological Terms' are separated from his entire material work, and are dealt with in isolation and misunderstood as 'the' Weberian sociology; and (2) The whole area of research material is detached from Weber's writings on the methodology of the social sciences and both are not understood as linked to one another.

Through this pervasive pattern in most interpretations, numerous misunderstandings, assumptions and foreshortenings have arisen since Weber's time until today, which we must briefly mention here. In other words, a single work, as for example the 'Protestant Ethic' cannot be understood *comprehensively* and adequately if

Weber's works on the legal, historical, social, economic and political premises and effects of modern capitalism, which were also written before 1904, are not included.

The methodological concepts of *Verstehen, Erklären* and the 'ideal-typical procedure' are not familiar.

The later works on 'The Economic Ethic of the World Religions' are not included.

The scientist Weber's (self-)understanding of the tasks and possibilities of scientific work, as recovered in his postulates on 'freedom from value-judgement' and 'relevance to values', is not acknowledged as the basis of interpretation.

The outcome of the high selectivity of the reception of Weber's work thus far comprises not only the effects mentioned of divisions in time and space and those of a separation of investigations and method. Added to this is the *fragmentation* of the entire oeuvre into 'instructive pieces' (*Lehrstücke*). It is doubtless this which leads us to today's *quantitatively* important impression of Weber the 'classic'. No internationally recognized work in the sociology of bureaucracy, domination, music, religion, the city or political parties etc., will fail to cite the name of Max Weber as one of the decisive historical precursors who worked on contemporary problems in the area of social science. The overwhelming majority of this kind of ritualized obeisances before Weber the 'classic' have no other function than that of legitimizing their own undertaking. Weber the 'classic' serves to establish the identity in both content and methodology of a discipline, of a research intention and of the respective scientist.[5] If, in *this* influence on today's and probably on future international sociology, we see a successful passing of the 'test of time', then Weber, the 'classic' has already passed the test.

However, a question emerges from all this: What does it prove, if for example in those social scientific works on the problem of 'charismatic domination' published between 1920 and today, the name of Max Weber is mentioned? This appears to be purely an antiquarian 'preservation of historical monuments', which prevents a *living* exchange with Weber's work and method. The 'vitality' of a classic cannot be proven purely by the number of times he or she is quoted.

If we proceed from the criteria we have ourselves created for determining a 'classic', then we end up with a very ambivalent picture:

1 Weber has passed the 'test of time'; over sixty years after his death, his works are still read and quoted today. Since 1945 we can see a pre-occupation with Weber which is gradually growing internationally.[6]

2 The continuing and increasing *reference* to Weber's works and the equally strengthened *exchange* with him is not actually a *re*naissance. Weber's *contemporary* reception and influence was incomparably less

strong and 'canonized' than in the period after 1945. Weber did not stand at the centre of the sociological discourse of his *own* age.

3   Weber developed no *new* sociological theory. In a strictly scientific–theoretical sense, he did not furnish sociology with *any theory* at all. In this respect, his work consists of an unending multitude of axioms, premises, suggestions, theses, hypotheses and a few theorems. The lack of a system, the existing contradictions and the differing levels of precision made and still make Weber's entire oeuvre into a huge 'quarry', which could be, and indeed was, exploited, protected, wondered at and inspected.

4   Weber did not discover *any* problematic area which had not already been discovered previously or independently of him. Research into the development and effects of modern capitalism, the restriction of the social action of the single individual with social rules, the normative preconditions for material circumstances and processes, the material and social preconditions for normative rules etc. were problems which sociologists before Weber and those after – independently of him – had dealt with.

9   Weber discovered neither the *method* of *Verstehen* nor that of the 'ideal-typical procedure'. However, he made both these research tools more precise for the sociology of his age and reflected them conceptually. But both heuristic aids were greatly changed and differentiated during the scientific–theoretical discussions and developments which took place after Weber, with the result that Weber's essays on these methods, while being certainly very exciting texts, have rather an archive or antiquarian value when compared with the systematic scientific–theoretical works, which start from a completely different (self-)understanding of today's natural sciences than there was during Weber's time.[7]

So what is left of Weber the 'classic' for the future development of sociology? We can see in Weber not so much the man who *introduced* a new viewpoint, through which new positions on problems, new concepts, and new methods were created, but rather the sociologist who has followed this viewpoint through all its consequences and does not assume that he has ever reached a comprehensive, exhausting answer. We can call Weber's viewpoint a form of 'mediation' – or we could also say 'dialectic' if this concept were not already burdened with even more connotations.

Weber wanted to mediate between *Verstehen* and *Erklären*; between 'causal adequacy' and 'adequacy on the level of meaning'; between 'individual' and 'society'; between 'subjectively intended meaning' and 'normative order'; between 'social action' and 'social order'; between 'communal social relationships' and 'associative social relationships'; between 'material' conditions/consequences and 'immaterial' conditions/consequences; between 'rationalization' and 'charisma'; between 'the extraordinary' and the 'everyday'; between the 'ethic of single-minded conviction' (*Gesinnungsethik*) and the 'ethic of responsibility' (*Verautwortungsethik*). In all these attempts at mediation, supplemented by the richness of universal–historical data, we can see both Weber the specialist sociologist as well as Weber, the 'classic'.

What is specifically *sociological* is his mediation of 'individual' and 'society'; for Weber, the one without the other is neither thinkable nor explicable. We can see in Weber's work the structuring of that mediation which proceeds from a *social* construction of reality,[8] and in which the individual on the one hand encounters an 'objective' reality confronting him or her, and on which, on the other hand, the individual can change and have an influence. The 'subjective' meaning is not a residual quantity of social reality, but a constitutive element for its creation and alteration. Thus the real object of Weber's sociology consists of grasping both the 'subjective' creation of meaning and also the 'objective' social reality.

The 'vitality' of Weber the 'classic' resides in the fact that he does not present this specific sociological viewpoint in a self-contained theory, but he undertook his 'attempts at mediation' in continually different ways. Thus Weber might be categorized in a context in which he has not been seen for some time: as an *essayist*.[9] Weber undertook his 'attempts at mediation' in the form of the essay, as that stylistic device with the help of which an object, theme or historical process may be placed in the centre of completely different perspectives and aspects. The experimental, hypothetical character of the essay is particularly important in this, as its professed goal is a synthesis, *tertium datur*, thus exactly what we want to indicate by 'mediation'. If we regard the essay as the art-form suited to the twentieth century, then Weber is immediately placed alongside authors such as Georg Simmel, Robert Musil and Georg Lukács, among others. They all shared the attempt to 'mediate', to build bridges, and thereby to open up new pathways. If, as a result, we regard the *Gesammelte Aufsätze zur Religionssoziologie*, for example, or *Economy and Society* as large, scientific essays, or rather collections of essays, and not as comprehensive, theoretical-empirical monographs, then many a sterile, interpretational dispute over the 'unity' or 'fragmentation' of the work would become unnecessary.[10] It is precisely this possibility *and* necessity of finding continually new ways of reading and interpreting his oeuvre which spark off new discussions with

Weber's work and method time and again. Through all the historical and contemporary limitations of his work, Weber the 'classic' will remain an excellent 'touchstone' for determining the professional identity of every sociologist. And thus any serious discussion of Weber's work will lead away from a narrow perspective limited only to its discipline, and draw us at the same time towards a rediscovery of the historical dimension of social reality.

Notes

1 Life

1 Much of Max Weber's life remains unresearched. Cf. Dirk Käsler, *'Der retuschierte Klassiker. Zum gegenwärtigen Forschungsstand der Biographie Max Webers'*, in J. Weiß (ed.), *Max Weber heute. Erträge und Probleme der Forschung* (Frankfurt, 1988). This sketch must be seen only as a fragmentary contribution to this research. Only the complete editing and publication of his private and academic correspondence will facilitate the solution of some obscurities. I am particularly grateful for the critical comments of the late Professor Eduard Baumgarten and Professor M. Rainer Lepsius.

2 A national legion founded in 1813. [Tr.]

3 Marianne Weber, *Max Weber: A Biography*, tr. Harry Zohn (New York: Wiley, 1975), p. 68.

4 Cf. Hermann Baumgarten, *'Der deutsche Liberalismus. Eine Selbstkritik'*, in *Preußische Jahrbücher*, vol. 18 (1866), pp. 455ff and 575ff.

5 Marianne Weber, *Max Weber*, p. 114. Cf. also Alfred Heuss, *'Max Webers Bedeutung für die Geschichte des griechisch-römischen Altertums'*, in *Historische Zeitschrift*, vol. 201, no. 3 (December 1965), pp. 536f, particularly note 5.

6 See bibliography for the proceedings of the *Verein für Sozialpolitik*, Leipzig 1893, p. 7.

7 *Geisteswissenschaften*: usually translated as 'the human sciences' or 'moral sciences' and understood as one half of the opposition between human sciences versus natural sciences. This conflict was at its height during the time of the *Methodenstreit*, when the newly expanding natural sciences caused the established human science disciplines to feel under threat. [Tr.]

8 *Reichstag*: the lower chamber of the German parliament. [Tr.]

9 Marianne Weber, *Max Weber*, p. 242.

10 See the letter of Professor Dr J. Hoops of 21 June 1917 to the Nominations

Commission of the Senate of Munich University in which Hoops gives evidence on Weber's state of health in the Munich University Archive, Sign. Sen. 346.

11 See section 3 of the bibliography, p. 235.

12 The intention to publish Weber's eighty or so letters to Marianne, his hundred or so to Else Jaffé and his one hundred and twenty or so to Mina Tobler will no doubt throw light on the problems of this area on Weber's development.

13 Marianne Weber, *Max Weber*, p. 425.

14 The *'Delbrück-Denkschrift'*, signed by Weber, Brentano, Troeltsch among others, opposed the extreme right's arguments for the prolongation of the war. [Tr.]

15 Marianne Weber, *Max Weber*, p. 598.

16 Wolfgang J. Mommsen, *Max Weber und die deutsche Politik 1890–1920* (Tübingen, 1959), p. 284.

17 Ernst Toller was a dramatist of the Expressionist movement. [Tr.]

18 Mommsen, *Max Weber und die deutsche Politik*, p. 293.

19 Marianne Weber, *Max Weber*, p. 630.

20 Mommsen, *Max Weber*, pp. 297ff.

21 Kurt Eisner, the prime minister of Bavaria, was assassinated by Anton Graf von Arco (auf) Valley on 21 February 1919. The young count's death sentence was initially commuted to life imprisonment and finally in 1924, because of ill health, he was released. Weber was critical of such leniency. See Marianne Weber, *Max Weber*, p. 672, n. 16. [Tr.]

2 Early writings

1 The numbers in brackets throughout the text after the titles of works or after quotations, refer to sections 1 and 3 of the Bibliography (pp. 235–6 and 242–74). References which are simply a number/number and lower-case letter (e.g. 215/215f) refer to section 3; numbers followed by upper-case E (e.g. 10E) refer to the English translations listed in section 1. [Tr.]

2 Weber was inspired in this study 'largely and originally' by the works of Karl Rodbertus (48, p. 18). Cf. Karl Rodbertus, *'Untersuchungen auf dem Gebiete der Nationalökonomie des klassischen Altertums. I. Zur Geschichte der agrarischen Entwicklung Roms unter den Kaisern oder die Adscriptitier, Inquilinen und Colonen'*, in *Jahrbücher für Nationalökonomie und Statistik*, 2 vols., ed. Bruno Hildebrand (Jena: Friedrich Mauke, 1864), pp. 206–68; and ibid., II. *'Zur Geschichte der römischen Tributsteuern seit Augustus'*, vol. 4 (1865), pp. 339–427; vol. 5 (1865) pp. 135–71, 241–315; vol. 8 (1867), pp. 81–126, 385–475; and ibid., *'Zur Frage des Sachwerts des Geldes im Altertum'*, vol. 14, pp. 341–420.

3 Alfred Heuss, *'Max Webers Bedeutung für die Geschichte des griechisch-römischen Altertums'*, in *Historische Zeitschrift*, vol. 201, no. 3 (December 1965), p. 534. For Heuss's own account see his *Römische Geschichte*, 4th edn (Braunschweig, 1976).

4 Heuss, *Max Webers Bedeutung*, p. 539.

5 See below, p. 000.

6 Heuss, *Max Webers Bedeutung*, p. 531.

7 Apparently Weber originally intended to take over the article using the keyword '*Kolonat*', as is clear from numerous cross-references (cf. *The Agrarian Sociology of Ancient Civilizations*, p. 330). However, Michael Rostowzew took over the article and later produced a comprehensive investigation on this theme, '*Studien zur Geschichte des römischen Kolonats*', in *Erstes Beiheft zum Archiv für Papyrusforschung und verwandte Gebiete*, ed. Ulrich Wilcken (Leipzig/Berlin: Teubner, 1910).

8 See *The Agrarian Society of Ancient Civilizations* and also 67 and 97 which are thematically linked in this area.

9 Heuss, *Max Webers Bedeutung*, p. 538.

10 Cf. below pp. 180-84.

11 See below, pp. 42-48.

12 Heuss, *Max Webers Bedeutung*, p. 540.

13 Cf. below, pp. 201-13.

14 Cf. above, pp. 18 and 22, and below p. 142f.

15 Cf. below pp. 142ff.

3 Social change in German society

1 Cf. Franz Boese, *Geschichte des Vereins für Sozialpolitik 1872-1932*, (Berlin, 1939).
Else Conrad, *Der Verein für Sozialpolitik und seine Wirksamkeit auf dem Gebiet der gewerblichen Arbeiterfrage*, (Jena, 1906).
Marie L. Plessen, *Die Wirksamkeit des Vereins für Socialpolitik von 1872-1890*, (Berlin, 1975)
Dieter Lindenlaub, *Richtungskämpfe im Verein für Sozialpolitik*, (Wiesbaden, 1967).

2 '*Die Verhältnisse der Landarbeiter in Nordwestdeutschland, Württemberg, Baden und in den Reichslanden*', in *Schriften des Vereins für Socialpolitik. LIII. Die Verhältnisse der Landarbeiter in Deutschland*, vol. I (Leipzig, 1892) p. viii.

3 Cf. the works by Oberschall and Lazarsfeld/Oberschall in the bibliography, pp. 000-000.

4 Alexander von Lengerke, *Die ländliche Arbeiterfrage*, (Berlin, 1849).

5 Theodor von der Goltz, *Die Lage der ländlichen Arbeiter im Deutschen Reich* (Berlin, 1874).

6 Cf. several examples in 8, pp. 737-48.

7 For Weber a community (*Gemeinschaft*) (which he later changed to *Verband*, usually translated as an organized group or association) does not necessarily mean a less developed or more rural grouping of people than a society (*Gesellschaft*), as the English words connote. In his studies of Wilhelminian Germany Weber calls a *Gemeinschaft* the complex mutual interdependence of estate-owner and free-wage labourers. A *Gesellschaft* emerges with the introduction of the division of labour and a competitive attitude to work. [Tr.]

8 Cf. especially Wolfgang J. Mommsen, *Max Weber und die deutsche Politik 1890-1920* (Tübingen, 1959), pp. 23-54.

9 Cf. the relationship with the Evangelical-social courses in Berlin in which Weber participated and the report by Göhre in 31, pp. 8f, and also 10.

10 Cf. the account of the proceedings in 18, p. 194.

11 Cf. below pp. 180-84.

12 Cf. the 'Foreword' by Herkner, Schmoller and Alfred Weber in the resulting first volume, Marie Bernays, *'Auslese und Anpassung der Arbeiterschaft der geschlossenen Großindustrie. Dargestellt an den Verhältnissen der "Gladbacher Spinnerei und Weberei" AG zu München-Gladbach im Rheinland'*, vol. 133, *Schriften des Vereins für Sozialpolitik* (Leipzig: Duncker and Humblot, 1910), pp. vii-xv.

13 Cf. in particular Emil Kraepelin (ed.), *Psychologische Arbeiten* (Leipzig, 1895-1914) 6 vols each of 4 nos.

14 Cf. the bibliographical details in 115, pp. 117-38.

15 Cf. Adolf Levenstein, *Die Arbeiterfrage* (Munich, 1912).

4 The sociology of religion

1 Werner Sombart, *Der moderne Kapitalismus*, 2 vols (Leipzig, 1902). A third volume appeared somewhat later, *Das Wirtschaftsleben im Zeitalter des Hochkapitalismus* (Munich, 1927).

2 Cf. in particular Eberhard Gothein, *Wirtschaftsgeschichte des Schwarzwaldes* (Strasburg, 1892); Werner Wittich, *Deutsche und französische Kultur im Elsass* (Strasburg, 1900); Georg Jellinek, *Die Erklärung der Menschen- und Bürgerrechte* (Leipzig, 1895) (2nd edn 1904).

3 Cf. Reinhard Bendix, 'The Protestant Ethic Revisited', in *Comparative Studies in Society and History*, vol. 9, no. 3 (1967), pp. 266-73.

4 Ernst Troeltsch, *Die Soziallehren der christlichen Kirchen und Gruppen* (Tübingen, 1912), previously published in the *Archiv für Sozialwissenschaft und Sozialpolitik*, ed. Werner Sombart, Max Weber and Edgar Jaffé, vol. 26, no. 1, pp. 1-55; no. 2, pp. 292-342; no. 3, pp. 649-92; vol. 27, no. 1, pp. 1-72; no. 2, pp. 317-48; vol. 28, no. 1, pp. 1-71; no. 2, pp. 387-416; no. 3, pp. 621-53; vol. 29, no. 1, pp. 1-49; no. 2, pp 381-416; vol. 30, no. 1, pp. 30-65; no. 3, pp. 666-720 (1908-10).

5 A close textual examination of the different historical editions between 1905 and 1920 is however necessary in order to deal comprehensively and in detail with these works.

6 Martin Offenbacher, *Konfession und soziale Schichtung. Eine Studie über die wirtschaftliche Lage der Katholiken und Protestanten in Baden*, (Tübingen/Leipzig, 1901) (Also vol. 4, no. 5 of the national economic proceedings of the universities of Baden.)

7   Benjamin Franklin, *Necessary Hints to those that would be Rich* (1736) and *Advise to a Young Tradesman* (1748).

8   Cf. 2E, p. 26.

9   Cf. for example, Hugh Martin, *Puritanism and Richard Baxter* (London, 1954).

10 Cf. above p. 81.

11 See 'The Protestant Sects and the Spirit of Capitalism', in 5E, p. 301.

12 For the continuing reception of Weber's work on Protestantism see below, pp. 202-4.

13 Here we are referring to Walter M. Sprondel's interpretation. See Walter M. Sprondel, *'Sozialer Wandel, Ideen und Interessen: Systematisierungen zu Max Webers Protestantischer Ethik'*, in C. Seyfarth and W. M. Sprondel (eds), *Seminar: Religion und gesellschaftliche Entwicklung*, (Frankfurt am Main, 1973), pp. 206-24.

14 Cf. 2E, p. 98, and below pp. 180-84.

15 The reader is referred for examples to the works of Löwith, Birnbaum, Giddens, Lüthy, Bosse, Zander and Kocka.

16 Cf. below pp. 175-80.

17 Cf. above p. 44.

18 In *The Protestant Ethic* the concept of charisma is used purely theologically, i.e. in reference to the priest's ability to confer absolution. Cf. 184, pp. 229f.

19 Cf. above pp. 90f.

20 The 'Veda' is used here as a collective term for the Vedas, the Indian collection of hymns, prayers and formulae etc.

21 Cf. above p. 111.

22 Cf. above p. 99.

5   Economy and Society

1   Marianne Weber, *Max Weber, Ein Lebensbild* (Tübingen, 1926), p. 424 (omitted in English translation).

2   For details on the editions see Marianne Weber's preface in 215, 215a, 215b, and Johannes Winckelmann's preface in 215c, 215e, and 215f; also his essay *'Max Webers opus posthumum'*, in *Zeitschrift für die gesamte Staatswissenschaft*, vol. 105 (1949), pp. 368-87. See also Friedrich H. Tenbruck, *'Wie gut kennen wir Max Weber?'*, in ibid., vol. 131 (1975), pp. 719-42; and his essay, *'Abschied von Wirtschaft und Gesellschaft'*, in ibid., vol. 133 (1977), pp. 703-36.

3   Cf. above pp. 74-141.

4   Cf. above pp. 42-8.

5   Cf. 3, 4, 16, 17, 27, 51, 59, 113.

6   Cf. Marianne Weber, *Max Weber. A Biography*, tr. Harry Zohn (New York: Wiley, 1975), pp. 675ff.

 7 Cf. below, pp. 180–84.
 8 Cf. 8E, p. 29.
 9 Cf. Weber on the sociology of law, above pp. 144–48.
10 Cf. 8E, pp. 35f.
11 Cf. ibid., p. 64.
12 Cf. ibid., p. 65.
13 Cf. ibid., p. 83.
14 Cf. ibid., p. 96f.
15 Cf. ibid., pp. 114–18.
16 Cf. ibid., pp. 118–30.
17 Cf. ibid., pp. 130ff.
18 Cf. ibid., pp. 166–211.
19 The presentation which follows takes its orientation in places from my argu-
    ment in *'Das Konzept der "Herrschaft" in den Weberschen "Grundbegriffen"'*, from
    my book *Revolution und Veralltäglichung* (Munich, 1977).
20 Weber provides only a sketchy description of the forms of appearance of
    'power' in the economy (cf. 8E, p. 110; 165), in terms of class, status group and
    party (cf. 8E, p. 926) and in bureaucracy (cf. 8E, pp. 956f). He affords the
    phenomenon of 'discipline' similar treatment in the military sphere (cf. 8E,
    p. 213) in the economic sphere (cf. 8E, p. 214) and in the area of religious
    communities (cf. 8E, pp. 1158f).
21 Cf. 8E, pp. 271–84.
22 Cf. ibid., pp. 217–26.
23 Cf. ibid., pp. 302–7.
24 Marianne Weber, *Max Weber,* p. 500.
25 Cf. 211, 211a, 211b.
26 Alphons Silbermann, *'Max Webers musikalischer Exkurs. Ein Kommentar zu seiner
    Studie "Die rationalen und soziologischen Grundlagen der Musik"'*, in *Kölner Zeitschrift
    für Soziologie und Sozialpsychologie*, special no. 7 (1963), p. 458.
27 Cf. below pp. 206–09.

6   **Methodological writings**

 1 The position was adopted first of all by Marianne Weber, and its major
    representatives were Alexander von Schelting in his *Max Webers
    Wissenschaftslehre* (Tübingen, 1934), and Dieter Henrich in his *Die Einheit der
    Wissenschaftslehre Max Webers* (Tübingen, 1952).
 2 In particular Friedrich H. Tenbruck, *'Die Genesis der Methodologie Max Webers'*,
    in *Kölner Zeitschrift für Soziologie und Sozialpsychologie* vol. 11 (1959), pp. 573–630;
    Johannes F. Winckelmann, *'Max Webers logisch-methodologisches Interesse'*, in 229,
    pp. ix–xix; and Hans Henrik Bruun, *Science, Values and Politics in Max Weber's
    Methodology* (Copenhagen, 1972).
 3 Cf. in particular 60, 68, 71, 75, 80, 85, 92.
 4 Cf. Dirk Käsler, *Wege in die soziologische Theorie* (Munich, 1974), pp. 8–11.

5   Cf. the documentation and systematization in Walter L. Bühl (ed.), *Verstehende Soziologie. Grundzüge und Entwicklungstendenzen* (Munich, 1972).

6   A particularly important historical example of this is Alfred Schütz, *Der sinnhafte Aufbau der sozialen Welt. Eine Einleitung in die verstehende Soziologie*, 1st edn (Vienna, 1932); paperback edn (Frankfurt, 1974), especially pp. 9–61.

7   Cf. in particular 60, 62, 68, 75.

8   Cf. above pp. 148–56.

9   Cf. above p. 151.

10 Cf. above pp. 149–56.

11 Cf. above pp. 74–94.

12 Cf. above p. 154.

13 Cf. above p. 32.

14 Cf. as an earlier formulation of the concept Weber's presentation in his 1903 essay on Roscher and Knies, 14E.

15 The *Methodenstreit* originated in a conflict between the human sciences and the natural sciences. The latter wished to extend their 'rational' methodology to other disciplines as, it was claimed, only this methodology led to the establishment of certain truths. 'Art', however, lay outside the realm of this methodology, and the new *social* sciences appeared to lie in neither the one camp nor the other. Menger's 'classical' school argued that political economy belonged to the natural sciences and could thus be schematized methodologically into concepts and laws. Schmoller's 'historical' school, by contrast, claimed that such laws were too simplistic to explain human behaviour which was complicated by the individual's freedom of will. [Tr.]

16 Cf. in particular Friedrich H. Tenbruck, '*Die Genesis der Methodologie Max Webers*', in *Kölner Zeitschrift für Soziologie und Sozialpsychologie*, vol. 11 (1959), pp. 573–630; Winfried Schulze, *Soziologie und Geschichtswissenschaft. Einführung in die Probleme der Kooperation beider Wissenschaften* (Munich, 1974), pp. 17–47.

17 Cf. on this and the following Judith Janoska-Bendl, *Methodologische Aspekte des Idealtypus. Max Weber und die Soziologie der Geschichte*, (Berlin, 1965), pp. 17ff.

18 Cf. above pp. 179f.

19 To be found first in Bernhard Pfister, *Die Entwicklung zum Idealtypus. Eine methodologische Untersuchung über das Verhältnis von Theorie und Geschichte bei Menger, Schmoller und Max Weber* (Tübingen, 1928), pp. 170ff.

20 For example Janoska-Bendl, *Methodologische Aspekte des Idealtypus*, p. 55.

21 Johannes Weiß, *Max Webers Grundlegung der Soziologie. Eine Einführung* (Munich, 1975), p. 71.

22 Cf. Bühl (ed.), *Verstehende Soziologie*, pp. 39ff.

23 Cf. a useful documentation of some strands of the discussion up to 1967, in Hans Albert and Ernst Topitsch (eds), *Werturteilsstreit* (Darmstadt, 1971).

24 Cf. on this and the following, Georg F. Iggers, *Deutsche Geschichtswissenschaft. Eine Kritik der traditionellen Geschichtsauffassung von Herder bis zur Gegenwart* (Munich, 1971); especially chaps 6 and 7.

25 Cf. the extensive discussion in ibid. pp. 175ff, 198ff.

26 In *Jahrbuch für Gesetzgebung, Verwaltung und Volkswirtschaft im Deutschen Reich*, ed. Gustav Schmoller, vol. 7, no. 3 (Leipzig, 1883) pp. 239–58.

27 Schmoller, ibid., p. 241.

28 Carl Menger, *Die Irrtümer des Historismus in der deutschen Nationalökonomie* (Vienna, 1884). For an account of the entire *Methodenstreit*, cf. Carl Brinkmann, *Gustav Schmoller und die Volkswirtschaftslehre* (Stuttgart, 1937); Gerhard Ritzel, *Schmoller versus Menger* (Offenbach, 1951).

29 Wilhelm Windelband, *History and Natural Science*, tr. Guy Oakes, in *History and Theory*, vol. 19 (1980), pp. 175ff.

30 Heinrich Rickert, *The limits of concept formation in natural science: a logical introduction to the historical sciences*, ed. and tr. Guy Oakes (Cambridge: CUP, 1986).

31 For the effects of the *Methodenstreit* on Weber's position, cf. Hans Henrik Bruun, *Science, Values and Politics in Max Weber's Methodology* (Copenhagen, 1972), pp. 94–144.

32 Cf. Paul Honigsheim, '*Die Gründung der Deutschen Gesellschaft für Soziologie in ihren geistesgeschichtlichen Zusammenhängen*', in *Kölner Zeitschrift für Soziologie und Sozialpsychologie*, vol. 11 (1959), pp. 3–10.

33 Marianne Weber, *Max Weber*, p. 425. For an account of the debates during the first seven conventions of the *Gesellschaft* cf. Dirk Käsler, *In Search of Respectability: The Controversy Over the Destination of Sociology During the Conventions of the German Sociological Society, 1910-1930*, in *Knowledge and Society: Studies in the Sociology of Culture Past and Present*, ed. by Robert A. Jones/Henrika Kuklick. vol. 4, (Greenwich, Conn./London: JAI Press 1983), pp. 227–272.

34 Cf. Michael Zöller, *Die Unfähigkeit zur Politik. Politikbegriff und Wissenschaftsverständnis von Humboldt bis Habermas* (Opladen, 1975), pp. 101–19.

35 Ibid., p. 106.

36 Ibid.

37 Ibid., p. 107.

38 Ibid.

39 Cf. Herrmann Lübbe, *Politische Philosophie in Deutschland* (Basel/Stuttgart, 1963), pp. 179ff.

40 Cf. Hans Kammler, *Logik der Politikwissenschaft* (Wiesbaden, 1976), pp. 200f.

7   The reception of Weber's work during his lifetime

1 My long-time assistant, Helmut Fogt, presented his investigations on this subject in October 1977, and the following section is based on this. Helmut Fogt, *Max Weber - Wirkung und Bedeutung, 1890-1933* (unpublished Master's thesis, Munich University, Faculty of Social Sciences, examined by P. Ch. Ludz).

2 Fogt, *Wirkung und Bedeutung*, p. 2.

3 Cf. Schnabel's work which presented a comparable analysis of Georg Simmel;

Peter-Ernst Schnabel, *'Georg Simmel'*, in *Klassiker des soziologischen Denkens*, vol. 1, ed. Dirk Käsler (Munich, 1976), pp. 267–311.

4   Fogt, *Wirkung und Bedeutung*, pp. 4f.

5   Cf. Walter L. Bühl, *Einführung in die Wissenschaftssoziologie* (Munich, 1974), pp. 22f.

6   Cf. Bühl, *Einführung*, pp. 152–62.

7   Cf. Fogt, *Wirkung und Bedeutung*, pp. 11–22.

8   Eduard Heyck, (review of) *'Max Weber, Zur Geschichte der Handelsgesellschaften im Mittelalter'* (1889), in *Historische Zeitschrift*, vol. 65, no. 29 (1890), pp. 299–301.

9   Leopold Menzinger, (review of) *'Max Weber, Zur Geschichte der Handelsgesellschaften im Mittelalter'* (1889), in *Historische Zeitschrift*, vol. 15 (XXXIV), no. 1 (Munich/Leipzig, 1892), pp. 28–9.

10 Max Pappenheim, (review of) *'Max Weber, Zur Geschichte der Handelsgesellschaften im Mittelalter'*, in *Zeitschrift für das Gesamte Handelsrecht*, ed. L. Goldschmidt et al., vol. 37, no. 22, (Stuttgart, 1890), pp. 255–9.

11 See Pappenheim, review of *'Max Weber'*, p. 258 and Fogt, *Wirkung und Bedeutung*, p. 12.

12 Levin Goldschmidt, *Handbuch des Handelsrechts*, 3rd completely rev. edn, vol. 1, *'Geschichtlich-literarische Einleitung und die Grundlehren'*, section 1, *Universalgeschichte des Handelsrechts, Part 1* (Stuttgart, 1891), pp. 240–90.

13 Levin Goldschmidt, *System des Handelsrechts mit Einschluss des Wechsel-, See- und Versicherungsrechts im Grundriss*, 3rd (rev. and enlarged) edn with individual case studies (Stuttgart, 1891 (first edition 1887, second edition 1889, third edition 1890), pp. 26, 29.

14 Lujo Brentano, *Gutachten betr. Aufnahme Webers in die historische Klasse der Bayerischen Akademie der Wissenschaften vom 12.7.1919.* Thanks to Dr Martin Riesebrodt, Project Director of the Max Weber Collected Edition at the *Kommission für Sozial- und Wirtschaftsgeschichte der Bayerischen Akademie der Wissenschaften* for permission to inspect this work.

15 Werner Sombart, *Der moderne Kapitalismus. Historisch-systematische Darstellung des gesamteuropäischen Wirtschaftslebens von seinen Anfängen bis zur Gegenwart*, 3 vols., 6th edn (Munich-Leipzig 1924–7), vol. 1, 1st board, pp. 286, 300; vol. 2, 1st board, pp. 87, 90f, 139, 145, 147.

16 Sir William J. Ashley, *The Economic Organization of England* (London, 1914). I am grateful for this reference to Christopher Bernert, 'The Diffusion of the 'Weber-Thesis', 1904–30, unpublished paper, State University of New York at Stony Brook, Department of Sociology, May 1976, p. 13.

17 Cf. above, p. 00.

18 Theodor Mommsen, *'Zum römischen Bodenrecht'*, in *Hermes: Zeitschrift für classische Philologie*, ed. G. Kaibel and C. Robert, vol. 27, (Berlin, 1892), pp. 79–117.

19 Paul Krüger, (review of) *'Max Weber, Die römische Agrargeschichte in ihrer Bedeutung für das Staats- und Privatrecht'*, in *Kritische Vierteljahrsschrift für*

Gesetzgebung und Rechtswissenschaft ed. A. v. Bechmann and M. Seydel, vol. 15 (XXXIV), no. 4 (Munich–Leipzig, 1892), pp. 481–93.

20   L. M. Hartmann, (review of) *'Max Weber, Die römische Agrargeschichte in ihrer Bedeutung für das Staats- und Privatrecht'*, in *Archiv für Soziale Gesetzgebung und Statistik*, ed. H. Braun, vol. 5 (Berlin, 1892), pp. 215–18.

21   Herman Schiller, (review of) *'Max Weber, Die römische Agrargeschichte in ihrer Bedeutung für das Staats- und Privatrecht'*, in *Wochenschrift für Klassische Philologie*, ed. G. Andresen et al., vol. 9, no. 3 (Berlin, 20 January 1892), pp. 66–70.

22   Robert Pöhlmann, (review of) *'Max Weber, Die römische Agrargeschichte in ihrer Bedeutung für das Staats- und Privatrecht'*, in *Historische Zeitschrift*, vol. 71; vol. 35 (1893), pp. 314–16.

23   Cf. 48, p. 18; 1E, pp. 385f.

24   Werner Sombart, (review of) *'Max Weber, Die römische Agrargeschichte in ihrer Bedeutung für das Staats- und Privatrecht'*, in *Zeitschrift für Social- und Wirtschaftsgeschichte*, vol. 1, nos 2, 3 (1893), pp. 349–56.

25   Fogt, *Wirkung und Bedeutung*, p. 15.

26   Benedictus Niese, *Grundriss der römischen Geschichte nebst Quellenkunde*, 5th edn, rev. by E. Hohl (in *Handbuch der klassischen Altertumswissenschaft*, ed. W. Otto, vol. 3, no. 5, (Munich, 1923), p. 169, n. 1.

27   Otto Hintze, *'Roschers politische Entwicklungstheorie'*, in Hintze, *Soziologie und Geschichte*, compiled and ed. by G. Oestreich, 2nd extended edn (Göttingen, 1964), p. 26.

28   Alfred Heuss, *'Max Webers Bedeutung für die Geschichte des griechisch-römischen Altertums'*, in *Historische Zeitschrift*, vol. 201, no. 3 (December 1965), p. 535.

29   Fogt, *Wirkung und Bedeutung*, p. 15.

30   Marianne Weber, *Max Weber: A Biography*, tr. Harry Zohn (New York: Wiley, 1975), p. 371.

31   Fogt, *Wirkung und Bedeutung*, p. 19.

32   Michael Rostowzew, *'Kolonat (Rom)'*, in *Handwörterbuch der Staatswissenschaften*, ed. J. Conrad et al., 3rd (fully rev.) edn, vol. 5 (Jena, 1910), pp. 913–21.

33   Michael Rostowzew, *Studien zur Geschichte des römischen Kolonats. Erstes Beiheft zum Archiv für Papyrusforschung und verwandte Gebiete*, ed. U. Wilcken (Leipzig/ Berlin, 1910).

34   Ibid., p. vi.

35   G. Wollheim, *'Aufstieg und Niedergang des Kapitalismus im Römerreich nach Max Weber und Michael Rostovtzeff'*, in *Jahrbücher für Nationalökonomie und Statistik*, vol. 138, 3rd series; vol 83, 1st series, (Jena, 1933), pp. 390–412, here p. 411.

36   Letter from Max Weber to Georg von Below of 21 June 1914, published in Georg von Below, *Der deutsche Staat des Mittelalters. Eine Grundlegung der deutschen Verfassungsgeschichte*, vol. 1, 'Die allgemeinen Fragen' (Leipzig, 2nd edn, 1925), p. xxiv.

37   Georg von Below, *Probleme der Wirtschaftsgeschichte. Eine Einführung in das Studium der Wirtschaftsgeschichte* (Tübingen, 1920), p. 254; and *'Agrargeschichte'*, in

Handwörterbuch der Staatswissenschaften, ed. L. Elster, A. Weber and F. Wieser, 4th completely rev. edn (Jena, 1923), vol. 1, p. 61. See also Fogt, *Wirkung und Bedeutung,* p. 18.

38   Ernst Troeltsch, *'Die Soziallehren der christlichen Kirchen und Gruppen',* in *Gesammelte Schriften,* vol. 1 (Tübingen, 1912, reprinted Aalen, 1965), pp. 22, 120, 250f, 355f.

39   Erich Fechner, *'Der Begriff des kapitalistischen Geistes und das Schelersche Gesetz vom Zusammenhang der historischen Wirkfaktoren. Vergleich und Ausgleich zwischen Sombart und Max Weber',* in *Archiv für Sozialwissenschaft und Sozialpolitik,* vol. 63 (1930), pp. 93–120, here p. 106ff.

40   Fritz Heichelheim, *'Welthistorische Gesichtspunkte zu den vormittelalterlichen Wirtschaftsepochen',* in Bechtel et al., *Festgabe für Werner Sombart zur 70. Wiederkehr seines Geburtstags 19. Jänner 1933,* Schmollers Jahrbuch, vol. 56, no. 6, special issue, pp. 994–1035, here pp. 169–74.

41   Marianne Weber, *Ehefrau und Mutter in der Rechtsentwicklung. Eine Einführung* (Tübingen, 1907).

42   Werner Sombart, *'Städtische Siedlung, Stadt',* in Alfred Vierkandt (ed.) *Handwörterbuch der Soziologie* (Stuttgart, 1931), pp. 527–31.

43   Franz Oppenheimer, *System der Soziologie,* vol. 2, *'Der Staat'* (Jena, 1922–7), pp. 323, 360, 395f, 402ff, 410, 424–8, 443, 514ff, 536f, 551–5, 588, 601f, 606, 620–4, 658ff, 753–6. Also Fogt, *Wirkung und Bedeutung,* p. 20.

44   Werner Sombart, *Der moderne Kapitalismus. Historisch-systematische Darstellung des gesamteuropäischen Wirtschaftslebens von seinen Anfängen bis zur Gegenwart,* 3 vols, 6th edn (Munich/Leipzig 1924–7), here vol. 3, section 1, p. xvii.

45   Waldemar Mitscherlich, (review of) *'Max Weber, Wirtschaftsgeschichte, 1923',* in *Schmollers Jahrbuch für Gesetzgebung, Verwaltung und Volkswirtschaft im Deutschen Reiche,* ed. A. Spiethoff, vol. 48, nos 1 and 2 (Munich/Leipzig, 1924), pp. 372–6.

46   Henri Pirenne, 'Economic History', in *Encyclopaedia of the Social Sciences,* vol. 5 (New York, 1949; first published 1931), p. 322.

47   Pitirim Sorokin, *Soziologische Theorien im 19. und 20. Jahrhundert,* (Munich, 1931), pp. 320ff.

48   Heuss, *Max Webers Bedeutung,* p. 554; and Fogt, *Wirkung und Bedeutung,* p. 22.

49   Karl Christ, *Von Gibbon zu Rostovtzeff. Leben und Werk führender Althistoriker der Neuzeit* (Darmstadt, 1972), p. 337.

50   Cf. Fogt, *Wirkung und Bedeutung,* pp. 22–38.

51   Proceedings for 1893 of the *Verein für Sozialpolitik* (Leipzig, 1893), p. 7. For precise bibliographical details see 18.

52   Proceedings for 1920 of the *Verein für Sozialpolitik* in Kiel, *Schriften des Vereins für Sozialpolitik,* vol. 161 (Munich/Leipzig, 1921), p. 4.

53   Otto von Zwiedineck-Südenhorst, *'Vom Wirken von Max und Alfred Weber im Verein für Sozialpolitik. Erinnerungen und Eindrücke',* in *Synopsis. Alfred Weber 30 July 1868–30 July 1948,* Heidelberg, no date [1948], pp. 765–87, here p. 784.

54 Salli Goldschmidt, *Die Landarbeiter in der Provinz Sachsen sowie den Herzogtümern Braunschweig und Anhalt dargestellt nach den Erhebungen des Evangelisch–sozialen Kongresses*, part I, philosophical dissertation presented at Heidelberg, published Tübingen, 1899.

55 Andreas Grunenberg, *Die Landarbeiter in den Provinzen Schleswig-Holstein und Hannover östlich der Weser, sowie in dem Gebiete des Fürstentums Lübeck und der freien Städte Bremen, Hamburg und Lübeck.* (After the proceedings of the *Evangelisch-sozialer Kongreß*, part I, philosophical dissertation presented at Heidelberg, published Tübingen 1902.

56 Alfred Klee, *Die Landarbeiter in Mittel- und Niederschlesien nach den Erhebungen des Evangelisch–Sozialen Kongresses*, 2 parts, philosophical dissertation presented at Heidelberg, Tübingen 1902. These three works were published in their entirety under the title *Die Landarbeiter in den evangelischen Gebieten Norddeutschlands. In Einzeldarstellungen nach den Erhebungen des Evangelisch–Sozialen Kongresses,* ed. Max Weber, nos 1–3 (Tübingen, 1899–1902).

57 Felix Gerhardt, *Die Landarbeiter in der Provinz Ostpreußen* philosophical dissertation presented at Heidelberg 1902, published Lucka, 1902.

58 Karl Bor. Breinlinger, *Die Landarbeiter in Pommern und Mecklenburg. Dargestellt nach den Erhebungen des Evangelisch-sozialen Kongresses,* part 1, *'Die Regierungsbezirke Stettin und Stralsund'.* Philosophical dissertation presented at Heidelberg 1903, published Heidelberg, 1903.

59 Eugen Katz, *'Landarbeiter und Landwirtschaft in Oberhessen',* in *Münchner Volkswirtschaftliche Studien,* vol. 64. Dissertation in state theory presented at Munich 1903, published Stuttgart, 1904.

60 Cf. Gert Schmidt/Burkart Lutz, *'Industriesoziologie',* in H. Daheim, B. Lutz, G. Schmidt and B. F. Hoselitz, *Beruf, Industrie, sozialer Wandel in unterentwickelten Ländern* (in *Handbuch der empirischen Sozialforschung* ed. R. König, vol. 8), 2nd completely rev. edn (Stuttgart, 1977), p. 111.

61 Cf. Paul F. Lazarsfeld, Anthony R. Oberschall, 'Max Weber and Empirical Social Research', in *American Sociological Review,* vol. 30, no. 1 (1930), p. 193. And Gert Schmidt, 'Max Weber and Modern Industrial Sociology: A Comment on some Recent Anglo-Saxon Interpretations', in *Sociological Analysis and Theory,* vol. 6, no. 1 (February, 1976), pp. 47–73. And Fogt, *Wirkung und Bedeutung,* pp. 37f.

62 Cf. Fogt, *Wirkung und Bedeutung,* pp. 71–107.

63 H. Karl Fischer, *'Kritische Beiträge zu Professor Max Webers Abhandlung "Die protestantische Ethik und Sozialpolitik,* vol. 25 (1907), pp. 232–42. Also Fischer, *'Protestantische Ethik und der Geist des Kapitalismus"',* in *Archiv für Sozialwissenschaft und "Geist des Kapitalismus". Replik auf Herrn Professor Max Webers Gegenkritik',* in *Archiv für Sozialwissenschaft und Sozialpolitik,* vol. 26 (1908), pp. 270–4.

64 Felix Rachfahl, *'Kalvinismus und Kapitalismus',* in *Internationale Wochenschrift für Wissenschaft, Kunst und Technik,* ed. Paul Hinneberg, vol. 3 (1909), columns 1217–38, 1249–68, 1287–1300, 1319–34, 1347–66. Also Rachfahl, *'Nochmals*

Kalvinismus und Kapitalismus', in ibid., vol. 4 (1910), columns 689–702, 717–34, 755–68, 775–94.

65   Felix Rachfahl, *Wilhelm von Oranien und der niederländische Aufstand*, 3 vols (Halle, 1906–24).

66   Lujo Brentano, *Die Anfänge des modernen Kapitalismus*. Address given to an open meeting of the *K. Akademie der Wissenschaften* on 15 March 1913, published Munich, 1916; especially pp. 117–57. Also Brentano, *'Puritanismus und Kapitalismus'*, in Brentano, *Der wirtschaftende Mensch in der Geschichte*, collected addresses and essays, (Leipzig, 1923), pp. 363–425.

67   Werner Sombart, *Der Bourgeois. Zur Geistesgeschichte des modernen Wirtschafts-menschen* (Munich/Leipzig, 1913). Also Sombart, *Der moderne Kapitalismus. Historisch-systematische Darstellung des gesamteuropäischen Wirtschaftslebens von seinen Anfängen bis zur Gegenwart*, 3 vols, 6th edn (Munich/Leipzig, 1924–7), see especially vol. 3. Cf. Erich Fechner, *'Der Begriff des kapitalistischen Geistes bei Werner Sombart und Max Weber und die soziologischen Grundkategorien Gemeinschaft und Gesellschaft'*, in *Weltwirtschaftliches Archiv*, vol. 30, no. 2 (Jena, 1929), pp. 194–211.

68   Leipzig, 1911.

69   Cf. n. 48. Also Ernst Troeltsch, *Die Bedeutung des Protestantismus für die Entstehung der modernen Welt*. Lecture given at the 9th conference of German historians at Stuttgart on 21 April 1906, in *Historische Zeitschrift*, vol. 97 (Munich, 1906), pp. 1–66.

70   Cf. for example Paul Barth (review of) *'Max Weber, Gesammelte Aufsätze zur Religionssoziologie'*, in *Jahrbücher für Nationalökonomie und Statistik*, vol. 118, 3rd series, vol. 63 (1922/I), pp. 474–81. Also Gerhart von Schulze-Gävernitz, *'Max Weber als Nationalökonom und Politiker'*, in Melchior Palyi (ed.), *Erinnerungsgabe für Max Weber. Hauptprobleme der Soziologie*, vol. 1 (Munich/Leipzig, 1923), pp. x–xxii. Here, on the other hand (p. xv) Weber's thesis is seen as a further development of Marx's central ideas. Also, Weber is even made into a Marxist, as for example by Alois Dempf, *'Religionssoziologie'*, in *Hochland* vol. 18 (1921), p. 747.

71   Cf. the survey in Fogt, *Wirkung and Bedeutung*, pp. 79f.

72   Ephraim Fischoff, *Die protestantische Ethik und der Geist des Kapitalismus. Die Geschichte einer Kontroverse*, tr. and printed in 224a, p. 365.

73   Cf. Christopher Bernert, *The Diffusion of the 'Weber-Thesis', 1904–1930*, unpublished paper, State University of New York at Stony Brook, Department of Sociology, May 1976.

74   In particular R. H. Tawney, *Religion and the Rise of Capitalism*, (London, 1926).

75   Talcott Parsons, *Der Begriff des Kapitalismus in den Theorien von Max Weber und Werner Sombart*. Philosophical dissertation presented at Heidelberg 1929. Published as ' "Capitalism" in recent German Literature: Sombart and Weber', in The *Journal of Political Economy*, vol. 36, no. 36 (December 1928), pp. 641–61; and no. 37 (February 1929), pp. 31–51.

76 Max Weber, *The Protestant Ethic and the Spirit of Capitalism*, tr. Talcott Parsons, Introduction by Anthony Giddens (London: Counterpoint, 1976) 1st published by Allen and Unwin in 1930 with a foreword by R. H. Tawney.

77 Joachim Wach, *'Religionssoziologie'*, in Alfred Vierkandt (ed.), *Handwörterbuch der Soziologie* (Stuttgart, 1931), pp. 479–94, here p. 494.

78 Hermann Kantorowicz, *'Der Aufbau der Soziologie'*, in Melchior Palyi (ed.) *Hauptprobleme der Soziologie* (Munich/Leipzig, 1923), vol. 1, pp. 73–96; here pp. 87, 92. See also Fogt, *Wirkung und Bedeutung*, p. 91.

79 Alois Dempf, *'Religionssoziologie'*, in *Hochland*, 18th year, vol. 1, no. 6 (October 1920 – March 1921), pp. 746–8; here pp. 747f.

80 Erich Rothacker, (review of) *'Max Weber, Gesammelte Aufsätze zur Religionssoziologie, 3 Bände, Wirtschaft und Gesellschaft 1. u 2. Lieferung 1921'*, in *Vierteljahrsschrift für Sozial- und Wirtschaftsgeschichte*, ed. St Bauer et al., vol. 16, nos 3/4 (Berlin *inter alia*, 1922), pp. 420–34; here p. 426.

81 Paul Barth (review of) *'Max Weber, Gesammelte Aufsätze zur Religionssoziologie'*, in *Jahrbücher für Nationalökonomie und Statistik*, vol. 118, 3rd series, vol. 63 (1922/I), pp. 474–81; here p. 476.

82 Andreas Walther, (review of) *'Max Weber, Gesammelte Aufsätze zur Religionssoziologie. 3 Bände'*, in *Theologische Literaturzeitung*, no. 24 (1923), columns 505–11; here column 476.

83 Ernst Troeltsch, *Der Historismus und seine Probleme. 1. Buch: Das logische Problem der Geschichtsphilosophie*, in *Gesammelte Schriften*, vol. 3 (Tübingen, 1922), p. 368. See also Fogt, *Wirkung and Bedeutung*, p. 92.

84 Arthur von Rosthorn, *'Religion und Wirtschaft in China'*, in Melchior Palyi (ed.) *Hauptprobleme der Soziologie* (Munich/Leipzig, 1923), vol. 2, pp. 220–33; here pp. 221–7, 230–3.

85 Julius Braunthal, *'Oekonomische und soziale Wurzeln des chinesischen Risorgimento'*, in *Der Kampf, Sozialdemokratische Monatsschrift*, vol. 18, no. 8/9 (Vienna, August–September 1925), pp. 307–23, here pp. 309–13.

86 Otto Franke, *Geschichte des Chinesischen Reiches. Eine Darstellung seiner Entstehung, seines Wesens und seiner Entwicklung bis zur neuesten Zeit. 1. Band. Das Altertum und das Werden des konfuzianischen Staates* (Berlin/Leipzig, 1930), p. 91.

87 Stefan Balázs, *'Beiträge zur Wirtschaftsgeschichte der T'ang-Zeit (618–906)'*, in *Mitteilungen des Seminars für Orientalische Sprachen an der Friedrich-Wilhelms-Universität zu Berlin*, ed. E. Mittwoch, (Berlin), section 1: *'Ostasiatische Studien'*, vol. 34 (1931), pp. 2–92; vol. 35 (1932), pp. 1–73; vol. 36 (1933), pp. 1–62; here 1931, pp. 2, 8, 21, 88; 1932, p. 24. See also Fogt, *Wirkung und Bedeutung* pp. 93ff.

88 Paul Honigsheim, 'Max Weber as Historian of Agriculture and Rural Life', in *Agricultural History*, vol. 23 (July 1949), pp. 179–213; here pp. 186f, 190. See also Fogt, *Wirkung und Bedeutung*, pp. 95f.

89 Gerhart von Schulze-Gävernitz, *'Max Weber als Nationalökonom und Politiker'*, in Melchior Palyi (ed.), *Hauptprobleme der Soziologie* (Munich/Leipzig, 1923), vol. 1, pp. x–xxii; here p. xvii.

90 H. Meinhold, (review of) *'Max Weber, Das Antike Judentum. 1921'*, in *Deutsche Literaturzeitung*, no. 33 (19 August 1922), pp. 720-6.

91 Erwin Kohn, (review of) *'Max Weber, Gesammelte Aufsätze zur Religionssoziologie. Bd III Das antike Judentum'*, in *Der Jude. Eine Monatsschrift* (Berlin, 1922), vol. 6, no. 8 (May), pp. 515-20.

92 Julius Guttmann, *'Max Webers Soziologie des antiken Judentums'*, in *Monatsschrift für die Geschichte und Wissenschaft des Judentums*, ed. I. Heinemann, vol. 69, vol. 33 (Frankfurt am Main, 1925), pp. 195-223.

93 Wilhelm Caspari, *'Die Gottesgemeinde vom Sinaj und das nachmalige Volk Israel. Auseinandersetzungen mit Max Weber'*, in *Beiträge zur Förderung christlicher Theologie*, ed. A. Schlatter and W. Lütgert, vol. 27, no. 1 (Gütersloh, 1922). See also Fogt, *Wirkung und Bedeutung*, pp. 96f.

94 Cf. Fogt, *Wirkung und Bedeutung*, pp. 107-43.

95 Rothacker, (review of) *'Max Weber, Gesammelte Aufsätze zur Religionssoziologie'*, p. 422 (see n. 80).

96 Hans Freyer, *'Typen und Stufen der Kultur'*, in *Handwörterbuch der Soziologie*, ed. Alfred Vierkandt (Stuttgart, 1931), p. 307.

97 Eduard Spranger, *'Die Soziologie in der Erinnerungsgabe für Max Weber'*, in *Schmollers Jahrbuch für Gesetzgebung, Verwaltung und Volkswirtschaft im Deutschen Reiche*, vol. 49, no. 6 (Munich/Leipzig, 1925), p. 161. See also Fogt, *Wirkung und Bedeutung*, p. 110.

98 Friedrich Gottl-von Ottlilienfeld, *'Freiheit vom Worte'*, in *Hauptprobleme der Soziologie. Erinnerungsgabe für Max Weber*, ed. M. Palyi (Munich/Leipzig, 1923), vol. 1, pp. 106, 117f, 123.

99 Andreas Walther, *'Max Weber als Soziologe'*, in *Jahrbuch für Soziologie, Eine Internationale Sammlung*, ed. G. Salomon, vol. 2 (Karlsruhe, 1926), pp. 3, 21f, 45-50.

100 Otto Hintze, *Gesammelte Abhandlungen. Bd II: Soziologie und Geschichte. Zur Soziologie, Politik und Theorie der Geschichte*, ed. and introduced by G. Oestreich (Göttingen, 1964), pp. 144f.

101 Karl Mannheim, article in the Prague press 28 March 1937, printed in Kurt H. Wolff, *'Karl Mannheim'*, in *Klassiker des soziologischen Denkens* ed. Dirk Käsler, vol. 2 (Munich, 1978), pp. 343f.

102 Otto Hintze, *'Max Webers Soziologie'* (review of *'Wirtschaft und Gesellschaft'*), in *Schmollers Jahrbuch für Gesetzgebung, Verwaltung und Volkswirtschaft im Deutschen Reiche*, vol. 50 (Munich/Leipzig, 1926), p. 91ff.

103 Richard Thoma, *'Der Begriff der modernen Demokratie in seinem Verhältnis zum Staatsbegriff'*, in *Hauptprobleme der Soziologie. Erinnerungsgabe für Max Weber*, ed. M. Palyi (Munich/Leipzig), 1923. vol 2, pp. 47, 52ff, 58f, 63f.

104 Herbert Sultan, *'Soziologie des modernen Parteiensystems'*, in *Archiv für Sozialwissenschaften und Sozialpolitik*, vol. 55, no. 1 (Tübingen, 1926), pp. 91-140, particularly, pp. 112-19.

105 Cf. particularly, Wilfried Röhrich, *'Robert Michels'*, in *Klassiker des soziologischen Denkens*, ed. Dirk Käsler, vol. 2 (Munich, 1978), pp. 232f, 241ff.

106 Robert Michels, *Zur Soziologie des Parteiwesens in der modernen Demokratie. Untersuchungen über die oligarchischen Tendenzen des Gruppenlebens*, in *Philosophischsoziologische Bücherei*, vol. 21 (Leipzig, 1911).

107 Cf. Dietrich Herzog, *'Max Weber als Klassiker der Parteiensoziologie'*, in *Soziale Welt*, vol. 17 (1966), no. 3, pp. 232-52.

108 Fogt, *Wirkung und Bedeutung*, p. 113.

109 Kantorowicz, *'Der Aufbau der Soziologie'*, pp. 78f, 81f., 84 (see n. 78).

110 Spranger, *'Die Soziologie in der Erinnerungsgabe für Max Weber'* (see n. 97).

111 Othmar Spann, article on class and status group in *Handwörterbuch der Staatswissenschaften*, vol. 5, 4th edn (1923), pp. 692-705, particularly, pp. 702f.

112 Hans Lorenz Stoltenberg, *'Tote und lebendige Wissenschaft'*, in *Zeitschrift für die gesamte Staatswissenschaft*, vol. 85, no. 1 (1928), pp. 133-41.

113 Hans Freyer, *Einleitung in die Soziologie* (Leipzig, 1931), particularly pp. 24f, 117-20.

114 Walther, *'Max Weber als Soziologe'* (see n. 99), particularly pp. 3f, 14, 19f, 23ff, 34, 37, 41f, 55, 62.

115 Max Scheler, *'Wesen und Begriff der Kultursoziologie'*, in Scheler, *Die Wissensformen und die Gesellschaft*, collected works, 2nd edn, vol. 8 (Berne/Munich, 1960), pp. 17-52.

116 Franz Oppenheimer, *System der Soziologie*, 3 vols (Jena, 1922-7). Particularly vol. 1, pp. 80f, 93, 197ff, 338f, 365, 369-72, 377f, 383f, 406ff, 637f, 924; vol. 2, pp. 234ff, 660.

117 Fogt, *Wirkung und Bedeutung*, p. 119.

118 Spranger, *'Die Soziologie in der Erinnerungsgabe für Max Weber'* (see n. 97), pp. 149f, 157, 164.

119 Hermann Kantorowicz, *'Max Weber'*, in René König and Johannes Winckelmann. (eds), *Max Weber zum Gedächtnis. Kölner Zeitschrift für Soziologie und Sozialpsychologie*, no. 7, special edn (1963), pp. 94-8, particularly, p. 97.

120 Scheler, *'Wesen und Begriff der Kultursoziologie'* (see n. 115), p. 47.

121 Fritz Heichelheim, *'Welthistorische Gesichtspunkte zu den vormittelalterlichen Wirtschaftsepochen'*, in Bechtel et al. (eds), *Festgabe für Werner Sombart zur 70. Wiederkehr seines Geburtstags 19. Jänner 1933*, in *Schmollers Jahrbuch*, vol. 56, no. 6, special edn, pp. 994-1035, particularly p. 172.

122 Oppenheimer, *System der Soziologie* (see n. 116), vol. 1, p. 1000.

123 von Gottl-Ottlilienfeld, *'Freiheit vom Worte'* (see n. 98), pp. 129f.

124 Robert Wilbrandt, *'Kritisches zu Max Webers Soziologie der Wirtschaft'*, in *Kölner Vierteljahrshefte für Soziologie*, vol. 5 (1925-6), pp. 171-86.

125 Karl Mannheim, *Wissenssoziologie*, ed. and introduced by Kurt H. Wolff (Berlin/Neuwied, 1964), particularly, pp. 642, 682ff.

126 Manfred Rehbinder, *'Max Webers Rechtssoziologie: Eine Bestandsaufnahme'*, in König and Winckelmann (see n. 119), pp. 470-88; here, pp. 470f, 481f.

127 Fogt, *Wirkung und Bedeutung*, p. 129.

128 Fritz Sander, *'Zum Problem der Soziologie des Rechts'*, in *Archiv für Sozialwissenschaft und Sozialpolitik*, vol. 55, no. 3 (Tübingen, 1926), pp. 800-18.

129 Carl Schmitt, *'Soziologie des Souveränitätsbegriffes und politische Theologie'*, in *Hauptprobleme der Soziologie. Erinnerungsgabe für Max Weber*, ed. M. Palyi (Munich/Leipzig, 1923), vol. 2, pp. 3-35.

130 Otto Benesch, *'Max Weber als Musikwissenschaftler'*, in *Österreichische Rundschau*, vol. 18, nos 9/10 (31 May 1922), pp. 387-402.

131 Arnold Schering, *'Musik'*, in *Handwörterbuch der Soziologie*, ed. A. Vierkandt (Stuttgart, 1931), pp. 393-9, particularly p. 399.

132 Fogt, *Wirkung und Bedeutung*, p. 142.

133 Cf. Guenther Roth, ' "Value-Neutrality" in Germany and the United States', in Bendix and Roth (eds), *Scholarship and Partisanship. Essays on Max Weber* (Berkeley/Los Angeles/London, 1971), pp. 34-54; here p. 43.

134 Cf. Rolf Engelsing, *Der literarische Arbeiter*, vol. 1, *'Arbeit, Zeit und Werk im literarischen Beruf'* (Göttingen, 1976), p. 461.

135 Fogt, *Wirkung und Bedeutung*, pp. 41-70.

136 Alfred Weber, *'Max Weber'*, in Alfred Weber, *Einführung in die Soziologie*, in association with H. von Borch et al. (Munich, 1955), p. 169.

137 Cf. for example Hans Paul Bahrdt, *'Schamanen der modernen Gesellschaft? Das Verhältnis der Wissenschaftler zur Politik'*, in Bahrdt, *Wissenschaftssoziologie - ad hoc. Beiträge zur Wissenschaftssoziologie und Wissenschaftspolitik aus den letzten zehn Jahren* (Düsseldorf, 1971), pp. 98-105.

138 Erich von Kahler, *Der Beruf der Wissenschaft* (Berlin, 1920), p. 45.

139 Fogt, *Wirkung und Bedeutung*, pp. 64f.

140 Ernst Robert Curtius, *'Max Weber über Wissenschaft als Beruf'*, in *Die Arbeitsgemeinschaft. Monatsschrift für das gesamte Volkshochschulwesen*, vol. 1 (1920), pp. 197-203.

141 Ernst Troeltsch, *'Die Revolution in der Wissenschaft'*, in *Schmollers Jahrbuch* vol. 45 (1921), pp. 1001-30.

142 Max Scheler, *'Weltanschauungslehre, Soziologie und Weltanschauungssetzung'*, in *Kölner Vierteljahrsheft für Sozialwissenschaften*, vol. 2, no. 1 (1922-3), pp. 18-33.

143 Heinrich Rickert, *'Max Weber und seine Stellung zur Wissenschaft'*, in *Logos. Internationale Zeitschrift für Philosophie der Kultur*, vol. 15, (Tübingen, 1926), pp. 222-37.

144 Cf. the review statistics in Fogt, *Wirkung und Bedeutung*, pp. 148-152.

8 Weber's importance for sociology today and in the future

1 Cf. note 76.

2 Max Weber, *The Theory of Social and Economic Organization*, tr. A. M. Henderson and Talcott Parsons, ed. with an Introduction by Talcott Parsons (New York/London, 1947).

3 Cf. Jere Cohen, Lawrence E. Hazelrigg and Whitney Pope, 'De-Parsonizing Weber: A Critique of Parsons' interpretation of Weber's Sociology', in *American Sociological Review*, no. 40 (1975), pp. 229-41. See also Parsons' commentary on this, in ibid., pp. 666-70 and Cohen, Hazelrigg and Pope's reply in ibid., pp. 670-4.

4 Karl Jaspers, *Max Weber. Politiker, Forscher, Philosoph* (Munich, 1958), p. 7.

5 On this and on what follows see my introduction to vol. 1 of *Klassiker des soziologischen Denkens* (Munich, 1976), especially p. 14.

6 Cf. the secondary bibliography in Constans Seyfarth and Gert Schmidt, *Max Weber Bibliographie* (Stuttgart: F. Enke, 1977), pp. 61-165.

7 Cf. for example Mario Bunge, *Scientific Research*, vos. I and II, (Heidelberg/ New York, 1967).

8 This phrase is the title of a work by Peter L. Berger and Thomas Luckmann, *The Social Construction of Reality* (New York: Doubleday Inc., 1966).

9 I am grateful to the late Professor Peter C. Ludz for drawing my attention to this possible interpretation: it was he who formulated this idea as the link between Arnold Hauser and Georg Lukács. Cf. Arnold Hauser, *Im Gespräch mit Georg Lukács*, with an Afterword by P. C. Ludz (Munich, 1978), in particular pp. 94-7, 117ff.

10 Cf. Friedrich H. Tenbruck, *'Abschied von Wirtschaft und Gesellschaft'*, in *Zeitschrift für die gesamte Staatswissenschaft*, vol. 133, no. 4 (December 1977), pp. 703-36.

Bibliography

The bibliography consists of the following sections:

1 Works by Weber available in English
2 Guide to the secondary literature in English
3 Weber's works in German
4 The Max Weber Collected Edition

The numbers in brackets throughout the text after the titles of works or after quotations refer to sections 1 and 3 of this bibliography. References which are simply a number/number and lower case letter (e.g. 215/215f) refer to section 3; numbers followed by capital E (e.g. 10E) refer to the English translations listed in section 1.

1 Works by Weber available in English

1 *The Agrarian Sociology of Ancient Civilizations*, tr. R. I. Frank (London: New Left Books, 1976).
2 *The Protestant Ethic and the Spirit of Capitalism*, tr. Talcott Parsons, introduced by Anthony Giddens (London: Counterpoint, 1985).
3 *Max Weber: Essays in Sociology* (including 'The Economic Ethic of the World Religions'), tr. H. H. Gerth and C. Wright Mills (London: Routledge Kegan Paul, 1967).
4 *The Religion of China*, tr. and ed. H. H. Gerth (New York: Collier and Macmillan, 1964).
5 *From Max Weber* (including 'The Protestant Sects and the Spirit of Capitalism' and 'Religious Rejections of the World and their Directions') ed. H. H. Gerth and C. Wright Mills (London: Routledge Kegan Paul, 1948).
6 *The Religion of India*, tr. and ed. by Hans H. Gerth and Don Martindale (New York: The Free Press, 1967).
7 *Ancient Judaism* tr. and ed. Hans H. Gerth and Don Martindale (Glencoe, Illinois: The Free Press, 1952).

8 *Economy and Society*, 3 vols, ed. Guenther Roth and Claus Wittich (New York: Bedminster, 1968).

9 *The Rational and Social Foundations of Music*, tr. and ed. Don Martindale, Johannes Riedel and Gertrude Neuwirth (London and Amsterdam: Feffer and Simons, 1958).

10 *The Methodology of the Social Sciences* (including 'The Meaning of "Ethical Neutrality" in Sociology and Economics'; ' "Objectivity" in Social Science and Social Policy'; 'Science as a Vocation'), tr. E. A. Shils and H. Finch (Glencoe, Illinois: The Free Press, 1949).

11 *Selections in Translation*, ed. W. G. Runciman (Cambridge: CUP, 1978).

12 *The Theory of Social and Economic Organization* (part 1 of *Economy and Society*), tr. A. M. Henderson and Talcott Parsons, ed. and introduced by Talcott Parsons (New York: The Free Press, 1964).

13 *Critique of Stammler* tr. with an introductory essay by Guy Oakes (New York: The Free Press, 1977).

14 *Roscher and Knies: The Logical Problems of Historical Economics* tr. and introduced by Guy Oakes (New York: The Free Press, 1975).

15 *On Charisma and Institution Building* ed. and introduced by S. N. Eisenstadt, (Chicago: University of Chicago Press, 1968).

16 *General Economic History* tr. Frank H. Knight (New York: Collier–Macmillan, 1961).

17 *On Universities: The Power of the State and the Dignity of the Academic Calling in Imperial Germany* tr., ed. and with an Introductory Note by Edward Shils (Chicago: UCP, 1974).

2   Guide to the secondary literature in English

The following bibliographic section is selective in two ways: First, it refers solely to English publications; second, it tries to list in the *chronological* order of their publication those works that concentrate on the area I have dealt with in the foregoing chapters. As published bibliographies on selected secondary literature on Weber up to 1976 reference should be made to Constans Seyfarth and Gert Schmidt, *Max Weber Bibliographie* (Stuttgart: F. Enke, 1977; 2nd unchanged edn, 1982) and as a bibliography of mainly English secondary literature on Weber, see Vatro Murvar, *Max Weber Today – an Introduction to a Living Legacy: Selected Bibliography* (Brookfield, 1983).

I   BIOGRAPHY

Mitzman, Arthur, *The Iron Cage. An Historical Interpretation of Max Weber* (New York, 1970; New Brunswick/Oxford, 1985).

Mommsen, Wolfgang J., Max Weber and German Politics 1890–1920. (Chicago, 1984).
Weber, Marianne, Max Weber: A Biography (New York: Wiley, 1975).

II THE WORKS

1 Early writings

Honigsheim, Paul, 'Max Weber as Historian of Agriculture and Rural Life, in Agricultural History, vol. 23 (1949), pp. 170–213
Roth, Guenther, 'Introduction', in Guenther Roth and Claus Wittich (eds), Max Weber, Economy and Society. An Outline of Interpretative Sociology (New York, 1968), pp. xxvii–civ
Momigliano, Arnoldo, 'New Paths of Classicism in the Nineteenth Century', in History and Theory, vol. 21 (1982), esp. pp. 29–31
Scaff, Lawrence A., 'Weber before Weberian sociology', in British Journal of Sociology, vol. 35 (1984), pp. 190–215
Finley, M. I., Ancient History, Evidence and Models (London, 1985)

2 Social change in German society

Honigsheim, Paul, 'Max Weber as Rural Sociologist', in Rural Sociology, vol. 11 (1946), pp. 207–18
Lazarsfeld, Paul F. and Anthony R. Oberschall, 'Max Weber and Empirical Social Research' in American Sociological Review, vol. 30 (1965), pp. 186–99
Dibble, Vernon, 'Social Science and Political Commitments in the Young Max Weber', in Archives Européennes de Sociologie, vol. 9 (1968), pp. 1–28
Munters, Q. J., 'Max Weber as Rural Sociologist', in Sociologica Ruralis, vol. 12 (1972), pp. 129–46
Oberschall, Anthony, Empirical Social Research in Germany 1848–1914 (Paris, 1965)
Schmidt, Gert, 'Max Weber and Modern Industrial Sociology: A Comment on some Recent Anglo-Saxon Interpretations', in Sociological Analysis and Theory, vol. 6 (1976), pp. 47–73
Tribe, Keith, 'Prussian agriculture – German politics: Max Weber, 1892–1897', in Economy and Society, vol. 12 (1983), pp. 181–226
Scaff, Lawrence A., 'Weber before Weberian sociology', in British Journal of Sociology, vol. 35 (1984), pp. 190–215

3 The sociology of religion

(a) The cultural significance of Protestantism

Bendix, Reinhard, Max Weber. An Intellectual Portrait (New York, 1962)
Green, Robert W. (ed.), Protestantism, Capitalism, and Social Science. The Weber Thesis Controversy, 2nd edn (Lexington, 1973)
Nelson, Benjamin, 'Weber's Protestant Ethic: Its Origins, Wanderings and

Foreseeable Futures', in Charles Y. Glock and Phillip E. Hammond (eds), *Beyond the Classics? Essays in the Scientific Study of Religion* (New York, 1973), pp. 71–130

Marshall, Gordon, *In Search of the Spirit of Capitalism: An Essay on Max Weber's Protestant Ethic Thesis* (New York/London, 1982)

Poggi, Gianfranco, *Calvinism and the Capitalistic Spirit. Max Weber's 'Protestant Ethic'* (Amherst, 1983)

Weber and Marx

Giddens, Anthony, 'Marx, Weber and the Development of Capitalism', in *Sociology*, vol. 4 (1970), pp. 289–310

Ashcraft, Richard, 'Max and Weber on Liberalism as Bourgeois Ideology', in *Comparative Studies in Society and History*, vol. 14 (1972), pp. 130–68

Mayer, Carl, 'Max Weber's Interpretation of Karl Marx', in *Social Research*, vol. 42 (1975), pp. 701–19

Löwith, Karl, *Max Weber and Karl Marx* (London, 1982)

Antonio, Robert J. and Ronald M. Glassman (eds), *A Weber–Marx-Dialogue* (Lawrence, 1985)

(*b*)   'The Economic Ethic of the World Religions'

Bendix, Reinhard, *Max Weber. An Intellectual Portrait* (New York, 1962)

Nelson, Benjamin, 'Max Weber's "Author's Introduction" (1920): A Master Clue to his Main Aims', in *Sociological Inquiry*, vol. 44 (1966), pp. 269–78

Warner, R. Stephen, The Role of Religious Ideas and the Use of Models in Max Weber's Comparative Studies of Non-capitalistic Societies', in *Journal of Economic History*, vol. 30 (1970), pp. 74–99

Turner, Bryan S., *Weber and Islam* (London, 1974)

Little, David, 'Max Weber and the Comparative Study of Religious Ethics', in *Journal of Religious Ethics*, vol. 2 (1974), pp. 5–40

Fahey, Tony, 'Max Weber's Ancient Judaism', in *American Journal of Sociology*, vol. 88 (1982), pp. 62–87

Zeitlin, Irving M., *Ancient Judaism. Biblical Criticism from Max Weber to the Present* (Cambridge, 1984)

4   *Economy and Society*

(*a*) Sociology of law

Rheinstein, Max, 'Introduction', in Max Rheinstein (ed.), *Max Weber on Law in Economy and Society* (Cambridge, Mass., 1954), pp. xxv–lxxi.

Kronman, Anthony, *Max Weber* (London, 1983)

Treiber, Hubert, ' "Elective Affinities" between Weber's Sociology of Religion and Sociology of Law', in *Philosophy and Social Criticism*, vol. 10 (1984), pp. 809–61.

(*b*) 'General sociology'

Parsons, Talcott, *The Structure of Social Action: A Study in Social Theory with Special Reference to a Group of Recent European Writers* (New York, 1937)
Freund, Julien, *The Sociology of Max Weber* (London, 1968)
Munch, Peter A., ' "Sense" and "Intention" in Max Weber's Theory of Social Action', in *Sociological Inquiry*, vol. 45 (1975), pp. 59–65

(*c*) Economic sociology

Mommsen, Wolfgang J., 'The Alternative to Marx: Dynamic Capitalism instead of Bureaucratic Socialism', in Wolfgang J. Mommsen, *The Age of Bureaucracy. Perspectives on the Political Sociology of Max Weber* (Oxford, 1974), pp. 47–71

(*d*) Sociology of domination

Bendix, Reinhard, *Max Weber. An Intellectual Portrait* (New York, 1962)
Blau, Peter M., 'Critical Remarks on Weber's Theory of Authority', in *American Political Science Review*, vol. 57 (1963), pp. 305–16

Max Weber's political writings

Mayer, Jacob P., *Max Weber and German Politics* (London, 1944; 2nd edn, 1956)
Loewenstein, Karl, *Max Weber's Political Ideas in the Perspective of Our Time* (Amherst, 1966)
Dibble, Vernon, 'Social Science and Political Commitments in the Young Max Weber', in *Archives Européennes de Sociologie*, vol. 9 (1968), pp. 92–110
Dronberger, Ilse, *The Political Thought of Max Weber* (New York, 1971)
Giddens, Anthony, *Politics and Sociology in the Thought of Max Weber* (London, 1972)
Scaff, Lawrence, 'Max Weber's Politics and Political Education', in *American Political Science Review*, vol. 67 (1973), pp. 128–41.
Mommsen, Wolfgang J., *The Age of Bureaucracy: Perspectives on the Political Sociology of Max Weber* (Oxford, 1974)
Beetham, David, *Max Weber and the Theory of Modern Politics* (London, 1974; 2nd edn, Cambridge, 1985)
Eden, Robert, *Political Leadership and Nihilism: A Study of Weber and Nietzsche* (Tampa, 1983)
Glassman, Ronald and Vatro Murvar (eds), *Max Weber's Political Sociology. A Pessimistic Vision of a Rationalized World* (Westport, 1984)
Mommsen, Wolfgang J., *Max Weber and German Politics 1890–1920* (Chicago, 1984)

(*e*) Sociology of music

Martindale, Don and Johannes Riedel, 'Max Weber's Sociology of Music', in Don Martindale, *Community, Character and Civilisation*' (New York, 1963), pp.365–93

III METHODOLOGICAL WRITINGS

(a) The concept of *Verstehen* or 'understanding'

Truzzi, Marcello (ed.), *Verstehen: Subjective Understanding in the Social Sciences* (Reading, 1974)

Outhwaite, William, *Understanding Social Life: The Method called Verstehen* (London, 1975)

Huff, Toby E., *Max Weber and the Methodology of the Social Sciences* (New Brunswick, 1984)

(b) The concept of the 'ideal-type'

Bruun, Hans Henrik, *Science, Values and Politics in Max Weber's Methodology* (Copenhagen, 1972)

Burger, Thomas, *Max Weber's Theory of Concept Formation. History, Laws, and Ideal-Types* (Durham, NC, 1976)

Rogers, R. E., *Max Weber's Ideal-Type Theory* (New York, 1969)

Hekman, Susan, *Weber, the Ideal-Type, and Contemporary Social Theory* (Notre Dame, 1983)

McLemore, Lelan, 'Max Weber's Defense of Historical Inquiry', in *History and Theory*, vol. 23 (1984), pp. 277–95

(c) The postulate of 'freedom from value-judgement'

Bruun, Hans Henrik, *Science, Values and Politics in Max Weber's Methodology* (Copenhagen, 1972)

Runciman, W. G., *A Critique of Max Weber's Philosophy of Social Science* (Cambridge, 1972)

Torrance, John, 'Max Weber: Methods and the Man', in *European Journal of Sociology*, vol. 15 (1974), pp. 127–65

Portis, E. B., 'Max Weber and the Unity of Normative and Empirical Theory', in *Political Studies*, vol. 31 (1983), pp. 25–42

Turner, Stephen P. and Regis A. Factor, *Max Weber and the Dispute over Reason and Value: A Study of Philosophy, Ethics, and Politics* (London, 1984)

Bryant, Christopher G. A., *Positivism in Social Theory and Research* (London, 1985)

IV THE RECEPTION OF WEBER'S WORK DURING HIS LIFETIME

Simey, T. S., 'Max Weber: Man of Affairs or Theoretical Sociologist?', in *Sociological Review*, vol. 14 (1966), pp. 303–27

Shils, Edward (ed.), *Max Weber on Universities. The Power of the State and the Dignity of the Academic Calling in Imperial Germany* (Chicago, 1974)

Schroeter, Gerd, 'Max Weber as Outsider: His Nominal Influence on German

Sociology in the Twenties', in *Journal of the History of the Behavioral Sciences*, vol. 16 (1980), pp. 317–32

Factor, Regis, A. and Stephen P. Turner 'Weber's Influence in Weimar Germany', in *Journal of the History of the Behavioral Sciences*, vol. 18 (1982), pp. 147–56

Schroeter, Gerd, 'Weber and Weimar: A Response to Factor and Turner', in *Journal of the History of the Behavioral Sciences*, vol. 18 (1982), pp. 157–62

V WEBER'S IMPORTANCE FOR SOCIOLOGY TODAY AND IN THE FUTURE

Honigsheim, Paul, *On Max Weber* (New York, 1968)

Lachmann, Ludwig, *The Legacy of Max Weber* (London, 1970)

Wrong, Dennis (ed.), *Max Weber* (Englewood Cliffs, 1970)

Bendix, Reinhard and Guenther Roth, *Scholarship and Partisanship: Essays on Max Weber* (Berkeley/London, 1971)

Coser, Lewis A., 'Max Weber', in Lewis A. Coser, *Masters of Sociological Thought. Ideas in Historical and Social Context* (New York, 1971; 2nd edn, 1977)

Sahay, Arun (ed.), *Max Weber and Modern Sociology* (London, 1971)

Stammer, Otto (ed.), *Max Weber and Sociology Today* (Oxford, 1971)

Eldridge, J. E. T. (ed.), *Max Weber: The Interpretation of Social Reality* (Exeter, 1972)

Macrae, Donald, *Max Weber* (London, 1974)

Roth, Guenther and Wolfgang Schluchter, *Max Weber's Vision of History: Ethics and Methods* (Berkeley, 1979)

Kalberg, Stephen, 'Max Weber's Types of Rationality: Cornerstones for the Analysis of Rationalization Processes in History', in *American Journal of Sociology*, vol. 85 (1980), pp. 1145–79

Tenbruck, Friedrich, 'The Problem of Thematic Unity in the Work of Max Weber', in *British Journal of Sociology*, vol. 31 (1980), pp. 313–51.

Levine, Donald, 'Rationality and Freedom: Weber and Beyond', in Sociological Inquiry, vol. 51 (1981), pp. 5–25

Turner, Bryan S., *For Weber: Essays on the Sociology of Fate* (London/Boston, 1981)

Schluchter, Wolfgang, *The Rise of Western Rationalism: Max Weber's Developmental History* (Berkeley, 1981)

Parkin, Frank, *Max Weber* (Chichester/London, 1982)

Ferrarotti, Franco, *Max Weber and the Destiny of Reason* (New York, 1982)

Hennis, Wilhelm, 'Max Weber's "Central Question"', in *Economy and Society*, vol. 12 (1983), pp. 135–80

Alexander, Jeffrey C., *Theoretical Logic in Sociology. Vol. 3: The Classical Attempt at Theoretical Synthesis: Max Weber* (Berkeley, 1983)

Habermas, Jürgen, *The Theory of Communicative Action* (Boston, 1984)

Andreski, Stanislav, *Max Weber's Insights and Errors* (London, 1984)

Brubaker, Rogers, *The Limits of Rationality: An Essay on the Social and Moral Thought of Max Weber* (London, 1984)

Collins, Randall, *Weberian Sociological Theory* (New York, 1986)

Collins, Randall, *Max Weber: A Skeleton Key* (Beverly Hills, 1986)

Aron, Raymond, *History, Truth, Liberty: Writings of Raymond Aron* (Chicago, 1986)

3   Weber's works in German

The following bibliographical section is based on the author's research during the years 1975–7 together with Helmut Fogt. A first version was published in *Kölner Zeitschrift für Soziologie und Sozialpsychologie* (KZfSS, vol. 27 (1975), pp. 703–30) and led to a first amendment in 1976 (KZfSS, vol. 28, pp. 807–8). In 1978 a revised version was published in vol. 2 of *Klassiker des soziologischen Denkens* edited by the author (München: C. Beck; pp. 424–46). This publication again led to several new findings which were incorporated in the bibliography of the German version of this book published in 1979.

This last version became one starting-point for the planning of the *Max Weber Gesamtausgabe* (MWG) (see the bibliographical section 'The Max Weber Collected Edition'). In the prospectus for the MWG published in 1981 several new findings were reported which have been inserted in the following bibliography organized according to my scheme of listing:

I   Publications by Max Weber 1889–1920 (in chronological order)
II   Unpublished works by Max Weber (in chronological order)
III   Posthumous publications and collections
IV   Abridged collections
V   Published letters

The scheme of order – primarily a chronological one according to the *year of publication* – within these paragraphs is organized according to the following order:

Articles in newspapers (in chronological order)
Articles in journals, yearbooks, dictionaries, *Festschriften*, and published speeches
   (in alphabetical order of the sources and in chronological order)
Articles in reports and minutes (in alphabetical order of the sources)
Books

The bibliography itself has not been translated. Besides using the standard German abbreviations, where superior numbers (e.g. $GAzW^{1-4}$) refer to the editions of the work, I have used the following abbreviations for the standard collections of Weber's writings (the numbers refer to the works labelled as such in this section):

GAzRS   =   180, 203, 204
GPS   =   206
GAzW   =   213
WuG   =   215

GAzSuW = 217
GAzSuS = 218
PE I = 223
PE II = 224

I PUBLICATIONS BY MAX WEBER 1889–1920 (in chronological order)

1889

1   Entwickelung des Solidarhaftprinzips und des Sondervermögens der offenen Handelsgesellschaft aus den Haushalts- und Gewerbegemeinschaften in den italienischen Städten. Inaugural-Dissertation zur Erlangung der juristischen Doktorwürde von der juristischen Fakultät der Königl. Friedrich-Wilhelms-Universität zu Berlin genehmigt und zugleich mit den angehängten Thesen am 1. August 1889 öffentlich zu verteidigen. Stuttgart (Kröner).

2   Zur Geschichte der Handelsgesellschaften im Mittelalter. Nach südeuropäischen Quellen. Stuttgart (F. Enke). [Enthält (1) als Teil 'III. Die Familien und Arbeitsgemeinschaften'.] In: GAzSuW S. 312–443.

2a   dass. [Fotomechanischer Nachdruck] Amsterdam (Schippers-Verlag) 1964.

1890

3   [Besprechung von] Friedrich Conze, Kauf nach hanseatischen Quellen. In: Zeitschrift für das Gesammte Handelsrecht, hrsg. v. L. Goldschmidt u.a., 37. Bd., 1. u. 2. Heft, Stuttgart (F. Enke), S. 268–71.

4   [Besprechung von] A. v. Kostanecki, Der öffentliche Kredit im Mittelalter. In: Zeitschrift für das Gesammte Handelsrecht, hrsg. v. L. Goldschmidt u.a., 37. Bd., 3. u. 4. Heft, Stuttgart (F. Enke), S. 592–8.

1891

5   Die römische Agrargeschichte in ihrer Bedeutung für das Staats- und Privatrecht. Stuttgart (F. Enke).

5a   dass. [Fotomechanischer Nachdruck] Amsterdam (Schippers-Verlag) 1962.

1892

6   Zur Rechtfertigung Göhres. In: Die Christliche Welt, Evangelisch-Lutherisches Gemeindeblatt für Gebildete aller Stände, 6. Jg., Nr. 48 v. 24. 11. Leipzig (Fr. W. Grunow), Sp. 1104–9.

7   'Privatenquêten' über die Lage der Landarbeiter. In: Mitteilungen des
         Evangelisch-sozialen Kongresses. Hrsg. vom Aktionskomitee des
         Evangelisch-sozialen Kongresses. Nr. 4 v. 1. April, S. 3–5; Nr. 5 v. 1.
         Juni, S. 3–6; Nr. 6 v. 1. Juli, S. 1–5. Berlin (Vaterländische
         Verlagsanstalt).

8   Die Verhältnisse der Landarbeiter im ostelbischen Deutschland.
         (Preußische Provinzen Ost- und Westpreußen, Pommern, Posen,
         Schlesien, Brandenburg, Großherzogtümer Mecklenburg, Kreis
         Herzogtum Lauenburg). Dargestellt auf Grund der vom Verein für
         Socialpolitik veranstalteten Erhebungen. Schriften des Vereins für
         Socialpolitik. LV. Die Verhältnisse der Landarbeiter in Deutschland. 3.
         Bd. Leipzig (Duncker & Humblot).

         1893

9   Die Erhebung des Evangelisch-sozialen Kongresses über die Verhältnisse
         der Landarbeiter Deutschlands. In: Die Christliche Welt, Evangelisch-
         Lutherisches Gemeindeblatt für Gebildete aller Stände, 7. Jg., Nr. 23
         v. 1. 6. Leipzig (Fr. W. Grunow), Sp. 535–40.

10   Die Evangelisch-sozialen Kurse in Berlin im Herbst dieses Jahres. In: Die
         Christliche Welt, Evangelisch-Lutherisches Gemeindeblatt für Gebildete
         aller Stände, 7. Jg., Nr. 32 v. 3. 8. Leipzig (Fr. W. Grunow), Sp. 766–8.

11   [Besprechung von] Th. Frhr. v. d. Goltz, Die ländliche Arbeiterklasse und
         der preußische Staat. In: Jahrbücher für Nationalökonomie und Statistik.
         hrsg. v. J. Conrad u. L. Elster, 3. Folge, 6. Bd., Heft 2, Jena (Gustav
         Fischer), S. 289–96.

12   Die Erhebung des Vereins für Sozialpolitik über die Lage der
         Landarbeiter. In: Das Land. Zeitschrift für die sozialen und volkstüm-
         lichen Angelegenheiten auf dem Lande. Hrsg. Heinrich Sohnrey, I. Jg.,
         Berlin (Verlag von Trowitzsch & Sohn), Nr. 1, S. 8–9; Nr. 2, S. 24–6;
         Nr. 3, S. 43–5; Nr. 4, S. 58–9; Nr. 8, S. 129–30; Nr. 9, S. 147–8.

13   Wie werden einwandfreie Erhebungen über die Lage der Landarbeiter
         angestellt? In: Das Land. Zeitschrift für die sozialen und volkstümlichen
         Angelegenheiten auf dem Lande. Hrsg. Heinrich Sohnrey, I. Jg., Berlin
         (Verlag von Trowitzsch & Sohn), Nr. 4, S. 59–60.

14   Zwei neue Schriften zur Landfrage im Osten. [Besprechung von] 1. Th.
         Frhr. v. d. Geltz, Die ländliche Arbeiterklasse und der preußische Staat.
         2. Max Sering. Die innere Kolonisation im östlichen Deutschland. In:
         Das Land. Zeitschrift für die sozialen und volkstümlichen Angelegen-
         heiten auf dem Lande. Hrsg. Heinrich Sohnrey, I. Jg., Berlin (Verlag von
         Trowitzsch & Sohn), Nr. 15, S. 231–2.

15   Monographien von Landgeistlichen über die Lage der Landarbeiter.

[Besprechung von] Quistorp, Die soziale Noth der ländlichen Arbeiter. Wittenberg, Die Lage der ländlichen Arbeiter in Neuvorpommern und auf Rügen. O. Fischer, Beiträge zur Kenntnis der Lage der ländlichen Arbeiter in Ostpreußen. In: Sozialpolitisches Centralblatt, hrsg. v. Heinrich Braun, III. Jg., Nr. 9, Berlin, den 27. 11., S. 101-3.

16   [Besprechung von] Wilhelm Kaufmann, Das internationale Recht der ägyptischen Staatsschuld. In: Zeitschrift für das Gesammte Handelsrecht, hrsg. v. L. Goldschmidt u.a., 41. Bd., 3. u. 4. Heft, Stuttgart (F. Enke), S. 595-7.

17   [Besprechung von] Georg Schaps, Zur Geschichte des Wechselindossaments. In: Zeitschrift für das Gesammte Handelsrecht, hrsg. v. L. Goldschmidt u.a., 41. Bd., 3. u. 4. Heft, Stuttgart (F. Enke), S. 627-9.

18   Referat [über "Die ländliche Arbeitsverfassung"]. Verhandlungen der am 20. und 21. März 1893 in Berlin abgehaltenen Generalversammlung des Vereins für Socialpolitik über die ländliche Arbeiterfrage und über die Bodenbesitzverteilung und die Sicherung des Kleingrundbesitzes. Auf Grund der stenographischen Niederschrift herausgegeben vom Ständigen Ausschuß. Schriften des Vereins für Socialpolitik. LVIII. Verhandlungen von 1893. Leipzig (Duncker & Humblot), S. 62-86. In: GAzSuW S. 444-69 [unvollständig].

19   [Diskussionsbeitrag auf der gleichen Tagung.] In: Verhandlungen der am 20. und 21. März 1893 in Berlin abgehaltenen Generalversammlung des Vereins für Socialpolitik . . . [Vgl. (18)], S. 128-33.

20   [Persönliche Bemerkung auf der gleichen Tagung.] In: Verhandlungen der am 20. und 21. März 1893 in Berlin abgehaltenen Generalversammlung des Vereins für Socialpolitik . . . [Vgl. (18)], S. 215-16.

20/I   Landwirtschaft und Agrarpolitik. Grundriß zu 8 Vorlesungen im Evangelisch-sozialen Kursus zu Berlin. Oktober 1893. In: Grundriß zu den Vorlesungen im Evangelisch-sozialen Kursus zu Berlin. Berlin (Vaterländische Verlagsanstalt).

20/II [Besprechung von] Silvio Perozzi, Perpetua causa nelle servitù prediali romane. In: Zeitschrift der Savigny-Stiftung für Rechtsgeschichte, Romanistische Abtheilung, hrsg. v. E.I. Bekker u.a., 14.Bd., Weimar (H. Böhlau), S. 290-2.

1894

21   Entwickelungstendenzen in der Lage der ostelbischen Landarbeiter. In: Archiv für Soziale Gesetzgebung und Statistik. Vierteljahresschrift zur Erforschung der gesellschaftlichen Zustände aller Länder, hrsg. v. Heinrich Braun, 7. Bd., Heft 1, Berlin (Carl Heymanns), S. 1-41.

22   Was heißt Christlich-Sozial? [Besprechung von] Gesammelte Aufsätze

von Fr. Naumann. In: Die Christliche Welt, Evangelisch-Lutherisches Gemeindeblatt für Gebildete aller Stände, 8. Jg., Nr. 20 v. 17. 5. Leipzig (Fr. W. Grunow), Sp. 472–7.

23   Zum Preßstreit über den Evangelisch-sozialen Kongreß. In: Die Christliche Welt, Evangelisch-Lutherisches Gemeindeblatt für Gebildete aller Stände, 8. Jg., Nr. 28 v. 12. 7. Leipzig (Fr. W. Grunow), Sp. 668–73.

24   Argentinische Kolonistenwirthschaften. In: Deutsches Wochenblatt, hrsg. v. O. Arendt, VII. Jg., Berlin (Hermann Walther). Nr. 2 v. 11. 1., S. 20–2; Nr. 5 v. 1. 2., S. 57–9.

25   Entwickelungstendenzen in der Lage der ostelbischen Landarbeiter. In: Preußische Jahrbücher, hrsg. v. Hans Delbrück, 77. Bd., Heft 3, Sept., Berlin (Hermann Walther), S. 437–73 [Umgearbeitete Fassung von (21)]. In: GAzSuW S. 470–507.

26   Die Verhandlungen der Preussischen Agrarkonferenz. In: Sozialpolitisches Centralblatt, hrsg. v. Heinrich Braun, III. Jg., Nr. 45, Berlin, den 6. 8., S.533–7.

27   Das Anerbenrecht auf der preussischen Agrarkonferenz. In: Sozialpolitisches Centralblatt, hrsg. v. Heinrich Braun, III. Jg., Nr. 48, Berlin, den 27. 8., S. 573–5.

28   [Besprechung von] Angelo Sraffa, Studi di diritto commerciale. Ders., La liquidazione delle società commerciali. In: Zeitschrift für das Gesammte Handelsrecht, hrsg. v. L. Goldschmidt u.a., 42. Bd., 1. u. 2. Heft, Stuttgart (F. Enke), S. 314–20.

29   [Besprechung von] B. Lehmann. Die Rechtsverhältnisse der Fremden in Argentinien. In: Zeitschrift für das Gesammte Handelsrecht, hrsg. v. L. Goldschmidt u.a., 42. Bd., 1. u. 2. Heft, Stuttgart (F. Enke), S. 326–7.

30   [Besprechung von] Otto Thorsch, Materialien zu einer Geschichte der österreichischen Staatsschulden vor dem 18. Jahrhundert. In: Zeitschrift für das Gesammte Handelsrecht, hrsg. v. L. Goldschmidt u.a., 42. Bd., 1. u. 2. Heft, Stuttgart (F. Enke), S. 330–1.

31   Die deutschen Landarbeiter. [Korreferat und Schlußwort]. In: Bericht über die Verhandlungen des 5. Evangelisch-sozialen Kongresses, abgehalten zu Frankfurt am Main am 16. und 17. Mai 1894. Nach den stenographischen Protokollen. Berlin (Verlag von Rehtwisch & Langewort), S. 61–82; 92–4.

32   Die Börse. I. Zweck und äußere Organisation der Börsen. Göttinger Arbeiterbibliothek. Hrsg. v. Fr. Naumann. 1. Bd., H. 2, 3. Gottingen (Vandenhoeck u. Ruprecht), S. 17–48. In: GAzSuS S. 256–88.

32/I   [Besprechung von] Vinogradoff, Villainage in England. Essays in English Mediaeval history. In: Zeitschrift der Savigny-Stiftung für Rechtsgeschichte, Germanistische Abtheilung, hrsg. v. E. I. Bekker u.a., 15.Bd. Weimar (H. Böhlau), S. 187–92.

1895

33 Die Kampfesweise des Freiherrn v. Stumm. (Eingesandt.) In: Neue Preußische Zeitung, Nr. 96 vom 26. 2. 1895, Ab.ausg.

34 Eingesandt. [Zur selben Sache wie (33).] In: Neue Preußische Zeitung, Nr. 119 vom 12. 3. 1895, Mo.ausg.

35 'Römisches' und 'deutsches' Recht. In: Die Christliche Welt, Evangelisch-Lutherisches Gemeindeblatt für Gebildete aller Stände, 9. Jg., Nr. 22 v. 30. 5., Leipzig (Fr. W. Grunow), Sp. 521-5.

36 Börsenwesen. (Die Vorschläge der Börsenenquetekommission.) In: Handwörterbuch der Staatswissenschaften. Hrsg. v. J. Conrad u.a., 1. Supplementbd., Abzahlungsgeschäfte – Wollzoll. Jena (Gustav Fischer), S. 241-52.

36/I Erklärung gegen die Umsturzvorlage. [Mitunterzeichnet von Max Weber.] In: Die Hilfe. Gotteshilfe, Selbsthilfe, Staatshilfe, Bruderhilfe. Eine Wochenschrift Hrsg. v. Fr. Naumann. 1. Jg., Nr. 9, Berlin, 3. 3. 1895, S. 3-4.

36/Ia dass. in: Die Grenzboten. Zeitschrift für Politik, Litteratur und Kunst. 54. Jg., Erstes Vierteljahr, Heft 11, Beilage. Leipzig (Fr. W. Grunow).

37 [Besprechung von] Karl Grünberg, Die Bauernbefreiung und die Auflösung des grundherrlich-bäuerlichen Verhältnisses in Böhmen, Mähren und Schlesien. 2 Bde. In: Historische Zeitschrift, hrsg. v. H. v. Treitschke u. Fr. Meinecke, 75. Bd., Heft 1, München u. Leipzig (Oldenbourg), S. 143-6.

38 Der preussische Gesetzentwurf über das Anerbenrecht bei Rentengütern. In: Soziale Praxis. Centralblatt für Sozialpolitik, hrsg. v. J. Jastrow, IV. Jg., Nr. 50. Berlin-Frankfurt/M. (C. Heymanns), Sp. 956-60.

39 Die Ergebnisse der deutschen Börsenenquete. Vorbemerkung. I. Organisation und Rechtsstellung der Börsen. II. Maklerwesen und Kursnotirung. In: Zeitschrift für das Gesammte Handelsrecht, hrsg. v. L. Goldschmidt u.a., 43. Bd. Stuttgart (F. Enke), 1. u. 2. Heft, S. 83-219; 3. u. 4. Heft, S. 457-514.

40 Der Nationalstaat und die Volkswirtschaftspolitik. Akademische Antrittsrede. Freiburg i. B. u. Leipzig (Mohr-Siebeck). In: GPS S. 7-30; GPS[2,3] S. 1-25.

1896

41 Die technische Funktion des Terminhandels. In: Deutsche Juristen-Zeitung, hrsg. v. P. Laband u.a., I. Jg., Berlin (O. Liebmann), Nr. 11 v. 1. 6., S. 207-10; Nr. 13 v. 1. 7., S. 248-50.

42 [Besprechung von] Dr. Vallentin, Westpreußen seit den ersten Jahrzehnten dieses Jahrhunderts. Ein Beitrag zur Geschichte der Entwicklung des allgemeinen Wohlstandes in dieser Provinz und ihren

einzelnen Theilen. In: Historische Zeitschrift, hrsg. v. H. v. Treitschke u. Fr. Meinecke, 76. Bd., Heft 2, München u. Leipzig (Oldenbourg), S. 308–9.

43   Die sozialen Gründe des Untergangs der antiken Kultur. In: Die Wahrheit. Halbmonatsschrift zur Vertiefung in die Fragen und Aufgaben des Menschenlebens. Hrsg. v. Christoph Schrempf. 6. Bd., 3., 1. Maiheft (Nr. 63), Stuttgart (Fr. Frommanns Verlag [E. Hauff]), S. 57–77. In: GAzSuW S. 289–311.

44   Die Ergebnisse der deutschen Börsenenquete. III. Das Kommissions-geschäft. IV. Zulassung von Effekten zum Handel und Emissionswesen. In: Zeitschrift für das Gesammte Handelsrecht, hrsg. v. L. Goldschmidt u.a., 44. Bd., 1. u. 2. Heft, Stuttgart (F. Enke), S. 29–74; 45. Bd., 1. u. 2. Heft, ebd., S. 69–156 [Fortsetzung von (39)].

45   [Diskussionsbeitrag zum Vortrag] Hans Delbrück, Die Arbeitslosigkeit und das Recht auf Arbeit. In: Bericht über die Verhandlungen des 7. Evangelisch-sozialen Kongresses, abgehalten zu Stuttgart am 28. u. 29. Mai 1896. Nach den stenographischen Protokollen. Berlin (Karl Georg Wiegandt), S. 122–3.

46   [Diskussionsbeitrag zur Gründung einer national-sozialen Partei.] In: Protokoll über die Vertreter-Versammlung aller National-Sozialen in Erfurt vom 23. bis 25. November 1896. Berlin (Verlag der "Zeit"), S. 47–9. In: GPS[2,3] S. 26–9.

47   Die Börse. II. Der Börsenverkehr. In: Göttinger Arbeiterbibliothek. Hrsg. v. Fr. Naumann. 2. Bd., H. 4, 5. Göttingen (Vandenhoeck u. Ruprecht), S. 49–80 [Fortsetzung von (32)]. In: GAzSuS S. 289–322.

1897

48   Agrarverhältnisse im Altertum. In: Handwörterbuch der Staatswissen-schaften. Hrsg. v. J. Conrad u.a., 2. Supplementbd., Agrarverhältnisse im Altertum – Zinsfuß im Mittelalter. Jena (Gustav Fischer), S. 1–18.

49   Börsengesetz. In: Handwörterbuch der Staatswissenschaften. Hrsg. v. J. Conrad u.a., 2. Supplementbd., Agrarverhältnisse im Altertum –Zinsfuß im Mittelalter. Jena (Gustav Fischer), S. 222–46.

50   Wertpapiere (Aufbewahrung). Das Bankdepotgesetz vom 5. Juli 1896. In: Handwörterbuch der Staatswissenschaften. Hrsg. v. J. Conrad u.a., 2. Supplementbd., Agrarverhältnisse im Altertum – Zinsfuß im Mittelalter. Jena (Gustav Fischer), S. 984–6.

51   Gutachten über die Frage: Empfiehlt sich die Einführung eines Heim-stättenrechtes, insbesondere zum Schutz des kleinen Grundbesitzes gegen Zwangsvollstreckung? In: Verhandlungen des 24. Deutschen Juristen-tages. Hrsg. v. dem Schriftführer-Amt der ständigen Deputation. 2. Bd., Berlin (Commissions-Verlag v. J. Guttentag), S. 15–32.

52   [Diskussionsbeiträge zum Vortrag] Karl Oldenberg, Ueber Deutschland
      als Industriestaat. In: Die Verhandlungen des 8. Evangelisch-sozialen
      Kongresses, abgehalten zu Leipzig am 10. u. 11. Juni 1897. Nach den
      stenographischen Protokollen. Göttingen (Vandenhoeck & Ruprecht), S.
      105–13; 122–3.

      1898

53   [Stellungnahme zur Flotten-Umfrage der Allgemeinen Zeitung.] Die
      Ergebnisse der von der Allgemeinen Zeitung veranstalteten Flotten-
      Umfrage. Außerordentliche Beilage zur Allgemeinen Zeitung, Jg. 1898,
      Nr. 3 v. 13. 1. 1898. München (Verlag der Allgemeinen Zeitung), S. 4–5.
      In: GPS[3]S. 30–2.

54   Agrarverhältnisse im Altertum. In: Handwörterbuch der Staatswissen-
      schaften. Hrsg. v. J. Conrad u.a., 2., gänzlich umgearbeitete Aufl., 1.
      Bd., Abbau-Armenwesen, Jena (Gustav Fischer), S. 57–85 [umgear-
      beitete Fassung von (48)].

54/I Grundriß zu den Vorlesungen über Allgemeine ('theoretische') National-
      ökonomie. [Heidelberg, Sommersemester 1898]. Ca. April 1898.

54/II Die begrifflichen Grundlagen der Volkswirtschaftslehre. Erstes Buch
      [des Vorlesungsgrundrisses über Allgemeine ('theoretische') National-
      ökonomie. Heidelberg, Sommersemester 1898]. Ca. April 1898.

      1899

55   Herr v. Miquel und die Landarbeiter-Enquête des Vereins für Sozial-
      politik. In: Soziale Praxis. Centralblatt für Sozialpolitik, hrsg. v. Ernst
      Francke, VIII. Jg., Nr. 24 vom 16. 3. 1899, Berlin (Duncker &
      Humblot), Sp. 640–2.

56   Vorbemerkung des Herausgebers. In: S. Goldschmidt, Die Landarbeiter
      in der Provinz Sachsen, sowie den Herzogtümern Braunschweig und
      Anhalt. Die Landarbeiter in den evangelischen Gebieten Norddeutsch-
      lands. In Einzeldarstellungen nach den Erhebungen des Evangelisch-
      Sozialen Kongresses, hrsg. v. M. Weber, 1. Heft, Tübingen (H. Laupp),
      S. 1–11.

56/I [Anmerkung des Herausgebers]. In: A. Grunenberg, Die Landarbeiter in
      den Provinzen Schleswig-Holstein und Hannover östlich der Weser, sowie
      in dem Gebiete des Fürstentums Lübeck und der freien Städte Lübeck,
      Hamburg und Bremen. Die Landarbeiter in den evangelischen Gebieten
      Norddeutschlands in Einzeldarstellungen nach den Erhebungen des
      Evangelisch-Sozialen Kongresses, hrsg. v. M. Weber, 2. Heft, Tübingen
      (H. Laupp), S. VI.

1900

57   Vorbemerkung des Herausgebers. In: Walter Abelsdorff, Beiträge zur Sozialstatistik der Deutschen Buchdrucker. Volkswirtschaftliche Abhandlungen der Badischen Hochschulen, hrsg. v. C. J. Fuchs, G. v. Schulze-Gävernitz, M. Weber. 4. Bd., 4. Heft. Tübingen u. Leipzig (Mohr-Siebeck), S. VII–IX.

58   Anmerkung des Herausgebers [zum Vorwort Marianne Webers]. In: Marianne Weber, Fichte's Sozialismus und sein Verhältnis zur Marx'schen Doktrin. Volkswirtschaftliche Abhandlungen der Badischen Hochschulen, hrsg. v. C. J. Fuchs, G. v. Schulze-Gävernitz, M. Weber, 4. Bd., 3. Heft, Tübingen, Freiburg i. B. und Leipzig (Mohr-Siebeck), S. VI.

58a   2., photomechanisch gedruckte Aufl., Tübingen (Mohr-Siebeck) 1925.

1902

59   [Besprechung von] Philipp Lotmar, Der Arbeitsvertrag, 1. Bd. In: Archiv für Soziale Gesetzgebung und Statistik. Zeitschrift zur Erforschung der gesellschaftlichen Zustände aller Länder, hrsg. v. Heinrich Braun, 17. Bd., 3. Heft, Berlin (Carl Heymanns), S. 723–4.

1903

59/I   [Besprechung von] A. Grotjahn, Über Wandlungen in der Volksernährung. In: Jahrbuch für Gesetzgebung, Verwaltung und Volkswirtschaft im Deutschen Reich. Hrsg. v. Gustav Schmoller. 27. Jg., 2. Heft, Leipzig (Duncker & Humblot), S. 728–32.

60   Roscher und Knies und die logischen Probleme der historischen Nationalökonomie. (Erster Artikel), Vorbemerkung u. I. In: Jahrbuch für Gesetzgebung, Verwaltung und Volkswirtschaft im Deutschen Reich. Hrsg. v. Gustav Schmoller. 27. Jg., 3. Heft, Leipzig (Duncker & Humblot), S. 1181–221. In: GAzW[1-4] S. 1–42.

1904

60/I   Die 'Bedrohung' der Reichsverfassung. [Zuschrift]. In: Frankfurter Zeitung, 49. Jg., Nr. 153 vom 3. 6. 1904, 1.Mo.bl.

61   Geleitwort [der Herausgeber zum Übergang des Archivs für Soziale Gesetzgebung und Statistik auf die neuen Herausgeber Werner Sombart, Max Weber und Edgar Jaffé]. In: Archiv für Sozialwissenschaft und Sozialpolitik, Neue Folge des Archivs für Soziale Gesetzgebung und Statistik, hrsg. v. Werner Sombart, Max Weber und Edgar Jaffé, 19. Bd., Heft 1, Tübingen (Mohr-Siebeck), S. I–VII.

62   Die 'Objektivität' sozialwissenschaftlicher und sozialpolitischer Erkenntnis.

In: Archiv für Sozialwissenschaft und Sozialpolitik, 19. Bd., Heft 1, S. 22–87. In: GAzW[1-4] S. 146–214.

63 Agrarstatistische und sozialpolitische Betrachtungen zur Fideikommißfrage in Preußen. In: Archiv für Sozialwissenschaft und Sozialpolitik, 19. Bd., Heft 3, S. 503–74. In: GAzSuS S. 323–93.

64 Der Streit um den Charakter der altgermanischen Sozialverfassung in der deutschen Literatur des letzten Jahrzehnts. In: Jahrbücher für Nationalökonomie und Statistik, hrsg. v. J. Conrad u.a., III. Folge, 28. Bd., Heft 4, Jena (Gustav Fischer), S. 433–70. In: GAzSuW S. 508–56.

1905

65 Die protestantische Ethik und der 'Geist' des Kapitalismus. In: Archiv für Sozialwissenschaft und Sozialpolitik, 20. Bd., Heft 1, S. 1–54; 21. Bd., Heft 1, S. 1–110.

66 Redaktionelle Bemerkung zu vorstehendem Aufsatz [G. Cohn, Über den wissenschaftlichen Charakter der Nationalökonomie]. In: Archiv für Sozialwissenschaft und Sozialpolitik, 20. Bd., Heft 3, S. 479.

67 Bemerkungen im Anschluß an den vorstehenden Aufsatz [R. Blank, Die soziale Zusammensetzung der sozialdemokratischen Wählerschaft Deutschlands]. In: Archiv für Sozialwissenschaft und Sozialpolitik, 20. Bd., Heft 3, S. 550–3.

68 Roscher und Knies und die logischer Probleme der historischen National-ökonomie. II. Knies und das Irrationalitätsproblem. In: Jahrbuch für Gesetzgebung, Verwaltung und Volkswirtschaft im Deutschen Reich. Hrsg. v. Gustav Schmoller. 29. Jg., 4. Heft, Leipzig (Duncker & Humblot), S. 1323–1384 [Fortsetzung von (60)]. In: GAzW[1-4] S. 42–105.

1906

69 'Kirchen' und 'Sekten'. In: Frankfurter Zeitung, 50. Jg., Nr. 102 vom 13. 4. 1906, 4. Mo.bl.

70 'Kirchen' und 'Sekten' (Schluß). In: Frankfurter Zeitung, 50. Jg., Nr. 104 vom 15. 4. 1906, 6. Mo.bl. [Fortsetzung von (69)].

70/I Zur Stellung der Frau im modernen Erwerbsleben. In: Frankfurter Zeitung, 51. Jg., Nr. 222 vom 13. 8. 1906, Mo.bl. [anonym].

70/II [Erklärung gegen die preußische Schulvorlage]. In: Pädagogische Zeitung, Hauptorgan des deutschen Lehrervereins, 35. Jg., Nr. 13 vom 29. 3. 1906, S. 264.

71 Kritische Studien auf dem Gebiet der kulturwissenschaftlichen Logik. In: Archiv für Sozialwissenschaft und Sozialpolitik, 22. Bd., Heft 1, S. 143–207. In: GAzW[1-4] S. 215–90.

72 Zur Lage der bürgerlichen Demokratie in Rußland (S. J. Giwago u. Max

252 BIBLIOGRAPHY

Weber, Zur Beurteilung der gegenwärtigen politischen Entwicklung Rußlands). In: Archiv für Sozialwissenschaft und Sozialpolitik, 22. Bd., Heft 1, Beilage, S. 234–353. In: GPS² S. 30–65; GPS³ S. 33–68 [unvollständig].

73   Rußlands Übergang zum Scheinkonstitutionalismus. In: Archiv für Sozialwissenschaft und Sozialpolitik, 23. Bd., Heft 1, Beilage, S. 165–401. In: GPS² S. 66–108; GPS³ S. 69–111 [unvollständig].

74   'Kirchen' und 'Sekten' in Nordamerika. Eine kirchen- und sozialpolitische Skizze. In: Die Christliche Welt, Evangelisches Gemeindeblatt für Gebildete aller Stände. 20. Jg., Marburg i. H. (Verlag der Christlichen Welt), Nr. 24 v. 14. 6., Sp. 558–62; Nr. 25 v. 21. 6., Sp. 577–83 [umgearbeitete Fassung von (69), (70)].

75   Roscher und Knies und die logischen Probleme der historischen Nationalökonomie. (Dritter Artikel). II. Knies und das Irrationalitätsproblem (Fortsetzung). In: Jahrbuch für Gesetzgebung, Verwaltung und Volkswirtschaft im Deutschen Reich, hrsg. v. Gustav Schmoller. 30. Jg., 1. Heft, Leipzig (Duncker & Humblot), S. 81–120 [Fortsetzung von (60) und (68)]. In: GAzW¹⁻⁴ S. 105–45.

76   The Relations of the Rural Community to other Branches of Social Science (translated by Professor Charles W. Seidenadel). In: Congress of Arts and Science. Universal Exposition, St Louis, 1904, edited by Howard J. Rogers. vol. VII. Boston-New York (Houghton, Mifflin and Company), S. 725–46.

76a   Capitalism and Rural Society in Germany. In: From Max Weber: Essays in Sociology. Translated, edited and with an introduction by H. H. Gerth and C. Wright Mills (New York, 1946), S. 363–85 [umgearbeitete Fassung von (76)].

76b   Kapitalismus und Agrarverfassung. In: Zeitschrift für die gesamte Staatswissenschaft Hrsg. v. F. Böhm u.a., 108. Bd., 3. Heft, Tübingen (Mohr-Siebeck) 1952, S. 431–52 [deutsche Rückübersetzung von (76a) durch Hans H. Gerth].

77   [Diskussionsbeitrag zum Thema] Das Arbeitsverhältnis in den privaten Riesenbetrieben. In: Verhandlungen des Vereins für Socialpolitik über die finanzielle Behandlung der Binnenwasserstraßen, über das Arbeitsverhältnis in den privaten Riesenbetrieben und das Verhältnis der Kartelle zum Staate. Schriften des Vereins für Socialpolitik. 116. Bd. Verhandlungen der Generalversammlung in Mannheim, 25., 26., 27. u. 28. 9. 1905. Auf Grund der stenographischen Niederschrift hrsg. v. Ständigen Ausschuß. Leipzig (Duncker & Humblot), S. 212–17. In: GAzSuS S. 394–9 [unvollständig].

78   [Diskussionsbeiträge zum Thema] Das Verhältnis der Kartelle zum Staate. In: Verhandlungen des Vereins für Socialpolitik . . . [Vgl. (77)], S. 371; 382–90; 432–3; 434–5. In: GAzSuS S. 399–407.

1907

79　　　[Zuschrift zum Thema] Die badische Fabrikinspektion. In: Frankfurter
　　　　Zeitung, 51. Jg., Nr. 24 vom 24. 1. 1907, Ab.bl.

80　　　R. Stammlers 'Ueberwindung' der materialistischen Geschichtsauf-
　　　　fassung. In: Archiv für Sozialwissenschaft und Sozialpolitik, 24. Bd., Heft
　　　　1, S. 94–151. In: GAzW[1-4] S. 291–359.

81　　　Kritische Bemerkungen zu den vorstehenden 'Kritischen Beiträgen' [H.
　　　　Karl Fischer, Kritische Beiträge zu Prof. Max Webers Abhandlung: 'Die
　　　　protestantische Ethik und der Geist des Kapitalismus']. In: Archiv für
　　　　Sozialwissenschaft und Sozialpolitik, 25. Bd., Heft 1, S. 243–249. In: PE
　　　　II[1,2] S. 27–37.

1908

81/I　　Der Fall Bernhard. In: Frankfurter Zeitung, 52. Jg., Nr. 168 vom
　　　　18. 6. 1908, 1. Mo.bl. [anonym].

82　　　Der 'Fall Bernhard' und Professor Delbrück. In: Frankfurter Zeitung,
　　　　52. Jg., Nr. 190 vom 10. 7. 1908, 4. Mo.bl.

83　　　Die sogenannte 'Lehrfreiheit' an den deutschen Universitäten. In:
　　　　Frankfurter Zeitung, 53. Jg., Nr. 262 vom 20. 9. 1908, 5. Mo.bl.

83/I　　Die Lehrfreiheit der Universitäten. I. In: Saale-Zeitung, Halle, Nr. 553
　　　　vom 25. 11. 1908, Mo.ausg.

83/II　 Die Lehrfreiheit der Universitäten. II. In: Saale-Zeitung, Halle, Nr. 554
　　　　vom 25. 11. 1908, Ab.ausg.

83/III　Die Lehrfreiheit der Universitäten. III. (Schluß). In: Saale-Zeitung,
　　　　Halle, Nr. 558 vom 27. 11. 1908, Ab.ausg.

84　　　Bemerkungen zu der vorstehenden 'Replik' [H. K. Fischer, Protestan-
　　　　tische Ethik und 'Geist des Kapitalismus']. In: Archiv für Sozial-
　　　　wissenschaft und Sozialpolitik, 26. Bd., Heft 1, S. 275–283. In: PE II[1,2] S.
　　　　44–56.

85　　　Die Grenznutzlehre und das 'psychophysische Grundgesetz'. In: Archiv
　　　　für Sozialwissenschaft und Sozialpolitik, 27. Bd., Heft 2, S. 546–58. In:
　　　　GAzW S. 360–75; GAzW[2-4] S. 384–99.

85/I　　[Besprechung Sign. 'W' von] H. Schumacher, Die Ursachen der
　　　　Geldkrisis. In: Archiv für Sozialwissenschaft und Sozialpolitik, 27. Bd.,
　　　　Heft 2, S. 597–8.

85/II　 [Besprechung Sign. 'W' von] Chr. von Ehrenfels, Sexualethik. In: Archiv
　　　　für Sozialwissenschaft und Sozialpolitik, 27. Bd., Heft 2, S. 613–17.

85/III　[Besprechung Sign. 'W' von] E. Kaufmann, Auswärtige Gewalt und
　　　　Kolonialgewalt in den Vereinigten Staaten von Amerika. In: Archiv für
　　　　Sozialwissenschaft und Sozialpolitik, 27. Bd., Heft 2, S. 618–19.

254   BIBLIOGRAPHY

86   Zur Psychophysik der industriellen Arbeit. In: Archiv für Sozial-
      wissenschaft und Sozialpolitik, 27. Bd., Heft 3, S. 730–70. In GAzSuS S.
      61–109.

87   Die Kredit- und Agrarpolitik der preussischen Landschaftern
      [Besprechung von H. Mauer, Das landschaftliche Kreditwesen Preussens,
      agrargeschichtlich und volkswirtschaftlich betrachtet, 1907]. In: Bank-
      Archiv, Zeitschrift für Bank- und Börsenwesen, hrsg. v. Dr. Riesser,
      VIII. Jg., Nr. 6 vom 15. 12., Berlin (Verlag v. J. Guttentag), S. 87–91.

87/I Sozialdemokraten im academischen Lehramt. In: Hochschul-Nach-
      richten, hrsg. v. Paul v. Salvisberg, XIX. Jg., Heft 218, Nr. 2,
      November, München (Academischer Verlag), S. 45.

88   [Glückwunschadresse zu Gustav Schmollers 70. Geburtstag.] In: Reden
      und Ansprachen gehalten am 24. 6. 1908 bei der Feier von Gustav
      Schmollers 70. Geburtstag. Nach stenographischer Aufnahme. Als Hand-
      schrift gedruckt. Altenburg (Pierersche Hofbuchdruckerei Stephan Geibel
      & Co.), S. 67–8.

88a   dass. in: Carl Brinkmann, Gustav Schmoller und die Volkswirtschafts-
      lehre. Stuttgart (W. Kohlhammer) 1937, S. 8–9 [unvollständig].

88b   dass. in: Kölner Zeitschrift für Soziologie und Sozialpsychologie. Hrsg. v.
      R. König. 27. Jg., Heft 4, Opladen (Westdeutscher Verlag) 1975, S.
      723–4.

88/I [Diskussionsbeiträge auf dem Zweiten deutschen Hochschullehrertag].
      Zweiter deutscher Hochschullehrertag zu Jena am 28. und 29. September
      (Bericht, erstattet vom engeren geschäftsführenden Ausschuß). In:
      Beilage der Münchner Neuesten Nachrichten, Jg. 1908, Nr. 146,
      München, 18. Dezember, S. 634–5.

89   [Diskussionsbeitrag zum Thema] Verfassung und Verwaltungsorgan-
      isation der Städte. In: Verhandlungen des Vereins für Socialpolitik über
      die berufsmäßige Vorbildung der volkswirtschaftlichen Beamten und über
      Verfassung und Verwaltungsorganisation der Städte. Schriften des
      Vereins für Socialpolitik. 125. Bd. Verhandlungen der Generalversamm-
      lung in Magdeburg, 30. 9., 1. u. 2. 10. 1907. Auf Grund der steno-
      graphischen Niederschrift hrsg. v. Ständigen Ausschuß. Leipzig [Duncker
      & Humblot], S. 294–301. In: GAzSuS S. 407–12 [unvollständig].

90   Erhebungen über Auslese und Anpassung (Berufswahl und Berufs-
      schicksal) der Arbeiterschaft der geschlossenen Großindustrie [Exposé zur
      Methodik der Erhebungen]. Als Manuskript gedruckt. Altenburg
      (Pierersche Hofbuchdruckerei Stephan Greibel & Co.). In: GAzSuS S.
      1–60 [unter dem Titel 'Methodologische Einleitung für die Erhebungen
      des Vereins für Sozialpolitik über Auslese und Anpassung (Berufswahlen
      und Berufsschicksal) der Arbeiterschaft der geschlossenen Großindustrie';
      unvollständig].

1909

90/I Prof. Weber-Heidelberg über die Erneuerung Rußlands. In: Neue Badische Landeszeitung, Mannheim, Nr. 158 vom 4. 4. 1909, Mo.ausg.

90/II Zum Hochschullehrertage. [Zuschrift]. In: Frankfurter Zeitung, 54. Jg., Nr. 290 vom 19. 10. 1909, 1. Mo.bl.

90/III Professor Ehrenberg. [Zuschrift]. In: Frankfurter Zeitung, 54. Jg., Nr. 291 vom 20. 10. 1909.

91 Zur Psychophysik der industriellen Arbeit. II., IV. [III. fehlt]. In: Archiv für Sozialwissenschaft und Sozialpolitik, 28. Bd., Heft 1, S. 219–277; Heft 3, S. 719–761; 29. Bd., Heft 2, S. 513–42 [Fortsetzung von (86)]. In: GAzSuS S. 109–255.

92 'Energetische' Kulturtheorien. [Besprechung von] Wilhelm Ostwald, Energetische Grundlagen der Kulturwissenschaft. In: Archiv für Sozialwissenschaft und Sozialpolitik, 29. Bd., Heft 2, S. 575–98. In: GAzW S. 376–402; GAzW$^{2-4}$ S. 400–26.

93 [Besprechung von] Adolf Weber, Die Aufgaben der Volkswirtschaftslehre als Wissenschaft. In: Archiv für Sozialwissenschaft und Sozialpolitik, 29. Bd., Heft 2, S. 615–20.

93/I [Besprechung von] Franz Eulenburg, Die Entwicklung der Universität Leipzig in den letzten hundert Jahren. In: Archiv für Sozialwissenschaft und Sozialpolitik, 29. Bd., Heft 2, S. 672–5.

94 Zur Methodik sozialpsychologischer Enquêten und ihrer Bearbeitung. [Besprechung von] A. Levenstein, Aus der Tiefe, 1908. Ders., Arbeiter-Philosophen und -Dichter, Bd. I, 1909. Ders., Lebenstragödie eines Tagelöhners, 1909. In: Archiv für Sozialwissenschaft und Sozialpolitik, 29. Bd., Heft 3, S. 949–58.

95 Agrarverhältnisse im Altertum. In: Handwörterbuch der Staatswissenschaften. Hrsg. v. J. Conrad u.a., 3. gänzlich umgearbeitete Aufl., 1. Bd., Abbau – Aristoteles, Jena (Gustav Fischer), S. 52–188 [umgearbeitete Fassung von (54)]. In: GAzSuW S. 1–288.

96 Die Lehrfreiheit der Universitäten. In: Hochschul-Nachrichten, hrsg. v. Paul v. Salvisberg, XIX. Jg., Heft 220, Nr. 4, Januar, München (Academischer Verlag), S. 89–91.

96a dass. In: Süddeutsche Zeitung, 29. Jg., Nr. 254 vom 3./4. 11. 1973, SZ am Wochenende.

97 Altertum. In: Die Religion in Geschichte und Gegenwart. Handwörterbuch in gemeinverständlicher Darstellung. Unter Mitwirkung v. H. Gunkel u. O. Scheel hrsg. v. F. M. Schiele. 1. Bd. Von A bis Deutschland. Tübingen (Mohr-Siebeck), Sp. 233–7.

97a Antike Agrarverfassung. In: Die Religion in Geschichte und Gegenwart. Handwörterbuch für Theologie und Religionswissenschaft. 2., völlig neu bearbeitete Aufl. In Verbindung mit A. Bertholet u.a. hrsg. v. H. Gunkel

u. L. Zscharnack. 1. Bd. A-D, Tübingen (Mohr-Siebeck) 1927, Sp. 158–61 [textgleich mit (97)].

1910

98 Antikritisches zum 'Geist' des Kapitalismus. In: Archiv für Sozialwissenschaft und Sozialpolitik, 30. Bd., Heft 1, S. 176–202. In: PE II$^{1.2}$ S. 149–87.

99 Antikritisches Schlusswort zum 'Geist des Kapitalismus'. In: Archiv für Sozialwissenschaft und Sozialpolitik, 31. Bd., Heft 2, S. 554–99. In: PE II$^{1.2}$ S. 283–345 [unvollständig].

99/I Die Deutsche Gesellschaft für Soziologie. [Beilage zum Archiv für Sozialwissenschaft und Sozialpolitik, 31. Bd., Heft 2]. [anonym]

100 [Diskussionsbeiträge auf dem 3. Deutschen Hochschullehrertag.] In: Verhandlungen des III. Deutschen Hochschullehrertages zu Leipzig am 12. u. 13. 10. 1909. Bericht erstattet vom engeren geschäftsführenden Ausschuß. Leipzig (Verlag des Literarischen Zentralblattes für Deutschland [Eduard Avenarius]). S. 6, 16–17, 20–1, 41–2, 47.

101 [Diskussionsbeiträge zum Thema] Die wirtschaftlichen Unternehmungen der Gemeinden. In: Verhandlungen des Vereins für Socialpolitik in Wien, 1909. I. Zum Gedächtnis an Georg Hanssen. II. Die wirtschaftlichen Unternehmungen der Gemeinden. III. Die Produktivität der Volkswirtschaft. Schriften des Vereins für Socialpolitik. 132. Bd. Verhandlungen der Generalversammlung in Wien, 27., 28. u. 29. 9. 1909. Auf Grund der stenograph. Niederschrift hrsg. v. Ständigen Ausschuß. Leipzig (Duncker & Humblot), S. 245, 282–7. In: GAzSuS S. 412–16 [unvollständig].

102 [Diskussionsbeiträge zum Thema] Die Produktivität der Volkswirtschaft. In: Verhandlungen des Vereins für Socialpolitik in Wien . . . [Vgl. (101)], S. 580–5, 586, 603–7, 610, 611, 614. In: GAzSuS S. 416–24 [unvollständig].

1911

102/I Eine Duellforderung an der Heidelberger Universität. [Zuschrift]. In: Heidelberger Tageblatt, 29. Jg., Nr. 7 vom 9. 1. 1911.

102/II Zur Affäre Dr. Ruge, Professor Weber. [Zuschrift]. In: Heidelberger Tageblatt, 29. Jg., Nr. 11 vom 13. 1. 1911.

102/III Ein Votum zur Universitätsfrage. In: Volksstimme. Sozialdemokratisches Organ für Südwestdeutschland, Frankfurt a. Main, 22. Jg., Nr. 146 vom 26. 6. 1911. [Abgedruckter Brief Max Webers an Max Quarck]

103 Professor Max Weber – Heidelberg über seine Rede auf dem Deutschen Hochschultag zu Dresden. In: Tägliche Rundschau, 31. Jg., Nr. 497 vom 22. 10. 1911, 2. Beilage.

103/I   Deutscher Hochschullehrertag. [Zuschrift]. In: Heidelberger Zeitung, 53. Jg., Nr. 246 vom 20. 10. 1911, Erstes Blatt.

104   Die Handelshochschulen. Eine Entgegnung. In: Berliner Tageblatt, 40. Jg., Nr. 548 vom 27. 10. 1911, Mo.ausg.

105   Max Weber über das 'System Althoff'. In: Frankfurter Zeitung, 56. Jg., Nr. 298 vom 27. 10. 1911, Ab.bl.

105a   Die Reverse des Kultusministeriums. In: Vossische Zeitung, Nr. 539 vom 28. 10. 1911. [textgleich mit (105)].

105/I   Die preußische Unterrichtsverwaltung und Prof. Max Weber-Heidelberg. In: Badische Landeszeitung, Nr. 504 vom 28. 10. 1911.

105/II   Die 'Reverse' des Kultusministeriums. In: Vossische Zeitung, Nr. 547 vom 1. 11. 1911.

106   Max Weber und das System Althoff. In: Frankfurter Zeitung, 56. Jg., Nr. 304 vom 2. 11. 1911, 1. Mo.bl.

106/I   Professor Weber über das System Althoff. [Zuschrift an die Nationalliberale Correspondenz]. In: Tägliche Rundschau, Berlin, 31. Jg., Nr. 519 vom 4. 11. 1911, Mo.ausg., 1. Beil.

107   Nochmals Weber – Althoff. In: Tägliche Rundschau, 31. Jg., Nr. 528 vom 9. 11. 1911, Ab.ausg., 2. Beilage.

107/I   Noch einmal die Erklärung des Herrn Professor Dr. Max Weber –Heidelberg. [Zuschrift]. In: Nationalliberale Correspondenz, Nr. 241 vom 10. 11. 1911.

107a   Nochmals das 'System Althoff'. In: Frankfurter Zeitung, 56. Jg., Nr. 312 vom 10. 11. 1911, 3. Mo.bl. [inhaltlich identisch mit (107)].

108   [Geschäftsbericht für die Deutsche Gesellschaft für Soziologie.] In: Verhandlungen des Ersten Deutschen Soziologentages vom 19.–22. 10. 1910 in Frankfurt a.M. Reden und Vorträge von G. Simmel, F. Tönnies, M. Weber, W. Sombart, A. Ploetz, E. Troeltsch, E. Gothein, A. Voigt, H. Kantorowicz und Debatten. Schriften der Deutschen Gesellschaft für Soziologie. I. Serie: Verhandlungen der Deutschen Soziologentage. I. Bd., Tübingen (Mohr-Siebeck), S. 39–62. In: GAzSuS S. 431–49.

109   [Diskussionsbeitrag auf der gleichen Tagung zu dem Vortrag von] Werner Sombart, Technik und Kultur. In: Verhandlungen des Ersten Deutschen Soziologentages . . . [Vgl. (108)], S. 95–101. In: GAzSuS S. 449–56 [unvollständig].

110   [Diskussionsbeiträge zu dem Vortrag von] Alfred Plötz, Die Begriffe Rasse und Gesellschaft und einige damit zusammenhängende Probleme. In: Verhandlungen des Ersten Deutschen Soziologentages . . . [Vgl. (108)], S. 151–7, 159, 161–5, 215. In: GAzSuS S. 456–62 [unvollständig].

111   [Diskussionsbeiträge zu dem Vortrag von] Ernst Troeltsch, Das stoisch-christliche Naturrecht und das moderne profane Naturrecht. In: Verhandlungen des Ersten Deutschen Soziologentages . . . [Vgl. (108)], S. 196–202, 210–11. In: GAzSuS S. 462–9, 469–76.

112 [Diskussionsbeitrag zu dem Vortrag von] Andreas Voigt, Wirtschaft und Recht. In: Verhandlungen des Ersten Deutschen Soziologentages . . . [Vgl. (108)], S. 265–70. In: GAzSuS S. 471–7.

113 [Diskussionsbeiträge zu dem Vortrag von] Hermann Kantorowicz, Rechtswissenschaft und Soziologie. In: Verhandlungen des Ersten Deutschen Soziologentages . . . [Vgl. (108)], S. 312–13, 320, 323–30, 333. In: GAzSuS S. 476–83 [unvollständig].

1912

114 [Diskussionsbeiträge zum Thema] Die von den deutschen abweichenden Einrichtungen an den nordamerikanischen Hochschulen. In: Verhandlungen des IV. Deutschen Hochschullehrertages zu Dresden am 12. u. 13. 10. 1911. Bericht erstattet vom geschäftsf. Ausschuß. Leipzig (Verlag des Literarischen Zentralblattes für Deutschland [Eduard Avenarius]), S. 66–77, 85–6.

115 [Diskussionsbeiträge zum Thema] Probleme der Arbeiterpsychologie unter besonderer Rücksichtnahme auf Methode und Ergebnisse der Vereinserhebungen. In: Verhandlungen des Vereins für Sozialpolitik in Nürnberg 1911. I. Fragen der Gemeindebesteuerung. II. Probleme der Arbeiterpsychologie unter besonderer Rücksichtnahme auf Methode und Ergebnisse der Vereinserhebungen. Schriften des Vereins für Sozialpolitik. 138. Bd. Verhandlungen der Generalversammlung in Nürnberg, 9. u. 10. 10. 1911. Auf Grund der stenograph. Niederschrift hrsg. v. Ständigen Ausschuß. Leipzig (Duncker & Humblot), S. 163, 176, 189–97. In: GAzSuS S. 424–30 [unvollständig].

1913

116 Ueber einige Kategorien der verstehenden Soziologie. In: Logos. Internationale Zeitschrift für Philosophie der Kultur. Hrsg. v. R. Kroner u. G. Mehlis. Bd.IV, Heft 3, Tübingen (Mohr-Siebeck), S. 253–94. In: GAzW S. 403–50; GAzW$^{2-4}$ S. 427–74.

117 [Bemerkungen zur Werturteilsdiskussion]. Äußerungen zur Werturteilsdiskussion im Ausschuß des Vereins für Sozialpolitik. Als Manuskript gedruckt, (o. O.), S. 83–120.

117a dass. in: Eduard Baumgarten, Max Weber, Werk und Person. Dokumente ausgewählt und kommentiert von Eduard Baumgarten. Tübingen (Mohr-Siebeck) 1964, S. 102–39.

118 [Diskussionsbeiträg zu dem Vortrag von] Paul Barth, Die Nationalität in ihrer soziologischen Bedeutung. In: Verhandlungen des Zweiten Deutschen Soziologentages vom 20.–22. 10. 1912 in Berlin. Reden und Vorträge von A. Weber, P. Barth, F. Schmid, L. M. Hartmann, F. Oppenheimer, R. Michels und Debatten. Schriften der Deutschen

Gesellschaft für Soziologie. I. Serie: Verhandlungen der Deutschen Soziologentage. II. Bd., Tübingen (Mohr-Siebeck), S. 49–52. In: GAzSuS S. 484–6.

119   [Diskussionsbeiträge auf der gleichen Tagung zu dem Vortrag von] Ferd. Schmid, Das Recht der Nationalitäten. In: Verhandlungen des Zweiten Deutschen Soziologentages . . . [Vgl. (118)], S. 72–3, 74–5. In: GAzSuS S. 487–8.

120   Rechenschaftsbericht für die abgelaufenen beiden Jahre [über die Tätigkeit der Deutschen Gesellschaft für Soziologie]. In: Verhandlungen des Zweiten Deutschen Soziologentages . . . [Vgl. (118)], S. 75–9.

121   [Diskussionsbeiträge zu den Vorträgen von] Ludo Moritz Hartmann, Die Nation als politischer Faktor. Franz Oppenheimer, Die rassentheoretische Geschichtsphilosophie. Robert Michels, Die historische Entwicklung des Vaterlandsgedankens. In: Verhandlungen des Zweiten Deutschen Soziologentages . . . [Vgl. (118)], S. 188–191. In: GAzSuS S. 488–91 [unvollständig].

1914

121/I   Eine Erklärung von Max Weber. In: Frankfurter Zeitung, 58. Jg., Nr. 181 vom 2. 7. 1914, Ab.bl.

122   Redaktionelles Nachwort [Zu Arthur Salz, In eigener Sache. Im selben Bd., S. 527–38]. In: Archiv für Sozialwissenschaft und Sozialpolitik, 38. Bd., Heft 2, S. 539–50.

123   Vorwort [von Schriftleitung und Verlag zum Erscheinen der I. Abteilung des 'Grundriss der Sozialökonomik', Heidelberg und Tübingen, 2. 6. 1914]. In: Grundriss der Sozialökonomik, I.Abt. Wirtschaft und Wirtschaftswissenschaft. Bearb. v. K. Bücher, J. Schumpeter, Fr. Freiherrn v. Wieser. Tübingen (Mohr-Siebeck), S. vii-ix.

1915

124   Bismarcks Außenpolitik und die Gegenwart. I. Dreibund und Westmächte. II. Dreibund und Rußland. In: Frankfurter Zeitung, 60. Jg., Nr. 357 vom 25. 12. 1915, 3. Mo.bl. In: GPS S. 31–47; GPS^2 S. 109–26; GPS^3 S. 112–29.

125   Zu dem redaktionellen Geleitwort im Märzheft 1914 S. 539f. gegen Herrn Prof. Dr. Sander in Prag (IV.). In: Archiv für Sozialwissenschaft und Sozialpolitik, 39. Bd., Heft 1, S. 231–52.

126   Geleitwort [der Redaktion zu den als Bd. 40 des Archivs für Sozialwissenschaft und Sozialpolitik unter dem Titel 'Krieg und Wirtschaft' erschienenen Abhandlungen]. In: Archiv für Sozialwissenschaft und Sozialpolitik, 40. Bd., Heft 1, S. 1–2.

126/I   [Namensliste der Unterzeichner der Gegenadresse zur sog. 'Seeberg-

Adresse', Sommer 1915; mitunterzeichnet von Max Weber.] In: Preußische Jahrbücher. Hrsg. v. Hans Delbrück. 162. Bd., Heft I, Oktober, Berlin (Georg Stilke), S. 169–72. [Der Text der Gegenadresse findet sich in: ebd., 169. Bd., Heft II, August, Berlin (Georg Stilke), S. 306–7].

1916

126/II   'Der Berliner Professoren-Aufruf' [Erklärung zu einem Aufruf Berliner Professoren, abgedruckt in der Frankfurter Zeitung, 61. Jg., Nr. 206 vom 27. 7. 1916, 2. Mo.bl.]. In: Frankfurter Zeitung, 61. Jg., Nr. 207 vom 28. 7. 1916, Ab.bl. In: GPS[3] S. 155–6 [anonym].

126/III   Kundgebung. [Protest gegen Anfeindungen des Reichskanzlers Bethmann Hollweg. Mitunterzeichnet von Max Weber.] In: Heidelberger Tageblatt, 35. Jg., Nr. 277 vom 25. 11. 1916.

127   Die Wirtschaftsethik der Weltreligionen. Religionssoziologische Skizzen. Einleitung; Der Konfuzianismus I–IV; Zwischenbetrachtung. Stufen und Richtungen der religiösen Weltablehnung. In: Archiv für Sozialwissenschaft und Sozialpolitik, 41. Bd., Heft 1, S. 1–87; Heft 2, S. 335–421.

128   Die Wirtschaftsethik der Weltreligionen. Hinduismus und Buddhismus, I–III. In: Archiv für Sozialwissenschaft und Sozialpolitik, 41. Bd., Heft 3, S. 613–744; 42. Bd., 1916/17, Heft 2, S. 345–461; Heft 3, S. 687–814. In: GAzRS Bd. II[1-5] S. 1–378.

129   Zur Erklärung der Prager Rechts- und Staatswissenschaftlichen Fakultät Bd. 39, S. 567. In: Archiv für Sozialwissenschaft und Sozialpolitik, 41. Bd., Heft 3, S. 927–8.

130   Zwischen zwei Gesetzen [Brief M. Webers an Dr. Gertrud Bäumer]. In: Die Frau, Monatsschrift für das gesamte Frauenleben unserer Zeit, hrsg. v. Helene Lange, 23. Jg., Heft 5, Februar, Berlin (W. Moeser), S. 277–9. In: GPS S. 60–3; GPS[2] S. 139–42; GPS[3] S. 142–5.

131   Deutschland unter den europäischen Weltmächten [Vortrag in München am 27. 10. 1916. Zensierte Fassung. In einem redaktionellen Vermerk heißt es: 'Mit Rücksicht auf die Zensur sind die Ausführungen gegen die Demagogie in rein militärischen Fragen fortgelassen']. In: Die Hilfe, Wochenschrift für Politik, Literatur und Kunst. Hrsg. v. Fr. Naumann. 22. Jg., Nr. 45 vom 9. 11., S. 735–41. In: GPS S. 73–93; GPS[2] S. 152–72; GPS[3] S. 157–77.

132   Deutschland unter den europäischen Weltmächten. Deutscher Kriegs-und Friedenswille. Drei Reden: Fr. Naumann, Rede über den Krieg. M. Weber, Deutschland unter den europäischen Weltmächten. W. Heile, Deutscher Siegeswille. In: Die Hilfe, Wochenschrift für Politik, Literatur und Kunst. Hrsg. v. Fr. Naumann. Sonderheft. Berlin (Verlag der 'Hilfe') o. J., S. 7–13 [umgearbeitete Neufassung von (131)].

133 [Diskussionsbeitrag zur] Generaldebatte. In: Die wirtschaftliche Annä-
herung zwischen dem Deutschen Reiche und seinen Verbündeten. Hrsg.
im Auftrage des Vereins für Sozialpolitik von H. Herkner. 3. Teil.
Aussprache in der Sitzung des Ausschusses vom 6. 4. 1916 zu Berlin.
Schriften des Vereins für Sozialpolitik. 155. Bd. 3. Teil. München und
Leipzig (Duncker & Humblot), S. 28–37.

134 [Diskussionsbeiträge zum Thema] Bedenken gegen eine Erleichterung des
Güteraustausches. In: Die wirtschaftliche Annäherung . . . [Vgl. (133)],
S. 42, 57–9.

1917

135 Deutschlands äußere und Preußens innere Politik. I. Die Polenpolitik. In:
Frankfurter Zeitung, 61. Jg., Nr. 55 vom 25. 2. 1917, 1. Mob.bl. In:
GPS S. 94–9; GPS² S. 173–8; GPS³ S. 178–83.

136 Deutschlands äußere und Preußens innere Politik. II. Die Nobilitierung
der Kriegsgewinne. In: Frankfurter Zeitung, 61. Jg., Nr. 59 vom
1. 3. 1917, 1. Mo.bl. [Fortsetzung von (135)]. In: GPS S. 99–106; GPS²
S. 178–86; GPS³ S. 183–91.

137 Ein Wahlrechtsnotgesetz des Reichs. Das Recht der heimkehrenden
Krieger. In: Frankfurter Zeitung, 61. Jg., Nr. 86 vom 28. 3. 1917, 1.
Mo.bl. In: GPS² S. 187–91; GPS³ S. 192–6.

138 Der preußische Landtag und das Deutsche Reich. In: Frankfurter
Zeitung, 61. Jg., Nr. 114 vom 26.4.1917, 1. Mo.bl.

138/I Eine katholische Universität in Salzburg. In: Frankfurter Zeitung, 61.
Jg., Nr. 128 vom 10. 5.1917, 1. Mo.bl. [anonym].

138/II Die russische Revolution und der Friede. In: Berliner Tageblatt, 46. Jg.,
Nr. 241 vom 12. 5. 1917, Ab. ausg.

139 Deutscher Parlamentarismus in Vergangenheit und Zukunft. I. Die
Erbschaft Bismarcks. In: Frankfurter Zeitung, 61. Jg., Nr. 145 vom
27. 5. 1917, 1. Mo.bl.

140 Vergangenheit und Zukunft des deutschen Parlamentarismus. II.
Beamtenherrschaft und politisches Führertum. In: Frankfurter Zeitung,
61. Jg., Nr. 157 vom 9. 6. 1917, 1. Mo.bl. [Fortsetzung von (139)].

141 Vergangenheit und Zukunft des deutschen Parlamentarismus. II.
Beamtenherrschaft und politisches Führertum (Schluß). In: Frankfurter
Zeitung, 61. Jg., Nr. 158 vom 10. 6. 1917, 1. Mo.bl. [Fortsetzung von
(140)].

142 Deutscher Parlamentarismus in Vergangenheit und Zukunft. III. Ver-
waltungsöffentlichkeit und politische Verantwortung. In: Frankfurter
Zeitung, 61. Jg., Nr. 172 vom 24. 6. 1917, 1. Mo.bl. [Fortsetzung von
(141)].

143 Die Lehren der deutschen Kanzlerkrisis. In: Frankfurter Zeitung, 62. Jg.,

Nr. 247 vom 7. 9. 1917, 1. Mo.bl. In: GPS S. 261-5; GPS³ S. 211-16; GPS³ S. 216-21.

143/I   Die Abänderung des Artikels 9 der Reichsverfassung. In: Frankfurter Zeitung, 62. Jg., Nr. 248 vom 8. 9. 1917, 1. Mo.bl. In: GPS³ S. 222-5 [anonym].

144   Die siebente deutsche Kriegsanleihe. In: Frankfurter Zeitung, 62. Jg., Nr. 258 vom 18. 9. 1917, 1. Mo.bl. In: GPS³ S. 226-8 [unvollständig].

145   Vaterland und Vaterlandspartei. In: Münchner Neueste Nachrichten, 70. Jg., Nr. 494 vom 30. 9. 1917, Einzige Ausgabe. In: GPS S. 266-9; GPS² S. 217-20; GPS³ S. 229-32.

146   Bayern und die Parlamentarisierung im Reich. I. In: Münchner Neueste Nachrichten, 70. Jg., Nr. 522 vom 15. 10. 1917, Ab.ausg. In: GPS S. 270-3; GPS² S. 221-4; GPS³ S. 233-6.

147   Bayern und die Parlamentarisierung im Reich. II. In: Münchner Neueste Nachrichten, 70. Jg., Nr. 525 vom 17. 10. 1917, Mo.ausg. [Fortsetzung von (146)]. In: GPS S. 273-6; GPS³ S. 225-8; GPS³ S. 237-40.

147/I   Gegen die 'Vaterlandspartei'. [Abdruck der 'Heidelberger Erklärung'. Mitunterzeichnet von Max Weber.] In: Frankfurter Zeitung, 62. Jg., Nr. 294 vom 24. 10. 1917, 1. Mo.bl.

148   'Bismarcks Erbe in der Reichsverfassung.' In: Frankfurter Zeitung, 62. Jg., Nr. 298 vom 28. 10. 1917, 1. Mo.bl. In: GPS² S. 229-32; GPS³ S. 241-4.

148/I   Eingesandt. In: Heidelberger Tageblatt, 35. Jg., Nr. 289 vom 10. 12. 1917, Einzige Ausgabe.

148/Ia   dass. in: Kölner Zeitschrift für Soziologie und Sozialpsychologie. Hrsg. v. R. König, 28. Jg., Heft 4, Opladen (Westdeutscher Verlag) 1976, S. 808.

149   Schwert und Parteikampf. In: Frankfurter Zeitung, 62. Jg., Nr. 344 vom 13. 12. 1917, 1. Mo.bl.

149/I   Volksbund für Freiheit und Vaterland! Aufruf! [Mitunterzeichnet von Max Weber 'Als Mitglied des Ausschusses'.] In: Heidelberger Tageblatt, 35. Jg., Nr. 298 vom 20. 12. 1917.

150   Die Wirtschaftsethik der Weltreligionen. Das antike Judentum. I. Die israelitische Eidgenossenschaft und Jahwe. In: Archiv für Sozialwissenschaft und Sozialpolitik, 44. Bd. 1917/18, Heft 1, S. 52-138; Heft 2, S. 349-443; Heft 3, S. 601-26. In: GAzRS Bd. III¹⁻⁵ S. 1-207.

151   Erklärung [zu dem Aufsatz von E. Jaffé, Das theoretische System der kapitalistischen Wirtschaftsordnung]. Zusammen mit Werner Sombart. In: Archiv für Sozialwissenschaft und Sozialpolitik, 44. Bd. 1917/18, Heft 1, S. 348.

152   Das preussische Wahlrecht. In: Europäische Staats- und Wirtschafts-Zeitung, hrsg. v. H. v. Frauendorfer u. E. Jaffé, Nr. 16 vom 21. 4., Berlin (Verlag der Europäischen Staats- und Wirtschafts-Zeitung), S. 398-402.

152a   dass. in: Kölner Zeitschrift für Soziologie und Sozialpsychologie. Hrsg. v. R. König. 27. Jg., Heft 4, Opladen (Westdeutscher Verlag) 1975, S. 724–30.

153   Rußlands Übergang zur Scheindemokratie. In: Die Hilfe, Wochenschrift für Politik, Literatur und Kunst. Hrsg. v. Fr. Naumann. 23. Jg., Nr. 17 vom 26. 4., S. 272–279. In: GPS S. 107–25; GPS² S. 192–210; GPS³ S. 197–215.

154   Das Reichstagswahlrecht für Preußen. In: Die Hilfe, Wochenschrift für Politik, Literatur und Kunst. Hrsg. v. Fr. Naumann. 23. Jg., Nr. 48 vom 29. 11., S. 709–10 [Vorabdruck aus (156), mit einem Vorwort von W. Heile].

155   Der Sinn der 'Wertfreiheit' der soziologischen und ökonomischen Wissenschaften. In: Logos. Internationale Zeitschrift für Philosophie der Kultur. Hrsg. v. R. Kroner u. G. Mehlis. Bd. VII, Heft 1, 1917/18, Tübingen (Mohr-Siebeck), S. 40–88. In: GAzW S. 451–502; GAzW² S. 475–526; GAzW³,⁴ S. 489–540 [umgearbeitete Fassung von (117)].

156   Wahlrecht und Demokratie in Deutschland. In: Der deutsche Volksstaat. Schriften zur inneren Politik. Hrsg. v. W. Heile & W. Schotte. 2. Heft, Berlin (Fortschritt [Buchverlag der 'Hilfe']). In: GPS S. 277–322; GPS² S. 233–79; GPS³ S. 245–91.

1918

157   Innere Lage und Außenpolitik. I. In: Frankfurter Zeitung, 62. Jg., Nr. 34 vom 3. 2. 1918, 1. Mo.bl. In: GPS S. 323–326; GPS² S. 280–3; GPS³ S. 292–5.

158   Innere Lage und Außenpolitik. II. In: Frankfurter Zeitung, 62. Jg., Nr. 36 vom 5. 2. 1918, 2. Mo.bl. [Fortsetzung von (157)]. In: GPS S. 326–9; GPS² S. 283–6; GPS³ S. 295–8.

159   Innere Lage und Außenpolitik. III. In: Frankfurter Zeitung, 62. Jg., Nr. 38 vom 7. 2. 1918, 1. Mo.bl. [Fortsetzung von (158)]. In: GPS S. 329–36; GPS² S. 287–93; GPS³ S. 299–305.

160   Die nächste innerpolitische Aufgabe. In: Frankfurter Zeitung, 63. Jg., Nr. 288 vom 17. 10. 1918, 1. Mo.bl. In: GPS S. 337–9; GPS² S. 432–4; GPS³ S. 444–6.

160/I   Waffenstillstand und Frieden. In: Frankfurter Zeitung, 63. Jg., Nr. 298 vom 27. 10. 1918, 2. Mo.bl. In: GPS S. 340; GPS² S. 435; GPS³ S. 447 [anonym].

161   Die Staatsform Deutschlands. I. In: Frankfurter Zeitung, 63. Jg., Nr. 324 vom 22. 11. 1918, 1. Mo.bl.

162   Die Staatsform Deutschlands. II. In: Frankfurter Zeitung, 63. Jg., Nr. 326 vom 24. 11. 1918, 1. Mo.bl. [Fortsetzung von (161)].

163   Die deutsche Staatsform. III. In: Frankfurter Zeitung, 63. Jg., Nr. 330 vom 28. 11. 1918, 1. Mo.bl. [Fortsetzung von (162)].

164   Die deutsche Staatsform. IV. In: Frankfurter Zeitung, 63. Jg., Nr. 332 vom 30. 11. 1918, 1. Mo.bl. [Fortsetzung von (163)].

165   Die deutsche Staatsform. V. (Schluß). In: Frankfurter Zeitung, 63. Jg., Nr. 337 vom 5. 12. 1918, 1. Mo.bl. [Fortsetzung von (164)].

165/I   Ein Aufruf der demokratischen Partei an Oesterreich. In: Frankfurter Zeitung, 63. Jg., Nr. 357 vom 25. 12. 1918, 1. Mo.bl.

165/II Der gebundene Privatgrundbesitz in der badischen Verfassung. In: Karlsruher Tagblatt, Nr. 50 vom 19. 2. 1919, 1. Bl.

166   Die Wirtschaftsethik der Weltreligionen. Das antike Judentum. I. Die israelitische Eidgenossenschaft und Jahwe (Schluß). II. Die Entstehung des jüdischen Pariavolkes. In: Archiv für Sozialwissenschaft und Sozialpolitik, 46. Bd. 1918/19, Heft 1, S. 40–113; Heft 2, S. 311–66; Heft 3, S. 541–604. In: GAzRS Bd. III$^{1-5}$ S. 207–400.

167   Parlament und Regierung im neugeordneten Deutschland. Zur politischen Kritik des Beamtentums und Parteiwesens. In: Die innere Politik, hrsg. v. S. Hellmann, München und Leipzig (Duncker & Humblot) [Umgestaltung und Erweiterung von (138), (139) bis (142) sowie Vorbemerkung]. In: GPS S. 126–260; GPS^2 S. 294–431; GPS^3 S. 306–443.

168   Der Sozialismus. Wien ('Phöbus', Kommissionsverlag Dr. Viktor Pimmer). In: GAzSuS S. 492–518.

1919

169   [Zuschrift betr. seine Nichtaufnahme in die Kandidatenliste der Provinz Hessen-Nassau zur Wahl in die Nationalversammlung.] In: Frankfurter Zeitung, 63. Jg., Nr. 12 vom 5. 1. 1919, 2. Mo.bl.

169/I   Erklärung! [Gegen antisemitische Propaganda. Mitunterzeichnet von Max Weber.] In: Heidelberger Zeitung, 61. Jg., Nr. 12 vom 15. 1. 1919.

169/II Aufruf. [Jugendwerbung für die DDP]. In: Heidelberger Tageblatt, 37. Jg., Nr. 22 vom 30. 1. 1919.

170   Zum Thema der 'Kriegsschuld'. In: Frankfurter Zeitung, 63. Jg., Nr. 43 vom 17. 1. 1919, 1. Mo.bl. In: GPS S. 381–9; GPS^2 S. 476–85; GPS^3 S. 488–97.

170/I   Professor Max Weber und die Couleurstudenten. In: Heidelberger Neueste Nachrichten, Nr. 22 vom 27. 1. 1919.

170/Ia [Erwiderung] In: Deutsche Corpszeitung. Amtliche Zeitschrift des Kösener S. C. Verbandes, 36. Jg., Nr. 2 vom 1. 5. 1919, S. 17f.

170/II Unitarismus, Partikularismus und Föderalismus in der Reichsverfassung. I. In: Heidelberger Zeitung, 61. Jg., Nr. 74 vom 28. 3. 1919.

170/III   Unitarismus, Partikularismus und Föderalismus in der Reichsverfassung. II. In: Heidelberger Zeitung, 61. Jg., Nr. 75 vom 29. 3. 1919.

170/IV   [Beitrag]. In: Das Gymnasium und die neue Zeit. Fürsprachen und Forderungen für seine Erhaltung und seine Zukunft. Leipzig/Berlin: B. G. Teubner 1919. S. 133–4.

171   Für eine Politik des Rechts. [Erklärung der 'Arbeitsgemeinschaft für Politik des Rechts (Heidelberger Vereinigung)'. Mitunterzeichnet von Max Weber.] In: Frankfurter Zeitung, 63. Jg., Nr. 117 vom 13. 2. 1919, 1. Mo.bl.

171/I   Aufruf. [Für den Ehrenausschuß des Roten Kreuzes, Abt. IX, Fürsorgestelle für elsaß-lothringische Flüchtlinge]. In: Heidelberger Tageblatt, 37. Jg., Nr. 59 vom 14. 3. 1919.

172   Der Reichspräsident. In: Berliner Börsen-Zeitung, 64. Jg., Nr. 93 vom 25. 2. 1919, Mo.ausg. In: GPS S. 390–3; GPS^2 S. 486–9; GPS^3 S. 498–501.

173   Die Untersuchung der Schuldfrage. In: Frankfurter Zeitung, 63. Jg., Nr. 218 vom 22. 3. 1919, 1. Mo.bl. In: GPS S. 394–5; GPS^2 S. 491–2; GPS^3 S. 503–4.

174   Die Schuld am Kriege. [Denkschrift der 'deutschen Kommission zum Bericht der Kommission der alliierten und assoziierten Regierungen über die Verantwortlichkeiten der Urheber des Krieges'. Zusammen mit H. Delbrück, M. Graf Montgelas und A. Mendelssohn-Bartholdy.] In: Frankfurter Zeitung, 63. Jg., Nr. 411 vom 5. 6. 1919, 2. Mo.bl.

174/I   Für die Aufhebung des Standrechts. [Erklärung der Arbeitsgemeinschaft für Politik des Rechts]. In: Münchner Neueste Nachrichten, 72. Jg., Nr. 227 vom 12. 6. 1919.

174/II   Der verstümmelte Bericht des Herrn von Schoen. Eine Erklärung der deutschen Viererkommission. Berlin, Würzburg und München, 3., 4. und 5. August 1919. In: Deutsche Allgemeine Zeitung, Berlin, 58. Jg., Nr. 377 vom 7. 8. 1919, Ab.ausg.

175   Deutschlands künftige Staatsform. In: Zur deutschen Revolution. Flugschriften der Frankfurter Zeitung. Sonderabdruck aus der Frankfurter Zeitung. Heft 2. Frankfurt (Frankfurter Societäts-Druckerei). [Umgearbeitete Fassung von (161) bis (165) mit einem Vorwort vom 15. 12. 1918.] In: GPS S. 341–6; GPS^2 S. 436–71; GPS^3 S. 448–83.

176   [Rede über die wirtschaftliche Zugehörigkeit des Saargebietes zu Deutschland.] Gegen Frankreichs Anspruch auf Pfalz und Saarbecken. Protestkundgebung von Lehrkörper und Studentenschaft der Ruprecht-Karls-Universität Heidelberg. 1. 3. 1919. Ansprachen v. Ch. Bartholomae, H. Oncken, W. Windelband, E. Thiel u. M. Weber. Heidelberg (Carl Winters Universitätsbuchhandlung), S. 30–8.

176a   Gegen Frankreichs Anspruch auf das Saarbecken. Auszug aus zwei Reden der Professoren Hermann Oncken und Max Weber gehalten bei einer

Protestkundgebung der Universität Heidelberg am I. März 1919. Berlin (H. Bergmann), S. 8–12. [Gekürzte Fassung von (1976).] In: GPS[3] S. 565–70.

177   Wissenschaft als Beruf. In: Geistige Arbeit als Beruf. Vier Vorträge vor dem Freistudentischen Bund. Erster Vortrag. [Mit einem Nachwort von Immanuel Birnbaum]. München und Leipzig (Duncker & Humblot).

177a   dass. 2. Aufl., München und Leipzig (Duncker & Humblot) 1921.

177b   dass. 3. Aufl. In: Wissenschaftliche Abhandlungen und Reden zur Philosophie, Politik und Geistesgeschichte. Heft VIII. München u. Leipzig (Duncker & Humblot) 1930.

177c   dass. Gedanken anläßlich einer Studentenversammlung 1919, die über Berufsfragen orientiert werden sollte. [Mit einem Zitat von Theodor Heuss als Vorwort.] In: SV-Schriftenreihe zur Förderung der Wissenschaft. Forschung und Wirtschaft. Partner im Fortschritt. 7. Jg., o. O. 1958/3.

177d   dass. 4. Aufl., Berlin (Duncker & Humblot) 1959.

177e   dass. 5. Aufl., Berlin (Duncker & Humblot) 1967.

177f   dass. 6. Aufl., Berlin (Duncker & Humblot) 1975. In: GAzW S. 524–55; GAzW[2] S. 566–97; GAzW[3, 4] S. 582–613.

178   Politik als Beruf. In: Geistige Arbeit als Beruf. Vier Vorträge vor dem Freistudentischen Bund. Zweiter Vortrag. München u. Leipzig (Duncker & Humblot).

178a   dass. 2. Aufl. [Mit einer Vorbemerkung Marianne Webers vom August 1926.] In: Wissenschaftliche Abhandlungen und Reden zur Philosophie, Politik und Geistesgeschichte. II. München u. Leipzig (Duncker & Humblot) 1926.

178b   dass. 3. Aufl. [Mit einer Vorbemerkung Marianne Webers vom August 1926.] Berlin (Duncker & Humblot) 1958.

178c   dass. 4. Aufl. Berlin (Duncker & Humblot) 1964.

178d   dass. 5. Aufl. Berlin (Duncker & Humblot) 1968. In: GPS S. 396–450; GPS[2] S. 493–548; GPS[3] S. 505–60.

179   Bericht der deutschen Schuldkommission. Endgültige Fassung vom 27. 5. 1919. Bemerkungen zum Bericht der Kommission der Alliierten und Assoziierten Regierungen über die Verantwortlichkeiten der Urheber des Krieges. In: Weißbuch, betreffend Schuldfrage. Korrekturexemplar. Berlin (Gedruckt in der Reichsdruckerei) o. J., S. 54–64 [identisch mit (174)].

179a   Bemerkungen zum Bericht der Kommission der alliierten und assoziierten Regierungen über die Verantwortlichkeiten der Urheber des Krieges. In: Weißbuch betreffend die Verantwortlichkeit der Urheber am Kriege. Auswärtiges Amt, Berlin, Juni (Gedruckt in der Reichsdruckerei), S. 36–46.

179b   dass. in: Weißbuch betreffend die Verantwortlichkeit der Urheber des

Krieges. Auswärtiges Amt, Berlin, Juni (Gedruckt in der Reichsdruckerei), S. 36–46.

179c   dass. in: Das deutsche Weißbuch über die Schuld am Kriege, mit der Denkschrift der deutschen Viererkommission zum Schuldbericht der Alliierten und Assoziierten Mächte. 'Materialien, betreffend die Friedensverhandlungen.' Teil VI. Amtlicher Text. Autorisierte Ausgabe. Im Auftrage des Auswärtigen Amtes. Charlottenburg (Deutsche Verlagsgesellschaft für Politik und Geschichte), S. 56–68.

179d   dass. in: Das Deutsche Weißbuch über die Schuld am Kriege, mit der Denkschrift der deutschen Viererkommission zum Schuldbericht der Alliierten und Assoziierten Mächte vom 29. März 1919. Im Auftrag des Auswärtigen Amtes. 2. Aufl., Berlin (Deutsche Verlagsgesellschaft für Politik und Geschichte) 1927, S. 63–77.

179e   dass. in: Deutschland schuldig? Deutsches Weißbuch über die Verantwortlichkeit der Urheber des Krieges. Hrsg. mit Genehmigung des Auswärtigen Amtes. Berlin (Carl Heymanns), S. 56–68. In: GPS[2] S. 551–6; GPS[3] S. 571–86 [Auf der Grundlage von (179 c, d).]

179/I   Die Demonstration in der Universität. [Zuschrift]. In: Münchner Neueste Nachrichten, 73. Jg., Nr. 32 vom 23. 1. 1920, Ab.ausg.

1920

180   Gesammelte Aufsätze zur Religionssoziologie [GAzRS]. Bd. I(1. Aufl.), Tübingen (Mohr-Siebeck) 1920.

180a   2., photomechanisch gedruckte Aufl., Tübingen (Mohr-Siebeck) 1922.

180b   3., photomechanisch gedruckte Aufl., Tübingen (Mohr-Siebeck) 1934.

180c   4., photomechanisch gedruckte Aufl., Tübingen (Mohr-Siebeck) 1947.

180d   5., photomechanisch gedruckte Aufl., Tübingen (Mohr-Siebeck) 1963.

180e   6., photomechanisch gedruckte Aufl., Tübingen (Mohr-Siebeck) 1972.

180f   7., photomechanisch gedruckte Aufl., Tübingen (Mohr-Siebeck) 1975.

181   Vorbemerkung [zu GAzRS Bd. I]. In: Gesammelte Aufsätze zur Religionssoziologie, Bd. I, Tübingen (Mohr-Siebeck), S. 1–16. In: GAzRS, Bd. I[2-6] S. 1–16, PE I[1-3] S. 9–26.

182   Die protestantische Ethik und der Geist des Kapitalismus. In: Gesammelte Aufsätze zur Religionssoziologie, Bd. I, Tübingen (Mohr-Siebeck), S. 17–206. [Umgearbeitete Fassung von (65).] In: GAzRS Bd. I[2-6] S. 17–206; PE I[1-3] S. 27–277.

183   Die protestantischen Sekten und der Geist des Kapitalismus. In: Gesammelte Aufsätze zur Religionssoziologie, Bd. I, Tübingen (Mohr-Siebeck), S. 207–36. [Umgearbeitete Fassung von (74).] In: GAzRS Bd. I[2-6] S. 207–36; PE I[1-3] S. 279–317.

184   Die Wirtschaftsethik der Weltreligionen. Vergleichende religionssoziologische Versuche. Einleitung; I. Konfuzianismus und Taoismus;

Zwischenbetrachtung: Theorie der Stufen und Richtungen religiöser Weltablehnung. In: Gesammelte Aufsätze zur Religionssoziologie, Bd. I, Tübingen (Mohr-Siebeck), S. 237–573. [Umgearbeitete Fassung von (127).] In: GAzRS Bd. I$^{2-6}$ S. 237–573.

II UNPUBLISHED WORKS BY MAX WEBER (IN CHRONOLOGICAL ORDER)

184/I [Vertrauliches Anschreiben mit Programmentwurf für die Gründung einer neuen Tageszeitung, verfaßt von einem vorbereitenden Komitee]. Februar 1896. In: Bundesarchiv Koblenz, Nachlaß Traub/41.

184/II [Beiträge zu den] Verhandlungen des provisorischen Börsenausschusses im Reichsamt des Innern in der Zeit vom 19. bis 26. November 1896, S. 24, 33f., 43f., 53–6, 66, 70, 74, 77, 82, 90, 109–13, 128f., 132, 147ff., 154, 158, 165ff., 170. Bayerisches Hauptstaatsarchiv, Abt. MH 11250.

184/III Bericht des provisorischen Börsenausschusses, betreffend die Neuordnung der Verkehrsnormen an den deutschen Produktenbörsen. [Berichterstatter Max Weber], In: Verhandlungen des provisorischen Börsenausschusses . . . a.a. O. S. 194–212.

185 [Einladung zum Beitritt zu der in Berlin gegründeten 'Deutschen Gesellschaft für Soziologie'.] Heidelberg, Juni 1909. Bundesarchiv Koblenz, Nachlaß Brentano/67.

185/I Vorbericht über eine vorgeschlagene Erhebung über die Soziologie des Zeitungswesens. [Für die Deutsche Gesellschaft für Soziologie, 1910] Nachlaß F. Toennies, Schleswig-Holsteinische Landesbibliothek, Cb. 54, B 30, 516ff.

185/II Anträge von Dr. Max Weber [eingereicht zur Sitzung des Unterausschusses für Preisuntersuchungen des Vereins für Sozialpolitik vom 16. Juli 1910]. In: Bundesarchiv Koblenz, Nachlaß Max Sering/104.

185/III Aufruf zur Begründung eines Verbandes für internationale Verständigung. Mai 1910. Frankfurt: Gebrüder Knauer. In: Bundesarchiv Koblenz, Nachlaß Jellinek, Nr. 6.

186 [Siehe (219)]

187 [Bemerkungen über die Handelshochschulen.] Heidelberg, den 7. 11. 1911. Max-Weber-Archiv, München.

188 [Siehe (223/I)]

188/I Handbuch der Sozialökonomik. [Internes Zirkular an die Mitherausgeber]. Heidelberg, den 8. Dezember 1913. In: Verlagsarchiv J. C. B. Mohr (Paul Siebeck), Tübingen.

188/II [Adresse an den Reichskanzler gegen eine Eroberungspolitik. Gegenadresse zur sogen. Seeberg-Adresse]. Berlin, den 27. Juli 1915. In: Bundesarchiv Koblenz, Nachlaß H. Wehberg, Nr. 15, Bl. 131.

189 [Austrittserklärung aus der Burschenschaft Allemannia vom 17. Oktober 1918]. In: 12. Kriegsbericht der Burschenschaft Allemannia zu Heidelberg. Februar 1919.

190 [Aufzeichnungen über Ausführungen zum Verfassungsentwurf.] Aufzeichnung über die Verhandlungen im Reichsamt des Innern über die Grundzüge des der verfassungsgebenden deutschen Nationalversammlung vorzulegenden Verfassungsentwurfs, vom 9. bis 12. 12. 1918 (I A 15607). Bundesarchiv Koblenz, Nachlaß Payer/11; S. 3, 12–13, 17, 20, 23, 25–7, 29, 31–2, 35.

190/I Wahlaufruf! [Aufruf der Deutschen Demokratischen Partei zur Wahl einer Nationalversammlung]. Januar 1919. In: Bundesarchiv Koblenz, Zsg 1–27/19(2).

190/II [Erklärung der Arbeitsgemeinschaft für Politik des Rechts gegen eine Beteiligung Deutschlands an der Blockade Rußlands]. Oktober 1919. In: Bundesarchiv Koblenz, Nachlaß H. Wehberg, Nr. 27.

III POSTHUMOUS PUBLICATIONS AND COLLECTIONS

191 [Siehe (81/I)]
192 [Entfällt]
193 [Siehe (126/II)]
194 [Siehe (138/I)]
195 [Entfällt]
196 [Entfällt]
197 [Siehe (143/I)]
198 [Entfällt]
199 [Entfällt]
200 [Entfällt]
201 [Siehe (160/I)]
202 Die Stadt. Eine soziologische Untersuchung. In: Archiv für Sozialwissenschaft und Sozialpolitik, 47. Bd. 1920/21, Heft 3, S. 621–772. In: WuG S. 513–600; WuG[2, 3] Bd. 2, S. 514–601; unter dem Titel: 'Die nichtlegitime Herrschaft (Typologie der Städte)': WuG[4] Bd. 2, S. 735–822; WuG[64] Bd. 2, S. 923–1033; WuG[2] S. 727–814.

203 Gesammelte Aufsätze zur Religionssoziologie. Bd. II. Hinduismus und Buddhismus. (1. Aufl.) Tübingen (Mohr-Siebeck) 1921.

203a 2., photomechanisch gedruckte Aufl., Tübingen (Mohr-Siebeck) 1923.
203b 3., photomechanisch gedruckte Aufl., Tübingen (Mohr-Siebeck) 1963.
203c 4., photomechanisch gedruckte Aufl., Tübingen (Mohr-Siebeck) 1966.
203d 5., photomechanisch gedruckte Aufl., Tübingen (Mohr-Siebeck) 1972.
203e 6., photomechanisch gedruckte Aufl., Tübingen (Mohr-Siebeck) 1978.

204 Gesammelte Aufsätze zur Religionssoziologie. Bd. III. Das antike Judentum. (1. Aufl.) Tübingen (Mohr-Siebeck) 1921.

204a   2., photomechanisch gedruckte Aufl., Tübingen (Mohr-Siebeck) 1923.

204b   3., photomechanisch gedruckte Aufl., Tübingen (Mohr-Siebeck) 1963.

204c   4., photomechanisch gedruckte Aufl., Tübingen (Mohr-Siebeck) 1966.

204d   5., photomechanisch gedruckte Aufl., Tübingen (Mohr-Siebeck) 1971.

204e   6., photomechanisch gedruckte Aufl., Tübingen (Mohr-Siebeck) 1976.

204f   7., photomechanisch gedruckte Aufl., Tübingen (Mohr-Siebeck) 1978.

205   Die Pharisäer (Nachtrag). In: Gesammelte Aufsätze zur Religions-soziologie. Bd. III. Das antike Judentum. Tübingen (Mohr-Siebeck) 1921, S. 401–42. In: GAzRS Bd. III$^{2-5}$ S. 401–42.

206   Gesammelte politische Schriften [GPS]. [Hrsg. v. Marianne Weber]. München (Drei-Masken-Verlag) 1921.

206a   2., erweiterte Aufl. Mit einem Geleitwort v. Th.Heuss, neu hrsg. v. J. Winkelmann. Tübingen (Mohr-Siebeck) 1958.

206b   3., erneut vermehrte Aufl. Mit einem Geleitwort von Th. Heuss, hrsg v. J. Winckelmann. Tübingen (Mohr-Siebeck) 1971.

206c   4., photomechanisch gedruckte Aufl., Tübingen (Mohr-Siebeck) 1980.

207   Zur Frage des Friedenschließens. [Erste Denkschrift, Ende 1915/Anfang 1916]. In: GPS S. 48–59; GPS^2 S. 127–38; GPS^3 S. 130–41.

208   Der verschärfte U-Boot-Krieg. Denkschrift unter Mitarbeit von Dr. Felix Somary. März 1916. Bundesarchiv Koblenz, Nachlaß Payer/10. In: GPS S. 64–72; GPS^2 S. 143–51; GPS^3 S. 146–54.

209   Begleitschreiben an die Frankfurter Zeitung vom 20. 3. 1919 zu seinem Artikel 'Die Untersuchung der Schuldfrage' [vgl. (173)]. In: GPS S. 487; GPS^2 S. 490–1; GPS^3 S. 502–3.

210   Grundriss der Sozialökonomik. III. Abteilung. Wirtschaft und Gesellschaft. I. Die Wirtschaft und die gesellschaftlichen Ordnungen und Mächte. Bearbeitet von Max Weber. Erster Teil. (Erste Lieferung). Tübingen (Mohr-Siebeck) 1921. S. 1–180.

211   Die rationalen und soziologischen Grundlagen der Musik. [geschrieben 1911]. Mit einer Einl. v. Th. Kroyer, München (Drei-Masken-Verlag) 1921.

211a   2., Aufl., München (Drei-Masken-Verlag) 1924.

211b   Neuauflage Tübingen (UTB/Mohr-Siebeck Bd. 122) 1972. In: WuG$^{2,\ 3}$ Bd. 2, S. 818–69; WuG^4 Bd. 2, S. 877–928.

211/I   Spätere Erklärung der deutschen Viererkommission. In: Bayerische Dokumente zum Kriegsausbruch und zum Versailler Schuldspruch. Im Auftrage des Bayerischen Landtages hrsg. v. P. Dirr. München u. Berlin (R. Oldenbourg) 1922, S. 23–4.

211/Ia   dass. in: ebd., 2., erweiterte Aufl., 1924.

211/Ib   dass. in: ebd., 3., erweiterte Aufl., 1925.

211/Ic   dass. in: ebd., 4. Aufl., 1928.

212   Die drei reinen Typen der legitimen Herrschaft. Eine soziologische

Studie. In: Preußische Jahrbücher, hrsg. v. W. Schotte, Bd. 187, Heft 1, Januar 1922, Berlin (G. Stilke), S. 1–12. In: GAzW[3, 4] S. 475–88.

213 Gesammelte Aufsätze zur Wissenschaftslehre [GAzW]. [Hrsg. v. Marianne Weber]. Tübingen (Mohr-Siebeck) 1922.

213a 2., durchgesehene und ergänzte Aufl., besorgt v. J. Winckelmann, Tübingen (Mohr-Siebeck) 1951.

213b 3., erweiterte und verbesserte Aufl., hrsg. v. J. Winckelmann, Tübingen (Mohr-Siebeck) 1968.

213c 4., erneut durchgesehene Aufl., hrsg. v. J. Winckelmann, Tübingen (Mohr-Siebeck) 1973.

213d 5., erneut durchgesehene Aufl., hrsg. v. J. Winckelmann, Tübingen (Mohr-Siebeck) 1982.

213e 6., erneut durchgesehene Aufl., hrsg. v. J. Winckelmann, Tübingen (Mohr-Siebeck) 1985.

214 Nachtrag zu dem Aufsatz über R. Stammlers 'Ueberwindung' der materialistischen Geschichtsauffassung. In: Gesammelte Aufsätze zur Wissenschaftslehre. Tübingen (Mohr-Siebeck) 1922, S. 556–579 [unvollendete Fortsetzung von (80); aus dem Nachlaß veröffentlicht]. In: GAzW[2–4] S. 360–83.

215 Grundriss der Sozialökonomik. III. Abteilung. Wirtschaft und Gesellschaft. Bearbeitet von Max Weber. [Hrsg. v. Marianne Weber]. Tübingen (Mohr-Siebeck) 1922 [WuG].

215a Grundriss der Sozialökonomik. III. Abteilung. Wirtschaft und Gesellschaft. Von Max Weber. [Hrsg. v. Marianne Weber]. 2., vermehrte Aufl., 2 Hbde., Tübingen (Mohr-Siebeck) 1925.

215b 3. Aufl. Unveränderter Nachdruck der zweiten vermehrten Aufl. 2 Hbde., Tübingen (Mohr-Siebeck) 1947.

215c Wirtschaft und Gesellschaft. Grundriss der verstehenden Soziologie. Mit einem Anhang: Die rationalen und soziologischen Grundlagen der Musik. 4. neu hrsg. Aufl., besorgt von J. Winckelmann, 2 Hbde., Tübingen (Mohr-Siebeck) 1956.

215d Wirtschaft und Gesellschaft. Grundriss der verstehenden Soziologie. Studienausgabe. Hrsg. v. J. Winckelmann. 2 Hbde., Köln/Berlin (Kiepenheuer & Witsch) 1964 [WuG[64]].

215e 5., revidierte Aufl., besorgt von J. Winckelmann. Studienausgabe. Tübingen (Mohr-Siebeck) 1972.

215f 5., revidierte Aufl., mit Textkritischen Erläuterungen hsrg. v. J. Winckelmann. 2 Hbde. und Erläuterungsbd., Tübingen (Mohr-Siebeck) 1976.

216 Wirtschaftsgeschichte von Max Weber. Abriss der universalen Sozial- und Wirtschaftsgeschichte. Aus den nachgelassenen Vorlesungen hrsg. v. S. Hellmann u. Dr. M. Palyi. München u. Leipzig (Duncker & Humblot) 1923.

216a 2., unveränderte Aufl., München u. Leipzig (Duncker & Humblot) 1924.

216b Wirtschaftsgeschichte. Abriß der universalen Sozial- und Wirtschafts-geschichte. Von Max Weber. Aus den nachgelassenen Vorlesungen hrsg. v. S. Hellmann u. Dr. M. Palyi 3., durchgesehene und ergänzte Aufl., besorgt von J. Winckelmann. Berlin (Duncker & Humblot) 1958.

216c 4., durchgesehene Aufl., besorgt von J. Winckelmann. Berlin (Duncker & Humblot) 1981.

217 Gesammelte Aufsätze zur Sozial- und Wirtschaftsgeschichte. Von Max Weber. [Hrsg. v. Marianne Weber] Tübingen (Mohr-Siebeck) 1924 [GAzSuW].

218 Gesammelte Aufsätze zur Soziologie und Sozialpolitik. Von Max Weber. [Hrsg. v. Marianne Weber]. Tübingen (Mohr-Siebeck) 1924 [GAzSuS].

219 Gedenkrede Max Webers auf Georg Jellinek bei der Hochzeit von dessen Tochter Frau Dr. Dora Busch am 21. 3. 1911. In: Marianne Weber, Max Weber. Ein Lebensbild. Tübingen (Mohr-Siebeck) 1926, S. 481–6 [unvollständig und verändert].

219a dass. in: ebd., [2. Aufl.] Heidelberg (L. Schneider) 1950, S. 517–23.

219a/I dass., in ebd., 3. Aufl., unveränd. Nachdr. d.l. Aufl. 1926. ergänzt um Register und Verzeichnisse von Max Weber-Schäfer. Tübingen (Mohr-Siebeck) 1984, S. 481–6.

219b dass. in: Max Weber zum Gedächtnis. Materialien und Dokumente zur Bewertung von Werk und Persönlichkeit, hrsg. v. R. König u. J. Winckelmann. Kölner Zeitschrift für Soziologie und Sozialpsychologie, hrsg. v. R. König, Sonderheft 7, Köln u. Opladen (Westdeutscher Verlag) 1963, S. 13–17 [nach der Originalniederschrift von Dora Busch].

219b/I dass., in ebd., 2. Aufl., unveränd. Nachdr. d.1. Aufl. Köln/Opladen (Westdeutscher Verlag) 1985, S. 13–17.

219/I [Bericht für die Reservelazarettkommission Heidelberg, 1915]. In: Marianne Weber, Max Weber. Ein Lebensbild. Tübingen (Mohr-Siebeck) 1926, S. 545–60.

219/Ia dass. in: ebd., [2. Aufl.] Heidelberg (I. Schneider) 1950, S. 589–93 [unvollständig und verändert].

219/Ib dass., in ebd., 3. Aufl., unveränd. Nachdr. d.1. Aufl. 1926. ergänzt um Register und Verzeichnisse von Max Weber-Schäfer. Tübingen (Mohr-Siebeck) 1984, S. 545–60.

220 Die protestantische Ethik und der Geist des Kapitalismus. Sonderdruck aus M. Weber, Gesammelte Aufsätze zur Religionssoziologie, I, S. 1–206. [Aus: I. Bd., 3., photomechanisch gedruckte Aufl., Tübingen (Mohr-Siebeck) 1934.] Tübingen (Mohr-Siebeck) 1934.

221 Rechtssoziologie. Aus dem Manuskript hrsg. und eingeleitet v. J. Winckelmann. Soziologische Texte, hrsg. v. H. Maus u. F. Fürstenberg, Bd. 2, Neuwied (Luchterhand) 1960.

221a   2., überarbeitete Aufl., Neuwied/Berlin (Luchterhand) 1967.

222   Soziologische Grundbegriffe. Sonderdruck aus 'Wirtschaft und Gesellschaft', 4., neu hrsg. Aufl., besorgt v. J. Winckelmann, 1956, S. 1–30. Tübingen (Mohr-Siebeck) 1966.

222a   2., durchgesehene Aufl., Tübingen (Mohr-Siebeck) 1966.

222b   3., durchgesehene Aufl. Sonderausgabe aus: Wirtschaft und Gesellschaft, 5., revidierte Aufl. besorgt v. J. Winckelmann, 1972, S. 1–30. Tübingen (UTB/Mohr-Siebeck Bd. 541) 1976.

222c   4., durchgesehene Aufl., Tübingen (UTB/Mohr-Siebeck Bd. 541) 1978.

222d   5., durchgesehene Aufl., Tübingen (UTB/Mohr-Siebeck Bd. 541) 1981.

222e   6., durchgesehene Aufl., Tübingen (UTB/Mohr-Siebeck Bd. 541) 1984.

223   Die protestantische Ethik. Eine Aufsatzsammlung. Hrsg. v. J. Winckelmann. München u. Hamburg (Siebenstern-Taschenbuch Bd. 53/54) 1965 [PE I].

223a   2., durchgesehene und erweiterte Aufl., München u. Hamburg (Siebenstern-Taschenbuch Bd. 53/4) 1969.

223b   3., durchgesehene und erweiterte Aufl., Hamburg (Siebenstern-Taschenbuch Bd. 53/4) 1973.

223c   4., durchgesehene Aufl., Hamburg (Siebenstern-Taschenbuch Bd. 53/54) 1975.

223d   5., erneut überarbeitete und mit e. Nachwort versehene Aufl., Gütersloh: Gütersloher Verlagshaus Mohn, 1979.

223e   6., erneut überarbeitete und mit e. Nachwort versehene Aufl;. Gütersloh: Gütersloher Verlagshaus Mohn, 1981.

223f   7., erneut überarbeitete und mit e. Nachwort versehene Aufl., Gütersloh: (Gütersloher Verlagshaus Mohn) 1984.

223/I   An die Herren Teilnehmer der Leipziger Besprechung. [Zirkular Max Webers an eine Sondergruppe des Vereins für Sozialpolitik vom 15. 11. 1912.] Max-Weber-Archiv, München. In: Bernhard Schäfer, Ein Rundschreiben Max Webers zur Sozialpolitik. In: Soziale Welt, 18. Jg., Heft 2/3, 1967, S. 265–71.

224   Die protestantische Ethik II. Kritiken und Antikritiken. Hrsg. v. J. Winckelmann. München u. Hamburg (Siebenstern-Taschenbuch Bd. 119/120) 1968 [PE II].

224a   2., durchgesehene und erweiterte Aufl., Hamburg (Siebenstern-Taschenbuch Bd. 119/120) 1972.

224b   3., durchgesehene und erweiterte Auflage, Gütersloh (Gütersloher Verlagshaus Mohn) 1978.

224c   4., durchgesehene und erweiterte Auflage, Gütersloh (Gütersloher Verlagshaus Mohn) 1982.

225   Georg Simmel As Sociologist. Introduction by Donald N. Levine. In: Social Research, Vol. 39, 1/1972, S. 155–63.

IV ABRIDGED COLLECTIONS

225/I   Schriften zur theoretischen Soziologie, zur Soziologie der Politik und Verfassung. Eingeleitet und mit Anmerkungen verhsen von Max Graf zu Solms. Civitas Gentium. Quellenschriften zur Soziologie und Kulturphilosophie. Hrsg. v. Max Graf zu Solms. Frankfurt a. M. (G. K. Schauer) 1947.

226   Aus den Schriften zur Religionssoziologie. Auswahl, Einleitung und Bemerkungen v. M. Ernst Graf zu Solms. Civitas Gentium. Quellenschriften zur Soziologie und Kulturphilosophie. Hrsg. v. Max Graf zu Solms. Frankfurt a. M. (G. K. Schauer) 1948.

227   Soziologie, Weltgeschichtliche Analysen, Politik. Mit einer Einleitung von Eduard Baumgarten. Hrsg. und erläutert v. J. Winckelmann (1. Aufl.). Stuttgart (Kröner Taschenausgabe Bd. 229) 1956.

227a   2., durchgesehene und ergänzte Aufl., Stuttgart (Kröner Taschenausgabe Bd. 229) 1960.

227b   3., Aufl., Stuttgart (Kröner Taschenausgabe Bd. 229) 1964.

227c   4., erneut durchgesehene und verbesserte Aufl., Stuttgart (Kröner Taschenausgabe Bd. 229) 1968.

227d   Soziologie, Universalgeschichtliche Analysen, Politik. Mit einer Einleitung von Eduard Baumgarten. Hrsg. und erläutert v. J. Winckelmann. 5., überarbeitete Aufl., Stuttgart (Kröner Taschenausgabe Bd. 229) 1973.

228   Staatssoziologie. Mit einer Einführung und Erläuterungen hrsg. v. J. Winkelmann. Berlin (Duncker & Humblot) 1956.

228a   Staatssoziologie. Soziologie der rationalen Staatsanstalt und der modernen politischen Parteien und Parlamente. Mit einer Einführung und Erläuterungen hrsg. v. J. Winckelmann. 2., durchgesehene und ergänzte Aufl., Berlin (Duncker & Humblot) 1966.

228/I   Staat, Gesellschaft, Wirtschaft. Quellentexte zur politischen Bildung aus Max Webers gesammelten Schriften. Ausgewählt, eingeleitet und erläutert von Ludwig Heieck. Heidelberg (Quelle & Meyer) 1967.

229   Methodologische Schriften. Studienausgabe. Mit einer Einführung, besorgt von J. Winckelmann. Frankfurt a. M. (S. Fischer-Verlag) 1968.

V PUBLISHED LETTERS

230   Jugendbriefe (1876–93). [Mit einer Einführung hrsg. v. Marianne Weber.] Tübingen (Mohr-Siebeck) o. J. [1936].

231   Politische Briefe (1906–19). In: Gesammelte Politische Schriften. [Hrsg. v. Marianne Weber]. München (Drei-Masken-Verlag) 1921, S. 451–88.

4   The Max Weber Collected Edition

Due to the preparation of the *Max Weber Gesamtausgabe* (*MWG*) (*Collected Edition*) our knowledge of the original sources and their availability has improved substantially. In Autumn 1976 the group of main editors was founded consisting of Horst Baier (Konstanz), M. Rainer Lepsius (Heidelberg), Wolfgang J. Mommsen (Düsseldorf), Wolfgang Schluchter (Heidelberg) and Johannes Winckelmann (Rottach-Egern). The edition will be prepared on behalf of the '*Kommission für Sozial- und Wirtschaftsgeschichte*' of the *Bayerische Akademie der Wissenschaften* in Munich, Federal Republic of Germany, and published by J. C. Mohr (Paul Siebeck) in Tübingen. A first outline of the edition explaining the general design and the state of preparations of the *MWG* was published in May 1981; a revision of this prospectus was published in February 1984. It indicates three divisions – Writings and Speeches, Letters and Lectures – with 22 volumes for division 1 (Writings and Speeches) alone. Further information can be obtained on application to:

Arbeitsstelle und Archiv der
Max Weber-Gesamtausgabe
Kommission für Sozial- und Wirtschaftsgeschichte
der Bayerischen Akademie der Wissenschaften
Marstall-Platz 8
D-8000 Munich 22
Fed. Rep. of Germany

To date of the publication of this book three volumes have been published:

Vol. 2: *Max Weber, Die römische Agrargeschichte in ihrer Bedeutung für das Staats- und Privatrecht 1891*. Herausgegeben von Jürgen Deininger. Tübingen: J. C. B. Mohr (Paul Siebeck) 1986.

Vol. 3: *Max Weber, Die Lage der Landarbeiter im ostelbischen Deutschland 1892*. Herausgegeben von Martin Riesebrodt. 2 Halbbände. Tübingen: J. C. B. Mohr (Paul Siebeck) 1984.

Vol. 15: *Max Weber, Zur Politik im Weltkrieg. Schriften und Reden 1914–1918*. Herausgegeben von Wolfgang J. Mommsen in Zusammenarbeit mit Gangolf Hübinger. Tübingen: J. C. B. Mohr (Paul Siebeck) 1984.

The Max Weber papers in any technical sense do not exist, but there are various collections of manuscripts, letters and first editions at different locations. Those Weber papers that were in the possession of Marianne Weber at the end of the Second World War were deposited in the *Preußisches Geheimes Staatsarchiv* and now form part of the *Zentralarchiv der Deutschen Demokratischen Republik*, in Merseburg, German Democratic Republic.

Index

Index by Fiona Barr